Charles Raven

Charles Raven

Naturalist, Historian, Theologian

by
F. W. DILLISTONE

HODDER AND STOUGHTON
LONDON SYDNEY AUCKLAND TORONTO

Contents

Illustrations

between pages 224 and 225

Acknowledgements

1 by courtesy of Liverpool Cathedral
2 Ramsay and Muspratt, Post Office Terrace, Cambridge
3 *Cambridge Daily News*

Preface

Two men possessed supreme qualifications for the writing of a biography of Charles Raven. One was Ian Ramsey who in 1933 went up as an undergraduate to Christ's, the College of which Charles had recently become a Fellow; the other was Max Warren who in 1936 was appointed Vicar of Holy Trinity, Cambridge, a church situated less than two hundred yards from the College gateway. Both became close friends and admirers of Charles and remained so to the end of his life.

But by the time that the possibility of a biography was being considered, Ian Ramsey was assuming new and heavy reponsibilities as Bishop of Durham and Max Warren was recovering from an illness. When, after much hesitation, I agreed to undertake the task, I was heartened by the knowledge that I could turn to them for information and sound judgment on matters about which I was largely ignorant. I had, in fact, never had any close links with Charles before the occasions when he came to visit us in Liverpool after his retirement.

Though Ian was characteristically generous in helping me in the earlier stages of my research, he did not live to see a draft completed and was not able to give me the comments and criticisms which would have been so valuable. On the other hand, Max not only kept in touch with the project as it developed but was the first to read the finished product and to register his general approval. To him more than to any other I owe an immense debt of gratitude for wise guidance and constant encouragement.

Next I must record my deep appreciation of the assistance received at every stage from the members of Charles's own family. They honoured me with the invitation to write the book, they entrusted me with his papers, they were always ready to answer my questions and they gave me generous help in the final negotiations towards publication. Through many visits and conversations the portrait of husband, father, brother, friend gradually took shape and it is this that I have tried to reproduce in the following pages.

So much of Charles's career was associated with Cambridge that it was clearly imperative for me to gain some first-hand acquaintance with the places in which he lived and the colleagues with whom he worked. This was happily made possible by my election to a Visiting Fellowship at Clare Hall for the Michaelmas Term of 1970. This term of residence gave me immense pleasure and supplied me with the basic information which I so obviously needed. To the Master and Fellows of Clare Hall I wish to express my continuing gratitude.

During the past four years I have visited or corresponded with many of Charles's friends in Cambridge, in London, in Liverpool and other parts of England, in Scotland, in New England, in India. I considered the possibility of including a comprehensive list of names in this Preface. But it finally seemed better to express to all who have responded to my enquiries an "omnibus" word of very sincere thanks and to confine myself to mentioning by name four personal friends to whom I owe a special debt.

Canon C. F. D. Moule, Lady Margaret's Professor of Divinity in the University of Cambridge has supported me in the enterprise from start to finish. Eric Heaton, formerly Chaplain of St. John's College, Oxford and now Dean of Durham spent much time in helping me to obtain my image of Christ's College during the period when he was an undergraduate and Charles was Master. Vernon Sproxton of the Religious Department of the B.B.C. gave me special assistance in the investigation of Charles's broadcasting activities. Harold Loukes, Fellow of Jesus College, Oxford nobly came to my rescue when it had become clear that the manuscript must be shortened but when I was at a loss to know how this operation should be performed.

No experiences during the writing of the biography have brought me greater pleasure than the forging of new links of friendship with those who were themselves friends of Charles. I have tried to collect scattered material and to give it a certain shape. But I am conscious that whatever has been achieved has come about as the result of the interest and co-operation of a great company of those who loved and admired him and have been eager that some permanent record should be made of a man who deserved to be regarded as one of the outstanding figures in Church and University circles in this century.

Prologue

In May, 1964, Charles Raven was in sight of his seventy-ninth birthday. On the second Sunday of the month he was due to preach the late evening sermon at the University Church in Oxford in a series entitled *Other Christs*. And the particular theme assigned to him was "Christ in the Laboratory".

During the weeks before the event his heart had caused him a certain amount of pain and breathlessness but he left Cambridge in good spirits on the Saturday afternoon. A friend travelling with him, however, felt considerable concern about his physical condition and when he arrived at our home it was clear that he needed both rest and sedation if he were to be fit for his Sunday evening engagement.

He himself seemed apprehensive and in spite of a reasonably quiet night was in some distress on Sunday morning. At midday, however, he managed to visit his granddaughter and her husband who were living temporarily at Christ Church and late in the afternoon he was taken by the Vicar of St. Mary's to the Vicarage for a meal before the sermon. There he stretched himself out on a sofa and had a light tea quietly by himself.

Yet in sharp contrast to his earlier anxiety his spirits began to rise as the time for the sermon drew near. He was no stranger to the University pulpit and once he was safely within it the old fire rekindled. With growing confidence he proceeded to deliver a closely reasoned forty-minute address with verve and with much of the magnetic power which had characterised his preaching over more than fifty years.

The text was taken from the chapter in the New Testament which appears more frequently than any other in his writings. It is the eighth chapter of the Epistle to the Romans, a chapter in which he discerned the unfolding of the whole pattern of the Divine purpose and in which he found the key to the whole mystery of cosmic evolution. Christ is the beginning and the end of the creative process: the Spirit is the agent through whose energy the Divine purpose moves towards its fulfilment. But, in his view, the "new theology", as it had begun to be called, was isolating the Christ from the created order and failing to bear witness to the ceaseless work of the Spirit both in bringing the created order to its consummation and in guiding the social order to its final unification.

From his earliest days of preaching and lecturing it had been his ambition to expose himself fully to the challenge both of the physical and of the social sciences. He had striven to present the Christ within the context of the structures which each of these groups of disciplines had gradually laid bare. So on this occasion, as he spoke on the theme "Christ in the Laboratory", he dealt in turn with recent developments in physics, in chemistry, in biology and in psychology. He touched upon the implications of relativity theory, of the D.N.A. molecule model, of ecological concepts and of life-in-community experiments. All led him to the conclusion that "the growing points of modern science are towards the unity of the cosmos," a unity consequent upon the assured pattern of co-operation and movement towards integration which belongs to every constituent part of the universe.
His final words were:

> We shall be able to see, I think, in the record of Jesus the outline of that pattern, the pattern which the fourth evangelist describes in the great three fold rhythm of his definition of life: I am come that ye might have life and have it abundantly: the whole creative process and adventure after fullness of life. Whoso loves his life, clings to his personal possession, loses it: only as you ride loose to your life and are prepared to spend it, will you find it fulfilled.
> And so to the life which is life indeed, the life of the blessed community, where God is all and in all and we all attain to the unity of our faith. We all come home (because the Pauline word in Ephesians is used of the ship coming into harbour) into the unity which is

supplied by our faith and our full knowledge of the Son of God, unto mature manhood, unto the measure of the stature of the fullness of the Christ.

It was a remarkable performance. Whatever may have been missing in its detailed analysis of the current state of scientific studies, it nevertheless revealed a clear understanding of important trends in the total scientific enterprise. It emphasised the key concepts of unity, wholeness, relation to environment, organic pattern, cosmic purpose which had played so large a part in his own thinking and writing over half a century. And it was delivered with such confidence and enthusiasm that the Vicar, recalling it some years later, was moved to say: "If there had been some one like that in my undergraduate days he would certainly have scooped me in!"

He returned to our home, buoyant and elated, and left for Cambridge after breakfast on the following day. Some eight weeks later he woke early one morning and talked happily with Ninette, his wife. They had their meal together and shortly afterwards she left the room for a short while to answer the telephone. When she returned he lay completely inert and this time the heart attack proved fatal. To use his own metaphor, he had reached harbour, having passed swiftly through the gateway of death, an experience which during his life-time he had never anticipated without some sense of fear and foreboding.

He had promised to preach at Westminster Abbey on the Sunday which followed his death but as it turned out the Oxford sermon was the last of literally thousands of efforts he had made in the course of his ministry to bring about the end which he had so passionately desired, the reconciliation of Christian theology and modern science, of Christianity and natural religion. Each, he believed, had a necessary and legitimate part to play within the total system created and sustained by God Himself. Each could help the other in leading men to an ever deepening understanding of the manifold wisdom of God.

PART ONE

1885–1919

THE FORMATIVE YEARS

CHAPTER ONE

The Introduction to Nature and the Classics

Charles Raven was born in 6 Kildare Terrace, Paddington on July 4th, 1885. He was proud to describe himself as a typical Londoner, "born within sound of Bow Bells." Though he was to become one of the most distinguished naturalists of his time, he never lost his sense of belonging to "the bustle of the streets and the beauty of their lamps 'shining double in the wet'. The inquisitiveness, the unrest, the passion of the dwellers in great cities, these are native to me; and though at times there comes a yearning for a ruminant or vegetable existence, my wife is certainly right when she answers my complaints with: 'My dear, you would be bored to death in a month'."[1]

The home in Paddington was a typical residence within what were then regarded as the suburbs of London. A member of the professional classes with only a modest income would often choose a house for his family in an area near the Parks and if possible within walking distance of his own work. Charles's father, a barrister who practised on the South East Circuit, walked to and fro daily to his chambers in Temple Court and when Charles was of school age he would go with him part of the way. The liveliness of the streets of London in sharp contrast to the quiet of the Parks—this was the general environment in which he grew up.

Within the home his mother reigned supreme. She had to exercise immense care over the family finances in order to maintain the standard expected of a middle-class household at that time. It was the normal practice to employ two servants and even extra help when there were young children. The expense associated with private schools might not present too great a problem for those who could send their children to day-schools in London but there was always the anxiety of what would happen when the time came for public boarding school and university. There was also the annual holiday whose character bore some relation to social prestige: books and equipment for some kind of recreation were regarded as reasonable extras.

The general pattern of the home was entirely typical of place and period. But there were unusual elements in the histories of both father and mother which could not fail to have had some influence upon the imagination of a young boy. John Earle Raven, the father, had spent his early years in New Zealand: Alice Comber, whom he married, had come from a merchant family whose trading concerns were principally with South America and she had herself been born in Buenos Aires.

Charles's grandfather, John Raven, went from Shrewsbury to Caius College, Cambridge in 1839 and was ordained in 1845. In 1847 he married Sara Hole, a younger sister of Samuel Hole, who became Dean of Rochester. (It was cause of great satisfaction to Charles that his grandmother had been so closely related to one of the nineteenth century authorities on rose culture. The Dean was one of the founders of the Rose Society.) Within five years four children had been born but this did not deter the parents from embarking on the long and tedious voyage to New Zealand. The *Minerva*, on which they sailed, took more than four months to make the voyage but all landed safely on February 2nd, 1853. Already the Canterbury Pilgrims, as they came to be called, were establishing a 'polite' settlement, a replica of English cultural life, at Christchurch and John set to work with enthusiasm to play his part in the new enterprise.

He was at once appointed Vicar of Kaiapoi with Woodend, a district north of Christchurch, and chose for his own personal estate an area between Woodend and Waikuku which he called Ravenswood. Life was not easy. Sheep died from eating poisonous weeds; a fire destroyed the house which was to have been the family home. For several years the family had to live in a wooden building that had originally been the steward's office at an agricultural show. Yet John Raven was a man of immense resolution as well as of practical skills. He took his full share in the building of his own house and later of theWoodend Church. And when his responsibility included the taking of services at Cust and Oxford.

"It was his custom on Sunday mornings to take two horses, ride one and lead the other to Cust; leave one there and ride the other to Oxford; hold service there and ride back to Cust, ride the other horse back to Woodend and conduct the evening service in the church at Woodend. There were no roads, only bullock dray tracks."

As a farmer he soon gained a high reputation. He imported his own sheep from Australia. He built the Ravenswood Flour Mill of wood and iron, with two stories and a basement. He cut the original water-race, and the plant, driven by a water wheel, produced about a sack of flour per hour. He built a road from Woodend to Ravenswood and as a reward received a grant of land comprising some 1200 acres. But not only was he occupied on his own estate: he was the business brains behind the establishment in 1861 of New Zealand's oldest metropolitan newspaper *The Press*. Most of the Committee concerned to organise the paper were theorists but John Raven was the practical man who made all necessary arrangements for its production.

At first, services for the Woodend parish were held in the house at Ravenswood but having donated a plot of land from his own estate, the Vicar set to work to build a church. He shared actively in the hewing of timber from the local bush and although he employed both architect and builders to assist him, all was under his general direction. At length in December 1860 the church was opened for worship though it was not until 1877 that it was actually consecrated. With all these achievements to his credit it is little wonder that Henry Sewell, the first Prime Minister of New Zealand, described him in his Journal as "the perfection of a colonist".

However he was offered no ecclesiastical preferment and by 1864 the two eldest boys in the family of nine were approaching the age for secondary education. He therefore sold his estate and returned to England. Both boys, John Earle and Tancred, were entered at Lancing College though subsequently Tancred transferred to Shrewsbury. Sara, their mother, died in 1868 and John the father soon afterwards resigned his living and never again accepted any formal ecclesiastical appointment. He returned to New Zealand in 1872 but travelled back to England via America in 1874, married Louisa Jane Hoskyns in 1875 and died in 1886 almost exactly a year after the birth of his grandson Charles.

John Earle's roots were in New Zealand and he loved to tell Charles about his earlier days in the colony. He was strong physically and became an excellent cricketer, playing later for his College at Cambridge, for the Incogniti and for the Gentlemen of Sussex. But although he seems to have done tolerably well in his studies, particularly in Latin, he reacted against the 'high-church' atmosphere of Lancing and did little to encourage religious interests in his own family in later years.

Yet Charles remembered him with deep gratitude. Writing about him in 1927 he says:

"Every morning he and I would walk to my day-school on his way to the Temple, furbishing up my home-work or discussing the news in the paper; and on Sundays there was always a visit to the park or, when friends gave us tickets, to the Zoo. Both parents made friends with us children, and encouraged us to enquire into and argue over books and ideas: both were singularly independent in outlook, free from all envy and ambition, looking with amusement upon the vulgarities of the merely rich, and content with a small circle of friends chosen quite irrespective of social position."[2]

To one enthusiasm of his father's Charles was perhaps indebted most of all. From the time he was seven years old Latin was the regular accompaniment of the breakfast table, at least in term. No doubt Charles's teachers at school were able to provide the necessary grammatical disciplines but it was his father who gave him the early enthusiasm for spoken Latin. In his thirtieth year Charles was still finding pleasure in writing Latin verse and when an occasion arose for him to act as substitute for the Public Orator at Cambridge his performance was quite outstanding. In a very real sense Latin had become part of the very structure of his being.

In this respect he fulfilled all that his father could have wished for him. In another respect, however, his performance was less than perhaps his father might have hoped. John Earle was not only a fine cricketer but also a good golfer and was interested in all athletic pursuits. His second son Edward in many respects emulated him. But though Charles longed to shine at some kind of sport and felt real envy of his brother's achievements, he was so constituted physically that no major success ever came his way. He loved to watch cricket and talk about it: he coxed boats and followed bumping races with an almost wild enthusiasm. But he could never either by skill of hand and eye or by speed and fearlessness of running measure up to the standards which he had unconsciously accepted as enviable in his early years. "I was always a coward: I hated pain: I was weak and weedy in a school crazy for athletics." These are frank confessions, half concealing a deeply-felt yearning to excel in adventures which the structures and sensitivities of his own body made impossible.

Charles's maternal grandfather was Edward Comber, a merchant whose commercial interests were linked mainly with Liverpool and South America but to some extent also with the southern United States. His daughter Alice, who was later to marry John Earle Raven, was less than five years old when her father died. Her mother continued to live in the comfortable family home, Myddleton Hall, in Lancashire until her death around the turn of the century. Alice and her sisters grew up and received their education at home. Reading and painting and music were substantial ingredients in the training of a 'young lady' at that time and Alice delighted to paint natural objects: it was from her that Charles learned to copy meticulously and later to build up his outstanding collection of water colour paintings of birds, plants and flowers. Until he went to day-school, each morning was spent in lessons with his mother. "My mother," he writes, "had the artist's passion for beauty in nature and literature: I was never so happy as in watching her paint or hearing her read."[3] And the simple inscription of his book *Bird Haunts and Bird Behaviour* reads: "To my Mother who first taught me to have pleasure in the works of the Lord."

She was not strong physically but she gave herself unstintingly to her children's welfare: Charles was born in 1885, Eleanor in 1886 and

Edward in 1889. To acquire knowledge through reading and through the study of nature: to reproduce it through written work, dictated or freely composed, and through painting—these were the ways by which a child might begin to advance towards true culture. Charles's parents were prepared for any sacrifice to make this possible.

He leaves us in no doubt about his own earliest enthusiasm:

"A Londoner born and bred I was bird-mad before I had seen anything but sparrows and at a very early age was fascinated by the portrait of a Puffin. Thereafter for many weeks my mother had to design for me elaborate pictures of precipices adorned with Puffins in rows, which I subsequently coloured with a box of chalks—their beaks being given full value. At the day-school that I attended till thirteen my half-holidays were spent at the National History Museum and the walk along Westbourne Grove was cheered by the presence of three poulterer's shops. One of the proudest moments of my life was when the proprietor of one of them, who must have noticed the small urchin gazing devotedly at his rows of corpses, suddenly seized two of them in his huge hands, held out the feet to me and invited me to tell him what they were, and when I not only distinguished the Golden Plover from the Grey, but took his breath away (horrid little prig!) by announcing their Latin names and giving him a disquisition upon their classification and habitats. Soon afterwards the family began to spend its holiday at Parkgate on the river Dee, and by great good fortune in the house of the local gunner; and I was able to see and handle many of the shore-birds that do not find their way into the London markets."[4]

To see and handle. By his own testimony, as well as by the witness of those who knew him intimately, Charles's ability to *see* the minutest details of his world of experience was quite extraordinary. His eldest daughter later expressed it quite simply: 'Father taught us to see.' A Liverpool friend occupying a responsible post in the Natural History Museum, often accompanied Charles on one of his expeditions. "He was so observant," he remarked in conversation years later, "that he would have noticed if you had only dropped an eyelash." In later life the whole man commanded attention—in any company his presence was immediately felt. But it was his eyes, piercing, pulsating with energy, always capturing new impressions, which constituted the most striking feature of his appearance. "I must register my impressions in pictures if they are to become a true part of my being," he was to write when around forty years old.[5] In fact he had been using his eyes for this purpose from the very beginnings of his sentient life.

The small boy in Bayswater was not only a seer he was also an avid collector. This enabled him not only to see but also to *handle*.

"If not born a collecting maniac," he wrote in 1931 "I was infected in infancy. Numbers and names of engines, numbers of policemen, crests, postmarks, postage stamps: born in a city it was natural that civic life should be the earliest field of interest. Nature soon took its place. Birds' feathers, wings, eggs, breast bones and skins; paintings of birds, bird photographs; butterflies, moths, bees and wasps, and, very half-heartedly, beetles and dragonflies; shells (but not with zeal); flowers (but the pressed plant is a monstrosity); rock plants and hybrid lupins (in the happy years when I had a garden): all of these I have collected; some few I still treasure. Then came another change when I became a husband and a householder, and the fascination of old furniture produced a final outbreak of the malady. Old furniture, old books, old china—until the children came I had enough cash, enough for mild indulgence, and even now it is safer not to linger in places where such things are for sale."

But Charles could not forbear to offer a modest defence of his 'madness'. The zest of the search for something that you can appropriate: "the joy of discovery is no bad equipment for the service of God." The aesthetic satisfaction to be derived from that contemplation: "it is good to gaze at them till every last detail lives in one's appreciation, to meditate upon their excellence, to discover fresh springs of wonder and joy." In short the collector *loves* his treasures; they have become a real part of himself. "He loves them as men love their homes or the priest his altar; they are bound up with the vital core of his being; they are mysteries in which he has found his heart's desire embodied, sacraments whereby the eternal has taken shape."

Whatever may be the psychological interpretation of the collector's urge there can at least be no doubt that one of its results in Charles's case was to strengthen and extend the range of his prodigious memory. Having *seen* an object or an event, he was determined to retain it as part of his own inner being. So he proceeded to *name* that which he had observed, sometimes in English, sometimes in Latin. Or he would *photograph* it: Charles was in fact a pioneer in bird photography in days when the task of the amateur was far from easy. Or he would *paint* it: the exact reproduction in shape and colour of innumerable plants and flowers was a means, more satisfying even than photography, of retaining the delight of the initial vision. For a while he made a collection of stuffed birds and skins but came to the conclusion that the practical difficulties of housing and preserving these objects were such as to outweigh any slight advantage they possessed over the painted or photographed image.[6] In time his own memory became in a sense a vast picture gallery of replicas of his collected objects, including their names. So much were they a part of his being that he could call them up and flash them forth in words which could create vivid visual impressions upon his hearers. He was a seer who was always helping others to see; he was a collector who was ever ready to project images of his collected data so that others could catch the vision and share his delight.

To see, to handle, to collect: but not to delight in rough and tumble with other boys. This may in a measure have been due to an extraordinary bodily sensitivity which was part of his make-up from early boyhood. When he was nine years old he became seriously ill with diphtheria and his tenth and eleventh years were marked by periods of weakness and ill-health. This seems to have made him nervous about disease and he shrank from pain of any kind. Yet in fact he later became extraordinarily tough physically, able to work far into the night and to manage with a minimum of sleep, able to expose himself to appalling weather conditions when in search of some prized object in the natural world. The bodily sensitivity, however, was always there and this was one of the causes of his dependence at all times upon feminine sympathy and care.

His relationship to his mother had from the beginning been exceedingly intimate; in times of her frequent sicknesses and of his own ailments this came to be accentuated. His sister, too, was his constant companion as she was only seventeen months his junior. They played together, chased butterflies together and above all enjoyed holidays together. Eleanor had her lessons at home until she was ten years old and this meant that her older brother would constantly have had the pleasure of bringing back to an eager listener his news of the outside world. They went out to the Green Pond together and watched birds; they went to cricket matches together and watched their father. On holiday at Parkgate in the Wirral, to which the family went all through school-days, they played cricket together on the Dee Sands and familiarised themselves with every detail of their particular portion of the estuary.

In concluding an eloquent passage on the love of Nature published in 1929 Charles admitted that amidst all the scenes that had imprinted themselves on his memory and which never failed, when recalled, to quicken his wonder and delight, one vista in particular held the place of honour. The lover of the whole panorama of nature had his own special object of devotion.

"So it is with the seriousness of the confessional that I avow my own queer preference (where all is beautiful) for the sand banks and mud flats of an estuary; a foreground of slobland and still water, tiny runlets and immature deserts, reflecting the changing radiance of the sky; beyond it a wide perspective of subdued but subtle colour where the gently tilted surfaces, the gradations from wet to dry and the passage of the shadows give an infinite variety of harmonious hues; in the distance hills across the river, their slopes skirted with a patchwork of tiny fields, their summits fading through purple moorland to blue horizon; and above a summer sky on which the clouds march solemnly past the sun to prepare for him his triumph at the close of day. With this for background and a company of waders and sea fowl as dramatis personae, my soul is utterly satisfied."

Who can doubt that the summers at Parkgate had provided for
Charles the prototype, the quintessential expression of natural beauty
which was always to retain the romance of first love?

"An infinite variety of harmonious hues"—a typically English scene,
a typical Englishman's delight. Meanwhile, at precisely the same time,
a small German boy was spending his vacation on the shore of the
Baltic Sea. There, summer by summer, he built his huge sand castle
and, enthroned on its summit, stayed gazing out to sea. What fascinated
him was the great deeps, the surging of immense forces below the
ocean's surface, the far-off horizon forming a boundary beyond which
all was mysterious and unknown. Perhaps this was not altogether a
typically German scene though for the East German the mysteries of
the dark forest and the wild open sea were never far away. Certainly it
was in the midst of such scenes that the young Paul Tillich lived and
grew. Later from New York his soul, his imagination, yearned for the
wideness of the sea and the sense of its depth. Environmental influences
in the 1890s had at least some part to play in the theological reconstructions of the 1930s.[7] Charles, it must be said, remained ill at ease with
Tillich's theology to the very end.

Granted then that Charles began life in particularly happy surroundings in home and school: what part in his upbringing did specifically
religious influences play? His mother was a devoted Church worker;
his father, something of a rebel, reacted against the religious forms of
his old public school. Charles's own experience can be recaptured only
through his words which, although they may be highly coloured,
reveal what he himself felt some thirty years later to have been the
major effects of his earliest encounters with institutional religion.

"My mother," he writes, "cared about God: somehow one's mother
naturally would: *her life was saturated with religion,* and though she
said little its influence upon her was infective. She went to church
when she was well enough; I liked going with her, and her faith was
far stronger than I knew. But my father seldom went, except in the
holidays; and though I sometimes wondered about him, it seemed

as if he didn't need it; he never talked about such things, but his opinion of parsons had been formed at a very 'high-church' school, and was not, I fear, too complimentary. Religion could hardly matter as enormously as the clergy claimed if its effects were not more evident. People were nice or nasty, quite irrespectively of their churchmanship; and some of the most religious were obviously unpleasant, fussy and irritable and inquisitive and far too interested in one's faults. Gradually the dread of God was forgotten: His existence hardly counted; and though there was still mystery and sometimes, at the sight of a moth emerging from its pupa or of the patterned feathering of a bird, wonder and admiration, He dwelt apart. The religion of the church and the spitirual quality of home life belonged to different worlds: *the conflict between institutionalism and the wider vision may be said to have begun in those early days.*"[8]

Charles came in time to love the fellowship of the Church and many aspects of its sacramental life. But he could never bring himself to be bound within any single form of religious expression. No party, no denomination, no school of thought was ever able to command his exclusive allegiance. He was to remain an individualist and at the same time a catholic in the fullest sense of that word.

Late in March 1898 Charles sat for the Scholarship Examination at Uppingham School. Not only the family honour but the family finances were at stake. Without a scholarship (even although in the first instance it amounted to only £30 a year) it is doubtful if his parents could have afforded to send him to boarding school. But as things turned out both Charles and his younger brother Edward relieved them of this particular anxiety by performing excellently in the examination and by making full use of their years at public school to prepare them for the time when they would be undergoing a more exacting test for entrance to University.

The choice of Uppingham for the first scholarship attempt might seem surprising. The school had sprung to prominence in the nineteenth century under the dynamic leadership of Edward Thring but at the time of Charles's entry a considerable proportion of its boys were drawn from families in the Midlands whose wealth had increased with the growth of industry. The fame of the former headmaster, ("He ennobled the smallest detail of school life") the good situation in open country 500 feet up, may have had some bearing on the parents' decision. But almost certainly the chief determinant was the fact that Charles's uncle Tancred was firmly established as a housemaster in this particular school. How far it was in the boy's interests to send him to a school where he would be constantly under the eye of a relation and inevitably regarded by other boys as occupying a place of some privilege may be open to question.

It was to his uncle's house, Fircroft, that Charles went in 1898 having gained fifth place in the Scholarship examination. The contrast to life in Bayswater and Kensington Gardens must have been almost overwhelming. Uppingham is a small and ancient country town in England's smallest county, Rutland. It is situated between the industrial area of Leicester and Birmingham on the west and wide-stretching farm and fen land on the east. At the end of the nineteenth century, the nearest railway station was four or five miles distant, and there were no cars to choke its streets.

The town is built around the intersection of roads coming from four directions. In one direction, about a quarter of a mile from the centre, Fircroft stands. It is a spacious Victorian private house converted and adapted for school purposes. Behind it is an acre or so of garden and beyond that fields and rolling country. By means of ingenious additions it became possible for the house master and his family to occupy one part of the house while the thirty boarders, each with a tiny den of his own, stayed in the newer part. It was a feature of the distinctive life of Uppingham that the boys, while sharing open dormitories, each had a study space to call his own. The ideal was that every house should be regarded as a large extended family.

By the time that Charles entered Uppingham, Thring had died (1887) but his influence lived on in every part of the school's life. It has been said that Thring "was the first man in England to assert openly that in the economy of God's world a dull boy had as much right to have his power, such as it is, fully trained as a boy of talent."

Certainly he had a passionate concern for the individual. "Every boy," he urged, "can do something well." But this was not just a vague sentiment. He was determined that the whole structure of the school should be developed and adapted with this aim in view. Houses and classes must be kept sufficiently small to allow each individual the chance to be known and to gain his own self-respect. Interests must be as widely varied as possible—though in the late nineteenth century this meant little more than games and music; the sciences and other arts still found little place in a school curriculum.

"Until very recent years," Charles wrote in 1935," it was almost impossible for a boy of any ability to escape from the classical tradition or to get any sort of acquaintance with the sciences. In my own school, where Thring had lived and laboured, there was in my time only one science master, Howson, afterwards the second founder of Gresham's School, Holt. Yet he failed to secure any pupils except those incapable of progress in classics or mathematics, and ruined by years of unprofitable drudgery; and, when he left, his successor found his laboratory a bear-garden, his apparatus grossly defective, hardly a single microscope, and no balances that weighed accurately. We grew up totally ignorant not only of biology, but of the whole scope, meaning and method of scientific studies."[9]

Thring expressed his own ideal in terms of a striking symbol.

"Whatever men may say or think," he wrote, "the almighty wall is the supreme and final arbiter of schools. I mean, no living power in the world can overcome the dead, unfeeling, everlasting pressure of the permanent structure, of the permanent conditions under which work has to be done. Never rest until you have got the almighty wall on your side and not against you."[10]

It was a fine ideal. The very openness of the Uppingham situation when Thring began—few existing buildings, room to expand in the small country-town, space for playing-fields all around—helped to make it possible. Perhaps by the time Charles arrived the first enthusiasm had begun to wane. The chapel was a dull building with a heavy stone

pulpit. The class rooms were uninspiring. The houses, though intended
to be homes in which the individual boy could flourish, were very
different from home as Charles had known it. Something at least of the
prison house descended upon him as he came to Fircroft in September
1898.

At first he was reasonably happy.

> "It was not till I was thirteen that I left home and London and was
> plunged into a public school. At first the change had little effect. It
> was all strange and full of pitfalls: but being nurtured on *Tom Brown*
> I had been so frightened beforehand that its novelty was rather
> bewildering than terrible ... At least the place was utterly unlike
> the Rugby of Arnold's day. People were kind—on the whole: I was
> neither bullied nor seriously ragged; the work was not hard; the
> country was delightful. The first few terms went quickly and happily.
> Indeed I felt like a changeling who had dropped into a queer world
> of topsy-turvydom where nothing was quite intelligible but every-
> thing could, with luck, be endured and might even be enjoyed."[11]

His letters home during his first year were natural and cheerful.
In one, he has advice to offer on young Ted's education. In another he
reveals his contempt for the crib. To wrestle with an author and his
original text remained one of his life-long principles for serious study.
In addition to studying classical authors he was making some acquaintance with Biblical literature and beginning to compare the contributions to civilisation of Jew, Greek and Roman. But the real excitement
of his letter-writing begins when he recounts some observation or
operation in the world of nature. Although he experienced some feeling
of constriction he seems in fact to have been remarkably free to walk
out into the countryside and to send home trophies of various kinds
that he had captured.

For example the gardener at Fircroft had one day found a Crossbill
hanging in a wire fence in the garden.

> "It is very thin and has evidently just migrated from the north. As
> you know they are not found except in winter and then are rare.

Please paint bird and head and foot and preserve wing-feathers and feet. I regard it as a very lucky find indeed. I feel quite intoxicated with joy after such a dull afternoon. It is the rarest bird I have ever seen and I hope joy has not made my demands too severe. I am sure you will enter into the rarity of the thing and if you have sufficient time will portray him nobly. Try and get a good position. My demands are of course absurd but I feel nearly paralysed with pleasure."

Towards the end of his first spring term he was stricken by one of the ordinary infectious ailments and had to spend time in the Sanatorium. From there he writes:

"I got out for the first time this morning. There is a huge garden and I went all over it. I saw a beautiful chaffinch, some tom tits, two great tits, some green finches, robins and thrushes, countless blackbirds and hedge sparrows and the common sparrow in plenty. I got a dead tom tit a few days ago and painted his head and foot, but I don't know if I can send it to you. If not I will look at it carefully and take measurements. It was a lovely specimen. Please could you copy out this note on it. Sunday last saw a blue tit. General colour above greenish grey. Lesser wing coverts like back. Remiges grey with blue edge on outer web. Greenish tinge on secondaries. Primary coverts bluish grey. Median and greater coverts blue. The latter with broad white tips forming a bar. Under wing coverts pale yellow. Undersides yellow. Tale (sic) blue grey. Top of head bright blue. Sides of face white with black eye stripe. Throat black as also a stripe round the head. Back of head below blue cap bluish black, below which is a patch of white. Bill greyish black. Feet black."

So the thirteen-year old boy was training himself, with his mother's help, to observe exactly. He was also making a few experiments in dissecting, and seeking her advice about "skeletonising a roach" which he had caught.[12]

"I cannot do it with a knife because it is not like a bird with proper thick bones and I might get into an ambush of bones waiting to be

broken off; chemicals I don't thoroughly understand. So please send
your advice. If you desire to be a participator in the smell I can bury
it and then bring it home. The whiffs of perfume which issue from
the box on its being opened are delicious. That rotten thrush's egg
we blew some time ago is nothing to it: nor is that teal. A quad-
rupled mixture of these and all other bad smells bring a slight resemblance of it before you." P.S. "The young rat was killed today and I
skinned and loosely stuffed it this afternoon as it is very wet. Please
keep it as it is my first animal stuffed."

The school authorities seem to have been lenient in allowing Charles
to carry on some of his activities in this field of exploration even though
he would dearly have loved to do more. His house master seems also to
have been sympathetic in permitting him to send some of his strange
treasures home. On February 10th, 1899 Tancred was writing to his
brother about his young nephew in these terms:

"Charles seems very well and is going on first rate. He is a regular
young needle and mops up things A1 quite unlike most of our boys.
It is soon to judge yet but it would seem as if he might have almost
anything before him. I fancy he is about the best boy I have taught at
Latin and Greek and I should say quite the best of the bunch I have
even now and that means giving away a year. He has the deltic mind
which is the main thing and retains and applies what he hears and is
taught. He sent you a brace of birds yesterday which will be a trifle
high I fancy when you get them. I told him to remove and bury them
which did not seem to meet his views at all."

So the first two years at Uppingham went by without undue strain or
unhappiness. Then however the coming of adolescence seemed to
change the whole situation.

"For two years I was in the school, though not in any real sense of it.
Then I ceased to be a sojourner and found my place in the community.
Of those later years it is less pleasant to write. There are from them a
few bright memories—an occasional innings at cricket, random

glimpses of wider interests, friendships that lasted for a month or so with boys who shared my keenness for birds and insects, a master or two who gave hints of knowledge and willingness to share it. But on the whole I hated it; and as I grew the hatred settled into a steady ache of loneliness and fear... It was my own fault—but not altogether. I was shy, and so people thought me conceited; keen about ideas, with not a soul to talk to; weak and weedy in a school crazy for athletics; passionately fond of nature, and never allowed to study her; eager for friendship, but never finding a friend; fastidious about sex in an atmosphere loud with indecency. Put it otherwise: a prig, a prude, a book-worm, a bug-hunter, who is no good at football and has on occasion a sarcastic tongue, is not likely to be popular. And probably his wretchedness is not only well earned but in the long run not unwholesome. It is good, up to a point, for those who are blessed or cursed with brains, to get the pride knocked out of them: and in my case the breaking-point was just not reached. Others of similar type were less fortunate. For me the wounds are old scars now: but the marks are still too sensitive to touch." [13]

Charles's comments on religion and morals at Uppingham, written more than twenty years after his experience of them, may be coloured by later reflection and selective in detail. But in all probability the account gives a fair representation of the public school situation in general and of Uppingham in particular at the beginning of this century. Compulsory chapel which inevitably became boring to high spirited boys; an excessively academic approach to the Bible which tended to make it inferior in quality to the classics; a taboo on speaking about religion in any unofficial context; confirmation, with preparation that was often inadequate and at times embarrassing followed by the service itself with its artificially induced emotional atmosphere; Communion with its manuals for self-examination—all these are described vividly, frankly and not unfairly. The religion that in his heart of hearts he wanted never came his way.

In part this may have been due to the dominating place which the classics held in the total educational system.

"It may still be doubted" he writes "whether any medium of education has greater power than the classics to foster both accuracy and
imagination. But the effect of the ostracism of the sciences was to
leave religion entangled with archaeology, to give us God in terms of
Sinai and Olympus rather than of evolution and experience and to
suggest that Jesus belonged only to the world of the first century.
It was not that I had rejected religion or disbelieved in God or
thought little of the church. Only, as before so now, religion and
life belonged to different worlds, and the world of life was full of interest, and of pain. I couldn't begin to think it out, and truth to tell was
not specially eager to do so. Practical problems were more urgent than
theological. Each day had its hopes and worries: there was always
plenty to keep me busy, and generally something, holidays or an
afternoon in the country, to look forward to. Existence was a difficult
business but the difficulties had nothing to do with God."[14]

The saddest defect of all in public school religion, Charles suggests as
he looks back, has been its inabiltiy to make the figure of Jesus strong,
noble and compelling. Julius Caesar, Hannibal, Hector had become
vivid and challenging personalities, arousing his admiration, even
evoking his hero-worship. But Jesus had remained a shadowy figure.
His divinity was generally so emphasised that His life and teaching
seemed unreal, "a stage-play, a fairy-tale, a series of oracles, an intrusion
from another world. We were allowed to conclude that Jesus did not
matter." Jesus as truly human, as the supreme figure in the life of
mankind, as the Lord of all good life, as the perfect example of fortitude
and heroic achievement, as the initiator of a world-wide kingdom, the
Kingdom of God—of such a figure Charles scarcely caught a glimpse
during his school-days. The career that challenged every human
convention had been largely passed by in silence.
     In due course Charles became a praepositor and captain of his house.
He played cricket, fives and hockey with some success. In the Speech
Day of 1903 he won prizes for Latin Declamation and Latin Epigram
and recited passages from Bridges and Molière. In 1904 the prize was
for English Essay (Is Tennyson the most classical poet since Milton?),

the recitation Milton's Samson. He had won a scholarship in Classics to his father's old College, Caius, Cambridge, and his father had received a letter from Uppingham referring to the "incalculable value" of his son's work as house-captain. To all outward appearances schooldays had been highly successful. But in dramatic contrast Charles records how a week after his last summer term he found himself reading Olive Schreiner's *Story of an African Farm*. The motto "A striving and a striving and an ending in nothing" seemed exactly to epitomise his mood at the moment. Had lessons learned at school brought him any nearer to the ultimate meaning of things? His task, he knew, was still to pursue in loneliness the white bird of truth.

NOTES TO CHAPTER ONE

1. p. 19: *A Wanderer's Way*, p. 10. (1927)
2. p. 22: Ibid. p. 7.
3. p. 23: Ibid. p.7.
4. p. 24: *In Praise of Birds*, p. 2.
5. p. 25: *The Ramblings of a Bird Lover*, p. 100.
6. p. 26: He even tried his hand at dissecting when on holiday at Parkgate. He found a dead cormorant and taught himself details of its anatomy experimentally.
7. p. 28: See e.g. Tillich's moving meditation "The Depth of Existence" in *The Shaking of the Foundations*.
8. p. 28: *A Wanderer's Way*, p. 5 f. His initiation into the regular services of the Church had been, to say the least, unfortunate. "It was only when religion led on to church-going that God became an object of dread, and a few well-intentioned sentences precipitated the shapeless awe of the numinous into an acute horror of a very definite tyrant. The children's service was taken by the curate, impressive in his strange robes, overwhelming as he warned us of the certainty and the pains of hell. Perhaps it was part of his creed; perhaps he merely found us tiresome and wanted to frighten us into better behaviour. But I was just beginning to wonder about life, and his words produced a reaction out of all proportion to their worth. The wrath of God eclipsed His love at once."
9. p. 31: *Evolution ond the Christian Concept of God*, p. 7.
10. p. 31: *The Life of Edward Thring*, p. 217.

11. p. 32: *A Wanderer's Way*, p. 10.
12. p. 33: This letter must have been written while on holiday but it is of the same period.
13. p. 34: Ibid. p. 11 f.
14. p. 36: Ibid. p. 21 f.

CHAPTER TWO

The Quest for Life's Meaning

In October 1904 Charles began the intimate association with Cambridge which was to last for almost exactly sixty years. Only during the decade 1921–31 was he absent for any extended period and even then sermons or lectures often brought him back to the University for short visits. He loved Cambridge: he contributed much to the life of the University in the twentieth century: it probably moulded him more than any other single institution, even including the Church of England.

As a scholar of his College Charles had to give more serious attention to his studies than was necessarily the case with many of his contemporaries. The Classical Tripos Examination, for which he had to prepare himself, came at the end of his third year but there were lectures and weekly supervisions and College examinations at regular intervals. The whole concentration was upon the languages and literatures of Greece and Rome and Charles, who had already reached a high standard in these disciplines in school-days, went on to gain ultimately the highest distinction that the University could offer, a first-class in the Tripos itself.

But it was not achieved easily. His memory for names and for detailed variations was phenomenal. His sense of rhythm and movement in language—the right word in the right place—was quite exceptional. These gifts stood him in good stead in all matters related to literary form and to historical reconstruction, especially in the realm of Latin studies. He was in his element with Caesar and Cicero. But he was never equally at home with Greek authors and never attained the same distinction in the Greek language. Subtleties of philosophical thinking, the to-and-fro movement of a dialectical pursuit of truth, the heights

39

and depths of Greek tragedy—these did not belong to Charles's native land. Probably this was the root difference between him and the man who was to become later so great a friend—William Temple. The latter was a Greek through and through. Charles had the strengths—and some of the limitations—of the Roman genius. The very word imperious, which it seems natural to apply to him, sets him firmly within the Roman tradition.

Whether he could ever have been content to concentrate all his energies on classical studies alone and to become a leading authority in that field is doubtful. Already when he entered the University his interest in natural history and English literature was considerable and his eager mind was in quest of some deeper interpretation of life's meaning than he had hitherto known. It only needed a rebuff or a disappointment in the area in which he had felt most confident to bring first disillusionment and then a determination to look elsewhere for the way to his own personal fulfilment. This rebuff was not long in coming.

"My first term started with what seemed a disaster. Picture me a shy and unimposing freshman, looking to be snubbed, accustomed to accept the idolatry of the athlete as a law of the universe, having lost what little comfort religion could give, and entering upon a new life for which my only qualification seemed to be a working knowledge of Latin and Greek. Weary as I was of the classics, they supplied a pedestal on which to base my self-respect: if all else was beyond me, I could at least do passable elegiacs and hexameters. How I laboured over that first copy of verses! Judged by school standards the result was, I knew, good; certainly the best that I could ever hope to produce. And so with it to my director of studies. A glance—purely formal: the slash of a blue pencil: and 'Never dare to show me up this schoolboy stuff again.' I realise now that it was his invariable practice, a good strong dose to purge the senior scholar of his pride. But for me it was devastating. If this was bad, then my whole standards of judgment were false: I no longer knew the difference between good and evil and had wasted years on misdirected labours. My interest in classical scholarship had perhaps never been very vigorous: it was killed at a stroke. Thereafter a minimum of drudgery should suffice: my interests should go elsewhere."[1]

In retrospect Charles may have exaggerated the influence of this one incident. But he was almost hyper-sensitive at this stage in his life. Schooldays may not have been as unhappy as he later imagined but the simple fact is that for as long as he could remember he had been struggling with what he regarded as physical and moral cowardice: shyness and self-depreciation constantly caused him misery; a word could cut him like a knife. So it is probably true that although his very sense of duty and responsibility to his family kept him steadily working at his classics, especially as the time of the Tripos drew near, he did it without that enthusiasm, that devoted specialisation which could have prepared him for some position of academic eminence in his field. He learned to handle most of the tools with competence and ease; he had no urge to use them for the construction of original works of classical scholarship.

If the classics were not to become the centre of interest what would be his attitude to the second, (sometimes the first) concern of university life—sport in all its forms? That he had wanted to excel at school but had never achieved more than moderate success seems obvious. He was genuinely fond of cricket and continued to play it whenever possible. But for a boy coming up from a non-rowing school, there was always the possibility that the river would prove to be the place of winning fame. Charles joined the Boat Club and to the end of his life never lost a sense of excitement when the Lents or the Mays were being rowed. Bishop Hans Lilje of Hanover has told of his astonishment at arriving in Cambridge after the Second World War to be guest of the Regius Professor of Divinity and finding himself being hurried at once to the banks of the Cam in order that his host might not miss the race in which his College boat was competing. A *German* Professor running along a tow-path was a sight beyond the Bishop's wildest imagination!

In February 1905 Charles was writing to his mother and his young brother. He had recently had his first experience of rowing a course under racing conditions and was quite elated. To his mother he writes:

"We had a very hard day yesterday which was extremely satisfactory in every way. I am personally bucked up because I was uncertain whether I could stand the strain of a course. I believe my heart must have outgrown its evil ways as I really did not feel at all abnormally bad. Our races are on Wednesday and I shall go to the extravagance of having a mutton chop for lunch till then, I think. My bills are smaller this term I think, so it will be worth it.

So sorry to bore you with all this but it is rather overwhelming at present. I send a list of the books read up till now that you may see that my time is not wholly taken up."

(Aeschylus, Homer, Thucydides, Pliny, Tacitus, Cicero—a list which shows that his director's shaft had not wounded his classical interests mortally.)

But with all his keenness Charles was never destined to become a great oarsman. He was wiry but not powerfully built. He was often to refer in later life to the team spirit engendered in rowing. When he became Master of Christ's he was delighted that the Boat Club gave him their confidence and their friendship. Yet athletic achievement was not to be the chief distinction of university days. Were there other fields, besides classical studies and games, in which he could make his mark?

In the first decade of this century music and drama had each a small band of devotees at the two ancient Universities but the two chief pursuits, outside strictly academic disciplines, in which fame could be achieved were the spoken or the written word. Every College had its debating society and for those seeking highest honours the Union at Oxford or Cambridge was the training ground for success in politics or at the Bar. Each College also had its own magazine while those with a literary flair, who hoped ultimately to succeed as writers or journalists, competed with one another in the columns of *Isis* or *Granta*.

Charles was not a debater. He embraced with zest the new opportunities which Cambridge afforded of discussions with intimate friends but he never enjoyed the cut and thrust of serious debate. He was too sensitive to take criticism of himself or of his position easily: in fact he could be deeply hurt by a phrase which had not been meant unkindly.

Perhaps there was a lurking feeling of insecurity in regard to the intellectual defence which he built up to support the causes which he advocated. He was destined, it is true, to master the art of rhetoric and to become an orator who impressed and charmed. But in undergraduate life the orator has little scope to display his gifts.

With the written word, however, the situation was far more favourable. Charles possessed a wide vocabulary, a command of rhythmic prose and plenty of ideas. He had first tried his hand at editing a magazine while still virtually in the nursery. So he grasped the opportunity to become Editor of *The Caian*, his College Magazine, and subsequently to rise higher still, to an editor's chair in the office of *Granta*, the most famous of Cambridge literary reviews.

Charles's earliest contributions to *Granta* were published in the May term 1906. Themes which later were to be taken very seriously were already being explored in a half-mocking style. The evils of competition, the folly of war, the boredom of club-life—essays touch on these subjects with a certain display of clever phrases but not yet with any depth of insight. Though he denounces cynicism there is more than a trace of the cynic in his own approach to the subjects he treats. "This is the true justification of a Debating Society: not that it gives instruction, not that it provides interest, not that it elevates the hearers: simply that to the despondent it is an opiate and to the cynical a holy joy." Undergraduate stuff? Possibly, but suggestive of a growing disillusionment with the surface activities of university life and a deepening concern for that which is more substantial and enduring.

Amongst his more serious interests the theory of evolution had evidently come to occupy a prominent place. An editorial introduction during his period of office finds space to comment on the great progress in the study of heredity over the past two years. And on South African Cycads he remarks: "The formation of cones seems to depend largely on drought and exposure to light, a fact which the horticulturist should note." Further he introduces what appears to be a new feature in the College magazine—reviews of recent scientific publications. He chooses two: *Life and Evolution* by F. W. Headley and *Variation, Heredity and Evolution* by Robert Heath Lock. The first is by a "classical scholar with a passion for things natural," who approaches very near to Hesiod's ideal of the man who found out everything for himself. "We would venture especially to commend his chapters on 'Gills and Lungs' and on 'The Flight of Birds' in each of which the author has given us many fresh and personal observations and experiments. And the wealth of pictorial is not less remarkable than the wealth of verbal illustrations. Some of the pictures are rather crude but on the other hand many are admirable. The most interesting are, perhaps, the author's snapshots of birds on the wing." A reviewer might in these words have been writing about Charles's own efforts twenty years later.

Of the second book he is much more critical. The chapter on evolution he thinks has been just thrown together—it is merely a series of disconnected parts. "Finally we venture to suggest that the idea of evolution has permeated far wider than he supposes. Is it necessary for him to have his pick at the dead horse of the special creation of species? The references to it are few, but we feel that the author is himself half-a-century out of date in what he terms 'religion'." Mr. Lock may have been behind the time but Charles may equally have been ahead of his time in assuming that the idea of evolution had already established itself firmly in the general outlook of the period.

These were Charles's earliest adventures into the realms of editorials and feature articles. He had an eye for important issues and considerable daring in commenting on them. One example became famous. During the time of his editorship he arranged for three Trinity men to write an article exposing a practice which was becoming common in the science laboratories: boys who were employed to prepare slides and exhibits for examination purposes were selling lists of them to candidates at half-a-crown apiece. The article was published and Professor Langley was furious. He threatened a libel action if Charles could not substantiate his case within twenty four hours.

"I spent them hectically collecting my witnesses and fortifying them to give evidence. Late that night we visited the Professor. He investigated, found the thing was true, withdrew his threat and asked me for the credit of the University to say no more about it. We made quite a lot of money over the *Granta* that term but a certain medical college (presumably his own!) wasn't a bit pleased."

Charles had become Editor jointly with R. M. Pattison Muir in May term, 1907—a bold undertaking when his Tripos was so near. The two continued in office through Michaelmas Term but then Charles resigned. During the term, however, the Editors had brought out a notable number to celebrate *Granta's* completion of twenty one years of publication. This included contributions from R. C. Lehmann and E. F. Benson, both of whom, in company with Owen Seaman who was later to become Editor of *Punch*, attended the celebration dinner. It was the first time in its twenty one years that *Granta* had been edited from Caius; there is every reason to suppose that it was a successful period in the magazine's history. So far as Charles was concerned it gave him a wide opportunity to become acquainted with literary figures such as Rupert Brooke and James Elroy Flecker (who had come over from Oxford to spend some time in Cambridge) and with Union figures such as H. Wilson Harris who was to become Editor of *The Spectator* and University Member of Parliament.

Contemporary records have preserved the essential facts about Charles's study of the classics, his cricket and rowing, his literary ventures. But had it not been for William Temple's strong pressure upon him some twenty years later to write an account of his own religious experience and development we should have known little of the most important aspects of his undergraduate days—the discovery of friendship and love and God. He came up to Cambridge lonely and hungering for friendship; he needed more than most the gift of a woman's love; and though he was inclined to discount the religion he had so far known—it was, he felt, Stoicism rather than Christianity—deep down there was a yearning for integration and meaning which was to be satisfied only through a disclosure of the presence of the living God. The story of his triple discovery is brilliantly told in the second chapter of *A Wanderer's Way*, a book which has been described by a distinguished modern historian as one of the classics of the twentieth century.

But before he attained what might be called his public freedom, the release which set him free to communicate his inner feelings through writing and speech, he experienced what might be called a private illumination, the first of a series in which from time to time his spirit was caught up into an almost rapturous sense of union with the plenitude of cosmic life. In August 1905 the Raven family changed the location of their annual holiday from the sands of Dee to the Lake District. It was Charles's first experience of acquaintance with the mountains at close range and initially it was by no means a welcome change. But then one day he set off alone to explore. He began to feel the lure of high places. And in the last week an unforgettable period of solitude on the summit of Great Gable constituted, he believed, the turning-point of his life. His moment of ecstasy was wholly unexpected; its significance was at the time unrecognised; but looking back he was sure that it marked a completely new stage in his life's journey from which there was to be no looking back.

"To be alone in such a place on such a day is to be drawn up from delight to rapture, and from rapture to adoration. When you have marked the lie of the land and spied out its secrets, when you have absorbed bit by bit every aspect of that glorious panorama, slowly the width of it and the far-off glimpses of plain and ocean give wings to your soul; the little hills rejoice on every side; the stark strength of the mountains ushers you into the presence chamber of the eternal. Free, joyous, abiding, their quality infects you with its own influence. You, this tiny, tragic, transient creature are at one with the universe, seized of its age-long glories, harmonised to its rhythm, enfolded in its peace. This is worship: here is holy ground.

Not that I took off my shoes. I was only a boy, suddenly integrated into manhood. Worship was still to me a thing of churches and clergy and the Book of Common Prayer. My God had been the deity of Jewry and the Creeds—I had disowned him and disowned him still. A boy lying on the rocks in the sunshine, what had he to do with religion? How could a new birth come so silent and unknown?

Yet it was with a joy wholly new, a radiance of face, a tingle of energy and a heart in heaven, that I scrambled at last down Windy Gap, raced over Great Gable and dropped back to the Tarn, to manhood and the earth."[2]

In August for the first time he had experienced this moment of ecstasy when alone with nature. But there was no consciousness that this had anything to do with formal religion. He had attended Chapel fairly regularly in his first year. He had met pagans on the one hand, fundamentalists on the other. But he felt in no way committed. Then came the more comprehensive and far-reaching revelation which not only brought moments of rapture but somehow lifted his whole life on to a new level.

"For my first eighteen months I was otherwise a pure pagan, and though growing fast was still very immature. The frost at school had nipped my buds severely, and though Cambridge was a spring-time it took me a long time to respond to its warmth. In the Christmas vacation of 1906 the miracle happened, and every shrivelled twig of me burst into bloom. I had come down a shy and awkward lad, self-conscious in company and rather morbid when alone. Suddenly the whole world seemed transfigured: people were kind and easy, friendliness was natural, life was bursting with beauty, the whole air was full of song; and I could take my place in it all simply and happily without fear or introspection, finding every common thing a new delight. The next two terms were spent in a haze of happiness."
"Amidst the natural beauties of Cambridge there would come to me something of what Wordsworth and the mystics have made familiar —the sense that for a moment time had stopped, that suddenly the visible world had become transparent, that the eternal reality, beyond and behind the things of sense, had been unveiled and in an instant of rapture had enfolded me into union with itself. Certainly those times, every little detail of their setting, is present to me as a possession for ever."[3]

The critical revelation had come early in January 1906. And then, in April, there was another moment whose effect upon his personal devel-

opment was to be incalculable. Calling in a purely formal way at the
Master's Lodge he met for the first time Miss Margaret Ermyntrude
Buchanan-Wollaston, the Master's niece. Immediately, so it appears, a
new love was born. But to pursue his love was not easy. Charles had
not yet reached the end of his second year. All comings and goings
inside College could be easily watched. Often it was a case of Charles,
having been let out by the front door after a tea party, being admitted
again by the back door which was out of sight of undergraduate eyes.
Somehow the lovers contrived to meet and to exchange letters and in
July, just after Charles' twenty-first birthday, they became engaged,
only however on condition that no announcement was to be made till
after he had taken the Tripos Examination in the following year.

The final year before the Tripos provided a foretaste of the kind of
life he would one day be living outside Cambridge. A constant turning
to Bee (as she was known to her relations and friends) for solace and
encouragement; concentrated attention upon reading and study;
high-pressure activities in journalism; a snatching of times for recreation
and expeditions to the country; membership of societies covering many
interests; it would have been hardly surprising if the final examination
result had brought disappointment. But happily, though failing to attain
the highest distinction of all (the first class was divided into three
divisions) Charles was placed in the second division of the first class
and an academic career became a lively possibility. It was normal for
anyone who hoped for a Fellowship to stay on in Cambridge and try
for another First. The question for Charles was what should be the
subject for this second course of study.

For whatever reason he rejected Classics. He was fascinated by the
Natural Sciences but knew that he had no kind of preliminary qualification for studying them at Tripos level. He had at one time considered
a career in law but had decided against it: the Law Tripos therefore was
of no interest. The most obvious remaining possibility was Divinity.
There seems to be some doubt as to whether Charles had by this time
decided to be ordained. If so it was not his immediate intention. Yet he
was undoubtedly interested in the history of Christianity and the
chance to study its origins made a strong appeal. He therefore decided

to read for a particular section of the Second part of the Divinity Tripos, a section which included extensive readings in the Greek and Latin Fathers, a period of modern doctrine and some history and philosophy of religion. The decision made, Charles launched himself with characteristic enthusiasm upon his new voyage of discovery.

The world of Cambridge divinity to which Charles now transferred his interests had become famous in the late nineteenth century chiefly because of the eminence of three outstanding figures. The great achievement of Westcott and Hort had been to produce a reliable text of the New Testament in 1881 and the result of their labours not only prepared the way for the Revised Version of the English Bible in 1885 but also gave scholars and students an indispensable tool for their further work. It had been Lightfoot's distinction to place the New Testament firmly within the context of its historical setting. In particular the Epistles of St. Paul gained an entirely new illumination when seen against the background of events and movements in the Graeco-Roman world. Hence to gain a mastery of the Greek language, to study texts and documents at first-hand, to interpret them by comparing their form and content with those of contemporary pagan writings—these were the ideals to which Charles was introduced as he began his theological studies and they remained with him throughout his career.

For such a task some knowledge of the Old Testament was required but Charles never became a Hebraist nor did he ever make an extended study of Old Testament documents. Though he worked devotedly in later life for reconciliation between Christian and Jew it is doubtful if he ever found the Hebrew approach to theology congenial. The majestic witness to Divine transcendence, the glad submission to Divinely ordained law, the recognition of Divine activity operating through critical events in history—these were never Charles's emphases. Immanence, evolution, freedom, worship—these were rather to become his watchwords. The Old Testament provided a shadowy background. The New Testament was the record of the living drama whose character and significance it was to be his task to unfold.

The teacher who became his supervisor and to whom he remained

ever devoted was John Henry Arthur Hart, Fellow of St. John's College.
In a letter to his son, Henry St. John Hart, Charles later wrote "I owe
more to your father than to any living teacher." Some ten years senior
to his pupil he shared his interests in natural history and Charles loved
to quote a passage from his book *The Hope of Catholic Judaism* in which a
parallel is drawn between the theologian and the biologist in their
methods of research. In the world of natural history, Charles points out,
elaborate theories had been built up in the early twentieth century about
animals' adaptation to environment. They seemed utterly convincing,
an irresistible deduction from the facts. "But the facts were dead
specimens not living creatures: and study of the life of animal and insect
exposed the fallacy of the whole hypothesis." It is the field naturalist
who has watched life and living processes at first hand who is best able
to explain puzzling phenomena.

So it is, Charles claims, following his former teacher, in matters of
Gospel criticism; a purely literary criticism can construct all manner of
speculative theories. What is needed is to get close to the society out of
which the Gospels were produced.

> "Literary criticism must always be pursued with the primary object
> of becoming familiar with the personalities behind the books, with
> the life reflected in them, with the experience of which they are the
> outcome. The critic must soak himself in the period he is studying,
> must share the society, the circumstances, the outlook of his authors,
> must know their time and place from within, see with their eyes and
> hear with their ears. Scientific compilation of words and phrases,
> elaborate disentangling of sources and editorships, a nice perception
> of inconsistencies and errors, these are neither his chief task nor his
> primary method. If he relies upon them to the exclusion of human
> and historical sensitiveness his work will be 'utterly unsympathetic,
> absolutely external and blind to the finest side of the literature that
> it treats'—and, it must be added, will reach conclusions manifestly
> absurd."[4]

This is an important exposition of Charles's own method and ideal.
It is clinched, interestingly enough, by the quotation from Hart to which

I have already referred. Hart has been commenting on Schweitzer's book, *The Quest of the Historical Jesus*, in which the many critical reconstructions of the nineteenth century are neatly labelled and assessed.

"Wheat and tares alike," Hart writes," are rooted up and dried and pressed and labelled and discussed—and you learn as much about the living plant as you can learn of a fox by contemplating its mask and pads and brush, each cured and mounted for display as the relics of an animal worthy to be hunted or shot or trapped according to the custom of the country. For scientific observation of living things, the systematist must wait upon the biologist. You must go to the earth and hide and wait if you want to see the vixen play with her cubs."

This emphasis on patient observation of life-situations Charles never forgot.

With Hart he began his study of the New Testament. Under J. F. Bethune-Baker he began to wrestle with the complexities of early Christian doctrine. This subject Bethune-Baker made very much his own and his lectures formed the staple diet for successive generations of theological students and ordinands. He was one of Cambridge's "characters", an individualist who could be exceedingly trying to his colleagues as he haggled over points of detail in committee—sometimes keeping them till midnight–yet who would give time and information to his students with the utmost kindness and generosity.

From him Charles learned particularly to read the text of the Fathers carefully, to work within a precise chronological framework, to seek by every means to become familiar with the rich variety of religious cults and speculative philosophies which flourished in the ancient world during the first three centuries of the Christian era and perhaps above all not to be hidebound by any system of Catholic "orthodoxy" but to be ready to form free and independent judgments after a full and honest weighing of the evidence. Bethune-Baker became one of the leading spirits in the Modern Churchmen's Union and although Charles never identified himself wholeheartedly with this movement there is no doubt that he had great sympathy with the so-called "modernist" approach to questions raised by advances in history and science.[5]

Bethune-Baker, Charles records, was always ready to give him the assistance of "his wide knowledge of patristics and his keen and candid criticism." But there was one other famous figure, then at the height of his powers in Cambridge, with whom Charles felt an even closer rapport. This was H. M. Gwatkin, the Dixie Professor of Ecclesiastical History, one of the last polymaths to survive amidst the explosion of detailed learning which the twentieth century has witnessed. [6] Theologian and historian, mathematician and entomologist, he was a man after Charles's own heart. "His learning, enthusiasm and generosity," Charles wrote later in the Preface to his *Apollinarianism*, "were an inspiration and remain an ever-honoured memory to generations of students."[7]

That Gwatkin did in fact exercise a great influence upon Charles's developing ideas in student days becomes evident as one reads his later writings. Gwatkin had severe things [8] to say about the medieval attitude to the world of nature and Charles never abandoned the conviction that the rise of modern science only became possible when the stranglehold of the medieval church had been broken and the new freedom of thought represented in Reformation and Renaissance had become a reality. Even more significantly we find Charles in an important peroration towards the end of his book *Jesus and the Gospel of Love* (1931), turning back to a passage from Gwatkin written in the early years of this century and describing the new attitude that modern science has made possible.

"First," Gwatkin writes," the witness of science would seem clear and decisive that the universe has one plan, one Power, behind it and no more. It is a coat without a seam. Physical evil is too closely woven into the fabric to be torn out, so that all polytheistic or dualistic explanations of it must be dropped. If that Power be personal, we must conclude that even moral evil is here by his permission. Its possibilities must be, so to speak, part of the plan. In the next place science has finally destroyed the conception of a God who acts on the world only from the outside. Either natural law is all divine or none of it is divine. Either God works in all or he works in none. For a third, there are some who say that God is unfeeling Law, while the Christians tell us that God is Love. At first sight the witness of science is all for rigid law: yet the right conclusion is not that love is not behind, but that if there be love it must be perfect love. We cannot believe now in a love divine which wavers and changes. You will see more and more clearly that the awful sternness of Nature is greater—and may well be no other—than the sternness of perfect love doing its work of love." (p. 411)

Such a vision gave Charles confidence to face what was to be for him a constant challenge—the existence of pain and suffering and apparently meaningless evil in the world. He could not accept Aquinas's distinction between a kingdom of nature and a kingdom of grace: his passionate concern was always for integration and unity. He could not entertain Origen's notion (much as he admired Origen) of a perfect creation followed and upset by a cosmic fall: this was sheer speculation with no basis in historical evidence. Most significantly of all (for Origen and Aquinas each shared the general world-outlook of his own age and those ages were now in the far distant past), Charles could not follow Bishop Gore, whose book *The Reconstruction of Belief* had gained wide acclaim in the 1920s, in his leading conception of a divine purpose being slowly and progressively realised on *the stage of the world;* for Charles the divine purpose was constantly being expressed and realised *in and through* the world. The universe was to be viewed not merely as a theatre in which God, the Church and mankind were playing out the drama of redemption; rather (and this Charles passionately believed and affirmed) the activity of the living God was being witnessed through every manifestation of light and life and love which the total world-order of nature and mankind reveals. In challenging Gore (and he returned to the attack on several occasions) Charles was running counter to one of the major influences in Anglican thinking in the first quarter of this century.

One other teacher captured Charles's imagination and admiration during the year that he was reading for the Divinity Tripos. This was Professor William Bateson, one of the world's outstanding geneticists in the early years of this century. Charles's interest in birds and insects and moths and plant-life had been a part of his very being for as long as he could remember. It had brought him relaxation, expansion of spirit, aesthetic delight.

"To spend a night alone in a summer woodland or a stretch of unspoiled fen is to experience an initiation into the life of the contemplative. Orthodox methods of meditation do not appeal to me: they produce boredom or coma—and platitudes. I can meditate best when there is something to occupy me without absorbing my interest, something which leaves the mind free to roam, to grapple with a difficulty, to disengage for a moment, and then to return to the encounter with fresh zest. Mothing is the perfect pursuit for such a temperament... No one can know what nature means until he has spent such a vigil alone and in the night: in the day-time the grandeur of her massed effect is concealed by the lavish wealth of form and colour, the glamour and fascination of each smallest detail; in the darkness the main lines of the whole are manifest, and make their appeal to the same qualities in yourself. There is a wealth of meaning in the cryptic sayings which declare that God dwells in thick darkness and that in darkness the Son of Man is revealed."[9]

But the study of natural history had gradually brought him also to a kind of intellectual crisis. Genetic determinism assumed the stature of a Goliath and Charles set himself to collect as many stones as possible to do battle with the giant. To learn the giant's ways he sat regularly in the lecture-room where Bateson championed the deterministic theory, and he also gained permission, though he was not officially a biological student, to carry out experiments in the laboratories.

"For it seemed to me then, and despite the critics it seems to me still, that if there is no room at all for use-inheritance in evolution, if our whole physical make-up is strictly conditioned by the immutable germ-plasm, and if therefore our struggles and hard-won virtues have no effect whatever upon the course of development, then to speak of the Creator as in any real sense the Father is impossible: Calvinism of so rigid a sort as to be irreconcilable with Christianity is the only possible theology."[10]

In sharp contrast Charles determined to make it his aim to construct what he called a "stereoscopic vision of reality," a reconciliation between his scientific convictions and his religious experiences.

The meaning and development of life, frustration and error, suffering and pain, alternate response and freedom, the individual and society, the emergence and development of a sense of value—these and above all the paradox of good and evil were common quests for me in both my main interests as they are for all normal human beings. And with the discovery that I was constantly asking the same questions in each field came quite suddenly the knowledge that in both I was being compelled to give similar answers. One looks through a stereoscope and at first sees only two blurred because separate pictures; as one alters the focus of the instrument or of one's eyes suddenly the two images come together and the whole scene stands out solid and in perspective. It would be an exaggeration to say that my sudden awareness of a stereoscopic vision of reality seen from the double standpoint of science and of religion was immediate or complete: but it came, and with it a sense of discovery and of satisfaction. The two worlds were one and the same. The process of creation, studied in its initial and physical aspect scientifically, was the same as that which reached its most revealing phase in the records of man's religious development and had its culmination in Jesus who proved to be what his followers had claimed, the mystery or illuminating event by which the nature of reality was unveiled and the meaning of evolution declared."[11]

What however had not yet become vivid and compelling to him was any vision of *the* (unique) Son of God. He could accept in theory that some personal energy exercising an immense influence had been abroad in the ancient classical world during the first century of our era. What he read about Jesus in the Gospels, what he learned about Paul's experience from his study of the Epistle to the Romans, seemed all of a piece. To try to explain the rise and spread of Christianity except in terms of such a dynamic figure as the Gospels portrayed seemed nothing less than preposterous. Yet so far all was theoretical and at second-hand: there was no conviction of a living, present, challenging Christ who could exercise an influence on his own life comparable to that which had utterly transfigured Paul.

Moreover the bulk of his theological studies were being devoted to the history of doctrine in the early Church. In this story he found much to admire. Origen and Clement of Alexandria were men of great intellectual stature whose reconciliation of Christian faith with Greek philosophy he found illuminating and convincing. But the shock was to come when he discovered that Origen had been condemned by the official church while Cyril of Alexandria, a man whom Charles found utterly base and contemptible, had been canonised! "If eternal salvation depended upon membership in such a church and the acceptance of such a verdict, then like the old Goth I would go to hell with my own people, to hell with Origen rather than to heaven with St. Cyril."

The first year of theological study had been a momentous one for Charles. He had stretched out one hand to grasp the discipline of historical theology, the other to embrace the discipline of a life-science. He was not an analytical philosopher, he was not a mathematician nor a logician. But with all his strength he was determined to hold together and bring into fruitful relationship his two consuming interests. When it came to the Tripos Examination he found himself hesitating between two questions. The first was concerned with Darwinism and Theology; the second with the bearing of the Logos Doctrine upon modern theories of the Person of Christ. He started on the former and wrote three pages. Then he decided that the latter was his real concern so started again and incorporated what he had already written into his final answer. This essay apparently gained him a star (denoting distinction) in the list of results which showed him occupying a place in the First Class. It was also a foreshadowing of the work of reconciliation which was to command his best energies for many years to come.

He had gained a thorough grounding in the doctrine of the early Church. He had fastened upon the model of evolution to provide him with the intellectual framework within which his detailed labours could be carried forward. But he was not yet conscious of any strong personal commitment beyond his love for his fiancée and his loyalty to friends. There was no compelling cause to command his devoted allegiance. And there was no sense either of any wider community calling for his services beyond the societies to which in the normal pattern of University life he had belonged. The year which followed the Divinity Tripos examination was to prove crucial in these respects. But before moving on to an entirely new adventure Charles was to enjoy a dreamlike existence on the Broads. To his mother he wrote: "The boat is large and luxurious and the whole a perfectly ideal experience: a complete slack and heavenly idleness—fishing, mothing, sailing and weather all good."

NOTES TO CHAPTER TWO

1. p. 40: *A Wanderer's Way*, p. 38 f.
2. p. 46: *Musings and Memories*, p. 148.
3. p. 47: *A Wanderer's Way*, p. 46 f.
4. p. 50: *Jesus and the Gospel of Love*, p. 131 f.
5. p. 51: Bethune-Baker attained a certain notoriety by what were regarded as the unorthodox views which he propounded at the Modern Churchmen's Union Conference at Girton College in 1922. The parents of a little girl, aged five, living in Cambridge were overheard by their daughter expressing their distress at the Professor's heretical utterances. A few days later she was asked in school to name four bad people in the Bible whose names begin with the letter B. She replied: Bathsheba, Beelzebub, and Bethune-Baker! The story gave the Professor immense delight.
6. p. 52: Charles lists Mahaffy in Dublin and Gwatkin in Cambridge as the last representatives of the "tradition of omniscience," with Sir D'Arcy Thompson at St. Andrew's deserving to be regarded as a worthy successor. He might have added L. W. Grensted of Oxford.
7. p. 52: A famous story went round among his students. He did not marry until he had become a well-established Cambridge figure. At the beginning of one new academic year he prefaced his first lecture by announcing to his students (who knew that he had been abroad during the Long Vacation): "I went to South Africa to look for bugs and I brought back Mrs. Gwatkin."

8. p. 52:   He uses the term "boorish dullness" of the Middle Ages in its apprecia-
            tion (or lack of appreciation) of the beauty of Nature.
9. p. 54:   *A Wanderer's Way*, p. 63 f.
10. p. 54: Ibid. p. 62 f.
11. p. 55: *Science, Religion and the Future*, p. 109 f.

CHAPTER THREE

Withdrawal and Return

Life in Cambridge in the Edwardian era could be extraordinarily sheltered. The majority of undergraduates came into residence straight from their public schools. They belonged to families who lived in ample and comfortable homes and in these they could spend their vacations. The scholarship system, of course, made it possible for a small number from grammar schools to enjoy the amenities of Oxford or Cambridge and this meant that there were always a few students in a College with first hand experience of life in an industrial town or of a system of education different from that of the public school. But they were very much in the minority. The average undergraduate had little knowledge of the social conditions of the East end of London or of the industrial North except through brief contacts, in School and College missions, with boys belonging to these areas.

As a double-first, Charles was now a marked man academically. The way was open for him to pursue advanced study in Britain or in Germany with a view to entering upon a career devoted to teaching and research. But with everything seemingly geared in this direction he suddenly and unexpectedly changed course. The drama of it is best recounted in his own words:

> "My advisers had urged me to go to Berlin, to learn German and read with Harnack: but I had returned to Cambridge to sit for the George Williams prize and to begin a thesis on Apollinarius of Laodicea. Clearly it was wise for me to use the year or so before the fellowship election for a visit to Germany: but I was unwilling to do so, partly from fear of strange places and a foreign tongue, partly because I was getting rather bored with academic life and found the

prospect of a further period as a student distasteful, and partly because desiring to be in a position to marry it was unsafe to count solely upon a fellowship. No reason weighed heavily, and I should doubtless have gone but for a sudden summons to the Appointments Board, where it was suggested to me that I should apply for a post as Assistant Secretary for Secondary Education under the Liverpool City Council. The salary was meagre; the prospects as uncertain as my own fitness for the work; my family and friends would obviously regard it as a disastrous mistake. I asked for twenty-four hours in which to decide, left the Board, walked a hundred yards, returned and requested the secretary to send in my name. At the time I hardly knew why I had done so: it was, I think, mainly the conviction that if I was ever going to be of any use in the world I must break away from the public school and university tradition and get a wider experience. I had definitely chosen educational work as my future: the new municipal and state schools were bound to play a large part in that future; Liverpool was a good centre in which to study them at first hand. That the choice was right, I have no doubt: had I realised that it would wholly change my way of life, I should nevertheless have taken it. A month later I settled into rooms in Canning Street and, less easily, into the routine of work in an office."[1]

The year that followed was probably the crucial period of his life. His lodgings were dingy. He was miserably lonely. His duties were monotonous and dull. He spent occasional week-ends with cousins who were Roman Catholics and wondered briefly if their pattern of religious devotion might perhaps satisfy his spiritual hunger. But he soon decided that it was quite impossible for him to give intellectual assent to certain of the Roman claims and pursued the matter no further. Instead he began to find warmth of religious expression and freedom of intellectual enquiry amongst sectarian groups and was glad to recall later that his first religious address had been delivered in the hall of a Congregational Church.

Yet he became increasingly uncertain about his future. In a letter to his mother in January 1909 he wrote:

"Cameron[2] tells me that I ought to get promoted before my two years are over: if only I could get settled down and be reasonably secure and comfortable it would be a different world. As it is I am perfectly right so long as I am fit but it isn't much catch when one doesn't feel very bright. The work is strange—just lately it has all been statistics for the grants to these blessed schools—the place beastly lonely, meals rather uncertain, comforts a pipe of an evening. I don't want to grumble. If only I knew when I could hope to get any further, it would be all right but until then I shan't be permanently cheerful, I am afraid."

But before ending his letter Charles refers to one of the influences which were destined to guide him towards the decision to be ordained, a decision, it appears, which was only finally made during the following summer.

"Did I tell you," Charles writes, "about my old 'bug' man, Mr. Pierce? He is absolutely unique. He is a tobacconist—a wonderful worker with a microscope—and runs an immense boys' club.[3] I went to the club last night and shall drop in again to-night." The club was less than half a mile down the hill from Charles's lodgings. The visits begun in January were to become a regular part of his life from then onwards.

These visits stirred Charles's soul to its depths. He could not resist the fearlessness, the naturalness, the buoyancy, the humour of the Liverpool boys. Yet he was appalled at the conditions under which they were compelled to live. He jumped at the chance to serve them by sharing their club activities; he began to see the possibility of extending this service into the future, not only by a fuller devotion to their immediate needs but also by crusading for the betterment of the conditions under which they were living. At last he was experiencing a new sense of *fellowship*, a word which was to remain central in his vocabulary for ever afterwards. He had known intimacy of personal fellowship in his home but never, it seems, in school or university life. He had talked with others, worked with them, rowed with them, danced with them but had never been able to surmount the feeling that he must stay within the barriers of convention and the rituals of an intellectual society. Now he felt free again. Life with the youngsters was comparable to life with his family: simple, direct, uninhibited. This was the kind of fellowship that he wanted above all else to promote and in no unworthy sense to enjoy. Could it be that the Church was the one supreme fellowship within which personal loyalty and sacrifical love were engendered and universalised? Had his conception of the Church (which he had hitherto taken for granted) as another institution with officers and an elaborate organisation been entirely wide of the mark?

"I had read enough of the Church of the first centuries," he writes, "to recognise at once its authentic quality. Bishops, orders, liturgies, creeds, forms of prayer, tests of membership, these were after all later developments, and had sprung up when fellowship and reality waned. They were necessary and useful; no one could deny that dogma and organisation had their place; I should not formally choose to join an undenominational body. But the real life of the church did not consist in these things but in love and glad serving, in doing good and bearing one another's burdens, in becoming as a little child, in walking humbly with God. I could not give up my post and apply for service in the Colosseum: somehow I must earn my living and find a stipend that would keep me. But surely in a parish there would be work like this; as a curate, I could run a Colosseum of my own and gather into it a host of youngsters like myself. There must be churches where the pomps and ceremonies mattered little, where a man could live simply among the poor without bothering about controversy or orthodoxy. I could not join even such a one yet: there were vows to take for which I was not ready. I could not yet even share fully with my friends in the Colosseum: they had a clear faith and mine was still hazy and insecure. But some day perhaps my convictions would take shape, and then I would try to find in the Church a whole-time ministry such as now filled three nights of my week. This was what the Church originally was and existed to do: this was what it should still be doing. There was no other body so plainly committed to the work: if only I had the spiritual experience to share however undogmatically its faith, I would offer my life to it at once."[4]

"Spiritual experience," another term which would constantly appear in his vocabulary, was, he felt, so far lacking. He had indeed sensed the expansion of his whole being in moments of communion with the source of the beauty and vitality of the natural world. But he had never known this in terms of a *personal* presence. So far the focus of *personal* relationship had been his mother, to some degree his sister, his college friends, supremely his fiancée; but he had never been aware of going beyond human relationships, of being grasped by a transcendent personal presence calling for his uncompromising loyalty and love.

Such an experience—and this to Charles was the paradigm of "spiritual experience"—came to him while visiting a friend of college days who had since taken orders and was a curate at Stoke-on-Trent.

"Liverpool has its squalid streets and I was used to slums. But for brute ugliness Stoke and its vast and dismal churchyard stand unique. My friend was ill: I wandered up to his rooms alone, and the grim tragedy of the place struck me cold with misery. He had loved the country, and music, and all beautiful things: and he was living in this hell. I found him, and behold he was not alone. No other phrase will express it. Here walking with him in the midst of the furnace was Jesus: and its flames were an aureole. He had found that which together we had sought. Jesus was alive and present to my friend as he had been to the eleven in the upper room. He was alive and present to me. I had studied the evidence for the resurrection with an unbeliever's critical scrutiny and had been persuaded of its validity but not of its consequences. Now I knew. It was not a dream for Saul of Tarsus, nor for a multitude of disciples through the ages. It was no longer a dream for me: for here was the reality of it. Such is a summary of the crucial event of my life."[5]

By the time that Charles was writing this personal confession of faith the tide of psychological explanations of abnormal ideas and unusual behaviour was running strongly. He felt bound therefore to examine his memories critically and to expose them to the light of the obvious objections which could be made against this type of "spiritual experience". Was it a case of wish-fulfilment, of subjection, as in revivals, to mass-hysteria, of auto-suggestion, of compensation, of sex transference, of heightened fantasy? With fairness and all honesty he weighs these various possibilities, urging what seem to be important considerations in favour of his own ultimate convictions. And finally he encapsulates his tested conclusions within a statement which is a not inadequate summary of his later detailed and developed Christology.

"To have known God vaguely but very really in nature and humanity, and then to discover Him translated into a human comrade, is to find awe quickened into devotion, and reverence into love. The Eternal may stir me in certain moods and certain elements of my being: only love of person for person can possess me entire. Art, reason, virtue, these appeal to particular functions: a friend, a lover, affects every fibre as my whole self goes out freely in response. If it be true that it is through relationship with others that we achieve personality, and that the quality of our friends determines our own, then the comradeship of Jesus should lift and integrate our nature as nothing else could do. And if in love we become what we love, and if Jesus be for us God, then indeed to love Him is to become in some sort divine."[6]

The practical outcome of the "heavenly vision" was ordination into the ministry of the Church of England. His passion to serve had to be expressed through a fellowship more comprehensive and enduring than the real but narrowly limited brotherhood of the Colosseum. (By a coincidence a building was beginning to arise on St. James's Mount not far from the Colosseum in which one day Charles would find perhaps the happiest of all his spheres of service. The foundation-stone of Liverpool Cathedral had been laid in 1904). His passion to see lives transformed through the discovery of a new loyalty and love needed to take form within a tradition which allowed the maximum of freedom in exploring the relation of the person and work of Jesus to every aspect of human life. Charles believed that with all its faults and defects the Church of England was the communion which offered him the fullest scope of ministry. He did not much approve of assent to the Articles though he could give the practice some historical justification. Many of the political connections and aesthetic adornments he disliked. But Rome and Nonconformity were alike impossible for him. "In fact it hardly occurred to me that there were other possibilities (i.e. than the Church of England) when I resolved to give up my post in the Education Office and apply for ordination and a curacy. The whole-time service of religion could mean nothing else."[7]

The decision seems to have been made in May or June 1909. For a short time he would continue to perform his duties in the Education Office. But this did not now prevent him from working on the subject which he had already chosen for his thesis: Apollinarianism. At the same time he began to familiarise himself with haunts which later on were to become oases of relaxation during the almost feverish activities of the late 1920s: Delamere Forest, Parkgate and Hoylake and Hilbre Island, the sands at Ainsdale, all were alive with objects of interest to the natural historian and few can ever have explored them with more enthusiasm and keenness of perception than did Charles. There was a blissfully happy fortnight in July when his mother and his fiancée came to stay at Parkgate, the place which had been the holiday retreat for the Raven family for so many years until the claims of golf lured the father to Rye. Ordination in due course to a parish, followed soon after, it was hoped, by marriage—this seemed to be the pattern of events now unfolding. And then suddenly all was again thrown into the melting-pot. News came that Charles's name was before the governing body of Emmanuel College for possible election to the vacant Dean-ship. All was in suspense until the election could be made at the beginning of Michaelmas Term. Then, almost too good to be true, the offer came. Charles immediately accepted and set his path towards a position in Cambridge which would combine academic with pastoral responsibilities and provide a field of service in which the new vision of the Liverpool days could be worked out in practice.

His feelings can be judged from his letter to his mother on October 15th.

c

"I am a bit dazed still. Dreams sometimes have no business to come true quite so fully and vividly, have they?

Chawner (Master of Emmanuel) writes most kindly. The election was unanimous and its only conditions are ordination at Advent and that I live in rooms until the summer and these of course are not hard to accept.

You know what it all means—the work I have above all desired, a position which, please God, I will try to fill, the ability to get married in June. The crooked ways seem plain, at last, don't they?"

Charles had no qualms or qualifications about becoming Dean of Emmanuel so far as the office was concerned. But to become Dean he must take Orders and in regard to ordination a good many reservations and uncertainties remained. His earliest experiences of parsons had been unhappy to say the least: his father had shown no particular interest in the Church; his relationship with his uncle—a parson—at Uppingham had not been at all easy; at Cambridge he had never belonged to a clerical "set" nor had his friends been budding parsons. He had entertained the idea of becoming a lay-theologian, perhaps after the example of the great F. C. Burkitt, one of his teachers, but there is no evidence, apart from a sentence in his fiancée's letter to her grandmother, that he regarded himself as an ordinand even at the time when he was reading theology. "I had," he frankly states, "never been a very regular or enthusiastic church goer: the recital of offices was a bore, and, though then (on the eve of ordination) I should not have said so, surely a bit of superstitious legalism: pious people still irritated me: my life had been thoroughly lay, full of secular interests and odd friendships"[8] and in many respects a layman he remained to the end of his life.

Yet he approached ordination very seriously. He was certain of his call to service; he believed that the taking of orders was the best way to fulfil it; he had made up his mind to seek ordination before any suggestion of the Emmanuel post had reached him. So he was made deacon by Bishop Chase in Ely Cathedral on the Third Sunday in Advent 1909. In subsequent years he often felt cut off from a free and natural relationship with lay folk: he often felt stifled in clerical circles. In spite of this he never seriously doubted his calling or that it was in the ordained Ministry that he could best accomplish it. He could never become a narrow churchman nor could he ever immerse himself in purely ecclesiastical affairs. One could imagine the expressions on his face if he had been doomed to sit in Convocation through the endless framing and re-framing of Canon Law in the 1950s! Yet he loved the Church of England, wanted to serve within its ranks, was above all eager to help reform it in order that it might become a better instrument in God's hands for the establishment of His Kingdom amongst men.

If the fifteen months in Liverpool had been the crucial period of Charles's life, the year which began in January 1910 was hardly less momentous. It brought him from the loneliness of rooms on Canning Street to the comparative luxury of a don's rooms in Cambridge; from the teeming and often pathetic social life of the Colosseum to the cultured and sometimes abrasive social life of a Senior Combination Room; from a routine job bearing little responsibility to a situation in which any day might bring problems of a highly personal kind to be handled with sympathy, and yet with firmness.

Emmanuel had its own character as distinct from Caius. It stands on the site formerly occupied by a Dominican monastery whose particular function it had been to train preachers in the fourteenth and fifteenth centuries. In 1540 the monastery was broken up but in 1584 it was re-founded as a college, now in order to train Protestant preachers. From the beginning it had a strongly Puritan character and by 1615 it had so grown in numbers as sometimes to outstrip even Trinity. Among the early emigrants to New England 100 out of 132 University graduates were Cambridge men and of these 35, including John Harvard, came from "The pure house of Emmanuel". After the Restoration its fortunes declined but not before its chief architectural glory had taken shape— the building of a cloister with a splendid picture gallery above and with the Chapel extending at right angles from its midsection, all to the plan of Sir Christopher Wren.

Like all Colleges it had its ups and downs in the eighteenth and nineteenth centuries but never lost its close association with Protestant divinity. Many sons of clergy came to Emmanuel; many went from it to be ordained into the ministry of the Church of England. It retained also a certain independence of character consonant with its Puritan tradition. But the general pattern of College life was entirely comparable to that with which Charles was already familiar and he could begin his new work with the confidence of understanding what it was all about.

Even in those days, however, the Press was quick to make headlines out of the unusual feature of his appointment: the *Daily Mail* not only gave three paragraphs to the "Youngest Don" in October 1909 but returned to the subject at still greater length in November 1910.

Under the head-line "Dean at 24: Success of a young Don" it first commented on his tact and moderation and then continued:

> "At the same time the Dean of Emmanuel has not erred on the side of weakness. When in celebration of the success of the Emmanuel College boat in the "Mays" the president of the leading Cambridge Undergraduate Theological Society, with some others, launched burning rafters as fire-rafts upon the college lake, he sent them down for a period of penitential reflection. It was a visible sign of his author-ity when these promoters of incendiary jubilation were convoyed in all the travesty of pomp and circumstance through the streets of Cambridge in the customary "funeral" procession.
>
> By straightforward reasonableness, by a keen interest in sport, by taking a firm line in more important cases, by showing a disposition to leniency in lesser ones, and, lastly, by complete lack of the fatal fault of "side" this young Dean of Emmanuel has founded his authority not only on respect but also on popularity."

The *Daily Mail* painted a rosy picture but it was by no means all roses for Charles. The exercise of discipline, whether in school or in college, is a mysterious process. Brute strength is of little use: a detailed knowledge of the rules makes little impression. Eyes, voice, and what is called "presence" all contribute to the establishment of authority and Charles was unusually endowed in each of these respects. There was a memorable occasion when the captain of the Rugby XV had trans-gressed and Charles called him to account. In physical build there was no comparison between the two men. Charles confessed afterwards to his own trepidation as he sensed the possibility of an actual violent attack. But within a few seconds the man was reduced to complete submission.

Charles could, indeed, be devastating with his tongue, and this was his chief weapon. He recognised that it could be too cruel a possession. "An undergraduate, meeting my brother but not realising his connection with me, when asked about the new Dean of Emmanuel replied "He's a sarcastic devil." Brotherly wisdom passed on the remark and I vowed then and there to keep my tongue severely bridled. God knows, I have often enough broken the pledge; indignation comes easily, and the power to wound with words is not an easy thing to lay aside." The capacity to wound was certainly there. Perhaps it was one of the greatest achievements of his life to keep it as firmly under control as he did.

Apart then from the occasional disciplinary problem his relations with undergraduates at Emmanuel, whom he found 'quiet and steady-going', were excellent. But with the senior members of the College, the governing body, he found himself almost at once in the midst of a veritable hornet's nest. The Chawner episode is still talked about as a kind of *cause célèbre* in Cambridge history.

The whole affair began on an evening in May 1909 when the Master, William Chawner,[9] read a paper to the newly formed Religious Discussion Society in the College. This he entitled *Prove All Things*. Probably like many radical effusions at College societies it would have made no more than a fleeting impression had not the Master decided forthwith to publish it in pamphlet form and to send it to a representative group of acquaintances for comment. When a large number of replies had been received, he proceeded further in November to publish a selection of these letters and by the time Charles arrived a situation existed similar to that which was to obtain in many quarters a half century later after the publication of *Honest to God*. The strange thing is that Charles seems to have been quite unaware of the feelings that had been aroused or of the complexity of the college situation until he actually came into residence. It is now known that Bishop Chase was gravely concerned about ordaining so young a deacon to so explosive a charge but whether he communicated his anxiety to Charles remains uncertain. At any rate within a month of his ordination he found himself involved in one of the most painful and exhausting controversies of his whole career.

What then in the Master's paper had created such a furore? Beginning with questions about man's origins and ultimate destiny he went on to affirm that "these and the like are questions to which most religions, certainly the Christian religion as we know it, profess to give a precise and definite answer—an answer in the case of Christianity based upon an infallible authority whether of book or institution or person. If we do not accept that authority, how little, if anything, we know." There is, he claimed, no absolute truth. During the past half-century there has been growing indifference and hostility towards orthodox Christianity. In Germany the churches are half empty and congregations consist only of women. In France any profession of religion is a bar to promotion in the Army or Civil Service. In England hostility varies in precise proportion to intelligence. Here also women are the mainstay of any religious assembly. And finally at Oxford and Cambridge the number of candidates for Holy Orders steadily diminishes, college chapels have many empty seats and dons reveal no more than a benevolent neutrality.

So far, he continued, there had been in Cambridge a conspiracy of silence about the real situation. Now however there was need for absolute frankness. Orthodox theology could no longer be defended. The only certainty was that provided by conscience, the moral sense of duty, the categorical imperative. This alone could be the rallying-point for those who desired to promote unity and harmony in the world.

As Charles was quick to see, there was nothing very original in this manifesto. The Master was "a layman, unmarried and in ill health, a great administrator, officially something of a martinet, privately a charming host and delightful companion, obviously the strongest member of the Governing Body." But he had gradually lost all confidence in the religious orthodoxy in which he had been reared. "He seemed like a man who had caught late in life the scepticism that affects most of us at eighteen; and like measles at his age it was a bad attack." He was sincere but no great thinker. What he had written on the negative side was in no way unfamiliar to discerning minds. "But he was the head of a Protestant college. He did not mince his words in denouncing the foolishness of conventional belief; and his pamphlet *Prove all things* came as a thunderbolt among the faithful. It set the college in ferment. The Governing Body was rent into parties and the whole atmosphere was tense with suspicion and excitement."[10]

The publication of the replies to the pamphlet in November did nothing to cool the heated atmosphere. In the main the replies were favourable to the Master's position. But one letter recalled the religious character of the foundation. "Whether you as Head of this institution ought to lead the discussion by an attack on the very principles which it was founded to promote and to which it still officially adheres is a question which I personally would have answered in the negative."

It needs little imagination to recognise how difficult was the position in which Charles now found himself. On one side the Master was the leader of a new attack on Christian orthodoxy; on the other side Charles was the official representative in the College of Christian faith. In between there was a variety of attitudes amongst the other dons with no desire to bring things to a head through some pronouncement for or against. The debate dragged on into the summer and then suddenly a real crisis arose.

No College can afford to be indifferent to the number and quality of those who seek to be admitted as undergraduates. It so happened that Emmanuel had an unusually large number of links with Evangelical homes and schools and many ordinands among members in residence. When new applications for admission were due to come in, it soon became evident that Emmanuel had experienced a heavy slump. And when Charles received a letter from a headmaster asking him whether Emmanuel was a fit place for a candidate for holy orders, he felt bound to raise the matter openly at a meeting of the Governing Body. From that moment the issue was joined. Nothing was decided immediately but in October the blow fell.

"The Master intimated that I had been appointed with full knowledge of his views and policy, and in accepting the post had done so without signifying any objection. I had just taken on the responsibilities of a married man, had no money, and if I left Emmanuel in disgrace, no prospects. Here was a merry greeting on our return from our honeymoon. Only one course was possible. I wrote to the Master asking him, if he regarded my opposition as disloyal or as infringing the terms of my appointment, to let me place my resignation in his hands. He replied generously, but without a direct answer. For the next six months I carried two letters in my pocket, one resigning my fellowship, and the other to the then headmaster of Rugby applying for a mastership under him.

Those six months were, I think, the most trying of my life, and that because of their isolation and insecurity. Had I been still unmarried a term of it would have broken me. Even as it was by March I was racked with neuritis and insomnia. When the Master died suddenly during the vacation I felt that he had only finished first by a short span."[11]

The Master had died in Switzerland on March 29th, 1911 while seeking renewal of health. So in a dramatic way the College was saved from what threatened to be a complete split in its Governing Body and Charles was saved from what would almost certainly have been an abrupt termination of his office as Dean. Matters calmed down and he was able to proceed with the task of constructing a reasonable intellectual undergirding of the profound spiritual experiences which had already given direction to his life. The crisis at Emmanuel had not been without value. It had challenged him to find a way of combining intellectual honesty with warm devotion and personal faith. This he would continue to do through the relatively short time that remained before another crisis, involving not just a small College but a whole world, would radically affect his total understanding of human experience and Divine reality.

Besides carrying on his duties as Dean, Charles had to undertake a considerable load of lecturing and tutorial responsibilities. To lecture regularly was for him a quite new experience. The range of subjects was extensive—The Gospels, Doctrine, and the life of the early Church. But more important for him at the moment were method and technique. Was he to rely heavily on carefully written material? How was he to judge the time factor? In what way would his sermons differ from his lectures? He was a complete novice in both areas of speaking for hitherto his medium of communication had been almost exclusively that of the pen and the essay.

The time problem resolved itself in an unusual but for him eminently satisfactory way. He found that he possessed a kind of built-in clock which told him precisely when to stop. Whether it were a five minute meditation or a three-hour service the instinctive mechanism always stood him in good stead. But the more important question was the *manner* of preparation and delivery. The lecturer's business, as he conceived it, was "not to supply a substitute for a text-book, but to arouse interest, to convey a personal interpretation of the facts and to make his hearers think for themselves."[12] So there was to be no dictation, no enslavement to a meticulously prepared text. He would master his material to the best of his ability and then present it in an orderly but not a formal fashion. Later (I do not know whether this was the case from the very beginning) he liked to walk about the platform or even up and down the aisle of the lecture-room as he talked. This could have a distracting effect on his hearers but an attitude of stillness was so unnatural to him—even when seated he was constantly changing position—that it was worthwhile enduring the rhythm of the walk in order to enjoy the orderly progress of his thinking. An actor is rarely still. His words are accompanied by movements. So it was with Charles. Even beyond the appreciation of the content it was fascinating for his hearers to move empathetically with the lecturer.

There was however one large difficulty. You do not interrupt an actor by challenging him or asking him questions. Occasionally in one of Charles's lectures a question would be asked or an objection raised. This had the effect (and the metaphor becomes almost literal in this situation) of putting him off his stride. The lecture was for him a dramatic presentation, not a dialogue. He was ready to deal with questions afterwards, though it was not always certain that he was really listening to the questioner's difficulty. His was the role of the actor to present truth through impersonation and through declamation; it was not that of the dialectician to discover truth through analysis and interchange.

It could of course be said that Charles was preacher first and foremost even in the lecture-room. That preaching was his supreme gift few would deny. During the Long Vacation of 1910, while still a deacon, he went to stay with his parents at Rye and was invited to preach at the Parish Church. He tells a story against himself of a lady who was present and claimed to be so impressed with the sermon that she asked that it might be printed—whereas the Vicar knew that she was so deaf that she could hardly have heard a word. But what Charles did not know was that a youth was present who was later to be a notable authority on preaching—Alec Vidler, for many years Dean of King's College, Cambridge. Recalling the sermon by this young deacon he described the effect as "electrifying". When Charles mounted a pulpit, wherever it might be, he seemed immediately to arrest attention—his eyes, his voice, his presence exercised a magnetic influence which few could resist. It is doubtful if any man in the Church of England in the twentieth century, not excepting even William Temple, could make the pulpit his throne more effectively than Charles succeeded in doing, not only in England but also in Scotland, Canada and the United States of America.

But it was a success not easily won. Charles has vividly described his agonising tension as the time of his ordeal drew near.

"The prospect filled me with such terror that for hours beforehand I could not swallow solid food, and while speaking my whole body was shivering. That first sermon took many hours of preparation; it was written out word for word, then read over and over again, and then rehearsed. Time after time with a watch beside me and a desk to represent the pulpit, I would go over the whole performance from invocation to ascription, locking myself into my room and speaking aloud as if to a congregation. For the first three or four years of my ministry that was my method; fortunately I did not have more than a dozen sermons a year; each of them was an agony. Then early in 1915 I was put in charge of a parish where I had to preach five times every Sunday to an overlapping congregation—five separate discourses. To learn them all was impossible: to prepare them all was difficult: I must improvise. The years of labour had not been in vain. I have only written half a dozen sermons since, and for many years have hardly ever used a note."[13]

During all this learning period from the beginning of 1910 to the end of 1914 he was strengthened and supported to a degree impossible to estimate or assess by the devoted care of Bee, his wife. In the summer of his first year at Emmanuel the long engagement came to an end and the marriage took place on June 22nd at Streatley-on-Thames. Bee was of more than average height, very thin, in some respects frail. Charles, indeed, seems never to have realised the limitations of her strength, so devoted was she to every aspect of his welfare. She never spared herself and conditions were by no means always easy. Money was often in short supply and she had her full share of moving from house to house. She soon had a growing family. Mary was born in 1912, Betty in 1913, John at the end of 1914, while Margaret the fourth child arrived in May 1918. The earliest home was 4 Park Terrace, and this was retained as the family residence until the move took place from Cambridge to Blechingley in 1920.

In contrast to Charles, who she often feared would run himself to death, Bee preserved an air of serenity which tended to hide the depth of her concern. She was the perfect foil to Charles and for thirty four years he depended upon her at every turn. Her sudden death, when it came, was the most shattering experience of his whole life.

NOTES TO CHAPTER THREE

1. p. 59:   *A Wanderer's Way*, p. 78f.
2. p. 61:   The senior man under whom he was working.
3. p. 61:   The Colosseum was the headquarters of a mission founded in 1877 by the Rt. Hon. Samuel Smith to carry on "religious and social work among

the very poor". It was refounded in 1907 and in addition to the many
week night activities in the Colosseum itself, a regular Sunday night
service with average attendance of eight hundred was held in the
Picton Hall. The Colosseum itself was situated in Fleet St. behind Bold
St, not far from Charles's lodgings. The hall seems originally to have
been built as a Unitarian Chapel in 1791, then converted into a theatre,
then demolished and rebuilt still as a theatre, and finally demolished
soon after 1920. The combination under one roof of religious, recreational and artistic activities has been a particular feature of social life in
Liverpool.

4. p. 62:   Ibid. p. 89 f.
5. p. 63:   Ibid. p. 71.
6. p. 64:   Ibid. p. 101.
7. p. 65:   Ibid. p. 105.
8. p. 66:   Ibid. p. 113.
9. p. 69:   William Chawner entered Emmanuel in 1867 and became Master in
             1895. He served as Vice-Chancellor from 1899–1901. His only publica-
             tion prior to *Prove All Things* was a prize essay entitled *The Influence of
             Christianity upon the Legislation of Constantine the Great*. On May 31st,
             1910 the Master received the following protest signed by seven (out of
             thirteen) of the Fellows: "Fellows of the College whose signatures
             appear below wish to represent to the Master their conviction that his
             recent practice of issuing to the undergraduates pamphlets and circulars
             dealing with questions of religious controversy is detrimental to the
             general interests of the College and specifically and gravely embarrassing
             to other officers of the College in the discharge of their statutory
             duties." Raven signed, as did F. W. Head, the Senior Tutor, who was
             subsequently to be Raven's colleague at Liverpool before becoming
             Archbishop of Melbourne. It was later represented to the Master that the
             greatest embarrassment was to the Dean who was charged with the duty
             of maintaining compulsory attendance at Chapel.
             An interesting account of the Chawner Affair appeared in the 1970–71
             issue of the Emmanuel College Magazine.
10. p. 71:   *A Wanderer's Way*, p. 133.
11. p. 71:   Ibid. pp. 138–9.
12. p. 73:   Ibid. p. 123.
13. p. 74:   Ibid. p. 124 f.

CHAPTER FOUR

A Descent into the Valley of Death

In August 1914 Charles had entered his thirtieth year. He was immensely happy with home and family. The troubles which had harried him during his early years at Emmanuel had been largely resolved. His research on Apollinarianism was going well. His fame as a lecturer was growing. All seemed set fair for a distinguished career in University and in the wider life of the Church.

Then came the sudden challenge of war. Probably no institution felt its effect more immediately and more devastatingly than the University. Undergraduates flocked to the colours. Charles himself felt a compelling urge to enrol as a combatant but for the time being was dissuaded from doing so by those in authority. Instead, when duties in College had been reduced to a minimum, he agreed to accept a temporary post at Tonbridge, teaching classics in the School during the week and deputising for the Vicar at the Parish Church on Sundays. (The Vicar had become a Chaplain to the Forces).

He seems to have enjoyed his work at the School and became form master of the Classical Middle Vth from September 1915 till the Spring of 1917. One boy who was in the Form at the time remembers him as "a rather austere, self-opinionated personality" who tended to over-awe the boys by his superior knowledge. But he admits that he was himself a "rather poor classic" and Charles was always at his best with those of keen intelligence who could respond to his own high standards of thought and speech. The brief return to Classical Studies was in some respects congenial. But his deepest interests were now elsewhere. It was at the Parish Church that his talents gained more characteristic expression.

In Cambridge his work had already compelled him to think ever more

deeply and radically about the central problem of Christianity: How
can we express in words our faith in Jesus as both human and divine?
Now his new relationships in Tonbridge with layfolk who were unaware of the subtleties of academic scholarship made him wrestle with
the problem even more sterenuously. How could he help them to
answer the question which Jesus is reported to have addressed to his
desciples: What think ye of Christ? In classes and discussions he
hammered out his language and ideas and at length presented them
to a wider public in 1916 under the title: *What think ye of Christ?*

He starts from the premise that the war is shaking everything. Reform
is in the air. How can individual, social, international life be truly
renovated? There must be certain principles or models to guide the zeal
of reformers. Dare Christians claim that in the person of Jesus the
Christ is to be found the only and all-sufficient pattern by which a new
humanity can be brought into being?

But how can people going about their daily work in London or
Liverpool or Tonbridge really see and experience the living Christ?
The academic constructs theories about the Incarnation in his study:
the parish priest goes about his daily work of caring for the souls of
men. Neither seems able to provide the needed re-statement of the
faith which could be adopted as the blue print for reform. So having
experienced life, as it were, in both camps Charles now attempts to set
forth in a readable way the central convictions which had come to
govern his own interpretation of ultimate reality.

As was often to happen in his written works he did not hesitate to
refer to stages of his own pilgrimmage. He had gone up to Cambridge
as an undergraduate, he says, in thoroughly sceptical mood, a mood
only relieved by certain momentary exaltations of a vaguely mystical
kind. Then through the influence of friends, through a careful reading
of the Epistle to the Romans, through his contacts with raw humanity
in the slums of Liverpool, he had gained a mental picture of Jesus as
image of the invisible God and it was that image that he wished now to
present to his readers in ordinary language.

His own convictions about the place of Christ in the universe had
not been easily won. At Emmanuel he had been a member of the

Religious Discussion Society, founded by Mr. Chawner, and in this group of twelve he had been the only one making a full profession of Christian faith. Indeed, to use his own words, they "all denied and would fain destroy the creed of Christ." Yet in this crucible of testing, his own beliefs became ever clearer and better defined. "I discovered that utter sincerity was the only possible method, that catch-words, ideas taken on trust and clothed in cant phrases were useless, nay subversive, that it was impossible to convince others of what I was not prepared to state logically and defend without appeals to external authority and that the personality and claims of Jesus came to mean more and more both to me and to my opponents while the metaphysics of the Creeds meant less and less." So as a result both of his work as teacher of the New Testament and of his struggles in discussions with unbelievers he reached an interpretation of Christ which he believed valid for his own time.

From its very beginnings Christianity has oscillated between two possible ways of interpreting the significance of Jesus. On the one hand it has assumed certain truths about the nature and purpose of God Himself, truths derived from what have been held to be His self-revelations either in the natural or the historical order; then with these truths assumed it has sought to integrate Jesus into the picture as being the particular image of the invisible deity whose general character nevertheless has already been made known. Alternatively it has come with as open a mind as possible to the records which bear witness to the "things concerning Jesus" and has then asked how the man revealed is different from ordinary men, whether there are indications that He was in some way more than man, in fact God in human terms, in human form. There is no doubt that Charles's sympathies were entirely with the second approach and that appeals either to the theology of the Old Testament or to the philosophical theology of the Greeks left him largely unmoved. His concern was to focus all his attention upon Jesus Himself and to see God through Him. "Angels or Martians," he declared, "may know God otherwise, that is no concern of ours: we can know Him only through our own natures and best as incarnate: that is all and that is enough. For us Jesus is God."[1]

In developing this conception more fully Charles appealed to the distinction often made between degree and kind. The early Greeks in general regarded the divine nature as different *in kind* from human nature and in 269 A.D. Paul of Samosata was condemned by a Church Council for affirming that Jesus differed from other men in degree but not in kind. This condemnation, Charles believed, was a dire mistake for it encouraged the belief that a rigid barrier existed between God and man. It inferred that Jesus was not really human in the sense of knowing the strains of growth and the struggles towards self-realisation. "If he never experienced the limitations under which we labour, if He never knew the fierceness of a life-and-death conflict with evil, if He never suffered the despair which is more bitter than bodily torment, if in fact he was never man but only "like man" then He is of no use to us. He has shared our griefs and carried our sorrows in name, not in reality."[2]

This insistence upon the reality of Jesus's manhood meant that transcendence could never for Charles imply existence on an altogether higher plane. He was ready to exalt Jesus to the very heights on the scale of humanity and then to see Him in His human perfection as the true representative of deity. But any kind of radical separateness he would not allow. "He transcends us as the perfect does the partial" — not as an imagined heavenly being might transcend an earthly. Moreover seeing that Jesus was always in complete union with the Father it follows that even the transcendence of God Himself is comparable to that of a father within a family rather than to that of a righteous Absolute over against a moral defaulter. Charles loved to speak of Jesus in terms of "height" and "perfection" but not of remoteness and difference in kind. He gloried in the many-sidedness of Jesus and the comprehensiveness of the salvation which He effected on behalf of mankind. But he was totally allergic to all dialectical ways of thinking which seemed to delight in radical opposition between the positive and the negative, between the holy and the profane, between justice and grace. Already he was making caustic comments on Schweitzer's and other German thinkers' attempts to make progress by dancing between alternatives. This rejection of German ways of doing theology was to become absolute when by the 1930s he had become acquainted with the works of Karl Barth. [3]

What think ye of Christ? placed Charles firmly on the theological "map." It was a difficult time for the thinker and the writer but Charles had managed to overcome war-time stresses and to produce a fresh and fearless treatment of a great theme. *The Guardian*, which at the time was the most scholarly of regular church newspapers, gave it a lengthy review, describing it as a "remarkable attempt to restate the primal verities of the Christian Faith" and referring to the author as being already well-known "among a rising and brilliant group of younger Cambridge Fellows."[4] Before this review had appeared in print however, Charles, whose writing career had begun so promisingly, had been admitted as a Chaplain to the Forces and soon was to be in the very midst of horror and suffering in the trenches of Flanders.

It is clear that the early days in France exercised a critical influence upon his whole apprehension of spiritual reality.

"It was during my first night in France on my way to Vimy Ridge in April 1917 that He vindicated for me my hope that when everything else failed He would stand sure. I am perhaps physically and certainly morally a coward; my wife knows it, whatever others may suppose; and when death looked me in the face, my manhood withered and collapsed. For what seemed hours I was in an agony of fear. Men talk of honour and a flag—I would have forsworn any earthly loyalty for the bare gift of life; or of immortality when one yearns for the dear small familiar things of earth, and the clutch of a baby's fingers on one's hand, and the smile in a woman's eyes; or of sacrifice and heroism, fine themes for talk, but poor consolation if all one's dreams are to end in a shattered pulp of blood and brain; or of God— *and suddenly as if in the very room His words "For their sakes I consecrate myself" and the fragrant splendour of His presence.*

I was overwrought, no doubt. The day had been too great a strain. I had parted from my wife, crossed the Channel at its worst, and been greeted at St. Omer with singular discourtesy; the authorities had urged me to take a job at a hospital, and I had chosen to go straight to a battalion; it was all new and strange and lonesome. I hope my behaviour will never again be so abject. But when kind friends murmur "reaction" or hint that tortured nerves play tricks with the imagination, I can only reply that neither of these comments is novel. Maybe, the visualising of the Lord was due to my mental state; maybe, the words were my own rendering of His impact; but *for the next nine months He was never absent, and I never alone, and never save for an instant or two broken by fear.* If He who was with me when I was blown up by a shell, and gassed, and sniped at, with me in hours of bombardment and the daily walk of death, was an illusion, then all that makes life worth living for me is illusion too; and I can only thank God that in this mockery of existence there has been a dream so beautiful, so realistic, so potent in its effects."[5]

The "gassing" to which he refers came about in the summer on the La Bassée front. This gave him a temporary respite from duty though he was allowed to 'hang about in the line.'

Subsequently he was granted leave and spent some weeks of ecstatic joy at home with Bee and the children. Returning to France early in September he found opportunity to do some sketching when not in the line. He also sent articles to *The Challenge*, the paper of which he was one day to become Editor.[6] The leave had restored his energies and he was feeling better than in a long time. But October brought a change of weather and a bad chill and he began to be apprehensive about his physical condition.

In early November he was at a Chaplain's School for three nights and this helped to prepare him for what was to be his sternest ordeal. Returning to his Battalion he found himself "in a beastly spot, dead flat fields and little farms scattered here and there and loosely connected by water logged roads and tracks. The whole land is so spongy with water and it has rained almost incessantly since we got here. However we probably shall not stay here very long—and we may well be in worse places before we've done." There was indeed a worse place—the sector around Bourton Wood where the 1st. Berkshires, Charles's battalion, were to be involved in bitter fighting towards the end of

November. "Few occasions," he was to write later, "have been more literally a descent into the valley of death . . . it was probably the most purifying week of my life . . . The impressions of those hours would take many pages to record: they surpassed my wildest dreams of hell and of heaven."[7]

Two impressions, with his subsequent comments, are worth recording.

"Twelve hours before I had been caught by shell-fire on a sunken road—a single howitzer was traversing it. In a scrape in the bank big enough to contain us I spent the next hour with an unknown private, huddled up and waiting for a direct hit. We could hear the gun fired, the flight of the missile, its scream and splash and roar, and the whizz of the pieces. Every half-minute a shell arrived, never more than a hundred yards away. The lad with me seemed unable to sit still: at last I warned him to stay quiet. A shell burst near: I saw his face: and realised that at each explosion he had put his body in the mouth of the hollow between it and me, offering his life for mine many times under conditions that try the manhood of the bravest. A day later—the night of the grand attack. I go out through the wreckage to bury a pal shot the day before. Reaching the grave a shell bursts fifteen feet away, throwing me over, leaving me unwounded, but unable to pronounce the letter "S". Going back to the cellar two young officers who have got hold of a German machine-gun want to test its action. "Come on, padre"—and I know that if I funk then it will be all up with my manhood. Most unwillingly I go off with them, stuttering my readiness. We set up the gun: a shell explodes a few yards off and covers us with dirt. I find myself alone: the others are in retreat: I follow at speed. A moment's sheer panic—the real rabbit-in-a-trap spasm for perhaps five yards: then a roar of laughter as I race to shelter. Ten minutes later when my comrades reappear I present them with two noble pictures of our gun going into action, and our gun-team in retreat. My lisp has entirely disappeared, and I sleep that night like a baby to find on waking that the colonel has wrapped me up in his own and only blanket."

After the intensity of these experiences there was a two week's lull at home—a perfect restorative. Back in France the cold was almost unbearable—"all the soda water frozen last night and the mustard a block of ice! However I slept in most of my clothes and piled the rest on to my blankets—Please God we shall never have another Christmas under such terrible conditions." But the worst of the ordeal was almost over. A few days after Christmas he was told that he would be withdrawn from the front line and given work at St. Omer, partly in the hospital and partly at the Chaplain's School, and that in April he would be allowed to return to England, perhaps for good.

January 1918, brought immense relief and many satisfactions. He had left behind the fearful rain and mud and was ensconced in a luxurious billet with every kind of comfort; he had a lovely little chapel in the hospital and enjoyed lecturing again in the School. News had come that his brother Ted was safely at home after grim experiences in the firing line. And he was able to report that he had been recommended for the Military Cross but only two were given in the battalion and "compared with lots of others who also got nothing I hadn't done much. However it meant that I left the battalion in the odour of popularity if not of sanctity and I'm jolly glad to have had the experience."

From now onwards time raced by. The work was exhilarating and the prospect of being in Cambridge for ten weeks in the summer term was almost too good to be true. The news of Bee was good: a fourth child was due to be born in May. What would happen after June was still uncertain.

"It will be horrible to have to face another year of loneliness and separation but I suppose some of us must share the discomforts of the fighting troops and I see no reason why I should choose a pleasanter path than the rest—though I hope it may not be thought necessary to send me back to the line. I shall of course offer to go; but don't expect that the Bishop will send me. I can't be in a much tighter place than I was at Bourton; and what one has done once, one can, if need be, do again. I don't want it or enjoy the prospect: but they tell me there is a great dearth of young chaplains and if so I can't keep a job that would suit an older man, unless they specially order me to do so."

Meanwhile a meeting at the School of the "élite" of the Chaplain's Department had enabled Charles to begin talking about plans for Church reform. A lovely March brought hedges into leaf with even the blackthorn flowering in sheltered spots. The euphoria was tempered however by the great German offensive and by Charles's realisation that if he had still been with his division he would have been in the very thick of the worst fighting.

At last he reached home soon after mid-April to a very different kind of life. Three mornings a week, for one hour a morning, he was lecturing to three undergraduates. In the afternoons he was taking Mary out into the country to pick flowers and hunt for butterflies. His preaching was attracting attention in the local press. And then on May 21st, the fourth child—a daughter—was safely born and the cup of happiness seemed full. But the war was not over. The hospital at St. Omer in which he had felt so safe had been smashed by bombs and two of his best friends killed. And it was still uncertain where he would be sent in July. (Though, in fact, he was not called to France again.)

There can be little doubt that war-service had a profound effect on Charles's whole interpretation of the human situation and of God's relations with man. Up to the time when he joined his regiment in the trenches his life had been relatively untroubled. The year at Liverpool had indeed introduced him to some of the grim realities of city slums; the controversy at Emmanuel had challenged him to think more radically about some of the beliefs which he had largely accepted on trust. But until he was thirty years old life had been extraordinarily rich in pleasures derived from both the natural and the social world. There was the constant delight in birds and plants; the almost ecstatic experiences in Lakeland and on the Norfolk Broads; many friendships in College; a growing confidence in lecturing and preaching; and above all a happy marriage and a healthy family.

Now, like so many of his contemporaries, he faced the real possibility that he would be snatched away from it all. As soon as the Channel was crossed old securities had disappeared. He tried to keep touch with his brother who was also in the Chaplaincy service but otherwise he was amongst strangers, most of them drawn from a completely different background from his own. And the physical fear which had haunted him from boyhood days now had its supreme opportunity to paralyse and disgrace him. Whatever happened in the trenches and in the rest periods behind the lines, he could never be the same man again.

As far as physical courage and endurance were concerned there is every reason to believe that Charles emerged triumphant. He had faced almost certain death without flinching and henceforward he knew that what he had done once he could do again.

As far as his relations with his fellow officers and other ranks were concerned there is again good reason to suppose that he gained their full confidence and that he experienced such a sense of intimate comradeship as had never come his way before. In the light of his later passionate espousal of pacifism it is interesting to find him writing in 1917: "Pacifists and C.O.s may talk of the sanctity of human brotherhood; we out here have discovered something at least of its reality." He never forgot the gaiety of men under stress, their willingness to sacrifice themselves for others, the quite unique sense of being bound together with them within a common purpose and a common constraint. There was little indication that this new experience of brotherhood would ever be translated into regular church-going but its potential was great for the cause of God's Kingdom and for the service of needy humanity.

The effect of involvement in war upon Charles's theological outlook can best be judged by reference to a remarkable essay which he wrote in scraps of leisure time largely on the battlefields of Artois. He had been invited by the editor, C. H. S. Matthews, to contribute a chapter on *The Holy Spirit* to a volume of "Constructive Essays in the application of Modernist Principles to the Doctrine of the Church," which was published in 1918 under the title *Faith and Freedom*. The invitation reached him on the eve of his departure for France and it is astonishing that with few books available he should have succeeded in preparing so original and so wide-ranging a treatment of the subject. In effect it can be seen as a preliminary sketch of his notable book *The Creator Spirit* which was to appear some ten years later.

Words which were to feature prominently in all his writings make their début. Process, evolution, corporateness, creative energy are employed to reinterpret the activity of the Holy Spirit and an appeal is made to the work of Bergson, whom Charles was already regarding as a philosopher after his own heart. He sees a remarkable parallel between "our account and Bergson's philosophy of evolution. Like the Spirit, his élan de vie makes for betterment, manifests itself in instinctive and direct action, gives unity and solidarity to all that lives, insinuates itself into, and adapts itself to the conditions of materiality, in order to overcome its opposition and impose upon it the impulse towards life." (p. 237)

Charles does not hesitate to speak of God's "involvement" in the world, of God "struggling" with the world, and supports such language by appealing to the Paraclete passages in the Fourth Gospel and to the great section of Romans 8 which includes the reference to "groanings which cannot be uttered." He is highly critical of the language of "omnipotence." "God has brought this world into being not as a marionette-show but as a training ground for free souls" and lays hold of Bergsons' central picture as worthy of being adapted for use within the context of the Christian doctrine of the Trinity.

"Probably Bergson's metaphor, if we may vary his interpretation of it, gives us the truth as fully as any, when he says that life which is really one superb picture flung in a rapture of creative impulse upon the canvas of the material world, yet appears to us as a mosaic of which we are the pieces, a mosaic apparently fitted together with the uttermost toil and only after the most laborious collection and perfectioning of the separate fragments, a mosaic so vast that we cannot grasp its meaning, so elaborate that we cannot credit the spasm of creative energy that called it into being. May we not venture to interpret the parable into the language of theology and say that the artist's will which purposes to create the picture and the impulse which prepares pigments and canvas is God the Father; that the artist's conception of the complete picture, his cartoon of the grand design on which the work is modelled is God the Son; that the artist's energy, the vital and creative activity whereby is produced upon the canvas of matter the perfect image which the will has planned and the vision conceived is God the Holy Spirit. And these three, separate in sphere and method, representing separate functions of the artist's personality, are yet one." (pp. 247–8)

This triadic analogy, later developed in detail by Dorothy Sayers in her book *The Mind of the Maker*, provided Charles with an altogether congenial framework within which to express his own growing understanding of the complex relationships between nature, man and God.

NOTES TO CHAPTER FOUR

1. p. 79: *What Think Ye Of Christ?* p. 194.
2. p. 80: Ibid. p. 95.
3. p. 81: Charles's passionate concern for co-operation rather than competition, combination rather than contention in every area of life leads him to pass this judgment on Schweitzer's method of setting up antitheses and rejecting one after another. "It is not altogether surprising that after this ruthless holocaust the final product is a theory of Jesus which has all the perverted ingenuity, all the colossal assurance and all the occasional brilliance of Bedlam."
Ibid. p. 139.
4. p. 81: *The Guardian* May 10th, 1917.
5. p. 81: *A Wanderer's Way*, p. 156 f.
6. p. 82: One article was written "on the firestep of a trench with a scream of shells perpetually passing." Charles comments: "Such conditions do not make for great literature."
7. p. 83: *Musings and Memories*, p. 166 f.

PART TWO

1920—1931

THE HERALD OF A NEW REFORMATION

CHAPTER FIVE

Academic Successes: Parochial Failure

With the War ended, Charles was free to fulfil an engagement to which he had committed himself early in 1917. It was to give the Donnellan Lectures in Trinity College, Dublin. There were elements of romance in his appointment to the Lectureship and he loved to tell the story of his first journey to Dublin in 1916 when he went to preach the University Sermon.

All arrangements had been made with the Provost who at that time was the distinguished classical scholar and famous character the Rev. Sir John Pentland Mahaffy.[1] Charles was to stay at the Provost's house but, the story runs, a few days before the event a telegram was delivered with the message, "Sorry cannot deliver the goods on time." signed Raven. Mahaffy assumed that this referred to his guest preacher and immediately arranged, as was customary, for a senior Fellow, a certain Canon Westropp-Roberts, to take Charles's place. Imagine the Provost's surprise—for by this time he had arranged to dine out on the Saturday evening—when a very young looking man arrived on Saturday afternoon and announced that he was Charles Raven! (It transpired that the telegram was from a seeds firm whose trade name was Raven.)

Charles appears to have been left in peace on the Saturday evening but after being treated to a gargantuan breakfast on Sunday morning was told the truth about the awkward situation. The substitute was still expecting to preach but Mahaffy proceeded to instruct his young visitor (to whom by this time he had taken a considerable liking) how to circumvent it. "He is an old man and I have not told him of your arrival. You must get to the pulpit before him."

During the hymn before the sermon Charles, in his normal and approved fashion, knelt to prepare himself for his solemn responsibility.

But almost at once the Provost's hand was on his shoulder and a whisper in his ear said, "Hurry up young man or he'll beat you to it."

Evidently the sermon was a great success for it led to his appointment to the Lectureship in immediate succession to the distinguished Scottish Old Testament scholar, Sir George Adam Smith. In due course a subject was chosen in consultation with the Provost but it was not until May 1919 (after Mahaffy had died) that the Lectures were actually delivered. They were ready for publication in much expanded form in 1919 under the title *Christian Socialism 1848–1854*.

In some respects this is the most astonishing book that Charles ever wrote—astonishing because its subject was outside his main area of research and yet the book itself was a detailed treatment of a large and important historical theme. It is clear that he had set two topics in the forefront of his programme of work—the Christology of the early Fathers and the challenge presented to Christian faith by certain forms of scientific determinism. How, in addition to his labours in these complex fields of study, he could have found time to engage in a thorough investigation of a highly significant yet complex social movement which took shape in the mid-nineteenth century is hard to imagine. He had carried heavy pastoral responsibilities during the War years and had been pressing forward with his work on Christology. Yet a major book on a quite different subject was ready for the press within a year of the Armistice in 1918.

How his interest in the Christian Socialists was first awakened is uncertain. Undoubtedly his year in the Liverpool Education Office stirred his social conscience deeply and he had long been familiar with the work of College Missions: in one of them, in Hoxton, his brother had been giving devoted service. But the book when it came was not simply an attempt to show how a group of concerned Christian men had faced the glaring social abuses of their own time; it was an ambitious survey of the development of social theories in the first half of the nineteenth century and of the particular contribution that Maurice and Kingsley and their friends made as *Christian* Socialists within this development. It revealed wide reading in the background works of Mill, Bentham, Carlyle, Marx and Huber as well as a mastery of the

literature and documents related to the special period 1848–1854. And
Charles was not slow to point out the implications of his study for the
theories being advocated by the Hammonds and the Fabians in his own
day.[2]

After an introductory chapter in which he defined the issues which
were to gain increasing prominence in the debates and controversies of
the nineteenth century—heredity versus environment, individualism
versus collectivism, freedom versus determinism, competition versus
cooperation, the spiritual versus the material, above all perhaps moral
education versus structural reform—Charles proceeded to what he
always found a congenial task and one which he always performed with
great felicity: the biographical description of the men who were
pioneers and leaders in the Christian Socialist movement. Possibly it was
his training in the close observation of nature and in photographic
reproduction which enabled him to become adept in painting pen-
portraits. Certainly some of his obituaries contributed later to the
Cambridge Review are models of this type of writing. And his portraits
of Ludlow, Maurice, Kingsley and Hughes constitute the most distinctive contribution of this his first major book.

Though he regarded Maurice as the greatest Churchman of the nineteenth century, it was Ludlow who stirred his enthusiasm. He it was
who had really created and fostered the movement. "He suggested it,
he planned its policy, he more than any other carried that policy into
effect. The achievements of Christian Socialism, though he neither
claimed nor received the credit for them, owe their accomplishment
to him; and the more closely one studies the records of the work, the
more does one become impressed."[3] His hero was a layman of brilliant
intellectual gifts, having an unusually wide cultural background,
always maintaining a deep and natural devotion to Christian faith. He
stood between Tractarianism, which he acutely disliked, and Bibliolatry, which set up the Bible as a mere dead idol instead of a living
witness to Christ. At the same time he stood between grandiose
theories of tailor-made Utopias on the one side and the severely
limited concentration upon individual conversions on the other. The
social order and its human members must be reformed together and

the only way in which this could be effected, he believed, was the way of *association*.

Association, co-operation, brotherhood were key words for Ludlow and they became key words for Charles. The fierce competition of capitalist society and its nemesis, open war, they feared and rejected. Equally the regimentation of communist or collectivist societies was anathema to them both. Ludlow's proposal was to begin with a small community, working together in decent conditions, and learning together the lessons of self-discipline and self control. Such a community, though small in size, would have a cell-like character. It would possess the potential of organic growth. Like Maurice, Ludlow believed "that humanity exists for fellowship, that if once the possibility of co-operation as a substitute for competition is demonstrated it will be welcomed and accepted, and that the method is capable of expansion until the whole constitution of society is rebuilt upon the lines of a world-wide self-governing brotherhood"[4]

It would not be unfair to say that Charles himself embraced this basic belief of the Christian Socialists and strove throughout his life to promote the spirit of comradeship and co-operation which he had seen in a well-organised team at Cambridge, in the work of the Colosseum in Liverpool, in the trenches in Flanders and in some of the better examples of the life of the Church. He believed that this spirit of true community was indeed the most impressive manifestation of the activity of the Divine Spirit. The Spirit who promotes life in the natural order by the generation and association of living cells seeks to operate in the same way in the social order by building up an ever expanding assembly of units which become transfigured through their intimate association with one another in a common enterprise.

The progress of the movement between 1848–1854 is described with great care and the question of how far Christian Socialism "failed" is fairly assessed. Charles's chief claim for the leaders is that they were in the best sense of the word educators, both in theory and in practice. They understood social theory and they were in close contact and sympathy with the human lives to whom their knowledge was to be made available. Other historians have disputed this claim, questioning how adequate was their appreciation of the importance of social structures and how far they were really in touch with the working classes.[5] And this is a criticism which could be directed against Charles himself for he tended to minimise the necessity for what might be called a scaffolding of society and only knew working-class culture under certain highly specialised conditions. Nevertheless both the Christian Socialists and Charles himself had a deep concern for the improvement of social conditions in the great industrial areas of Britain and were surely right in using the organic model to guide and direct their educational activities. Probably their greatest mistake was in believing that this was the only possible model for use in this situational context.

In the final ten pages of his book Charles tries to assess the continuing significance of the thought and work of the Christian Socialists.

"Quite apart from the merits or demerits of their actual schemes of reform, few will venture to dispute that they are infinitely the most highly qualified, alike in intellect and character, of all those who have studied such problems in this country and that they need not fear comparison in these respects with the world's greatest sociologists."[6]

Alas, many *have* ventured to dispute the high claim that Charles makes for his heroes! So far as the detailed history of the movement is concerned no comparable survey has since been undertaken except by the Scandinavian writer T. Christensen in his *Origins and History of Christian Socialism 1848–54* and he adds little of substance to what appears already in Charles's book. (It is noteworthy that *Christian Socialism* was reprinted in 1969 nearly half a century after its first appearance). But much work has been done on the history of the development of ideas in the nineteenth century and many detailed surveys of its social conditions have been made. In the light of these researches Charles's estimate of the influence of the Christian Socialists may need to be revised. At the same time his book was a fine pioneering attempt to focus attention upon an important movement and in particular, perhaps, to show the greatness of Frederick Denison Maurice as thinker and practical reformer. Since 1920 Maurice's influence has gained increasing recognition and this man, who had obviously captured

Charles's imagination, is now widely regarded as worthy to be classed with Coleridge and Newman as one of the leading seminal religious thinkers of the nineteenth century.

Back in Cambridge Charles took up his regular duties again at Emmanuel and during the first part of 1919 shared in the task which confronted all Colleges—that of dealing in special ways with men who had been on war-service while gradually restoring normal patterns of entry and study for boys coming straight from school. By Michaelmas Term the life of the University was in full swing. Charles had been appointed Proctor and was drawing large numbers to his lectures. All seemed to point to further progress in his academic career.

However he had many wider interests. The various Christian societies were renewing their activities and beginning to look towards the future. To some, the time seemed propitious for a great unified Mission to the University. After the disruption of so many careers and the tragic loss of so many promising lives it seemed an appropriate time to attempt a complete Christian re-assessment of the situation and to call for a renewed dedication of life to the service of Christ. So plans were drawn up for the launching of a mission in January 1920, plans to which Charles gave his enthusiastic support. He hoped that it would lead not only to individual conversions but also to a new experience of unity amongst the various Christian societies then active in Cambridge.[7]

It was the great religious event of the academic year 1919–20 and Charles had been fully involved. But a change in his affairs was imminent. With a family of four children, housing and finance in Cambridge were becoming a serious problem. Calls for his services were coming from outside the University and it would not be easy to respond to them while remaining responsible for the regular daily duties in College. It was not surprising therefore that when an attractive College living fell vacant, the living of Blechingley in Surrey, Charles decided to leave Cambridge and combine the work of a country parish priest with other forms of ministry—one in particular—which had been offered to him.

The Emmanuel College Magazine bade him farewell in these words:

"For some time it had been evident that Mr. Raven's gifts and ener-

ies as preacher, thinker, writer and editor were being unduly hampered by the exacting and irregular claims of his college duties as dean
and theological lecturer. Blechingley which has with few exceptions
regularly been held by an ex-Fellow of the College, will give fuller
scope for the exercise of those gifts and energies. We wish to offer to
Mr. Raven our warmest good wishes for the future and to express
cordial recognition of the part he played in the religious, intellectual,
social and athletic life of the College during the ten years since he
first joined it."

But if he was being unduly hampered by College routine would the
situation be in any way different when he found himself in charge of a
tightly—knit parish community in rural Surrey?

It was late in the year 1920 that Charles and his family moved to
Blechingley. For few men of his age can the future outlook have seemed
brighter. He had fulfilled the duties of his office in Cambridge with
distinction. He had written a major work on Christian Socialism whose
merits had been widely acclaimed. And to crown all, the year had
brought him the coveted distinction of being appointed Chaplain to the
King. From now onwards the scarlet cassock would be in constant use,
providing him with a certain ceremonial dignity which he was not
loathe to enjoy. The tall slim figure with coal-black hair looked so
youthful that when he first went to preach at Sandringham their
Majesties were astonished to find that he had daughters of school-
going age.

Blechingley is situated in the midst of the lovely downland area of
England where the three counties Surrey, Sussex and Kent converge and
is near enough to Redhill to be within reach of a fast train service to
London. The Church itself is most attractive, standing as it does in a
spacious church yard, well back from the main thoroughfare but intimately related to the village houses and shops. The Rectory to which the
Raven family came was of a size more than sufficient for their needs—
the top storey was in fact given over to the Scout Troop as a Headquarters.

Although Charles possessed a real pastoral concern and doubtless had

D

every intention of serving the Church and the community in Blechingley to the best of his ability, his mind was set on much wider issues as they affected the total life of Christendom. He had no intention of becoming the quiet country parson who studied in the mornings, went visiting in the afternoons and occupied himself with village social interests in the evenings. His vision was much more akin to that of John Wesley who saw the world as his parish.

In the first place he had agreed to become the Editor of *The Challenge*, a task that entailed constant journeys to London and much public speaking on behalf of the causes which it was seeking to promote. Secondly he was committed to assist in a series of missions which were being planned by Dr. David, the new Bishop of St. Edmundsbury and Ipswich, for his Diocese. And thirdly Charles soon undertook to be organising secretary, in company with Miss Lucy Gardner, a member of the Society of Friends, of the great Conference on Politics, Economics and Citizenship which was to take place in Birmingham in the spring of 1924. With these three major responsibilities demanding constant attention it is hardly surprising that his parishioners did not see as much of their Rector as they tended to expect.

It is true that he had as assistant a man of some seniority and that he made available out of his own stipend a considerable sum of money for the payment of deputies when he was absent. Nevertheless the records reveal that by the end of his first year in Blechingley the situation had become sufficiently critical as to demand a thorough appraisal of his whole policy in regard to the parish. At a meeting of the Parochial Church Council the Rector reviewed the past 12 months, expressed his happiness in the work, and his gratitude for much kindness received, and ventured to claim that matters generally had "enlivened up," the social work in particular having made real progress. Yet because of the stress and strain caused by his work outside Blechingley, he had felt it right to consult the Bishop of Southwark about the future and he had advised him to talk matters over with the Council. After a preliminary discussion a special meeting was arranged for December, 1921. "The Rector, after reporting the progress made during his first year in Blechingley, retired and the Chair was taken by Mr. S. G.

Sneezum, Churchwarden and Vice-Chairman. It was proposed seconded and carried unanimously that the meeting of the members of the
P.C.C. desire to express their appreciation of the very frank statement submitted to them by the Rector and wish to express their
unabated confidence in him. They concur in the continuance of his
outside work as proposed by him and sanctioned by the Lord Bishop
provided proper provision is made for the needs of the Parish during
such absence and appoint the Churchwardens to confer with him as to
the best means of so doing."[8]

One could wish that a movie-camera had been on hand to make a
permanent record of the withdrawal of the Rector and Mrs. Raven
while their fate was being decided by Mr. Sneezum and his colleagues
of the P.C.C. Charles always walked with a certain air of majesty. A
slight toss of the head might have indicated his defiant lack of concern
about which way the decision went. But the members of the Council
were probably aware that a very unusual man had come to be their
Rector and that they would be ill-advised to dispense abruptly with his
services, even though they seemed little more than part-time. So
democratic procedures were vindicated and Charles could continue his
programme of outside activities with greater confidence and peace of
mind. One suspects that it was Mrs. Raven who in the end did much to
keep the parishioners satisfied.

As it turned out the incumbency was not to be long extended. During
the next two years real progress was made in ordinary parish affairs. A
troup of Boy Scouts was formed; the number of confirmation candidates was well above the average; the financial position vastly improved
and a new interest in missionary giving was created; special lectures
were arranged; and somewhat surprisingly, in view of Charles's limitations musically, congregational hymn practices were introduced and a
better standard of musical offering achieved—though not without the
dismissal of the organist and troubles about the introduction of lady
choristers.

In his final letter published in the Parish Magazine in April 1924
Charles admits that by Easter 1923 he had realised that the parish
ought to have a different kind of rector. "It is always well to know

one's limitations. You will, please God, find in Mr. Crawshaw (who had been appointed as his successor) a man who can succeed where I have failed: a man with no outside duties, with health and strength and with wider experience of parish work." At the same time he did not exonerate his parishioners completely. "Blechingley folk are very critical and I think very easily pessimistic: they dwell on the failures more than on the encouragements. By all means let us see our failings and criticise our position; but we must not forget that no obstacles are insuperable and that the resources of God are available for us if we will use them."

So with a characteristic exhortation to his people to "pull together" Charles said good-bye to Blechingley. The P.C.C. in a recorded resolution referred with gratitude to all he had done to awaken enthusiasm and good fellowship in the Parish and to the improvement in church finances under his leadership. But the other side of the picture appears in the communication to their Patrons when they ask that their new Rector shall be a man "who understands and will visit and sympathise with country people." This final reference to country people came near to the heart of the matter. Though he loved country sights and sounds and rejoiced whenever the opportunity arose for him to absorb himself in the study of nature, Charles was at heart a towns-man who was never content for long to be away from the bustle of human affairs and the places where community decisions were being made. The discharge of his responsibilities at Blechingley had really only been tolerable within the context of the crowded programme of activities which he had been carrying on in London and Ipswich and other towns. It must have been an immense relief to him when towards the end of 1923 Dr. David, the newly appointed Bishop of Liverpool, invited him to become a residentiary Canon of the Cathedral. His country incumbency ended on May 1st, 1924.

During his final year at Blechingley Charles brought to a conclusion two major tasks. The first had occupied him steadily for some fifteen years and had finally issued in the publication of the book *Apollinarianism* for which he was awarded the Cambridge D.D. The second had engaged his attention for roughly four years and had reached its

climax in the meeting of Copec in the Central Hall at Birmingham
during the week April 5–12, 1924. The first set him in the forefront of
research on the development of early Christian doctrine. The second
marked him out as a leader in the new movement amongst Christians
of all denominations towards understanding more fully the nature of
their responsibility in relation to the growing complexity of economic
and political problems within the life of society.

Turning first to the book which has remained the most important
single treatment of the subject during the past half century: the theme
had been first suggested to him as a research project in 1908 but had
been prevented from an earlier completion by the coming of the Great
War. Yet the project had never been abandoned and had probably
gained in depth by the process of revision which had become necessary
after his return to more normal life. Possibly it gained also in piquancy
by the fact that it was a young Cambridge man's challenge to views
which had for long been strongly held in Oxford, the traditional home,
as it likes to think, of sound patristic scholarship.

It was characteristic of Charles that his chief contribution to historical
theology should have been the defence of a man who had been officially
repudiated as a heretic. Throughout his life he was ever quick to
spring to the side of anyone who seemed to him to be unjustly accused
or trampled upon. Something of his own sensitivity to physical pain
and to personal criticism transferred itself to any weaker brother,
whomsoever he might be, who was under any kind of attack. So
having come to the conclusion that Apollinarius was a far more
admirable person than many of his denigrators, he set to work to
place him within a true perspective and to determine just how far his
views were identical with those of men who claimed to be his disciples
and how far they contributed to a proper understanding of the person
of Christ.

A second type of human experience which Charles intensely disliked
and which he never hesitated to pillory was that which manifested
itself in an extreme authoritarianism on the one side and a passive
submission on the other. His historical investigations led him to the
conclusion that Rome and the imperial power had been mainly respons-

ible for throttling the spirit of free enquiry which had characterised the early Greek theologians and that a kind of mechanical efficiency had taken the place of creative growth and a constantly expanding life. Again there may well have been a love-hate attitude on Charles's part to the whole Roman tradition. He was a fine Latinist and had an excellent knowledge of Roman history. Contrary to a fairly widely held impression he was an excellent organiser and loved order in worship, in language and in life. Yet he reacted fiercely against any forms of absolute authority or of imposed closure of an issue. He was acutely sensitive to attempts being made in his own Church to limit the freedom of the individual person in thought and action. Still more did he feel a complete antipathy to the authoritarian tradition of the Roman Church. Its almost mechanical structures and its imperviousness to change seemed to him utterly inimical to the development of the true life of the Spirit. So in *Apollinarianism* he did not hesitate to name the chief culprit, as he believed, both in heresy-hunting and in imposing uniformity—it was the genius of Rome incorporated into the Christian Church.

At Rome, he said, "speculation was taboo": every citizen owed "implicit obedience to constituted authority": "discipline", "solidarity", "conformity", "efficiency", "formulated dogma", were key concepts. All this meant that when Rome gained the upper hand in Christian counsels, Christianity came more and more to be identified with "the creed, the canons and the constitution of the Church".

> "To reduce Christian morality to the observance of a code of rules was the business of the organisers of monasticism: to translate the specula-tions of Christian philosophy into a series of precise definitions was an equally desirable task: in all departments there must be systematic organisation and a recognised authority. Greece had been conquered by Rome before: confronted by the alternative, Rome or chaos, she would again make her submission." (p. 236)

Many years were to pass before Charles allowed himself to regard the Church of Rome in a more favourable light. What he saw of its opera-tions in Liverpool and Ireland did little to improve its image in his eyes.

His passionate interest in the history of scientific advance led him to the conviction that only when the dominating imperialism of the medieval church had been breached was real progress in man's understanding of the universe made. Furthermore the development of his own theology was essentially in terms of life, spirit, personality, progress rather than of tradition, consensus, dogmatic formulation, establishment. Though, somewhat ironically, Charles's own philosophic position was nearer to that of Aristotle than of Plato, to that of Aquinas than of Augustine—and Aquinas has been regarded as the official philosopher—theologian of the Roman communion—it was only when he became familiar with the works of Teilhard de Chardin that he recognised how similar his own approach was to that of a neo-Thomist within a liberal Catholic tradition.

Of the ancient writers portrayed in his book one stands out as specially akin to Charles in his approach and general outlook. This was Paul of Samosata, a man who found his chief interest, "in the concrete and particular not in the abstract and general, in the scientific analysis of human nature rather than in the metaphysical principles of which it is or may be the embodiment, in the study of the facts of history and experience more than of the eternal relationships by which those facts are to be interpreted." (p. 55)

In so describing Paul, Charles provided an almost exact definition of his own leading interests. Speculations about pre-existent relationships within the godhead, about the possibility of a pre-mundane fall, about a pre-natal conjunction of the logos with the humanity of Jesus, he regarded as unedifying and unprofitable. What was central for him was the story of Jesus as told in the Gospels: a human babe, a naturally growing child, a mature person capable of ethical choice and decision, a man struggling to understand God's will for his vocation and destiny, a heroic figure standing firm in the fight against evil and nobly faithful even unto death. To interpret the meaning and implications of that story became his own overmastering concern. So far as possible he eschewed all preconceptions, orthodoxies, philosophical traditions. He tried to fix his gaze upon the Jesus of the Gospels and of Paul's Epistles and then to view the whole of reality—the physical universe, human behaviour, personal relationships—in the light of that vision. Like many other historians of his own time Charles scarcely realised how difficult, if not impossible, it is to dispense with presuppositions and to avoid dependence upon some framework of reference. Yet his challenge was salutary in a period when new knowledge of man —his history, his physiological and psychological make-up, his place in the universe—was flooding in from so many sources. It was useless to spin webs of discussion around theoretical concepts of divine nature and human nature while failing to ask what could be said with confidence about human nature in the light of scientific research.

Charles allied himself with Aristotle in a common concern for careful obsevation of all manifestations of life, of growth, of progress towards a goal. He could not, however, accept his dualistic outlook in which he made a sharp distinction between mind and body, between a substance which is imperishable and immortal and another substance which is passible and corruptible. For him the unity of the human personality must in no way be compromised. If the divine had indeed been manifested in and through a human being then there must have been a complete assumption of humanity and a complete subjection to its restraints and limitations. Divinity is not something utterly separate from and apart from humanity. Rather, only through Jesus's perfect humanity has man seen that which is truly divine. In and through identification with the living Christ man can ascend towards that union with the highest which is his true end.

While *Christian Socialism* had attracted a good deal of favourable attention the reception given to *Apollinarianism* was all that an author could have wished. Naturally there were criticisms of some of his historical judgments and of what *The Tablet* described as "tendentious prejudices". But lengthy reviews appeared, not only in Church papers and theological journals, but also in such secular organs as *The Times Literary Supplement*, *The Spectator* and the *New Statesman*: and their general consensus was that a highly important subject had been treated in a competent and in many respects an original way. *The Spectator* for example declared:

"English theologians are few and far between. This is more particularly the case since theology has ceased to be a deductive science. The English mind has great qualities; but it is not speculative, and does not easily move among ideas. Dr. Raven's treatise on Apollinarianism has, therefore, the charm of novelty: here is an English writer who is unmistakably a theologian; and an English work which is an important contribution to theology, in the European sense of the word." (March 1, 1924)

All reviewers were impressed, I think, by the lucidity of his expositions, by the vigour of his language, and in particular by the vivid pen-portraits which he had been able to sketch of the leading thinkers and controversialists of the early Church. Inevitably his more caustic comments aroused animosity and from about the year 1921, when his writings began to reach a wide public, he became a marked man. Many hailed the advent of a new prophet: not a few, while recognising his ability, dismissed him as a modernist or a revolutionary. Some quotations from *Apollinarianism* will illustrate the type of comment or judgment which could hardly fail to stir hostile reactions.

"The real Apollinarius went almost unscathed: a man of straw created by his opponents and bearing only the most distant resemblance to him was gibbeted in his place."
"The Cappadocians never hesitated to reinforce the arm of the spirit by a timely appeal to the arm of the flesh."
Gregory of Nyssa: "A peacemaker not wise enough to be honest and too simple to escape being found out."

Perhaps most scathing of all was a purple passage which did nothing to endear Charles to his 'orthodox' critics:

"Among the wars of history there are few more significant than the miserable campaign which the Bishop of Salamis, and under his instigation his illustrious admirer Jerome, waged against the memory of Origen. With its virility sapped by monasticism and its honesty corrupted by state patronage, cowed by threats of persecution in this world and hell in the next, seduced by pomps and ceremonies, by ritual and relics, pilgrimages and image-worship, miracle mongering

and the cult of the saints, bewildered by its manifest disunion and
betrayed by the lying and intrigue, violence and vanity of its leaders,
the glory of Greek Christendom was outraged and destroyed.
Apollinarius, Chrysostom, Nestorius are the principal victims: but
the war was not so much against them as against the free search for
truth, the wide horizon and clear vision of God, the hope and faith
and love which Christian Hellenism had laid at the feet of Christ.
Efficiency triumphed and the splendour faded. Christ was exiled and
the Church Catholic reigned in his stead." (p. 239)[9]

As early as 1907–8 Charles had sensed that one of the supreme issues
of the twentieth century was likely to be that of determinism. How
far could it be proved by scientific investigation that man's subsequent
behaviour was controlled by his initial genetic endowment? To what
extent could it be said that man was free to orient himself either towards
righteousness or towards damnation? If this issue was destined to become
crucial for the ordinary interpreter of the human condition (and
developments in this century have confirmed that this is indeed the
case) then all the more should religious interpreters be careful not to
play into the hands of secular determinists by advocating some kind of
metaphysical or transcendental determinism instead. While attracted by
the more mystical side of Platonism Charles had a deep-rooted aversion
to all notions of changelessness and impassibility and pre-determined
"forms". In particular, if Jesus's humanity was not a real humanity but
was controlled from the outset by a supernatural "Logos" taking the
place of the faculty of "reason" which belonged to man as man—then
the Incarnation was in the last resort a theophany and in no way a true
identification with man in the inescapable conditions of his lot.

There may be more than a little significance in the fact that Charles
often appealed to the realm of dramatic experience to show how he
differed from certain traditional interpretations of the Incarnation.
Whether he was aware at that time of his own histrionic gifts it is
impossible to say. Certainly in his later years he knew it: he once said
"If I had not been a parson, I should have been an actor." He always
enjoyed dressing up and had a great sense of occasion. This led his

critics to suggest that all too often he was putting on an act and that he was sometimes playing to the gallery. Did he half feel this temptation and did it make him, if only unconsciously, the more antagonistic to any theory which implied that Jesus Himself was acting a part rather than sharing to the fullest degree in the human nature which He came to redeem?

In the first chapter of *Apollinarianism* he commits himself to a general statement about Greek Christians in the early centuries of the Church's life.

"Their whole interpretation of Christ was dramatic: He came as a spectacle for men to behold, an example to copy, a teacher to obey. And in so far as stress is laid on this side of His mission, the significance of His humanity falls into the background. The evidences of that humanity, invaluable as they are to the sinful and the despairing, to those whose discipleship is of the heart rather than of the intellect, must be explained away lest the presence of His human limitations cast a slur upon the infallibility of His divine authority. And in that fact is contained the whole burden of the history, the whole secret of the failure of the Greeks." (p. 29)

And when he comes to the last chapter of his book, where he singles out Theodore of Mopsuestia as the most appealing and satisfying of Apollinarius's opponents, he again makes use of dramatic imagery. Theodore, he points out, was the champion of Antiochene theology and in the theology the human element was vitally important.

"To him (Theodore) as to all the Antiochenes, the efforts of Christian Platonists to see life in all its manifestations as one great act of divine self-revelation seemed alike false to history, unworthy of the dignity of man, and subversive of all sense of the reality of the moral struggle. If the universe were simply a theatre on which a single author spoke his plot through the mouths of puppets, what a mockery it all was! What was the value of prayer, of the fight against sin, of holy purpose and high endeavour, if all men were alike empty masks speaking a pre-arranged part, unable to swerve a hair's-breath from their allotted places in the play? If the fall of a soul into sin is merely an incident giving variety to the drama, if it is not an outrage in the sight of God and an act of rebellion against His will, then saints have toiled and martyrs perished in vain."[10]

Charles felt so deeply the danger of viewing the Incarnation in terms of drama that he made special reference to it when giving his Gifford Lectures some thirty years later. He recalled a conversation he had had with William Temple at about the time when *Apollinarianism* was published.

"We had been discussing the change of outlook that was coming over theology as a result of the development of science and the changes in the social order. I put it to him that, whereas Christendom down to and including our immediate predecessors like Bishop Gore had regarded the Universe as the theatre on the stage of which was played out the drama of Man's Fall and Redemption, our generation, taking evolution seriously, must see the theatre not as a mere setting, itself subsidiary and irrelevant, but as an essential and integral part of the play; and that this must in fact enlarge our whole concept of the scope and character of religion."[11]

The world a stage on which a Divine Actor from another world played out a drama of certain well-defined acts—Incarnation, Transfiguration, Crucifixion, Resurrection: this whole conception Charles found himself utterly unable to accept. For him there were not two worlds but one. This one world, not to be regarded as a static stage but as a dynamic process, as part of the drama itself, was best conceived as the outward vesture of the one Eternal Spirit who through it was forever travailing to bring into being the perfection of personality, a travail which reached its initial fulfilment in the Christ and which would reach its final fulfilment in the creation of a great family of children bearing the image of the Christ and dwelling in perfect communion with Him and with one another. To develop this conception in detail—by immersing himself in scientific and historical studies and by presenting the results of his labours in appropriate forms of speech and writing—became the compelling constraint of Charles's subsequent career.

NOTES TO CHAPTER FIVE

1. p. 91: Stories about Mahaffy are legion. When Charles first met him he found himself confronted by a figure wearing "slack trousers, red braces and nothing else". Yet Charles once declared that in no social setting in which he had ever found himself had he listened to more brilliant and exhilarating conversation than in the Senior Common Room at T.C.D. in the time of Mahaffy. He possessed an international reputation as a classical scholar but he did not always endear himself to his fellow scholars by the frankness of his utterances. The Dictionary of National Biography records a famous instance which Charles, with his suspicion of German methods, must have greatly enjoyed. Those who were present at the Historical Congress at Berlin in 1908 are not likely to forget the scene that was occasioned by his remark that the reason why English scholars, in dealing with questions of authorship, attached far more importance than the Germans to the argument from style, was that English scholars had been drilled in writing Latin and Greek prose while the Germans had never written a piece of either in their lives.

2. p. 93: He launches a vigorous attack on Beatrice Webb for being guilty of what he always regarded as one of the worst faults of any would-be historian: relying on second hand reports about the Christian Socialists rather than taking pains to study their works at first hand.

3. p. 93: *Christian Socialism*, p. 55.

4. p. 94: Ibid. p. 64.

5. p. 95: e.g. "The weakness of most Christian Socialists was one they shared with other types of socialists: their middle-classness."
Peter d'A. Jones. *The Christian Socialist Revival. 1877–1914.* p. 458.

6. p. 95: *Christian Socialism*, p. 369.

7. p. 96: The account of the Mission which was ultimately published was actually written at speed by Charles himself.

8. p. 98: The Council Minutes.

9. p. 105: Dr. Henry Chadwick, Dean of Christ Church, has sent me the following note on the continuing value of the book:

"At first there was considerable criticism of Raven's view that the bishops who condemned Paul of Samosata in 268 anticipated the Apollinarian position. But subsequent research, especially the book by H. de Riedmatten, has entirely vindicated Raven's position.

My own view, in short, would be that it remains a very good book and, although much water has passed under the bridge since then, it was a landmark in the study of a great subject."

10. p. 107: *Apollinarianism*, p. 279.
11. p. 108: *Natural Religion and Christian Theology, II* p. 20.

CHAPTER SIX

The New Reformation

On February 20th, 1921 Charles preached the University sermon at Cambridge and this was subsequently printed in *The Challenge*, a paper of which he had recently become Editor. It was given the significant title *The New Reformation*, a title which brought into sharp focus ideas and hopes which since the latter part of the War had been stirring in his mind. It would not, I think, be unfair to say that this prospect dominated his life and outlook throughout the next decade. He was not paranoiac —there is no evidence that he conceived himself as the great Reformer in the style of a Luther or a Calvin. But that he had a real part to play as a leader in the New Reformation seemed clear to him. Erasmus was to him the most congenial type of reformer. If like Erasmus he could bring the Church to study and appreciate the new learning—and this in the twentieth century meant the new discoveries of experimental science—and to apply the methods of science to its own problems and to those of society at large then indeed a new era might dawn. The disappointment of this hope in the thirties was to make the period from 1935–1945 the darkest in his whole life.

Meanwhile what he had outlined in his University sermon was given full expression in a brilliant essay contributed to a book entitled *Anglican Essays: A Collective Review of the Principles and Special Opportunities of the Anglican Communion as Catholic and Reformed* which was published in 1923.

In this he began by sketching the leading characteristics of what he called 'the present crisis'. The crisis is concerned with the very nature of *life* itself. Whereas in the nineteenth century the concentration on material things and material ends had almost throttled the life-process, the twentieth century, especially since the conclusion of the War, had witnessed a notable revival of *life* in all its aspects. On all hands now there were signs of a new desire for life—and what could be more encouraging to those whose major concern was to bear witness to Him who came that men might have life and have it more abundantly? The experiences of war had indeed been terrible but the sacrifices had not been in vain if now new life could come forth out of the pain and suffering which had been endured.

"With body broken and blood outpoured mankind shattered the tyranny of materialism and in a grim sacrament of pain, dying to live, gained communion with its God." (p. 250)

But has the Church, he asks, understood the new revelation of the fundamental principles of the universe—that only through death can new life be generated?

"If she (i.e. the Church) is to rise again after her confessed failure and to seize the opportunity of the present crisis she must cease busying herself about 'side-shows' and concentrate her resources upon the fundamental duty of evangelism. To be the instrument of God's Spirit in the world and to mediate His life to mankind through the sacramental means of grace, that is through her every activity, to proclaim her Lord as Life and Light and Love (Charles's favourite triad) and to bring all her members into living communion with the risen Christ, this is her supreme task." (Ibid.)

Charles was not alone in making this kind of appeal for evangelism in the post-war period. Studdert-Kennedy was burning himself out in impassioned addresses all over the country; Tubby Clayton was trying to present the Christian message through the particular symbolism of Toc H; Dick Sheppard was using the newly discovered medium of broadcasting to speak to mass audiences. What distinguished Charles, however, from the other evangelists of his time was the highly trained intellect which sought always to set the evangelistic appeal within the context of the best theological understanding of his time. Perhaps the nearest parallel in the Anglicanism of the twenties was William Temple. But whereas he was primarily concerned with the philosophical climate within which the Christian message must be proclaimed, Charles was constantly seeking to relate the Gospel to the world of the scientist, to the particular method of seeking truth which he came to regard as alone valid.

Having then defined the Church's task he went on to admit that it is beset with difficulty because of the great intellectual advances which have been made during the past century.

"The new physical sciences have rendered untenable the traditional ideas of authority, of the supernatural, of miracles, and in fact of the whole method of God's operation... The new history has profoundly modified the traditional portrait of Christ ... The new philosophy has made the traditional language of dogmatic theology almost unintelligible without an apparatus of translation and exegesis; technical terms like substance and person have either become meaningless or are now used with an altered significance ... The new psychology is challenging many of the traditional concepts as to the nature and relationships of men, of the character of sin and the process of salvation. And if psychic research should emerge from the empirical stage of its development and become psychic science, we shall certainly have a vast deal of readjustment in almost every department of Christian thought." (pp. 262–3)

I have quoted excerpts from this passage because it illustrates vividly the main lines on which Charles's thinking was developing. His *bêtes noires* were impassibility, immutability, magic, mechanism, determinism, legalism, authoritarianism, dogmatism. His hopes were pinned on the life-sciences, on history, on psychology, on evolutionary philosophy, possibly on psychic research. He rejects both the primitive ethics of the Hebrews and the primitive theology of the Greeks. The methods associated with modern science—observation, experiment, criticism, verification—he accepts whole-heartedly.

This did not mean that he was an unrestrained iconoclast. He was too well-grounded in the culture of Greece and Rome, too great an admirer of the early Greek Fathers, especially Origen, to want to jettison the inheritance from the past completely. But he was convinced that there had been a great apostasy in Christendom during the Dark Ages and much of the Middle Ages, an apostasy which had enthroned dogma and canon law and sacramental automatism. To seek the truth openly, patiently, unfettered by past rigidities and present prejudices, seemed to him to constitute the central challenge of the new day. The pangs of the Great War had been so terrible that he could not but believe that in God's providence a new Pentecost had now become possible for the Church. ("We have prayed and believed that the Calvary of war would lead to a new Pentecost.")

While Charles was often critical of the Church he seldom spoke hard words about the Universities. But in this essay on *The New Reformation* he castigates the academic world on account of certain of its preoccupations.

"Unfortunately the theological faculties of our Universities, to which naturally the Church would look for guidance, are still in the grip of a rigid and tyrannical convention. When they ought to be pressing on to meet the needs of the time they are refusing to leave the beggarly elements of Hebrew and Greek. Theology to its professors seems to mean little more than a minute acquaintance with the linguistic and textual problems of the Scriptures and with the niceties of fourth century controversies, as if a detailed study of the authorship of Isaiah or of the manuscript evidence for a few verses in the Gospels helped a man to see God or to preach Christ." (p. 263)

Already Charles is expressing something of the frustration that he was to feel later when called to a position of high responsibility in the divinity faculty at Cambridge.

But in spite of all his criticisms, Charles was full of hope for the future. The immediate task as he conceived it was not so much hard thinking about the Church's relation to the social and economic problems of the time, though he was in fact devoting much of his energies to the organisation of the greatest effort that had so far been made in this direction. Rather he saw the immediate task as "the promotion of a strong and if possible united evangelistic movement within the Church, a movement planned with the sympathy and, if practicable, the concurrent support of the Free Churches." Yet for the time being Copec and *The Challenge* and the responsibility for the regular services at Blechingley held him fast. An occasional mission was possible but not until he took up his new appointment in Liverpool at the beginning of June 1924 was he free to give more time to the evangelistic task which seemed to him more urgent than any other in the life of post-war England.

Charles occupied the editorial chair of *The Challenge* for approximately fifteen months. This paper had been launched in May, 1914. It was definitely a Church paper but aimed to be independent of all party allegiances. It sought to include a wide range of interests and to deal with them in untechnical language, hoping thereby to attract a lay readership.

But almost from the beginning it ran into difficulties. Financially it suffered from its lack of capital resources and from the rapid rise in costs caused by war. Editorially it changed its direction twice in its first year and was only saved from collapse by the willingness of William Temple to undertake the task from July 1915. With remarkable resourcefulness he managed to keep things going until late in 1918 but then felt bound to resign. The outlook was grave unless a man could be found who would gather new readers by the sheer dynamic of some new appeal. At last after two years of further struggle the committee of management prevailed upon Charles to attempt what seemed almost the impossible (He called it "a bankrupt venture"). Could he stir up amongst church members (for inevitably the paper must direct itself primarily to those who would hear of it through their church connections) sufficient interest in the application of Christian principles to current affairs to make them willing to pay threepence a week (for costs had steeply risen) and to give time to serious thought about matters which might often seem remote from their immediate experience?

During most of the first year his editorials were vigorous, his notes on current affairs critical but also constructive, his comments on moral problems fearless. But then came ominous references to Charles being in the doctor's hands. He has had only six days holiday in the past eighteen months. Through the kindness of a friend he is spending three weeks in the Engadine before taking up his job again. Meanwhile however the paper's financial situation has become desperate. Unless new funds can be found within a few weeks it cannot continue to operate.

For the moment the situation was saved and Charles returned to his task. But by the end of April 1922 the doctors were deciding the question so far as he was concerned. He must cut down somewhere and the editorship was the responsibility which he could most easily relinquish. So his last editorial was written for the April 28th issue and at the end of September *The Challenge* passed into new hands and took on a new form. He had made a heroic effort but to be in charge of a parish and to combine with it two major tasks besides his mission preaching and writing was more than any man could stand. He continued to make occasional contributions to *The Challenge* but to all intents and purposes this phase of his career had come to an end.

Yet it was in no way a failure. Within a short space of time he had brought to the attention of thoughtful Church members some of the issues which were to assume increasing importance in the next twenty years. Reunion, Christianity and War, Religion and Science, the new relationship between the sexes, the Ministry of Women, Planned Parenthood, Christianity and Eastern Cultures, Christ and Modern Philosophy—about them all he wrote with conviction, with insight and above all with a firm grasp of what were the *theological* issues involved.

His final leading article from the Editorial Chair was entitled *The Origin of Species*. He had not often referred to his scientific interests but now, in response to certain views on evolution which had recently appeared and which seemed to be of a wholly deterministic kind, he seized the opportunity to outline his own convictions on a subject which would constantly figure in his writing in the coming years. It was a strange farewell. The theologian, evangelist, social reformer made his final bow as a natural historian and apologist. And he showed as complete a command of the vocabulary of lepidoptera as of the technicalities of early patristic controversies. It was a mark of the many sidedness of this man who would increasingly devote his gifts to the inter-relationship of the realms of Christian experience, scientific observation and historical theology.

Though nearly fifty years have passed since the Christian Conference on Politics, Economics and Citizenship was held in Birmingham, the name Copec has established itself firmly in the records of twentieth century British church history and by general consent has come to symbolise one of the most notable efforts ever made to apply Christian principles to contemporary social problems. It was this Conference which was never far from Charles's mind from the time when he agreed to be one of its joint secretaries in 1920 until the event itself took place from April 5–12, 1924.

The direct antecedents of the Conference are well described by William Temple's biographer.

"It was first mooted in 1919 while Temple was at Westminster and officially launched at an Interdenominational Conference of Social Service Unions of which Gore was president. Its object was to seek the will and the purpose of God for men and women in every relationship of their lives—political, social, industrial and the rest. Four years were allowed for study and campaigning. Twelve commissions were set up; 200,000 questionnaires were dealt with at 75 centres, and the whole of 1923 was spent in studying the replies and producing the commissions' reports; Temple, as Chairman of the Movement (with Dr. Hugh Martin as Chairman of the Executive Committee and Lucy Gardner and Dr. Charles Raven as Joint-Secretaries) was involved in much of the preparatory work."[1]

And it has been affirmed by the Editors of *A History of the Ecumenical Movement, 1517–1948* that "no preparation of equal thoroughness had been carried out anywhere else in the world." Indeed in the same context they claim that "Copec was the most considerable effort made up to that date anywhere in the world to focus Christian thought and action on the urgent problems of the day."[2]

The Commission which owed most to Charles was that which dealt with the Nature and Purpose of God. Though the identity of the final writers of the volumes prepared by the commissions was not disclosed it would require little detective work to see his hand at work on its particular Report. (It is in fact known that he was made responsible for the drafting of this volume.) The text is copiously sprinkled with Latin quotations! The key-concepts are Fatherhood, Personality, Sacrifice, Fellowship. The writing is lucid, the style distinguished. It is a simple straightforward testimony which begins significantly enough with God's revelation in Christ and goes on to deal successively with God and nature, God and man, God and sin, God and present conduct. Though the Editors had been warned that this book of doctrine would be unsaleable it proved in fact to be the best seller of all.[3]

Some 1500 delegates attended the Conference which met in the Birmingham Town Hall. Extraordinary public interest had been aroused and messages of greeting were received from the King, the Archbishop of Canterbury and the Prime Minister. William Temple's Chairmanship was superb; a high level of presentation and debate was sustained throughout; and the reports of the Commissions were weighty enough in themselves, whatever the outcome of the Conference might prove to be. An interesting record of the reflections of a distinguished visitor from abroad is to be found in the biography of Nathan Söderblom, the Archbishop of the Church of Sweden, a man already playing an outstanding part in ecumenical affairs and destined to achieve still greater fame by his wise leadership of the international Conference on Life and Work to be held in Stockholm in 1925. His biographer writes:

"He was impressed by what he saw: 'Bishop Temple, broad, with thin lips and with will-power, presiding. Raven spoke with spiritual power. Copec has been prepared with British thoroughness and common sense and a simple, straightforward interpretation of our Lord's prayer without much theology! At the end of the conference Söderblom was tempted to meditate on the significance of the initials, Copec. This was not Esperanto, he said, but English and meant Conference Obviously Prepared with Extraordinary Care. It was a living thing, he suggested, with a father, Bishop of Manchester, a mother Lucy Gardner, and a soul, Charles Raven."[4]

This focussing of attention upon three of the participants is significant.

Charles often opposed Temple on matters of ecclesiastical or social policy but he never ceased to enjoy his friendship and to accord him the utmost respect. Many years later he was to write:

"The future Archbishop who was our Chairman had been established before the war as the representative and leader of the generation which was coming to terms with the cosmology and anthropology of modern science, which had renounced the individualism of the older liberalism without confusing the crowd with the community or authoritarianism with orthodoxy. His profound humility which, all his life, never really admitted that anyone was less Christian or less intelligent than himself, his astonishing memory especially for every sort of written word, his eloquence at once architectural in its sense of mass and felicitous in its control of phrase, which was as evident in any impromptu utterance as in his fully prepared discourses, gave him a power of maintaining personal relationships, of appreciating difficult problems, and of guiding conflicting interests which were in my experience unique. He was never unwilling to listen to critics and never tried to evade or to misrepresent them; he never professed to find difficulties easy or to admit them insoluble; if he never quite outgrew the need for his tutor Pickard Cambridge's warning "Mr. Temple you must never suppose that you have solved a problem when you have found a formula," he was never, I think, unaware of the danger of doing so and never willing to use his resourcefulness unfairly. If I may speak from some thirty years of affection, co-operation and controversy, I have not known anyone so ready to give himself to any cause that he knew to be serious or more generous in admitting the value of arguments and even reproaches which he could not himself accept. And at Copec he was in his freedom and his prime."

Lucy Gardner, whom Söderblom described as the 'mother' of the movement, never attained public recognition as did the 'father.' But she stood very high in Charles's roll-call of distinguished women. Of her he was to write:

"The genius of the whole movement was Lucy Gardner. Certainly she mothered and sustained our whole community but she had also gathered and organised it. I do not believe that any man could have shown such ruthless and untiring efficiency without losing the human touch. Lucy never for a moment treated her staff as less than persons: even when we disappointed or failed her (and she was both sensitive and temperamental) she never behaved as if we were instruments or conveniences. Politics were for her always secondary to human relationships. So she got out of us work of a quality, and quantity, that no male employer would have asked or received. Her power of work seemed almost unlimited: three days with her in Scotland involving two night journeys without sleepers, breakfast with David Cairns in Aberdeen, meetings at Perth and Stirling, Edinburgh and Glasgow, and a night in Herbert Gray's cottage on the mountain above Lochearnhead, left me exhausted: she went back having sat up all night in the train, to the office in Pimlico as if she were coming home from a holiday. Only once did I know her exhausted—on the first night of the Birmingham Conference when she fell out of bed in a sort of delirium, and at breakfast was obviously broken. And then a wire to my wife who had an almost miraculous control over neurotics brought her to the Conference Hall from Surrey, and restored Lucy to a child's night of unbroken sleep."

The Conference convened on April 6th, 1924 and dispersed after the morning meeting on April 12th. Nearly four years of Charles's life had been spent with this great event in view. He had attended Commissions, addressed meetings, written memoranda, organised all kinds of detailed arrangements. Had it been worth while? The preparatory written material and the volumes endorsed by the Conference were a solid achievement which were to be used at Stockholm in 1925 and valued as works of reference by all who were concerned about better conditions in the life of society. The Copec report could well be regarded as a blue-print for the Welfare State which was before long to be established in Britain and many of its recommendations have in fact been implemented in the last thirty years.

Yet it is hard not to feel that Charles experienced a certain sense of disillusionment as the whole enterprise came to an end. The tension between planning for social reform and seeking to lead individuals to a living faith in Christ remained unresolved. His words at the close of the Conference were significant. He declared that the delegates had been attempting a restatement of the Augustinian *City of God* and thereby providing a syllabus for future action. But this achievement had been surpassed by an even greater discovery—that of their fellowship one with another in Christ. The splendour of this fellowship must colour all the practical proposals now being proposed. "I have feared lest we might be rushed, through lack of faith and vision, into creating a mere inanimate machine, so that we could say, 'At least, if we have done no more, we have done a few practical things'" Proposals for a Continuation Committee, a Research Bureau, a Study Programme, would indeed be made. But most important of all would be the transformation of their own lives. "I have been haunted in these past years by one image of the Master. 'They were in the way going up to Jerusalem; and Jesus went before them: and they were amazed.' We are not sure where this strange Master is leading us. Are we going to betray Him? The only way of escaping this great betrayal is that for love of Him we are, each of us, ready to mount the Cross!" Though the organisation of the Conference had to all outward appearances been brilliantly successful there was still the fear, in Charles's inner consciousness, that the living organism which had been brought to birth would be smothered by formal structures and lifeless machinery. The personal, the spiritual, the sacrificial—these were his watchwords. The Cross symbolised his final challenge to the Conference.

The great mission at Cambridge in 1920, the thrilling experience at a mission in Ipswich in 1921, remained vividly in his memory. Could it be that his own particular vocation was now to be more in the direction of evangelism in the fullest sense of that word—to confront men with the claims of the living Christ and to draw them together within a new experience of fellowship in the Spirit? When late in 1923 Bishop David invited him to come to Liverpool and share in the work of the Cathedral which was so soon to be consecrated, Charles must have felt that this would offer just the opportunity that he needed to establish right priorities while he would still be free to face the social challenges which belonged to the life of a great city. There would be the regular duties of preaching in the Cathedral, freedom to share in the Bishop's plans for renewal in the Diocese, opportunity to exercise a preaching and teaching ministry when called upon to do so in other parts of the country—the Cathedral seemed to provide just the base that he needed for carrying on the evangelistic ministry which he loved and to be relieved of the struggle which he had endured for roughly three years to balance the rival claims of a circumscribed country parish, a dying newspaper and a vast planning enterprise about whose ultimate effectiveness he may well at times have had considerable doubts.

Whatever struggles may have been going on in his mind the fact remains that after the conclusion of the Copec Conference there is no record of his being actively engaged in follow-up activities or indeed of keeping in touch with the organisations which were trying to improve conditions in society at large. He had done a magnificent job of organisation for Copec. He wanted now to speak directly to men and women, presenting to them the saving Christ of the Gospels and promoting amongst them the creative life of the Spirit.

Towards the end of his life he looked back on Copec. He felt, probably rightly, that whereas the foundations of a Christian sociology had been well and truly laid, no group of thinkers had carried on the task of raising the building above ground. This is hardly surprising. The study of sociology was only at its early stages in Britain and was regarded with a good deal of suspicion. The era of Keynes had not yet dawned and Christians, though sometimes aware of the evils of the system under which they were living, could feel no confidence that either Marxist economics or some kind of Social Credit would make things any better.

But Charles's primary interest was theology, not sociology, and it was in this area, he believed, that a great opportunity had been missed. He speaks of "the essential weakness of our work at Copec".

"We had relied upon selected biblical texts rather than any relevant theology; when applied to the new cosmology, anthropology, psychology and sociology of the twentieth century our equipment, though less archaic than that of Christendom in general, could not stand the strain. We had no understanding of the modern technological world-wide aggregates, productive of benefits which we could not wisely use and evils which no one individual could restrain or cure. Like Haig at Cambrai we were using men on horseback against barbed wire and machine guns."[5]

He did not lose all interest in problems of politics and citizenship. Indeed, as we shall see, he was prepared to speak out forthrightly in Liverpool when some particular abuse captured his attention. But he was not willing to identify himself with particular programmes of social action. For example we find him late in 1926 addressing a meeting of the League of the Kingdom of God in Coventry on "The Church's Intervention in Social Affairs and Industrial Affairs" and using the occasion to define his own attitude to Labour politics. At an early stage of his life, he said, he had thrown himself ardently into the campaign in support of Labour policies. But he had discovered that the *spirit* in which he wanted to intervene was not *their* spirit. So he had abandoned the advocacy of direct intervention or of some particular piece of social reform. He had tried rather to press for such ideals as beauty, knowledge and the development of character; for a true understanding of Christ and His message; for the right of every human being to realise to the full his own personal union with God. He never ceased to believe that if only the individual could be brought to live according to the highest part of his nature, to identify himself with the Kingdom of God and His righteousness, then and only then could society be redeemed and healed.

Some twenty five year later Charles returned to the question, *Is there a Christian politics?*[6] Still we find him hesitant to call particular forms of social action, particular patterns of social organisation, "Christian". This does not mean that he wanted to keep his religion or his Christianity *separate* from his life in society. But again it is a question of priorities. "Religion in its essence is essentially a personal experience and a personal relationship." (p. 349). Only when such a relationship with the Eternal has been established is man in a position to take a creative part in social affairs. This creative role will then be double-sided. On the one hand he will have the courage to say a firm and uncompromising "No" in certain circumstances.

"It is perfectly clear that there are points at which we are bound to say:
"No, I cannot do that. You can argue with me until you are blue in the face, and for you it may be a perfectly legitimate thing to do. I am not at the moment challenging your obligation. What I am saying is that for me there is an absolute obligation: 'I cannot do that'."

This is the negative side of Christian social action. On the positive side the great aim is to transform the whole spirit of democracy from "what I call the spirit of a committee into the spirit of a fellowship." Again there is the suspicion of form, machinery, rules of representation and of procedure, all that belongs to organisation man through his councils and boards and committees. Charles is still the idealist: "I believe that *the* essential condition for success is what the Navy calls the creation of a "happy ship". I believe that where you have—a common loyalty, a humbling and exalting task, something which you know you are not up to, and a trust and affection holding the people together, there creative possibilities beyond all expectation become possible." (p. 353)

So he concludes:

"The function, therefore, of the Christian man in the political world is not to get out of it, but to go into it knowing that there are certain things that we cannot do, prepared to say:
'There is never a choice of two evils because there is always the martyr's way and I may have to take it? That is on the negative side. On the positive side, there is the belief that if we can infect one another with great ideals, plain tasks and a spirit of fellowship, we can release in the community resources adequate even for such times as these." (p. 354)

Thus speaks Charles the individualist, the idealist, the visionary. Form in nature, form in art, form in language, form in ceremony,—of all these he was not only aware: he gloried in them. Yet he was terribly afraid of being restricted and enclosed by *social* forms—the school, the business, the church, the state. He could submit himself to the study and reproduction of form in nature with almost infinite patience: his endurance of form in any kind of social situation soon reached breaking-point. It was this contrast which constituted the seeming contradiction and at the same time the abiding fascination of Charles's life.[7]

NOTES TO CHAPTER SIX

1. p. 117: F. A. Iremonger. *William Temple*, p. 334.

2. p. 117: Ibid. p. 540. f.

3. p. 118: Nevertheless Lord Tavistock pleaded in one of the open sessions for greater allowance to be made for the limited vocabulary of the masses. This was not their fault: it was the result of inadequate education. Let that be improved and they might be able to understand that page of one of the Reports which referred to "synoptic criticism", "eschatological colouring," and to "immanental teleology". He urged that the writers of the Reports should take as their regular prayer: "God who made me simple, make me simpler yet!"

4. p. 118: B. Sunkler. *Archbishop Söderblom*, p. 331.

5. p. 123: *The Crucible*, January 1963.

6. p. 123: In *The Hibbert Journal*, July 1951.

7. p. 125: Maurice Reckitt comments shrewdly on Lucy Gardner's words: "We want to establish a norm of Christian thought and action for the further working out of a Christian order" (i.e. through Copec). He says: "The ambition was noble, but the question was whether the necessary theological, metaphysical and sociological formulation had been provided or even envisaged, and the answer which Copec suggested to many who attended it was not reassuring. The conference in fact represented rather the climax of a phase of social idealism than the initiation of a new phase of Christian realism." *From Maurice to Temple*, p. 172.

CHAPTER SEVEN

A New Approach to Natural Theology

With his formal responsibilities to Copec ended, Charles seized the opportunity to return to his first love, the attempt to draw together into a living synthesis the two disciplines of theology and natural science. He determined to apply himself afresh to the task of relating traditional Christian affirmations to the new knowledge derived from studies in genetic and evolutionary theory on the one side, psychology and corporate experience on the other. Happily this task could be carried on within the context both of his official duties at the Cathedral and of the demands created by two forthcoming engagements of a more personal kind. He was to be responsible for organising the Church Congress to be held in Southport in 1926; in addition he was to give the Noble Lectures at Harvard in the same year and to be Hulsean Lecturer at Cambridge in the academic year 1926–7.

The Church Congress had been an annual event since 1861, meeting in different Dioceses from year to year. Liverpool was to be the host Diocese in 1926 and Southport, a popular seaside resort with ample hotel accomodation, was chosen as the venue. As for Copec in 1924, the preparation seems to have been extraordinarily thorough; the Diocese was made vividly aware of the Congress theme through courses of study and preparatory meetings in the organisation of which Charles was actively engaged.

How far he was responsible for the theme *The Eternal Spirit* is not clear but it is hardly likely to be sheer coincidence that it was so closely linked with his own central interest at that time. Every effort was made to include the many aspects of the Spirit's operations—in nature, in mystical experience, in art, in the ethical and sacramental life of the Church, in its social and missionary activities. Nearly two thousand were present at the Congress which continued for a week and concluded with a closing service of dedication at the Cathedral on October 8th. An astonishing postlude was provided by the organising genius of the event—Charles himself—working almost day and night to prepare a report and interpretation of the Congress which ran to more than two hundred pages in its published form but which was ready for the printer on October 20th. After admirable chapters on the background of the great meeting, adequate summaries are given of all the addresses and much of the atmosphere is conveyed by lively and informed comment. The book can still be read as a sketch-plan of what any full-orbed treatment of the Holy Spirit in action must contain.

The Hulsean Lectures at Cambridge and the Noble Lectures at Harvard were brought together to form one volume—*The Creator Spirit*. In Cambridge the focus of attention was the relation of Christian Doctrine to the Biological Sciences: for twenty years Charles had been disturbed and challenged by the brilliant attempt made by Professor Bateson to construct a system of genetic determinism. At Harvard the focus was the relation of Christianity to the rapidly developing psychological and sociological sciences: William James had attained international fame by his Gifford Lectures on *The Varieties of Religious Experience* and his colleague in the Department of Philosophy, William Ernest Hocking, had written what Charles called a "great book" on *The Meaning of God in Human Experience*. It was to say the least a bold decision to lecture on biology in Cambridge and on psychology at Harvard.

Yet it is arguable that *The Creator Spirit* was the most original, most constructive and, considering the date of its appearance, most impressive of all Charles's many writings.[1] Up to this time no theologian had grappled seriously with the challenge to traditional forms of doctrine presented by the advances of the life-sciences; no sustained examination had been made, from the Christian point of view, of the new psychological theories which had been gaining currency in England since the first translations of Freud's works appeared not long before the outbreak of the First World War. Charles could justly claim to possess a thorough knowledge of the development of early Christian doctrine

and of the formulations which had remained the expressions of orthodoxy down through the centuries. At the same time he had tried in every
way possible to acquaint himself with the most recent developments of
biological methodology and theory. He had also, as is clear from the
second part of *The Creator Spirit*, read widely in the rapidly expanding
literature of psychology and had in particular followed the advice which
he constantly gave to others to go to the original sources which in this
case meant to the works of Freud himself.

The first paragraph of the Preface provides an excellent summary of
his total concern:

> "The purpose of this book is simple, if its scope is ambitious. It is an
> attempt to show that the work of the Holy Spirit is to be traced in
> the creative as well as the inspirational energies of the Godhead; that
> creation, incarnation and inspiration reveal the same eternal values;
> that biology and psychology bear witness to love rather than to will.
> It therefore deals with what must be for the Christian a fundamental
> task, the effort to formulate and defend a Christ-centred view of the
> Universe in such ways as to heal the breach between science and
> religion."

In this brief statement Charles outlined what had become his overmastering ambition. First and foremost it was to set Christ at the very
centre of man's new view of the universe. Christ, he believed, was the
key to the interpretation of the total cosmic process. Christ, he believed,
was the paradigm of what the human personality in its fullest development could be. So his book really reaches its climax in the seventh
chapter where, in one of his most exalted passages, he devotes some
seven pages to a confession of the way in which he had himself come to
acknowledge Christ as Very Man and Very God.

But although the figure of Christ is at all times utterly central,
Charles is at pains to draw out the implications of this fact for a much
needed re-interpretation of the work of the Spirit. He had been almost
astonished in his study of early Church history at the failure to give
more than lip-service to the place of the Spirit in the divine economy.

"It is an exaggeration to say that He is a mere name; but there is in all patristic literature a conspicious absence of any large and clear conception of Him, and until the middle of the fourth century, when study had already begun to decline, the greatest hesitation as to His relation to the Godhead or His function in the world."[2]

The Greeks, with their glorification of Reason, had hardly felt the need for any extended doctrine of the Spirit: the Latins, with their glorification of Order, had relegated the Spirit to the position of supernatural operator of ecclesiastical institutions. A comprehensive doctrine of the Spirit had never been developed. Might it not be the case that the new knowledge which had come to man through his advances in the biological and psychological sciences was now for the first time making this possible?

The introductory paragraph reveals the existence of a further motif which was the driving force of much of Charles's work: he had a passion for *unity*. He could not bear division and dissension. Nothing brought him greater joy than the spirit of unity in his own family. Nothing distressed him more than antagonisms and alienations in the world around. This meant that any kind of dualistic interpretation of the universe was for him unthinkable. It also meant that any interpretation of the Doctrine of the Trinity which seemed to suggest division of nature or function within the Godhead was also inconceivable. The unity of the Godhead, the unity of the universe, the unity of humankind, the unity of man himself—these were postulates which Charles could never allow himself seriously to question. It might be necessary to conceive unity in ways different from what had been common in the earlier history of mankind but to imagine an apotheosis of evil or a continuing dialectic of contraries was a sheer impossibility for someone of Charles's background and outlook.

His aim and ambition then was to set forth afresh the splendour of the Divine unity in terms of creation, incarnation and inspiration. These words immediately call up to our minds and imaginations the order of nature, a man in history, and a form of human experience: their relationship to one another is not immediately obvious. But it was for

E

Charles axiomatic that the same God was involved in each and that His method of operation must be the same in each. They must be regarded as different phases of the same process. He could not believe that God had created and sustained the universe by the exercise of His almighty power and had then acted in a quite different way at a particular point in history in order to redeem and to save. To conceive personality in a unified way was for him imperative and the principle of unification in God and man could only be expressed as spirit. *The Creator Spirit* was the unifying title of this definitive book.

In the biological section Charles pins his faith to the interpretation of the evolutionary process advanced by Professor Lloyd Morgan in the two volumes of his Gifford Lectures, *Emergent Evolution* and *Life, Mind and Spirit*. He repudiates entirely the earlier materialistic and deterministic theories which had gained wide acceptance towards the end of the nineteenth century. But this does not drive him into the arms of the Vitalists and Animists, attractive as some of their ideas of a universal life-force may have seemed. Instead he accepts a model of the evolutionary process, propounded by Morgan and in general supported by Whitehead, in which the definitive terms are phases or stages or levels, combination and emergence, organism and growth, diverse modes and degrees of manifestation, the Nisus directing the course of events. God is All and in All, creating and controlling the total life-process from its beginings in the lowly atom to its consummation in a perfect human being. The fact that the unique humanity of the Christ reflects the Divine Nature perfectly at a comparatively early stage of history does not constitute any great difficulty, for the emergence of the highest reveals the pattern to which the human person is being constantly persuaded (Nisus) to conform by the One Spirit who is working all and in all. "From embryo to saint" Charles exclaims "is man's Pilgrim's Progress; if we could see it whole and complete, we should resolve the antithesis of organism and environment, of nature and nurture, of freedom and determinism, of process and deity." (p. 87)

This architectonic schema is undoubtedly impressive, bearing many resemblances to two of the most famous cosmologies of this century— Whitehead's *Process and Reality* (which had not yet appeared in 1926 though Charles was familiar with *Science in the Modern World* and *Religion in the Making*) and Teilhard de Chardin's *The Phenomenon of Man*. Indeed, as we shall see, Charles later accepted Teilhard's interpretation with enthusiasm, believing that he and the Jesuit priest had for long been working with the same general model, even though each had been ignorant of the labours of the other. But all such unified schemas can hardly avoid two criticisms. In the first place there is the question of interpretation. The scientist is dedicated to the pursuit of facts through observation and experiment and questioning and comparison. But by what standards are his *interpretations* of the facts to be judged? Can all the "facts" at his disposal be included within one over-all synthesis? In the second place there is the question of evil, of contradiction, of disorder, of death. How can the contraries which seem to challenge the very idea of a universe or a unified process be explained? Some of the most significant sections of *The Creator Spirit* are concerned with these problems.

In regard to the first Charles put forward a very interesting theory which may perhaps be called the theory of the two stories. Being passionately opposed to any kind of dualism he would not allow that the physical and psychic aspects of the human personality could be regarded as belonging to separate compartments and therefore as merely allied to or interacting with one another. He insisted that between them there was "an absolute correlation as of two concomitant aspects of a single whole" (p. 78). To speak of the physical operating in isolation would imply a mechanistic view of man; to speak of the psychic as so operating would imply a pure animism or vitalism.

The man who wishes to make sense of his experience must therefore be prepared to direct his attention first to the facts as perceived by direct observation, facts which may be called physical, objective, historical or scientific. Concerning these he will tell a "plain tale", as truthfully and objectively and comprehensively as possible. But there is a second story to be told—the psychic. "Next will come an attempt to expound the same facts in their psychical aspects, to give a faithful presentation of the psychology of our subject, of its emotions, instincts and intelligence so far as any or all of these are appropriately discoverable" (p. 98). The first story, the "plain tale" will be couched in scientific language which tries to give an exact and accurate representation of the physical aspects of the reality observed; the second story must be told in symbolic language which tries to create correspondences between experiences of the human psyche and psychic aspects of the outwardly observed reality. "The two stories, if faithfully told, will each include all the facts and will each be equally true—though they will be couched in totally different language" (p. 80). But

> "in the correlation of the two stories, as we try to enter into the indivisible life which they disclose, we shall find not only aesthetic joy in what is in all its manifestations beautiful, nor rational satisfaction in understanding fresh evidence of ordered harmony, nor ethical enlargement as we gain richer appreciation of suffering and struggle, and catch glimpses of the paradox of goodness and severity; beyond all these, beyond the extending and unifying of our thought of God, we shall gain new avenues of communion with Him, new insight into the reality of Spirit, new stimulus to spiritual growth". (p. 98)

It is extraordinary that Charles, with his hostility to all forms of dualism, could use such a phrase as "couched in totally different language." How *could* there be a vital correlation between the two stories if the language of one was "totally different" from that of the other? His idea of telling a story about observed data is entirely consonant with the description of the scientific method expounded for example by Sir Peter Medawar in his book *The Art of the Soluble* some forty years later. But to suggest that the psychic story could be told in language totally different from that of the scientific or physical story is to re-introduce the very dualism between body and psyche which Charles was at pains to avoid. The technical analysis of language had hardly begun in philosophical circles and questions about religious language had not yet become urgent amongst theologians. Charles's theory of the two stories was therefore very suggestive and in many respects ahead of its time. If he could have shown more clearly how language referring primarily to objective and physical realities could be correlated with language referring primarily to subjective and psychical realities he might well have made a major contribution to the debates about language which were so soon to become one of the most prominent features of Western intellectual life. Ironically it was probably the constant weaving together of physical and psychic elements in his own speaking and writing which gave them much of their attractiveness and power. The language he used in describing bird-behaviour was not "totally different" from that which he used in describing spiritual experience. Every story which he told included the two elements. His physical-psychic correlation was at its maximum when he was addressing an audience. If ever a personality was totally involved it was when Charles was telling a story.

In regard to the second it would be no exaggeration to say that Charles was wrestling with the problem of suffering from the time when he first saw squalor and deprivation at first-hand in the slums of Liverpool, on through two wars and two post-war disillusionments, through two shattering personal bereavements, through frustrations and disappointments which tortured him to the very end of his life. This does not imply that he was a permanently unhappy man. He experienced endless delight through his exploration of the world of nature—though there were mysteries of pain and conflict even in that realm which he did not find it easy to explain. He rejoiced in all that his home and family and friendships brought him and responded almost boyishly to the many marks of appreciation and recognition which were bestowed upon him in public life. Yet a consciousness of pain and travail was always present in the background of his thinking and speaking and writing. How could suffering, both physical and mental, be honestly integrated into the total evolutionary system which had come to express for him the ultimate nature of God's relation to the universe?

In *The Creator Spirit* he develops the general lines of the theodicy which he was to amplify and illustrate and in some minor respects revise in his later books. Fundamentally he argues that no true progress is possible anywhere except through pain and suffering and even death. The writer of the Epistle to the Hebrews enunciated a principle of the widest possible application when he declared, in an inspired moment, that it was necessary even for a captain or pioneer of salvation to be perfected for his task through the experience of suffering.What men of insight in the world of ancient Greece had expressed through the famous aphorism that one can learn only through suffering, what the writers of the New Testament had seen supremely manifested in the passion of Jesus Himself, had, Charles believed, been further illustrated and re-inforced by the discoveries of modern science. "From the study of the neo-Darwinians we may learn to see the grand pattern of the Cross woven into the whole fabric of the natural order, to rediscover the wisdom of the sage who spoke of suffering as the only true learning, and of the Master who bade us lose life if we would find it." (p 58 f.)

In expounding his own theodicy further Charles turns first the to question of how far animals can be said to *suffer*. No one can doubt his own intense empathy with birds; deliberate cruelty to animals he abhorred. Yet he had never shrunk from capturing, killing, dissecting, skinning and stuffing, insects, moths, butterflies, fish and birds. He was convinced that these activities did not result in "pain" on the part of the animal creation any more than the pruning activities of the gardener caused "pain" to his roses. A kind of "suffering", yes: but not "pain" in any sense comparable to that of the pain of humanity.

"Pain is due in us to three chief factors, to the highly sensitive nervous system which accompanies the development of the higher areas of the brain, to the anticipation of hurt due to our foreknowledge of what is to come, and to the sympathy which enables us to share the sufferings of our fellows—these are attributes of humanity." (p. 120)

Many today would feel that this dismissal of the possibility of "pain" in animals is too easily made. No man is perfect and with all his sensitivities in certain directions Charles seems to have had curious insensitivities in others. His love of the chase, his delight in landing a struggling fish, his sharpness of verbal attack, his air of contempt for intellectual inadequacy—all these reveal aspects of his character in which there seems to have been a real insensitivity to suffering and possibly even to "pain" in other living creatures. He revolted against any conception of the Spirit as being "soft-hearted, and in consequence often soft-headed": he may perhaps have been less than just to those who were troubled by much that seemed ruthless in man's treatment of sentient creatures and much that seemed unnecessarily cruel in the overall disposition of the world.

His second line of defence is constructed by a reconsideration of the concept of freedom. He does not try to exaggerate the evidences for "freedom" which can be deduced from the behaviour even of lowly forms of life. But he is convinced that

"life at whatever level must imply, in however lowly a degree, alternative possibilities of reaction to environment. That there will be degeneration as well as progress, mistakes involving the side-tracking of a whole race into a blind alley, disasters which can only be undone by ages of suffering, is the price that has been paid for growth in capability, in freedom, in sensitiveness" (p.121 f.).

Freedom at any stage in fact cannot be easily won. But there must be the possibilities of alternatives if freedom is to be won at all.

Again it may be urged that Charles resolves too easily the terrible dilemma which is created for those who would fain choose freedom, by the existence in the world of cold, callous and enormously efficient systems of apparently impersonal law. There may be indeterminism and random-ness at the sub-atomic level but as aggregates are formed, the larger their size the more rigid in their structure and functioning they seem to become. He could claim that "in spite of a myriad delays and a myriad failures, through bloodshed and horror, organisms have achieved the ascent of man" but to apply this same principle of develop-ment to justify the existence of suffering and heartbreak and despair among the downtrodden and oppressed of the world as necessary for their "ascent" to beatitude is surely dangerous in the extreme. The word "sacrifice" can be too lightly employed. Charles believed that he could see "sacrifice" in the very texture of the universe of living things which he loved to observe. But it is open to question whether he would have called it "sacrifice" if that word had not already become sanctified and honoured through its use in the context of the great event of Calvary itself.

We might have expected in conclusion a direct appeal to the passage from the New Testament which more than any other summed up

Charles's philosophy of life. But although there is no direct quotation from Romans 8, the imagery of the whole creation groaning and travailing in pain and waiting expectantly for the emergence of the perfected family of God can hardly have failed to influence him in setting forth his considered interpretation of the universal process. A generation earlier a distinguished Anglican theologian R.C. Moberly had interpreted the work of the Spirit in terms of family relationships, laying stress upon the experiences of alienation and penitence and forgiveness as he had observed them within his own family circle and using these to illuminate the reconciling and re-creative operations of the Divine Spirit in the general life of humanity. Charles's perspective was even wider. The human family was for him the highest manifestation of unification and differentiation that could be conceived within the evolutionary process. The perfect Son had been revealed at a particular point in time. And just as in nature a new mutation becomes the prototype of a wholly new species so, now that the perfect Man, the human life wholly inspired by pure Spirit, has appeared, it becomes possible for a new family to emerge bearing His likeness, the family enjoying ever more fully the glorious liberty of the children of God.

And what are the essential features of this likeness? What are the utterly distinctive characteristics of the New Man?

"Beyond all other aspects one is for me at least dominant. Jesus is supremely the sufferer whose suffering redeems. The picture that haunts me is not that of the gentle Shepherd gathering His lambs to His bosom, nor even the heroic adventurer striding before the frightened group of disciples on the road to His Passion at Jerusalem (This latter had been the "haunting" picture at the time of the Copec Conference) It is the Jesus of Gethsemane, striving to hold and be held by God's will, striving for the soul of Simon lest Satan sift him like wheat, and for the soul of Judas that the traitor too may come to repentance." (p. 236)

The psychological chapters in *The Creator Spirit* are less impressive than the biological. This is not surprising. For nearly twenty years

Charles had been wrestling with the problems of genetic determinism and creative freedom, of evolution and divine intervention. He had been a keen observer of natural phenomena and had made his own experiments. He was therefore able to speak out of first-hand knowledge when discussing the relation of the biological sciences to religion. But in the field of psychological studies his position was very different. The subject itself was at an early stage of its development in Britain, and Charles, though remarkably well-informed when compared with other theologians of that period, could not claim first-hand experience of analysis or of developing psychological techniques. He had been wracked by dreams as a result of his war experiences and he tries to give an objective account of these dreams as they were related to changes in his own life-situations. He had also been deeply moved by his experiences of group-loyalties and group-enthusiasms while serving with his battalion in France and was convinced that under the stress of common danger or common suffering a spirit of fellowship emerges which far transcends any bonds of community created by law or convenience. He welcomes the attention being given by psychologists to the problem of integrating the individual personality and by sociologists to the means of fostering a true group-mind. But he had no specialised knowledge in these fields.

However in one respect he felt the challenge of the new psychology quite acutely. Not only in *The Creator Spirit* but also in *A Wanderer's Way* (which was written two years later) he tries to face squarely the possibility that his own religious experience and that of all those who have been vaguely called "mystics" could really be explained in psychological terms. Might it not be that what he had regarded as experiences of communion with the living God or of encounter with the living Christ had in fact been the products of heightened emotion such as can be engendered by drugs or alcohol or hypnosis or suggestion? Was it not possible that the mystics had suffered from delusions, from fancies stimulated by fasting or other austerities?

His defence in *A Wanderer's Way*, where he felt that his own spiritual integrity was at stake, is more impassioned and more convincing than perhaps is the case in *The Creator Spirit*. Nevertheless his analysis and assessment of mystical experiences in the latter book are both honest and judicious. He does not claim too much. Equally he does not yield ground easily. He deprecates any limitation of the word "mystical" to ecstatic and paranormal experience: instead he includes within it any "sense of wonder as at something not wholly of the earth" as well as the "clear conviction that for a timeless moment" there has been "union with infinite reality". Mysticism he claims is the essential element in religion and quotes with approval Whitehead's fine definition: "Religion is the vision of something which stands beyond, behind and within the passing flux of immediate things". "Suddenly, we know not when or why, the presence breaks in upon us." (p. 207)

Yet it is possible to prepare oneself for such visitations and this not only through the long discipline which has come to be traditionally associated with the great mystics. Every aspiration towards authentic values, every concentration of attention upon the discovery of truth, every turning away from the trivial towards the real can help to prepare the way of the Lord, can serve as the preliminary to the "moment one and infinite" (here Charles quotes Browning, his favourite poet) when "the presence breaks in upon us". "He takes us, and fills us with a life not our own, a life which is beyond sorrow and romance: He takes us, and in His grip we live abundantly, sharing for a moment the activity of His overwhelming love." (p. 218)

Of course it is always possible, as Charles well knew, to interpret mystical experience in terms of auto-suggestion, of eroticism, of psychic strain, of fanciful illusion, of projection. But in the end he leaves us in no doubt about what for him is the ultimate criterion in judging all so-called "spiritual" manifestations. Do they serve towards aesthetic, intellectual and moral expansion of the personality? Do they promote acts of graciousness and self-giving towards others? Above all do they lead towards the kind of communion with God which Jesus enjoyed not fitfully but throughout His earthly career? "Perspective and proportion, sanity and stability, integration and universality—these are the qualities of the true mystic" (p. 247). These were pre-eminently the qualities that characterised the "religious" life of Jesus and only these constitute the authentic marks of "religious" experience today.[3]

NOTES TO CHAPTER SEVEN

1. p. 127: Dean Inge reviewed the book favourably in the Church of England Newspaper and subsequently wrote to Charles:

   "You have a great work to do for your generation; I am preparing to take the back seat appropriate to an old beetle of sixty-seven. I ought really to have praised your book more unreservedly. The philosophy is not very clearly defined, but whose is in the present impasse? I doubt whether "Emergent Evolution" is much more than crypto-vitalism. W. Morgan is rather obscure and Whitehead (to me) almost unintelligible, though I feel that he is a deep thinker. I can't make out Needham. He is a Christian and yet will have nothing to say to mediators like John Haldane. The whole situation is most perplexing."

2. p. 129: *The Creator Spirit*, p. 2 f.

3. p. 138: Charles's note on alcoholic and ecstatic mysticism (p. 244 ff.) is astonishingly relevant to questions which have arisen nearly half a century later through the use of drugs either under medical prescription or in clandestine ways. He writes frankly about his own uncertainties. Could there be direct connection between the ecstacy of the mystic and the exaltation of the partially drugged or intoxicated? Charles may have rationalised his own experiences and interpreted them too favourably. He could not be accused of failing to consider other possible interpretations realistically or of being unwilling to expose the records of his own mystical experiences to public scrutiny.

CHAPTER EIGHT

The Challenge of a New Cathedral

A certain visitor to Liverpool in 1926, reflecting later on his experiences, accused its people of being such a modest crowd that they did not realise the growing importance of their city in the eyes of the world. He was not referring primarily, he said, to the great dock system or to the many new buildings. What struck him rather was that Liverpool has a "personality" such as few other towns possessed. He commented on the success of its young artists and architects; the fact that it had become a testing-place for music and plays: the scientific work in cancer research and tropical medicine. Liverpool he declared was on the way to becoming "the most progressive city in the World".

It was to this city that Charles had come for a very limited period in 1909. It was to this expanding city that he returned in 1924 for a period of eight years which, in my judgment, proved to be the happiest years of his life. The very cosmopolitan character of Liverpool appealed to his own cosmopolitan outlook for in no other city of the United Kingdom is there such a mingling of its four peoples while to these have been added the representatives of many nations coming into the port and often electing to stay permanently as immigrants. Ecclesiastically the city also contained the widest variety of traditions outside London: within a half mile radius of the Anglican Cathedral are churches and chapels representing the Church of Scotland, Welsh Methodism, Roman Catholicism, Greek Orthodoxy, Congregationalism, English Methodism, Unitarianism, the Jewish faith, the Catholic Apostolic Church and Christian Science, together with chapels of an undenominational kind. And in the 1920s most of these were still flourishing. Charles could rejoice in his friendships with the ministers and people of these richly varied religious emphases.

But what made his life in Liverpool supremely satisfying and exciting was his association with the new Cathedral whose Consecration took place within a few weeks of his arrival in the city. Charles loved a new adventure; he delighted in wide horizons; he was at his best when working as a member of a harmonious team (even though he was in many respects a strong individualist); and he flourished in a situation in which he could be free to go hither and thither on special assignments but still could return to a base where he felt completely at home and where he could share in the privileges and responsibilities of a common life.

Both the Diocese and the Cathedral had reached a critical stage in their respective histories in 1924. The Diocese which covered the south west corner of Lancashire, had originally been part of the ancient diocese of Lichfield, (920–1542), then of Chester (1542–1880) before gaining its independent status. Its first two bishops had been men of outstanding qualities: John Charles Ryle (1880–1900) had been a man of heroic stature, physically and in evangelistic zeal, a champion of the Protestant cause in an area where the Roman Church was strong; Francis James Chavasse (1900–1923) had been a man of diminutive physical stature but the possessor of immense strength of character, extraordinary gifts of personal understanding and sympathy, beloved and honoured as the chief pastor of a rapidly expanding population. When Albert Augustus David (1923–1944) came to Liverpool he faced the great task of maintaining the impetus within the Diocese created by his predecessors but of doing this in new ways appropriate to the changing conditions of the post-war world. New churches would need to be built; the central organisation of the Diocese, especially on its financial side, would need to be strengthened; above all (and this was particularly congenial to Dr. David, a former Headmaster) a new and extensive programme of education would need to be planned if the Church was to play its part in a world where education was becoming increasingly important. No man was to give him greater assistance in this last-named task than Charles Raven whom he was soon to appoint as one of the residentiary canons of the Cathedral.

These were the longer term objectives of the new Bishop. For the present, however, virtually everything centred upon the Cathedral.

He had come to Liverpool in the autumn of 1923; the consecration ceremony was to take place in July 1924. No such event had taken place in English life since the consecration of Salisbury Cathedral in the thirteenth century for when other new Dioceses had been formed an existing church had been taken over to serve as Cathedral, either in its original or in some extended and expanded form. In Liverpool the site had no tradition of ecclesiastical use and the part of the building already erected was entirely new.

The foundation-stone was laid on July 19th 1904, the Lady Chapel was opened in 1910, work went forward without a complete break even in the darkest days of the First World War and by 1924 the Choir and the Eastern Transept were ready for use. An immense temporary wall was erected to close in the western archway of this section and a gallery was built against it. This meant that although only roughly one third of the total building was so far in existence, its grandeur of conception could already be envisaged and a congregation of at least a thousand could be accomodated within it. When Bishop David moved to Liverpool the first section was nearing completion. But where was the man with the genius adequate to devise forms of worship and ceremonial appropriate to this new building, in a new age, in a city possessing none of the ancient traditions associated with such famous centres as Durham, Chester and York? The bishop might have called to his assistance one of the established liturgists of the Church of England or one of the experienced members of an ancient Cathedral Chapter. Instead, by an inspired judgment, he chose an incumbent of his own Diocese, Frederick William Dwelly, Vicar of Emmanuel Church, Southport, and gave him the title of Ceremonarius. In so doing he not only secured for the new Cathedral a man of genius; unwittingly he provided for Charles the opportunity to develop a friendship which was to become one of the most treasured possessions of his life. Though Fred Dwelly and Charles Raven were to pass through many harrowing experiences during the next twenty-five years, when loyalties in other directions were strained to the limit, their intimate regard for and affection towards one another were never broken. "Fred, my dear", "Beloved Charles", may appear sentimental as modes of address in correspondence. That they were sincere expressions of a deeply-felt relationship is beyond doubt. Charles was often a lonely figure. There is no evidence that any *man* entered so deeply into his life as did his fellow Canon who, in 1931, became the first Dean of Liverpool.

Few would have prophesied before 1920 that Dwelly was likely to be the man for the job. A native of Chard in Somerset he had moved to London after leaving school to work as a salesman in one of the great stores near Oxford Circus. He became associated with All Soul's, Langham Place whose incumbent at the time was a noted Evangelical leader, Prebendary F. S. Webster. Evidently realising the potentialities of the young man who had passed through a crisis of religious experience, Webster encouraged him to go up to Cambridge and prepare for ordination. Although his academic career was not distinguished he soon revealed in his ministry as a curate remarkable powers of youth leadership and a gift of speaking to people through his sermons in a way they could understand and in a spirit to which they seemed ready to respond. In 1916 he was called from Cheltenham to become Vicar of Emmanuel, Southport, a church which had been built in 1898 to serve one of the new districts of a rapidly expanding seaside resort and here his genius soon found possibilities of expression not only in the parish itself but in the wider life of the town.

In November 1918 a great Armistice Thanksgiving was held in the Palladium. It was Dwelly who marshalled Scouts, Guides and Boys Brigades for the ceremonial bringing in of all the standards of the nations. In 1922 a Dickens Carnival was mooted as one of the town's side shows for the summer. It was Dwelly who took it over and made it a pageant for the whole town. In November 1923 came his supreme opportunity when Southport's War Memorials were to be unveiled and dedicated. His "Order of Solemn Ceremonial and Service" provided Southport, according to a newspaper report, with one of "the most solemn and stately ceremonials which will always be remembered by the many thousands who participated in it." One of those involved was Dr. David, the new Bishop of Liverpool. Within a short time he had invited Dwelly to prepare the order and ceremonial for the Consecration of the Cathedral on July 19, 1924.

Charles scarcely had time to familiarise himself with his new surroundings before the great event took place. One of the best-known
photographs of the occasion shows Charles in his Doctor's robes,
standing to read the Deed of Consecration in the presence of the King
and Queen, the two Archbishops, some forty Bishops of the Anglican
Communion from all parts of the world, the Lord Mayors of London
and Liverpool, an Armenian Archbishop and a Greek Archimandrite,
and many other dignitaries. This was the central ceremony in a week of
varied services designed to bring as many sections as possible from
within the Diocese into a living relationship with the Cathedral. All
this had been organised by Dwelly so successfully that the *Manchester
Guardian* described the Consecration Ceremony as "an affair of ecclesiastical pomp such as this realm has not seen for many centuries nor for
many years is likely to see again." It was an astonishing achievement
which set a new pattern of Anglican ceremonial, a pattern which has
increasingly been followed in Cathedral worship since the Second
World War. Not all of Dwelly's innovations were to prove permanently useful, especially perhaps some of his verbal compositions. But
as an organiser of dignified and colourful pageantry he has had no
equal in this century. When Cosmo Gordon Lang, the Archbishop of
York, visited the Southport Church Congress in 1926 he declared that
it was Dwelly who "had taught the Church of England how to process."
And this was done in no ostentatious or pretentious way. Dwelly
loved naturalness as much as Charles loved nature. He trained his boys
and young men to play their parts in an orderly but wholly unself-
conscious way. And in such a context Charles, in spite of his aversion to
formality or *rigidity* or *artificiality* of any kind, felt completely at home.

The story has often been told that when rehearsing for a certain
great occasion Dwelly became aware of the need for colour in a certain
blank area of the Cathedral. "What we need over there," he exclaimed,
"is a splash of colour. You, Charles, in your chaplain's red cassock are
just what we want. Please go and stand over there." To which Charles's
answer is supposed to have been: "I was not aware, Mr. Dean, that when
I was ordained to the sacred ministry it was in order to be a splash of
colour in any situation." But in general Charles accepted and delighted

in the splendour of what he felt was a living pageant related to the contemporary world and not an imitation of some ancient glory. There were other services of the Cathedral in which the altogether dominant note was *informality* and in these he was equally at home. What he would never allow in worship was anything sloppy or untidy or casual. His experiences in Liverpool Cathedral were to stand him in good stead when he came to play a leading part on some of the great ceremonial occasions at Cambridge during his reign as Vice-Chancellor.

So far as his regular work in Liverpool was concerned Charles carried two special responsibilities. The first was to supervise the training of newly ordained clergy; the second was to share in the preaching at the famous 8.30 p.m. service on Sundays in the Cathedral. The scheme of training worked out in Liverpool constituted the first serious attempt in England to extend disciplined study from a man's theological college to his first two years in the ordained ministry. Men were required by the Bishop to attend regularly at the Cathedral on Tuesday mornings for specified terms and although another Canon was nominally in charge the main burden of teaching and lecturing was borne by Charles and his friend Dwelly.

To be lecturing regularly again brought Charles immense satisfaction. Of the young men some possessed able and lively minds and were destined to exercise considerable influence in the Church in later years. Chief amongst these was Michael Ramsey, who was ordained to a curacy at Liverpool Parish Church and attended the classes regularly. Often these assumed the character of a dialogue between Charles and this young man who was to be his successor in the Regius Chair at Cambridge. While others listened, the representative on the one side of the Gospel and its relation to Science, faced the challenges of the representative on the other side of the Gospel and its relation to Church order. Their concern for the Gospel provided their common ground; their differing views of the nature of the Church provided constant opportunities for debate.

Others trained in these classes included John Tiarks who in 1962 became Bishop of Chelmsford, Douglas Harrison who was to gain distinction in the field of liturgical scholarship and to become Dean of Bristol, Joseph McCulloch who was to gain wide publicity by inviting celebrities to occupy his pulpit at St. Mary-le-Bow in the City of London and Max Dunlop who became Archdeacon of Birmingham. It was Dunlop who composed a memorable sally, which the class treasured, by taking up a popular verse[1] and adapting it to their own circumstances.

> O happy happy country
> Come waft me to the shore
> Where the Ravens cease from raving
> And the Dwellys dwell no more.

One who remembers Charles's course on the teaching of Jesus describes it as in many ways brilliant. It was above all intended to show young men at the beginning of their ministries that Jesus's method was inductive rather than deductive and therefore the fore-runner of the modern scientific approach. Jesus did not impose his ideas: He constantly asked His hearers What do you think? What would you do? There was no trace of any insistence upon learning by rote or assenting to dogma. Rather there was the constant meeting of mind with mind and the stimulating of the learner to engage with truth to the utmost of his capacity.

With the members of the class who had received a disciplined intellectual training this was altogether beneficial but to those who had not had this opportunity Charles could sometimes seem superior and even cruel. He was in revolt against the system which was allowing men to be ordained after what seemed a very inadequate intellectual pre-paration and his own Bishop was by no means guiltless in this respect. And just across the water there was St. Aidan's College, Birkenhead, a College which had been specially designed to train for the ministry men who had not received a University education. A fair proportion from this College came into the Liverpool Diocese and their inad-equacies could become all too evident when Charles was riding the high horse intellectually (as he was quite capable of doing) by parading his own resources of a historical or scientific or linguistic kind. To the man who was humble and freely admitted his ignorance Charles would be generous to a degree and would take great pains in giving personal help. But if a man put up any pretence to knowledge, either superficial or second hand, then Charles could be quite devastating. On one occasion a student ventured some remark about the Gospel sources. Charles called him out and questioned him before the Class. "Now let us look at the Synopticon—but no, you wouldn't of course understand what a Synopticon is." Such treatment was deeply resented, not only by the victim but by intellectuals and non-intellectuals alike. With all his straining after intellectual integrity, Charles could descend to the level of an intellectual snob. It is never easy for one whose own standards of exact scholarship are so high to suffer fools gladly.

But all in all the post-ordination scheme worked wonderfully well. Dwelly talked in a heart-to-heart manner about the pastoral and devotional ministry; Charles lectured in his own dramatic way about the New Testament and Doctrine. And what was done for the young clergy through these regular classes was extended to lay folk through courses of instruction in parishes and still more through the late Sunday evening services, inaugurated by Charles in July 1924, which soon became one of the most distinctive activities of the new Cathedral. "The 8.30", indeed, became a catchword on Merseyside. Sunday by Sunday folk travelled from all over Liverpool (young people were there in force) on dark wintry nights in order to be present for this great occasion.

There was music on the magnificent new organ before the Service began; there was the atmosphere of the Cathedral itself which is never more impressive than when shafts of light and dark shadows compete with one another in the vast internal spaces; there were visits from men of high distinction—and at least one woman, Dr. Maude Royden—in ecclesiastical and public life. But what held the congregation together was undoubtedly the double influence of two strangely disparate personalities. Dwelly would lie flat on one of the great oak tables in a darkened vestry before going in to preach; Raven would pace up and down, almost physically sick, rehearsing his words and gestures like an actor. Dwelly captured his audience by his sheer informality of approach, talking to them as his friends for whom he really cared, about important matters which they had not perhaps sufficiently taken into account. Raven captivated them by his looks, his gestures, his command of his subject, perhaps most of all by his ability to relate the great themes of the New Testament to personal needs and duties. Men and women felt that the teaching of Jesus and St. Paul did not simply belong to the world of the first century but that it bore directly on the problems they were facing in their daily lives. One who was a student at the time tells how the Christian message suddenly became strong and important for the world in which she was actually living. The Incarnation became related to the here and now.

Charles's influence on school-boys, especially sixth-formers, was similar and was ultimately to become one of the most remarkable features of his ministry. At Liverpool it revealed itself particularly through the regular visits of boys from Shrewsbury to their School Mission. This was situated in the Scotland Road area, one of the grimmest sections of Liverpool's slumdom. Charles would go on occasion to speak to the regular members of the club and would magnetise them by his eloquence even when they had little understanding of what he was saying. But when the Shrewsbury boys came at weekends it was a regular feature of their programme to attend Sunday morning service at the Cathedral. As the then leader of the Club has recorded, boys would often lack all interest while the choir and the precentor performed their parts. But when Charles came into the picture—reading, leading prayers, preaching—the whole thing seemed suddenly to spring to life. There seemed to be in Charles a quality of incandescence; his burning spirit set his whole personality alight and this communicated itself in an extraordinary way to his audience. Incandescence, magnetism, charisma, electrifying—these are words which have been used by people of widely different backgrounds in an attempt to describe the effect of his preaching. The ultimate secret, as for all forms of genius, remains a mystery.

Occasionally on a Sunday evening Charles would draw attention to some public issue—but he preferred to deal with controversial matters in writing. And for this purpose an organ was readily available—the newly-founded *Liverpool Review*. This was a monthly periodical, first issued in 1926 under the editorship of Dr. David and designed to deal with matters of importance not only in the life of the Diocese but also in the civic and artistic life of Liverpool and its neighbouring towns. It was an ambitious project but the Bishop kept it well in hand and it enjoyed a good measure of success until rising costs of printing and the need for wider circulation made its continuance impossible.

Charles was a frequent contributor. He reviewed books, recorded experiences of bird-watching, gave voice to his theological and social concerns, and on two occasions made allegations which gained him wide publicity in the secular press. In January 1926 an article appeared under his name entitled *Cult or Craze? Plain words on Psycho-Analysis*. Immediately the Press scented a startling news item. "Snares set for Youth", "Psycho-Analysis condemned", "Psycho-Therapeutists astounded over insinuations." Charles had really touched a raw nerve especially as he had located charlatanism in consulting-rooms no farther away from the Cathedral than in Rodney Street, the Harley Street of Liverpool.

It was in fact an intemperate outburst. That there were grounds for protest few would deny and Charles scored some obvious hits. But his rhetorical exaggerations and sweeping generalisations left him open to serious refutation by those who were patiently using the new methods of therapy which had become available through advances in psychological knowledge. Dr. H. Crichton—Miller, the Honorary Director of the Tavistock Clinic for functional nerve cases and himself a distinguished Christian apologist, sprang to the defence of his profession in the next number of the Review through an article which, though highly critical of Charles's evaluation, contrived to be moderate and constructive at the same time. He dissociated himself from Freudian psycho-analytic methods while recognising the immense contributions made by Freud to the understanding of human behaviour. He accused Charles of confusion in his use of terms, of an imperfect understanding of psychology generally and of a surprising intolerance in his judgments of others. He then proceeded to give a brief and admirably clear summary of the theory of unconscious motivation and its repression before delivering a direct attack on Charles for his venture into the realm of dream-interpretation.

A foot-note to the article contained a short rebuttal by Charles. It mainly consisted in a series of quotations of a rather sweeping kind from the works of established scholars and a complaint that Dr. Miller had simply concentrated attention upon unconscious motives in general and upon Charles's in particular so that the main drive of the article had been obscured. But it is hard not to feel that in this case at least Charles had blazed away at psycho-analysis without either a proper sight of his target or sufficiently effective ammunition. When it was a matter of the external visible world he was meticulous in making his observations, checking them, recording them, and using them to construct provisional theories. But when it came to matters of the internal world of emotion and motivation he often seemed unwilling to adopt comparable methods. He recoiled from any kind of sustained introspection and this is understandable. But in his attempts to approach psychological problems scientifically he could have gathered data from plays and novels and biographies and subjected his findings to careful analysis before dismissing Freud and his disciples in so summary a fashion. It became easy for his critics to say that he was for some reason afraid to face *ugly* aspects of human nature and as a consequence found it possible to entertain a too facile and optimistic estimate of human progress.

The second issue brought to prominence through an article in the *Liverpool Review* was social rather than personal: it concerned Irish Immigration. This indeed was no new problem. Merseyside and Clydeside had during the nineteenth century been the twin foci towards which the North Atlantic sea routes had been directed and this meant that there had always been a need in each area for casual and unskilled labour. They became poles of attraction for poverty-stricken Irish families.

But the possibilities of callous exploitation of such a situation were enormous and Charles, who may not have been over-anxious to explore the ugly aspects of human nature within, was always quick to observe injustice or oppression without. So in the Spring of 1931, not long before the end of his Liverpool career, he wrote an article for the Review entitled *The Irish Problem*. By the autumn of the previous year a "very grave economic situation" had developed. Whereas in the summer the mood on Merseyside had still been optimistic—whatever depression there was could be remedied by sufficient human effort—by September a wave of pessimism had engulfed the city: "that Liverpool would never recover prosperity was now almost an axiom."

What had been the results? Religious and racial bitterness between Protestant and Catholic, erupting in some cases to open violence, and still more serious the emergence of a "widespread belief that our social progress is being hampered and our financial stringency increased by the influx of immigrants from the Irish Free State." Charles does not pass any judgment on this belief. He simply raises a series of questions asking for information on four important points.[2]

Not unnaturally the article created no small stir. In the succeeding issue the Bishop as Editor gave his full support to the call for accurate information. He began to make personal approaches to leading figures in commerce on Merseyside (in particular Sir Benjamin Johnson, Head of the Dye Works and a great friend of the Cathedral) seeking their help towards the clarification of what was obviously an explosive social issue.

As a result of his own and the Bishop's enquiries Charles was able to return to the subject within three months of the appearance of his original article. He writes firmly but moderately. That there had been a rapid increase in immigration since 1927 had become abundantly clear. The causes were not far to seek: no unemployment insurance or national relief in the Free State; the rigid enforcement of the Quota by the United States; the imposition of certain restrictions on Clydeside; the willingness of Irish foremen and gangers in Liverpool to give preference of employment to their own fellow countrymen. That a disproportionate amount of public money had been spent in supporting "poor Irish" was also scarcely open to question in the light of information gathered by a Social Survey and disclosed by the returns of a Public Assistance Committee.

Charles's main conclusion was expressed in terms which may have seemed logically inescapable but which still left unanswered certain awkard questions in regard to the Christian's responsibility towards his neighbour. Who is the neighbour? This is Charles's answer.

"With every desire to relieve suffering, whoever the sufferer, many of us feel that in the present distress and shortage we have too plain an obligation to our own ex-service men to be morally justified in undertaking responsibility which should fall upon the Irish Free State. Furthermore at a time when every far-seeing citizen is anxious to encourage emigration among our own people 'it appears a little incongruous that the Government and various estimable societies should have spent large sums of money in emigrating people of a fairly high standard from this district when no steps have been taken to restrict the entry of labour of an inferior quality through the port of Liverpool.' (Social Survey No. 2. P. 9.)"

Liverpool's problem in 1931 had become a national issue forty years later. In exposing it Charles may have performed a public service. He was certainly touching an inflammable issue and his proposal to restrict immigration was open to question when viewed in the light of Christian moral principles. It is strange that one who so consistently sprang to the support of the underdog seemed to display a less than generous attitude to those whom he described as "Irish invaders".

NOTES TO CHAPTER EIGHT

1. p. 146: "Where the Rudyards cease from Kipling
   And the Haggards ride no more."
   J. K. Stephens.

2. p. 151: 1. What is the actual number of immigrants from the Free State entering Merseyside at the present time?
   2. Has the occupation by immigrants of dwellings near the river prevented the progress of slum-clearance to which the city had been committed?
   3. A recent enquiry has revealed how large a surplus of unemployed labour already exists in the docks. Is it justifiable to allow fresh immigrants to crowd in?

4. It is commonly stated that there are businesses in which the immigrant can procure employment for sufficient time to enable him to qualify for Unemployment Benefit; that he is then discharged, and his place taken by a newcomer; that in this way the English taxpayer is being charged with the support of the poor of the Free State. Are these statements true?

CHAPTER NINE

What Next?

In 1924 Charles had become a *national* figure by virtue of the prominent part which he played in the preparation for and the direction of the Copec Conference in Birmingham. In 1928 he gained *international* recognition in the world missionary movement as the result of an outstanding address which he delivered at short notice to the International Missionary Council's extended meeting held in Jerusalem at Eastertime that year. William Paton who was one of the chief organisers of the Conference referred afterwards to "the brilliant argument by which Canon Raven took the meeting into the heart of the teaching method of our Lord as the ground of all our thinking about religious education."

When the Conference convened, "there were over two hundred and eighty delegates in the big hall of what had been Government House. Raven had a seat on the far side from the entrance and often took part shortly in discussions. There was disagreement at times and the day was coming when the subject was Education and there was some apprehension at to how it would go. John Mott had one of his inspired moments and as the delegates parted for the night he beckoned to Charles Raven and said that he wanted Raven to open the session next morning with an address on *The Teaching Method of Jesus*. He was up most of the night and what he said set the tone for the discussion."

In characteristic fashion he focussed attention upon three distinctive notes in Jesus's teaching method:

1. *The note of Life.* He is concerned with the development of *personality* and with instruction only as this serves the large end. He enlightens minds by enlarging their outlook rather than by formal lessons.

2. *The note of Freedom.* He never compels or forces upon His hearers

what they have not ears to hear. With infinite *sensitivity* He offers a wealth of educational resources, leaving them free to assimilate or to reject.

3. *The note of Fellowship.* His richest teaching is given within the *community* of His followers. They share with Him and with one another a way of life, in which not only by His lessons but by the intimate contacts of close intercourse and common pursuits their individualities are expanded.

He then went on to describe the *stages* by which this educational programme was carried out. First, he claimed, Jesus spoke simply and authoritatively about the kingship and fatherhood of God. "As in a nursery school His purpose is to make family life real, and to bring every child into contact with the Heavenly Father." Secondly He chose the Twelve and developed the teaching method of the parable. This method, Charles suggested, was appropriate to the later years of childhood when horizons were expanding and interests quickening. Thirdly He brought His disciples to the stage of the supreme parable, namely Himself. "Having learnt to see God in leaven and mustard-seed they now learn to see in Him their comrade and leader and to confess Jesus as the Christ." Such a discovery can be associated with the beginning of adolescence. Finally there comes the revelation of the place of service and suffering in life, the way of the Cross. In the later stages of adolescence a pupil is ready "to reach a Christian outlook upon the whole range of life personal and corporate."

This schema, prepared at remarkably short notice, made a profound impression on the Conference. It would doubtless be heavily criticised today as correlating far too simplistically an assumed sequence of events in the Gospel story and a hypothetical sequence of stages in child and teenage development. It was given at a time, however, when New Testament scholarship still held out the possibility of constructing a life of the Jesus of history and when psychologists had succeeded in defining certain stages through which, it seemed, a normal personality grew towards maturity. Charles's correlation of these two fields of scholarly enquiry was fresh and arresting and appeared to provide a framework within which positive programmes of Christian education could be developed. It was agreed that his presentation should be incorporated *in toto* into the findings on religious education and subsequently he was urged to expand his thesis into a book which was to bear the title *Christ and Modern Education*.

One other public action which Charles performed at Jerusalem is worthy of note, expressive as it was of his courage, his conviction and his future policy. On Easter Sunday morning a United Service of Holy Communion took place. Officially the Churches of the Anglican Communion did not allow participation in such services and the hostile reaction to what had been done at the Kikuyu Conference was still fresh in men's minds. But Charles was firmly convinced that the sacrament of unity should be one of the means towards attaining unity and not simply the seal of unity already achieved. So although the Service was not announced until late on Easter Eve and many delegates may justifiably have felt that they could not make a hurried decision about whether or not to share fully in it, Easter Sunday morning found Bishop Mc.Connell of the American Methodist Church presiding with Charles assisting him. "The elements were administered by the then Moderator of the Church of Christ in China, S. K. Datta from the Presbyterian Church of India, The Secretary of the Baptist Church of Eire and the Rev. William Paton as Secretary of the International Missionary Council. As the delegates filed past Dr. and Mrs. Mott at the door after the service we heard Dr. Mott say: This is what we have been waiting for for forty years."[1]

After the days of exaltation in Jerusalem, days which included Charles's own personal triumph and the great joy of participating actively in the missionary adventure, but also the solemn re-treading of the path to Gethsemane and the imagined Via Dolorosa to Calvary, he left for Cairo and the pyramids. His account of his experiences there is set in a somewhat lower key.

"The city full of kites—dozens circling overhead; nesting in all the larger foliage trees, hens already sitting; one bird with long streamers of paper several yards behind, another swooping for a dead branch; nests small—hardly bigger than those of the grey crow. Watched a crow and a lesser kestrel stooping at kites, saw kite roll clean over in the air as kestrel struck, kites use the tail freely in steering; are very tame; and chiefly haunt the city. In suburbs crows and bronze doves very common —saw also black and white kingfisher, great reed warbler and flock of eglets, not yet fully crested."

So from this memorable visit to the Holy Land Charles returned to his duties at the Cathedral and to the preparation of the book on religious education which the Council had asked him to write. As it turned out, the book was not the most successful of Charles's writings. His address in Jerusalem had given his hearers a new vision of the possibility of reproducing what appeared to be the method of Jesus in the training of the Twelve within the context of their own teaching responsibilities. This was positive and reassuring. But advances soon to be made, both in New Testament scholarship and in the study of the psychology of education, meant that the expansion of the address into book-form had only a limited appeal and a temporary value.

Two years later Charles was abroad again and this time encountered an unexpected challenge which affected his whole future. His first crossing of the Atlantic in 1926 introduced him not only to Harvard College but also to the famous Church which had risen to such eminence through the ministry of Phillips Brooks—Trinity Church in the city of Boston.[2]

Within the life of this Church Charles immediately felt at home and part of the hospitality for his Harvard visit was provided by a leading Trinity family—Mr. and Mrs. John F. Moors of Brookline. Mr. Moors was a leading Boston stockbroker; Ethel Moors, daughter of Robert Treat Paine, who had been Churchwarden of Trinity in the time of Phillips Brooks and a generous supporter of theological scholarship, was a gracious and vivid personality, highly intelligent, a lover of nature and deeply interested in the social outreach of Christianity; it was not surprising that Charles became almost at once an intimate friend of this Brookline couple. It may have come as a surprise to many but not to their closest friends that in 1954, Ethel Moors, then a widow, should have become Charles's second wife.

The associations made at this time with Trinity Church were soon to

involve Charles in one of the most important decisions of his life. His
preaching had made an immediate impact upon its great congregation.
His skilful use of analogies and illustrations drawn from his knowledge
of the natural world appealed to his American audience. His conduct of
a Three Hours Service on Good Friday was for many an unforgettable
experience. So when in 1930 Henry Sherrill, its Rector, was elected
Bishop of Massachusetts and the search for a successor began, the name
of Charles Raven, especially in the influential circle of the Paine
family, was often mentioned. In many respects it was the leading pulpit
in the Episcopal Church and indeed scarcely any Church of any
denomination in the United States was more famous for its tradition of
bringing Christian standards and values to bear upon the life of the
community. Would Charles regard this as the place where his preaching
and his scholarship could find their fullest expression and scope? Even
on the lowest level the stipend offered was such as would have relieved
him of all the anxiety which he was beginning to feel with his young
family and the burden of educational fees.

Matters came to a head in July 1930. Charles was lecturing on the
Philosophy of Religion in Union Theological Seminary, New York,
and this made it easy for negotiations to take place. How far he had been
consulted before the Vestry made its final decision is not clear but on
July 17, 1930, after careful consideration of three names, it was voted by
seven votes to two—and this was subsequently made unanimous—to
call Canon Raven to the Rectorship. A committee was instructed to
take the night train to New York and to confer with him on July 18th.

What transpired at the meeting is not recorded. It is known that
Mrs. Raven was strongly opposed to the idea of leaving England and
taking up residence in the U.S.A. Possibly Charles, though attracted by
the prospect of the preaching ministry, recognised how great would be
the demands of an administritive and pastoral kind and how difficult it
would be for him to continue his work of scholarship. Whatever his
reasons, his answer was firmly negative. In many ways he would have
been in his element in New England. Whether Boston and Cambridge,
Massachusetts, would have proved a more congenial environment for
him in the thirties than Ely and Cambridge, England, is a question

about which it is interesting to speculate but whose answer it is impossible to guess. But it was to the other Cambridge that he was soon
to go.

The time was in fact approaching when a change of far-reaching
significance would take place in the Cathedral with which Charles had
been so closely associated since its Consecration in 1924. The pioneering
stage of which the key-notes had been fellowship and freedom must be
succeeded by a second stage in which form and order would assume
new importance. If Liverpool was to gain full recognition as a Cathedral
within the establishment it must be governed in ways acceptable not
only to the Church but also to the Crown. During the period 1928–30
much attention was given to the drafting of Statutes for the constitution
of a formal Chapter. In 1931 the first Dean would be appointed.

But such a constitutional change could easily lead to friction. The
Bishop had acted as Dean for nearly eight years. He had been the
leader of the team, the final authority. He was an exceedingly capable
administrator and had been intimately concerned with every feature of
the Cathedral's developing life. He had given to his assistants an
unusual measure of freedom to experiment and had supported them
even when these experiments aroused critisism. But a new Dean
formally appointed would enjoy the rights and privileges laid down in
the Statutes and would naturally expect to exercise the kind of leadership in his own Cathedral such as other Deans exercised in theirs. It
would not be easy for the Bishop, however saintly, to hand over the
direction of an enterprise in which he had himself been so deeply involved, especially as he would continue in all kinds of ways to be
so closely related to it.

Obviously much depended on the question of who would be chosen
as first Dean of the new Cathedral. Three names have been mentioned
as having received consideration. It appears that Dick Sheppard was
either approached or actually offerred the Deanery but he declined. The
other names were those of Dwelly and Charles himself. The choice
fell on Dwelly who was installed on October 4, 1931. This may have
been a disappointment to Charles but there is not the slightest indication
that he begrudged his friend his distinction. He continued to be his

loyal colleague on the Chapter and after leaving Liverpool supported
him through many vicissitudes to the very end of his life.

Yet the appointment had two consequences. Although Charles was
given the title of Chancellor in the officially constituted Chapter he
must have known that it was unlikely that he would for long continue
in the office. He had served for seven years in a distinguished but
subordinate position. It was highly probable that he would soon be
invited to undertake a major responsibility of his own. Would it be a
Bishopric or a Deanery? The Deanery of St. Paul's might soon fall
vacant. Where would his gifts be most usefully employed? The
answer came in 1932 in a surprising way.

The other consequence unhappily was a rift in the cordial relationship
which had hitherto existed between the Bishop and Dwelly. To put it
bluntly the Bishop found it difficult to keep his hands off the Cathedral;
Dwelly on his part was determined to exercise the authority which had
now been officially delegated to him. The Crown had appointed him,
not the Bishop. Its New Statutes were now in operation. In addition
there were difficulties in the Diocese itself which tested the Bishop's
patience and endurance severely. The Prayer Book controversy in
1927–8 had caused a deep cleavage amongst the clergy. A Synod in
1929 voted by a large majority to regard three beneficed clergy as
having put themselves outside the diocesan fellowship by reason of
their refusal to submit to episcopal regulations on matters of ritual. It
must have been particularly galling to him when his old friends at the
Cathedral seemed to be determined to establish their own independence.

So there were clouds on the horizon at the beginning of 1932 and
two major storms were soon to break, one in the summer of the same
year, the other more serious in the late autumn of 1933. In both of
these Charles found himself involved, even though in neither case did
he bear any direct responsibility for the outbreak of hostilities. It
seems best to give a brief account of the two episodes at this stage even
though the famous Unitarian controversy really belongs to a later
period of our story.

I have already referred to the Tuesday morning classes at the Cathedral which newly-ordained deacons were required to attend. In Charles's

final year a young man Joseph McCulloch was ordained to a curacy in Blundellsands and thereby came to his notice as a member of his course. Some months after McCulloch's ordination a novel was published under a pseudonym, but as a result of a betrayal of confidence the press learned the name of the real author. This need have caused no trouble had it not been that the novel was in the nature of a satire on suburbia and it was not hard to imagine the possible identity of some of its characters; it seemed all too evident that they were members of the parish in which the author himself was serving his curacy! The effect was sensational not only in the Parish but also in the Diocese at large. There were cries of indignation from laity and clergy alike and McCulloch's whole future was in jeopardy. As he had not yet been ordained priest the Bishop was strongly urged to excercise discipline by refusing to allow him to assume this higher office within the sacred ministry. And although it appears that in personal ways the Bishop did everything in his power to help the man under attack, it would have scandalised large sections of the Diocese if he had admitted him to the priesthood.[3]

The immediate outcome was that McCulloch quietly left the Diocese. But Dwelly and Raven were both determined that he should not be lost to the service of the Church. Dwelly went to great lengths to help him, simply showing him that he cared and that he was willing to extend to him the marks of true friendship whatever the circumstances. Charles tried to probe deeper. Although he was on the point of leaving Liverpool and was snatching a holiday before his final departure he spent a considerable amount of time in corresponding with McCulloch, reading his novel, trying to encourage him by positive suggestions. Ten years later this was to be misinterpreted by a disaffected priest of the Diocese who claimed in a public manifesto that Charles knew about the writing of the novel and had actually read it in manuscript form before its publication. This accusation was quite baseless. The first inkling that Charles had that the novel was about to be published was when the author showed him the page proofs. Even if he had wished to do so he could scarcely have taken preventive action at this stage.[4]

The second event was far more serious. It involved well known and

F

highly respected public figures. It challenged the whole concept of freedom to experiment. It touched an issue which was to be one of the thorniest in the whole development of ecumenical relationships. It threatened to obstruct the free flow of subscriptions to the Cathedral which were so urgently needed if the building of the great central space and tower were to go forward without hindrance.

From the beginning those associated with the Cathedral had hoped that this great building would serve as a centre of worship not only for Anglicans but also for members of all denominations who wished to come together with their fellow-Christians on special occasions to offer united prayer and thanksgiving to God. After the Lambeth Appeal of 1920 this seemed a very natural policy to pursue. But there was one difficulty which could arise more easily in Liverpool than in any other city. It was the problem that many of its most prominent citizens were Unitarians and that two leading Unitarian churches were within easy reach of the Cathedral. Were Unitarians to be excluded from the friendship and hospitality extended to others?

It is true that Birmingham and Manchester had also been centres of Unitarian influence in the nineteenth century but the strength of the movement, socially and financially, was more fully represented in Liverpool in the early twentieth century than in either of these. The Mellys, the Holts, the Rathbones were all household names. Some from these families had become Anglicans but the older generation still loyally supported the important church on Ullet Road which had attained a certain fame by reason of its possession of fine stained-glass windows by Burne-Jones. Laurence Holt, the ship-owner, was perhaps the most prominent figure of all and he had married the daughter of L. P. Jacks, one of the best known of all Unitarian scholars. The Holts were devoted friends of the Cathedral and its Dean.

One other fact about Unitarianism in Liverpool deserves to be mentioned. No other denomination had a finer record of charitable and welfare work in the city's worst areas. Just below the Cathedral there was a University Settlement closely related to a social centre directed at the time by the future Lord Woolton. A mile away along Mill Street there was another vigorous educational and recreational mission. In

fact no denomination was more actively represented in the neighbourhood of the Cathedral than was the Unitarian. Was the Cathedral to
exclude it rigidly from its ecumenical outreach?

In 1931, when the Chapter was constituted, the minister of Ullet
Road was a very distinguished preacher, the Rev. Laurence Redfern. In
1932-3 he acted as Chaplain to the High Sheriff and it had become a
normal practice at Liverpool to invite the Sheriff's Chaplain to preach
at one of the special Assize Services which were held on one of the
Sundays when the Judges were in residence. These Services were not
regarded as *statutory* according to the strict requirement of the Prayer
Book; Mattins had been said at an earlier hour. It is not hard to see,
therefore, that to exclude Mr. Redfern from the customary invitation
would have seemed invidious and the fact that the Service was occasional or, as it was called, "vocational", seemed to make it the more
possible to invite him to the Cathedral pulpit on this occasion.

It was the actual Assize Sermon which sparked off the national
controversy but in the indictment against the Cathedral it was linked
with an earlier series in which Dr. Jacks had on three Sunday evenings
addressed University Students on the subject "The University of the
Spirit." This was at the late 8.30 Service which was in no sense statutory. It had been addressed by ministers of various denominations and
by laymen who were without commitment to any institutional form of
Christian faith.

Such in brief was the background of the general religious and social
situation in Liverpool. It was, it need hardly be said, complicated by the
more intangible factors of personal friendship and relationship which
existed for example between Dwelly and Redfern and the Holts,
between Raven and Jacks and the Rathbones. Charles had not hesitated
to criticise the working conditions within one of the businesses over
which a leading Unitarian presided. At the same time he had a profound
admiration for many whose lives manifested the fruits of the Spirit
even though their creeds were in certain respects unorthodox.

In December 1933, the storm broke when Lord Hugh Cecil, a leading
ecclesiastical layman whose family had certain Liverpool connections,
called upon the Convocation of York to take formal action to prevent

any repetition of the "offence" of a Unitarian minister being allowed to preach in an Anglican Cathedral. A judicious account of what followed may be read in Iremonger's *Life of William Temple:* the Archbishop as President of the Convocation was bound to be the individual most deeply involved. He had a great affection for Liverpool Cathedral, its Bishop and its Dean; at the same time he had already received many letters of protest about the whole affair before the gravamen had been submitted by Lord Hugh Cecil in an official way.

A characteristic letter from Charles to Dwelly shows that he was prepared to leap into the debate even though he no longer held any official position in the Cathedral. But nothing that he could do could now prevent the legal and constitutional process from going steadily forward. Temple handled these with consummate skill but not even he could find a way of preventing some motion of disapproval which would seem to reflect adversely on what had happened in Liverpool. This was actually confined to the statement that "this House cannot approve the invitation to preach in any Cathedral or parochial church within the Province of any person, however devout or distinguished, who acknowledges membership in a denomination which is known not to accept that Faith or to administer that Baptism, and hope that no such invitations will be issued in future." But there had been a curiously vehement speech by Hensley Henson, the Bishop of Durham, in which he saw fit to attack his brother of Liverpool, Dr. David. And Dr. David himself had, contrary to the view of Dwelly and his colleagues on the Chapter, allowed the interpretation that "Mr. Redfern had been asked to preach at one of the *statutory* services of the Cathedral." This Dwelly strenuously denied, as it seemed to undermine his whole policy of arranging *special* services for special occasions.

There was a further complication which unhappily served to strain to the limit the relationship between Bishop and Dean. It was the question of who held the final responsibility for inviting Redfern to preach. In effect Dwelly said: "I was responsible and will accept blame but I still believe I was right in taking this action." David said: "No, I must accept the final responsibility and I acknowledge that I was wrong in allowing this invitation to be extended." Each was in his way displaying a fine spirit. But the question of ultimate responsibility remained unsolved. And so far as the Cathedral was concerned the most unfortunate legacy from the whole controversy was not the outcry in certain quarters about Liverpool and Unitarianism but the tragic widening of the gulf which had begun to separate Bishop and Dean in the affairs of the Cathedral. If they could have stood together in a united front on this occasion the criticsims from outside would have done little damage. It was the division on the home front that had become more acute and more serious.

Charles's part in the unhappy affair was really confined to producing a final public manifesto in which he associated himself with his friend Dwelly in expressing apologies to Dr. Jacks for any hurt or indignity he might have suffered. (At the close of the controversy, when in June 1934 Lord Hugh Cecil withdrew his protest, he wrote to Dr. Jacks assuring him that the question he had raised was one of intramural church discipline and in no way a personal attack on his views.) This is an interesting document which still has relevance to the place of Unitarianism within the ecumenical movement. Charles hardly perhaps realised how near his own struggle for a theology of unity in contrast to any kind of dualism brought him to the theological position of the best Unitarian scholars of whom none was more distinguished than Dr. Jacks himself.

Although in 1931 Charles's star seemed to be altogether in the ascendant it was, in fact, a year of mounting strain for him .Questions about the Christian attitude to war, which had been stirring in his mind ever since his experiences in 1917–8, had finally been resolved by an uncompromising acceptance of the pacifist position. The nature of the varying influences which led to this decision can only be surmised even though he leaves us in no doubt about the theological rationale. One may assume that he had frequent discussions with his friend and colleague Lucy Gardner, herself a Quaker and a pacifist, during the years when they worked together for Copec. His friendship with Ethel Moors, which began when he visited Harvard in 1926, may well have led him to consider more deeply the pacifist outlook which she espoused. And it is known that in the late 1920s he was often in contact with Percy Bartlett, also a Quaker and prominent in the Fellowship of Reconciliation. Whatever may have brought him to his final decision, the commitment itself proved to be irrevocable. There is no evidence that he ever afterwards deviated from the absoluteness of this dedication which he believed to be according to the mind of Christ. But it could not fail to divide him from many of his friends who, even when their sympathies were in the pacifist direction, could not follow him to the limit which he now regarded as logically necessary.

In other ways, too, he was experiencing stress as can be seen expressed with a certain amount of self-pity in a letter to his friend Dwelly in December 1931.

"For the whole of this year I've felt, as you know, almost broken by the rush and the loneliness of my work. I've not had any real rest of more than a few weeks since I left France in 1918, and have spent the whole time in starting things. It's been great fun—but a bit exhausting; and I *know* that I ought to settle down to something definite. Till a year ago I knew I was useful here: since then my only job has been to make it as easy as possible for you to become Dean. It has been sheer joy to see you taking control; and it gave me time to tackle a big bit of research and writing, and to work at the Way of Renewal and at starting a lot of small things up and down the country. Now Mervyn (Mervyn Haigh later Bishop of Winchester) has warned me that I must drop out of the W. of R.: my big book is nearly done: things here go better without me: and nothing new has come along: and my brain and body are getting old. All of which means depression of spirits and irritability of temper: and you, poor dear, stand the racket."

Amongst other things the letter reveals Charles's conviction that a change in his sphere of work was imminent and in the spring of 1932 the question which had hung over him for many months was at last resolved. The Regius Professorship of Divinity at Cambridge was falling vacant. This was no longer in the gift of the Crown though it bore the Regius title. The appointment was in the hands of a Board of Electors. It appears that their choice finally lay between two men.

Charles was one. The other was J. K. Mozley, a man distinguished in the field of the history of Christian Doctrine. Charles represented a much more liberal and adventurous school of theology but there could be no doubt about his academic competence in the light of his already published works. After a lengthy debate the formal proposition that Charles should be appointed to the Chair was agreed.

Normally the Professorship would have involved no duties outside Cambridge. But the new Professor of Hebrew, Stanley Cook, was a layman and could not occupy the Canonry at Ely which his predecessor had vacated. It was therefore proposed that the new Regius Professor should undertake the duties of the Canonry and be granted the use of the residence attached to it. This meant that Charles in accepting the Chair agreed also to become a Canon Residentiary of Ely Cathedral and to live in an ancient and lovely house—The Prior's House—which, while it possessed many charms, also presented many problems. The Raven family would not only struggle to keep warm in winter; they would constantly be faced with the problem of transporting "Pa" to and from Cambridge. But Cambridge and Ely it was to be.

NOTES TO CHAPTER NINE

1. p. 156: Information supplied by the Rev. E. F. F. Bishop.

2. p. 157: Phillips Brooks was Rector from 1869–1891. The present building opened for worship in 1877.

3. p. 161: Mr. McCulloch has briefly recounted the story in his book *We Have Our Orders*, p. 188.

4. p. 161: In a letter to McCulloch at the time Charles reveals something of his own attitude to the established Church:

   "It is extremely hard for people like you and me who are not built on normal curatical lines to fit into the ecclesiastical frame. But the whole future of the Church depends upon its power increasingly to assimilate and use us, and this again depends on our refusing to be cast down or cast out. The easy way out, the coward's way is to say "This institution that knows not the Christ is accursed." If we say it, we surrender our chance of reforming it."

CHAPTER TEN

Bird-Lover and Botanist

"A Londoner born and bred I was bird-mad before I had seen anything but sparrows." And coupled with the bird-madness was an ambition to write a bird-book. The first attempt was made at the age of nine— the biography of a family of ducks; the second at the age of thirty-nine —a collection of memories of bird-watching and bird-photographing published under the title *In Praise of Birds*.[1]

It is one of the strange ironies of Charles's life that no book that he ever wrote evoked such a chorus of praise as this his first venture into natural history. Newspapers and periodicals, religious and secular, reviewed it enthusiastically. Even experts writing in such journals as *The Field* and *Country Life* had few criticisms to offer and *G. K's Weekly* probably summarised the feelings of most when it said: "We have read many and varied treatises, and otherwise on bird subjects, but none has held us more deeply enthralled, more amused or interested." It is true that by present day standards the photographs seem very amateurish but when one considers the technical facilities available at the time and Charles's inevitable dependence on his own skills and resources, the results he obtained by patience and sheer perseverance are quite remarkable. As for the accompanying narrative, not only is it written in his felicitous style; it is also based upon an extraordinarily keen observation of details and succeeds in conveying a sense of real drama and excitement as it describes the habits and movements of birds.

The drama, however, was not confined to the birds. Charles himself was never able to settle for long quiet periods in country surroundings to watch the regularities of nature. For him the pattern was rather that of snatching a day between engagements or of an hour or two before a meeting, thereby refreshing his own spirit and at the same time gathering precious information which he could duly record and on some

future occasion use. Equally he refreshed himself after committees by
rushing home to paint another flower or grass.

His books are full of accounts of these "snatched" days and of the
way he used his many journeys to other parts of Britain, to Ireland, to
Holland, and to America, to gain new information about eggs, nesting,
peculiarities of flight, hatching processes, relations between male and
female and their young. Dr. Alan Richardson who, in the late twenties,
was Secretary to the Student Christian Movement in the University of
Liverpool has told how when Charles came to speak at one of the
frequent conferences at Parkgate on the Wirral the most careful watch
had to be kept on the movement of tides. Charles was wont to slip out
from the Conference house and would soon be far away on the sands
photographing birds. Students would comb the beach searching for
him for, as he confesses in one of his essays, he was constantly under
temptation to get one more look or one more shot and so run the risk
of being late for his engagements.

A friend, Mr. Reginald Wagstaff, who has occupied a distinguished
position in the Liverpool Museum, remembers many expeditions in his
company. As they walked along the shore at Ainsdale Charles would
talk about the wonders of creation. How little could be known about
nature's mysteries in one short life! And how impossible it was to think
that death could bring an end to the exploration and appreciation of the
amazing wealth of the beauty of the universe! He possessed an uncanny
power of observation, even to the recognition of the number of feathers
of a bird in flight. But he also had a passion for naming: "Before you
can speak about anything," he said, "you must know its name." He
followed Linnaeus's system and stored his memory with the Latin
name of every species he encountered. And besides his photography he
was constantly engaged in bird-sketching and bird-painting—work in
which no pains were too great to establish as exact a representation as
possible of line and colour.

His sheer physical endurance was quite phenomenal.[2] He was subject
to neuritis and ulcers and never appeared to be robust. Yet he would
stay in a hide amidst pouring rain even when his companion could
stand it no longer and would finally emerge out of the tent like a

drowned rat. Bishop Launcelot Fleming, who later became a close friend, has recalled his first meeting with Charles in his cottage on the edge of Loch Rannoch. He opened the door to find a sodden and dripping figure who had been spending hours on the mountain side chasing the rannoch rambler. Taken in and provided with a hot bath he was soon captivating every one in the cottage with the record of his day's adventures. So his enthusiasms, which no adverse circumstances seemed able to dampen, were conveyed to others through conversation, through lectures, through essays and finally through his books. He helped countless people to see more clearly, to appreciate more fully the orderliness of nature's patterns and to gain at least some awareness of the grand operations of that Creator Spirit to Whom Charles delighted to bear witness.

Charles's first love was for birds.[3] But at public school, egg collecting was forbidden and bird-watching expeditions were out of the question. He therefore switched his interest to moths and butterflies and until war came in 1914 seized every opportunity he could to collect and classify the lepidoptera of the Cambridge neighbourhood. The sheer delight of finding a pair of swallows building their nest in the front line of the trenches however was enough to restore his enthusiasm for birds and this was reinforced when he found himself at Blechingley in the midst of the Surrey Downs. Throughout his Liverpool days the great source of refreshment in his incredibly busy life was an expedition to watch or photograph birds and by the time of his return to Cambridge he had made himself an acknowledged authority on the birds of the British Isles, of Holland and to a lesser extent of the Eastern United States. It was then that another interest became predominant—the identification and collection of plants and flowers. His knowledge of botany, rein-forced by his study of the history of this particular science, led amongst other things to his appointment to be President both of the British Botanical Society and of the Council for the Promotion of Field Studies. Few if any of his contemporaries can have had so detailed a knowledge of the names, behaviour and habitats of birds, plants and lepidoptera in the British Isles such as Charles possessed by the time he reached his sixtieth year.

He writes engagingly about his early keenness as a collector in one of his essays in *Musings and Memories*. But his passion to collect gradually changed direction as he came to see that the all important object of study in nature was life rather than death, the marvellous intricacies of a living situation rather than an accumulation of dead specimens, however skillfully classified and arranged. In one of his essays he gives a vivid account of the incident when any desire he may have had to shoot birds was forever dispelled; in another he argues convincingly that the piling up of stores of birds' eggs and skins is of little scientific value. "It is from knowledge of the live bird, from close observation of habits, of courtship and nest-construction, of adaptation and diet, that advance (i.e. scientific) is possible. Bird psychology is far more profitable and far less studied than changes of pigment or plumage. And for this living and accessible specimens in their wild state are the material."[4]

These sentences, written in 1925, establish him as one of the earliest British ethologists while he returned to the theme of comparative psychology in the Preface to *The Ramblings of a Bird Lover* in 1927. Already he was aware of the fact that the study of the behaviour of birds and animals could be of value not only as a means of happy relaxation but also as a discipline which, under proper rules and controls, could throw increasing light on the life of man in society. Very few of the technical aids which have become available in the past half-century for the recording of sights and sounds were then even dreamed of. But Charles saw what was needed: the best possible use of photography or sketching or painting to capture impressions of the living organism, coupled with the most detailed written record of observations which could to some extent serve to represent the behaviour of the individual bird or animal in its actual environment. He therefore made heroic efforts to develop photographic skills with what today would be regarded as almost crude apparatus and methods; at the same time he took infinite pains to log the behaviour of birds in particular though also, for example, of wasps and spiders, so that he might build up a store of information for the use of any who shared his concern to understand the nature of universal life—its origin, its processes, its goal.

For Charles, then, the order of things was first to observe—and no man ever had sharper or more discriminating eyes; next to name—and no man can ever have had a more retentive memory for Latin names; then to make some kind of pictorial representation ("It is perhaps true," he wrote, "that one never really sees a thing until one has sketched it"; and again "I must register my impressions in pictures if they are to become a true part of my being")—and no man, at least in recent times, can have built up a finer collection of paintings of birds and flowers, accurate in shape and colour and features; finally to record in writing patterns of behaviour which could not (before the days of films) be represented pictorially—and no man can have taken greater pains to report exact details of flight, places of perching, relations to other birds, particularly the mate, location of nest, method of its construction etc.[5]

It is interesting to speculate why the fully written-up account of his expeditions and discoveries and his reflections upon them were confined to his Liverpool years (1924–32). The four books published during that period were immensely popular and years afterwards people were still writing to thank him for the pleasure they had derived from them—perhaps the most moving being that from an officer serving in the desert in the Second World War who had received a copy of *In Praise of Birds* and had gained from reading it not only the "greatest pleasure" but also the determination "to force the barren and stubborn desert to yield me a biological harvest." And in a deserted quarry he discovered birds nesting! The essays were beautifully written; for sheer elegance of style and richness of vocabulary they stand out amongst all his literary efforts. They maintain a wonderful balance between detailed observations and perceptive applications. They must have seemed an admirable medium for the transmission of spiritual truths.

Yet *Musings and Memories* was the last book of this kind that Charles wrote. Henceforward the appeal to *history* and to the careful interpretation of scientific evidence were to be the dominant notes in his speaking and writing except perhaps when visiting schools or youth clubs or when speaking to audiences known to be open and friendly to his message. Informal talks about birds or plants he never attempted to publish and none of his writings after 1932 compare in style or content with the "bird-books". Many people, I suspect, would have been prepared to forego some of the records of his excursions into history if they could have received instead more examples of his observations and reflections gained from direct contacts with nature herself.

For to the end of his life Charles never slackened in his enthusiasm for the hunt—to see some new aspect of bird behaviour (as for example when he allowed himself to be suspended from a third floor window of a house in Cambridge, Massachusetts on a wintry day in order to photograph an owl) or to identify some rare flower in Anglesey or on Snowdonia or in Scotland. In September 1943, after his heart attack in the spring, he wrote to his friend Launcelot Fleming: "We had a grand fortnight in Glen Clova last year but still want Carex microglochin and three other Perthshire rarities. For twenty years of my youth Rannoch was my dream-place; and I've never collected there. One day, Launcelot, you must take me to find nubeculosa and Lapponaria and the twins Cordigera and Melanopa—if I can manage to crawl to their homes. I caught a Clouded Yellow on the Downs last week; so I'm not really quite bed-ridden." With his son John and an inner circle of friends who shared his enthusiasms he carried on a continuous interchange of news of fresh treasures discovered and pictured, while he was always ready to deal with questions about natural phenomena whether they came from learned historians seeking his judgment on a point of detail or from a school-boy wanting to know why, when he put out nuts into a nut-hopper, greenfinches arrived within a quarter-of-an-hour though none had been seen in the district for months. Can birds smell?[6]

In the latter part of his life Charles's contributions to natural history were not confined to the study of its history and the interpretation of its significance for the study of theology, though these enquiries occupied much of his time. On the more practical side he was immensely interested in the plans for developing the usefulness of the Botanic Garden in Cambridge at the time when a new era of expansion had become possible through the munificent bequest of a benefactor, Mr. Reginald Cory. Charles offerred various detailed suggestions for siting and planting but perhaps his most significant contribution was an urgent plea that the Garden should be developed not only as a reserved area to be admired and enjoyed but also as an invaluable instrument for teaching and research, not least through its Library.[7]

Another project which owed much to his enthusiasm and wise guidance was the preservation of Wicken Fen as an almost unique example of a total system of inter-related natural life. Land and water, trees and grass, birds and insects support one another within a fascinating ecological complex. Through the efforts mainly of Charles and his friend Professor W. H. Thorpe, the Fen has become Trust property, has been equipped with an excellent building for display and administration and has been given a measure of control for the convenience of interested observers. Charles was prepared to give generously of his time to such projects, as well as to societies such as the Linnaean and the John Ray and the Botanical Society of the British Isles because of his profound conviction that the study of life in all its aspects, of living phenomena in their natural environments, rather than dead specimens in museum or laboratory, was the most worth while of all human disciplines.

He expressed this conviction in an impressive way in a paper which he read to the Cambridge Natural History Society on the occasion of its centenary in May 1957. He first spoke charmingly of his earliest associations with the Society when the secretary was a certain William Farren, a taxidermist who later became an enthusiastic bird photographer and with whom Charles established a most cordial friendship. From this he went on to describe the way in which the study of natural history had changed since the beginning of the century when he joined the Society: from the collecting and study of lifeless exhibits to the controlled observation of the living animal in its natural environment. (In another context Professor C. H. Waddington has referred to the typical biological text-book of the late nineteenth century as consisting largely of descriptions of the *morphology* of plants and animals.[8] Charles's point could well have been expressed in terms of the change from morphology to ecology.) "At the beginning of the century," he declared, "the tide had begun slowly but surely to turn and though the gulf between the men of museums and the men of the open-air was still wide, the liveliest minds in biology were already moving towards a denial of the antithesis, towards ecological and psychological problems and to that sense of wholeness which is now influencing every department from medicine to nuclear physics." And in an interesting (and typical) peroration he expressed his hopes for the future of education generally.

"If, as I often think and say, natural history widely interpreted might well become the finest of all instruments for the training of children and if its pursuit has educational value for developing observation, memory and range of interests, for promoting aesthetic and moral as well as intellectual qualities, then we may see what is still too often regarded as a harmless hobby or even a sign of eccentricity take the place in cultural life which some of us believe it to deserve."[9]

Ecology and comparative psychology—these disciplines were only in their infancy in the 1920s when Charles was writing his "bird-books" but he already discerned, with a kind of prophetic insight, that the importance of wholeness in nature and of community—through—relationship were likely be become key issues before many years had passed. In 1927 we find him registering a bitter protest against the "horrors of the oil menace" on the Lancashire coast. Walking one afternoon amongst the sandhills he counted some forty corpses of dead birds left high and dry after the previous night's high tide. "The gulls and perhaps the heron may have been victims of a scoundrel with a gun: for the gulls I at least shall not mourn. The rest are victims of refuse oil, a melancholy sample of the havoc that goes on round our coast, and a silent protest against man's carelessness and greed."[10]

But his even deeper interest was in the wholeness of the great evolutionary movement of universal life. If, as he firmly believed, the *general* theory of an evolutionary universe was the only one that could be deemed to correspond with the known evidence, then it could be one of life's greatest excitements and satisfactions to seek further evidence which could throw light on *the nature and method* of the evolutionary process itself. This, without question, was Charles's underlying passion in his study of nature and of natural history. He delighted in nature, he rejoiced in the beauties of nature, he shared the collector's enthusiasm to discover a new plant or to see a rare bird. But all of these were, in a sense, subordinate to the never ending *quest for truth*. He sensed that the great struggle ahead would be that between a purely materialist—mechanist—behaviourist and a holist—organicist—personalist interpretation of the universe.[11] Anything that he could discover by careful observation and comparison about the nature of bird-life and plant-life might serve to throw light on the detailed processes of evolution and their relationship to the whole design.

This is the hope he expresses in an impressive passage in *Bird Haunts and Bird Behaviour* where he argues that "natural selection," interpreted in a rigidly mechanistic way, is inadequate to account for variations in the life of nature itself. He reveals his own fascination with the evidence for some kind of use-inheritance and for the transmission of acquired characteristics. He is not content with simplistic formulae such as "trial and error", "the struggle for existence", "natural selection". Each is a useful description of certain observable processes; it is not sufficient to encompass the whole. Charles refuses to be dogmatic on the other side by imagining that such formulae as "special creation", "life-force" or "universal purpose" are to be adopted instead.

> "Better an attitude" he writes, "of what some call agnosticism and others natural piety, an attitude which observes, and wonders, and questions, and admits itself ignorant. As accurate knowledge advances, as the results of many lines of enquiry are brought together, the truth of the matter may be discovered. Meanwhile bird-watching besides its aesthetic charm has about it the excitement of discovery and the delight of speculation. We begin with the joy of the mountain-stream; its genius takes shape in the Dipper (he had been examining a dipper's nest): and the dipper sets us on to the quest for truth."[12]

This was written in 1929. Nearing the end of his life, when speaking as President to a Conference of the Botanical Society, he returned to the same general theme, this time in relation to the collection and study of flora. Concluding his paper with what he called a "personal confession" he said:

"As primarily an ornithologist I have spent many years pleading that the business of adding new and casual visitors to the Fair Island list or of splitting the tits into insignificant sub-species was a relatively childish and scientifically valueless pursuit—as compared at least with the study of behaviour. I cannot but make a similar plea to a Conference like this. By all means let us collect and identify and classify our flora and note additions to it and calculate their chances of survival. But let us remember that this is only preliminary investigation: we do not learn from it anything of scientific value, unless we use our experience to throw light upon the problems of the relationship of the plant to its environment, of its adaptation and survival, and of the parts played by nature and nurture in its constitution."

The field worker and the expert, the amateur and the professional he urged, could all take a part in observing and recording and, as far as possible, co-ordinating the behaviour of the living organisms each in its particular environment, each a constituent element in the vast living whole.

Interestingly enough, in his own interpretation of nature he made use from time to time of the model of the drama, even though he had firmly rejected the way it had been employed by certain theologians who had spoken of the intrusion of a Divine Actor upon the stage of history. For Charles the total process of evolution was to be viewed as drama. Life cannot exist apart from an environment but life can develop as the organism comes to play an increasingly *conscious* part in the drama of life.

"The actions of insects in their standardised precision and in the total lack of ingenuity if the routine is upset make it hard to believe that the agent is not merely an actor playing a part created for it but not by itself or by its ancestors. For there is nowhere among any of their kin evidence of inventiveness such as could ever have produced the surgery of the predatory wasps or the engineering feats of the spiders. And if not, whence comes the design which they put into effect? Who wrote the drama that they play? What is the cause and source of their skill?

In birds it is much easier to believe that the performer is also the playwright, or rather that through many generations and by many little innovators the drama has been brought to its present perfection. As compared with the insects the bird shows a great advance: if it has lost the mechanical perfection of routine activity it has gained elasticity, initiative, freedom outside the range of any insect. Experiment consciously willed, if not in the full human sense purposive, intervenes upon and modifies the representation of a standardised performance."[13]

This is an important passage for the understanding of Charles's total philosophy of life. He conceives the whole evolutionary movement in terms of three stages: reflex action, conscious action, purposive action. In the initial stage the parts played by living organisms conform to a given script (and in such a conception Charles was not far from the whole idea of a genetic code) as in a play. But gradually the players experiment with small variations, write minute parts of the play themselves: this is the stage of consciousness. Finally consciousness rises to the level of intelligent purpose in which the organism gains an ever deepening appreciation of the meaning of the play and seeks to be fully identified with it: this is the stage of personal purpose. It is a suggestive model not devoid of difficulties but better than either a purely mechanistic or an exclusively organismic framework for the interpretation of the distinctive quality of the human amidst other forms of life. Again Charles does not dogmatise but concludes:

"Probably in birds we have a good cross-section at which to study the whole process; for the whole seems to display a development by which behaviour originally given or, as some would say instinctive, is supplemented and finally replaced by actions deliberately discovered, controlled and acquired. If so, the origins of instinct remain inscrutably mysterious; but we can perhaps see how intelligence has arisen out of it, how nurture has influenced nature, and man's relative freedom of adjustment to circumstances been won."[14]

Although Charles tended to regard his sheer love of nature and his delight in its aesthetic aspects as subsidiary to his passionate search for ultimate truth, truth which could only be apprehended by a ceaseless attention to all the available evidence whether provided by nature or by history, it is hard not to regret that he did not write up more of his experiences just for the joy of sharing with others his feelings and his reflections. What he reveals about his own personal life in his 'Birdbooks' is always of intense interest. "Every man has his own private terror, some one thing that stirs up ancient and unreasoning panic: a big vertical drop has always been mine; and looking at that awesome cliff I could hardly believe that I had ever worked my way from top to bottom of it."[15] Or, after a nasty fall when climbing to photograph, he had been helped back over a distance of three miles by his wife and a friend while his groin was shooting with pain all the way; "It was worth while to have seen my peculiar fear face to face and to have gained a new experience of pain. There is, even at the worst of it, a certain joy in overcoming, a certain exaltation in the testing of manhood which is, I think, an authentic, though not the finest, part of fortitude."[16]

Most interesting of all in this respect are his references to the features in nature which evoke his most rapturous response. Daringly he suggests that if one is able to discover what feature draws out from a man the quintessence of his homage, one will have found the secret of his real self: a man can be truly mirrored in a scene. For what then is his own preference when so much in the world is beautiful? It is the seaboard, the place where land and water meet. "Here in the marriage-bed of land and water life first had its origin; we hardly need the scientists to assure us of it; even mankind feels the sanctity of it, and goes to the seaside as to his home, his nursery, his playground, where he can forget his dignity and be a child again, with a child's freedom to dream and to enjoy." In these periods of detachment it is possible to recover perspective and a sense of the eternal. "Where sea meets earth under an ever-changing, ever-changeless sky, there if anywhere is the mystery that will reveal to us the parable of our being. Even a day at Blackpool is in some sort an initiation."[17]

The mirror of the man, the parable of his being; the emergence of life out of the marriage-bed of land and water; the return to the place where sea meets earth. Such self-revelations help to the understanding not only of Charles's psychology but also of his theology. That which is most worshipful for him is the fount and source of *life:* and the source of life is the feminine. To that source Charles had constantly to return, even though in another sense he was constantly struggling away from it. Again his theology came to be expressed in evolutionary, immanental, organismic, terms with "union" and "communion" as its determinative concepts. The meeting of land and water becomes both a mirror and a parable of ultimate union and beatitude. I cannot refrain from referring again to the vivid contrast between this man, returning in spirit and imagination to the estuary where wet and dry, sea and land, hill and mud-flat, sky and water, all seemed to merge into one another in a supremely harmonious *communion* and another man (Paul Tillich) returning in imagination to the sea-shore from whence he looked out towards stupendous *contrasts*—the watery deep and the starry height, light and dark, time and eternity, sea and sky, only meeting one another at the far mysterious horizon of cosmic being. No wonder that their theologies came to such different forms of expression. Yet who dares to say that one was wholly right and the other wholly wrong?

There are lovely passages in each of the four bird books. One is the story of the prisoner who possessed an uncanny power of imitating the songs and cries of birds. Charles was lecturing on birds and showing some of his slides when suddenly the cry of the curlew was heard in the prison assembly hall as its picture appeared on the screen. It was a perfect reproduction, just as Charles had first heard it one moonlit night on the banks of the Dee. And he comments:

"The call that more than any other contains the secret of the life of the wild. There is no melody on earth that can touch it unless it be the lilt and yearning of an Irish song; there is passion in it and a broken

heart, endurance and defiant fortitude, even a touch of exultation and
of life tortured but unsubdued."[18]

Another is the reference to the rock-garden he created at Blechingley
but only possessed for three years. "Dear little corner of rock-set bank—
how I loved every inch of it—And how wonderfully the tiny place
repaid me. Eighteen species of gentian I grew there: and in my last
season thirteen of them flowered for me: and with them all the choicest
of their neighbours."[19] But for sheer beauty of writing, with a superb
capacity to hold before our imaginations the scene about which he writes,
the two passages which follow seem to me to touch the heights and
give Charles a rightful place not only amongst theologians and natural
historians but also amongst artists and masters of the written word. In
the first he is telling of his visit in Holland to a colony of spoonbills:
in the second he tries to recapture the delights of his holiday in Texel.

"We came upon the colony through secret byways from behind;
and I shall never forget the moment when the glorious creatures rose
glitteringly and sailed over our heads. There were said to be a hundred
pairs in residence: but many were away fishing and many more
refused to leave their nests. Yet enough sprang up to greet us to make
a spectacle intolerably beautiful. The great white wings, the long
slender shapes, the ease and grace of their motion, the silence of their
ordered advance—so might Dante emerging from the steeps of
purgatory have been welcomed by a host of angels. And when the
unforgettable moment of their passing was over, we could study at
our leisure those that remained. There they stood erect upon their
nests, the strange beak adding a curiously mischievous touch to the
seraphic loveliness of their plumage. The flowing plumes, the amber
glow upon the breast, the slimness of line, the pure perfection of
feathering, how grand a sight they made! We must not stay long: for
young spoonbills have delicate digestions and a vigorous habit of
expressing disapproval of strangers. But we had been allowed to see
a nest, and one was conveniently situated some distance from the main
city. To it very gently we made our way: and in it were a single egg
and three babies perhaps a couple of days old, covered in patches with

white down, with queer tufts like young herons upon their heads and short straight beaks of glowing orange. To look down upon such a nursery was a fitting climax to a day of wonders. After it one could utter a silent "Nunc dimittis" and on the way home resign oneself to the beauty of the mere and the glow of happiness which comes from hopes fulfilled. There is no joy like it—those quiet and leisurely returns when an achievement long desired has been accomplished, and when the whole self is steeped in a peace too deep for thought. And if such a day ends in a bout when repose of motion and the calm of the fenland with its wide sky and open levels match the mood and give the soul room for its expansion, then all life's disappointments, all its demands upon courage and endurance, are infinitely worth while: for after all it is the very rarity of such gifts of God and the impossibility of planning their occurrence that keep for them their wonder. We cannot command such joy: it comes, and we are thankful."[20]

"A week later when I was back at work in England and the pair of avocets had been duly enlarged and hung upon my study wall, it all seemed a dream. Indeed, in the busy days that followed I caught myself gazing at their portrait incredulously. It must have been in some previous incarnation that I had sat out in my tent in the rain and waited and watched and failed, and at last succeeded. There are places and scenes which one can revisit merely by turning one's gaze inward: the sights and sounds and smells, the very reality of it all, come back at once and without effort. Texel, alas! is not such. I know as a fact that it exists and that I have visited it: my room holds proof indisputable. Were it not for my pictures I could not believe; and even with their help I cannot do more than think myself into knowledge. If only here in Liverpool the chorus of the waders would break upon the silence—if only I could slip away to my hide on the Waal en Burg! It is vain desire. We cannot force that strange subconscious self of ours. I suppose that only what is native to us and in keeping with our general habit can be freely and fully recovered. The great experiences, the events that we long to retain for ever, fade and elude us. Texel cannot be absorbed by a Cockney Briton. He has there no abiding heritage. But even so, and if he must remain an alien at heart, it is good for him to know that for a moment, once and again, he has seen and heard. And by and by if Browning speaks truth he will recapture it all in its fulness. Heaven, for me, must surely have its avocets.

And perhaps some winter evening when the house is still and the day's work done my birds will come down from their frame and set me free to fly with them to Texel; and I shall feel again the sting of the rain on my face and the lash of the wind on my tent, and look up and see her sitting there so humbly proud of mate and eggs and watch him stealing near and stooping to wish her well. My chairs and books will fade and the walls of my room dissolve in luminous mist, and out of it the long green flats of the Waal en Burg, and its fringe of distant dunes and low farmsteads will take shape before my inward eye; and the pale gold of the buckwheat and the sungleam of the buttercups will shine out in the meadows; and the clamour of the birds will echo in my ears, and all the air be filled with the wonder of their wings."[21]

NOTES TO CHAPTER TEN

1. p. 168: *In Praise of Birds* was published in 1925. *Ramblings of a Bird-Lover* in 1927. *Bird Haunts and Bird Behaviour* in 1929. *Musings and Memories* in 1931. In 1946 a revised volume entitled *In Praise of Birds* was put out by George Allen and Unwin. It was a selection of the best papers from these four books brought up to date with a new series of photographs.

2. p. 169: "I once rode (on a bicycle) the fifty miles two days running to photograph a crippled stone curlew at Icklingham."

3. p. 170: On the lighter side it is worth recording that when Charles gave a lecture in Liverpool on seabirds and declared in passing that in his opinion, through the imposition of certain controls, gulls had multiplied to an undesirable degree he provoked an indignant lady correspondent to reply: "You say there are too many gulls; I say there are too many ravens."

4. p. 171: *In Praise of Birds* p. 132.

5. p. 172: e.g. "Ravens in Belstone Cleave near Sticklepath, Devon. April 12th, 1935. Cock bird soaring over hillside and trees— croaked and made evidence of size and hackles certain. Flight more masterly, turns more acrobatic than crow. Perching tree a small thorn on further slope. Hen soon appeared and after perching on slope, glided down into trees and was lost to sight— I guessed in one of a clump of tall spruces by water side."

6. p. 173: In the mid Twenties Charles was a member of an Anglican delegation to Helsinki. Finding one of the conference sessions unusually boring he went outside and encountered a minister's son aged twelve or thirteen who knew no English but was obviously interested in plants and birds. They struck up an immediate friendship by using Latin names with which they were both familiar.

7. p. 174: Towards the end of his teaching career in Cambridge Charles was invited to give lectures on the history of botany to undergraduates formally enrolled in the Tripos. This he did without notes, showing himself to be word perfect in recalling names and periods.

8. p. 174: *The Twentieth Century Mind*, I. p. 343.

9. p. 175: *Cambridge Review*, Oct. 12th, 1957.

10. p. 175: *Ramblings of a Bird Lover*, p. 151.

11. p. 176: cp. *Ramblings of a Bird Lover*, p. 167 f.

12. p. 176: *Bird Haunts*, p. 47.

13. p. 177: Ibid. p. 47 f.

14. p. 178: Ibid. p. 87.

15. p. 179: *Ramblings*. p. 81.

16. p. 179: Ibid. p. 133.

17. p. 179: *Ramblings*, p. 103 f.

18. p. 180: *Musings and Memories*, p. 60.

19. p. 181: Ibid, p. 132.

20. p. 181: *Bird Haunts*, p. 151 f.

21. p. 182: Ibid, p. 181 f.

PART THREE

1932–1952

THE
CREATOR OF A NEW INTEGRATION

CHAPTER ELEVEN

The Critical Transition

The change from Liverpool to Ely was revolutionary. The Raven family had for eight years lived in a rambling Victorian house in what at the time was considered one of the better middle-class areas of Liverpool. The wide open space of Sefton Park was within easy reach in one direction, the Mersey River in the other. Yet the slums of Toxteth sprawled between the Park and the Cathedral and a damp, smoke-laden pall frequently hung over the city. Fenland indeed could often be clothed in mist but clean air and bracing winds were the rule rather than the exception.

Again where virtually every aspect of Liverpool bore witness to the rapid industrial expansion of the nineteenth century, Ely was steeped in tradition and the glories of the Middle Ages were always in sight. The Prior's House, which was assigned to the new Canon, is one of the historical houses of Cambridgeshire.[1] It stands within the Close on the south side of the Cathedral and its windows allow wonderful glimpses of this ancient building in one direction, lovely views of a walled garden with beech, birch and pine trees in another. There is an arched dining-room on the ground floor, strange passage-ways, a haunted room, the kind of house in which one feels that anything might happen. Adjacent is the Prior's Chapel with Norman undercroft. The main structure dates from the twelfth and thirteenth century.

It was into this romantic setting that the Raven family moved. There was ample room for the four children now in their teens, a splendid study for Charles and still plenty of space to spare. Had it been possible to employ a full domestic staff, life could have been idyllic. But this was quite beyond the family means. Once at least they tried the experiment of having a paying-guest in residence and a brief reference to it appears in a book of reminiscences by the Duke of Bedford entitled *A Silver Plated Spoon*. His father, he writes, was "a committee member of something called the Conference on Politics, Economics and Citizenship where I think he first met Canon Raven who became Master of Christ's College, Cambridge and played a brief part in the curious plan of education my father devised for me." The plan, in fact required him to live for a while at The Prior's House and to be tutored by Charles.

"It was rather a pleasant old house, although freezing cold like every other house I have lived in since the day I was born. It was full of stone flags, refectory tables and rush seats and I have never known people drink quite so much tea. They used to have early-morning tea and tea for breakfast, tea in the middle of the day, tea after lunch, tea for tea, tea after dinner and tea before they went to bed. I did not see much of the good canon but he was in fact the agent of my first visit to Woburn, our ancestral home."

To be warm and comfortable in this ancient home was one problem; to journey to and fro to Cambridge was another. To travel by rail was one possibility but this involved the long journey from station into town at the Cambridge end and in any case the times of duties in the University were irregular. The car was the obvious answer to the problem if only Charles could have mastered the art of driving. The undisturbed roadways within the Close seemed to offer an excellent course on which to practise and he was let loose on an apparently fool proof track with railings on one side and a meadow on the other. Within yards however the car had swerved into the railings and it soon became evident that Charles could never change gear unless he could first look down and see exactly what needed to be done. His family and friends realised that the task of making him into a confident driver was hopeless and that the only solution was to be found in the joint-chauffeurship of wife and daughter.

Often no less than three times a day the Raven car went to and fro on the fenland road covering the thirteen miles from Ely to Cambridge. It might have been expected that once Charles had been safely deposited in Cambridge he would have remained there throughout the day for his various engagements. But the family circle drew him back like a magnet. He loved to be in the midst of whatever was going on at home and actually did much of his work sitting in the drawing-room rather than his study while incessant talk was in process round about him. In between he loved to argue and dispute with members of the family, retaining thereby the habit which he had formed in his own early life of engaging with his father and brother in lively discussions. He was happy to do this in the intimacy of the family circle; he found it difficult if not impossible to enter into debate in an environment which was unsympathetic or in any way hostile.

His duties in the Cathedral were not onerous. For only two months of the year was he officially in residence though he naturally attended meetings of the Chapter and shared its general life at other times. Dr. Kirkpatrick had been in Ely for roughly half a century, first as Canon, then for nearly thirty years as Dean and the contrast between the traditional rites and ceremonies of Ely on the one hand and the almost startling innovations at Liverpool on the other could hardly have been more extreme. Charles never really adjusted himself to the order of the ancient régime and was immensely relieved when in 1938 the Regius Chair was severed from the Canonry and he was free to live in Cambridge, untrammelled by association with what must often have seemed to him a moribund institution. Once, indeed, he exclaimed in a moment of exasperation: "Ely Cathedral is a great white elephant which feeds on the souls of men."

Moreover it was not only the Cathedral and its Close which provided so great a contrast to Liverpool. The people of Liverpool have become famous for their friendliness, vivacity, humour, resilience. The people of East Anglia were still conservative, insular, exceedingly slow to recognise an immigrant as one of themselves. It was commonly said that it was necessary to live in Fenland for at least twenty years in order to gain acceptance as an authentic member of the community. Charles's mental processes worked at lightning speed; his body was scarcely ever still. To be a patient, withdrawn researcher in a quiet medieval close was certainly not the life for him. So in many ways he lived the life of a commuter. Ely had to be the place of residence; Cambridge and the wider world were the spheres of his work and influence.

But where was to be his pied-à-terre in Cambridge itself? In Oxford a Fellowship in a particular College is allocated to a particular Chair but such has never been the general custom at Cambridge. When a new Professor is appointed, he must wait for an invitation from a College which happens at the time to be in a position to elect him into a Fellowship. In the case of Charles the invitation came from Christ's, a College with which he had previously enjoyed no special associations but which was from now onwards to constitute part of his very existence to the end of his life.

Though deprived of the site which the original founder had intended for the erection of "God's-house" on the banks of the Cam, the College is centrally situated close to the busiest part of the trading and commercial life of the city. Its ancient and noble gateway leads into a court dating mainly from the early sixteenth century, on whose far side the Master's Lodge and the Hall combine dignity with a certain homeliness; the Lodge itself must be one of the most attractive houses in Cambridge. The College has two inner courts and beyond these there is the Fellows' Garden, perhaps the most beautiful to be found in either of the two ancient Universities. Its most prized possession is a splendid mulberry tree associated with Milton[2] but all of its trees are noteworthy; together they provide a vertical dimension for one of the most harmonious horizontal landscapes that could be designed.

Besides the splendour of its natural features the College possesses fascinating links with historic figures of the fifteenth and sixteenth centuries. Though the initiative for establishing a training-college for schoolmasters to be known as God's-house came from a certain cleric, William Byngham, the official founder of Christ's College was King Henry VI and what had been begun by Henry was extended in scope in 1505 and fully establlshed in law by his niece, Lady Margaret Beaufort, famous patroness of learning and mother of King Henry VII. The College therefore possesses as its full title: "Christ's College in the University of Cambridge by Henry the Sixth King of England first begun and after his decease by Margaret Countess of Richmond, Mother of King Henry the Seventh augmented finished and established." It was with an institution inheriting the doubly religious title of God's House and Christ's College that Charles was now to become intimately associated.

Yet the attraction for him was to be found not only in its religious and royal traditions (as Chaplain to the King he could feel at home with both) but also in the names of those who had entered the society as undergraduates and had gone on to achieve fame in varying walks of life. Of these by general consent the most famous was John Milton. But there were also the Cambridge Platonists of whom the three greatest had been Benjamin Whichcote, Henry More, and Ralph Cudworth: of these More had been an undergraduate at Christ's, Cudworth had become its Master in 1654. And Charles felt a deep affinity with the ideals and achievements of these seventeenth century scholars as he was to show in his own later writings. Perhaps even more exciting was the fact that Charles Darwin, whose evolutionary doctrines he had embraced so wholeheartedly, was a Christ's man. And finally it must have been a considerable satisfaction to him that General Smuts, whose doctrine of "Holism" had already captured his attention and interest, had spent his formative years in Cambridge as a member of this particular College—a College of which Charles, little imagining it at the time, was one day to become Master.

The Fellowship at Christ's gave him a base in Cambridge and the convenient facilities of College life. It also brought him close into touch with scholars of distinction in fields other than his own. The Governing Body was still small enough to make it possible for all its members to have a reasonable acquaintance with one another and to some degree to share each other's interests. In 1932, when Charles became a Fellow, the Master was a Scotsman, Norman McLean, a noted authority on Syriac and Aramaic and a man deeply interested in the history of religion. But McLean was in poor health and it seemed unlikely that he would long continue in office. His death in 1936 was the prelude to an election which, through its fictional dramatisation, has become more widely known than any other of a comparable kind in this century.

For another new Fellow had been elected at Christ's not long before Charles. This was Charles Snow who had come from Leicester to Cambridge, first to research, then to teach in the field of molecular physics. Soon however his name was to become famous in the world of letters and when, in 1951, *The Masters* was published, it was clear enough that the general background bore close similarities to that of the Christ's election in 1936, even though the game of seeking to identify individual characters was capable of being played indefinitely. Snow was senior to Charles in date of election. Two years his junior was C. H. Waddington who, when he came to the College, was already distinguished in the field of embryology and was destined to go on later to Edinburgh to become one of the world's leading geneticists. But not only so. By his book *Behind Appearance* Waddington has established himself as a remarkably gifted interpreter of modern painting. It must be without parallel in this century that within one College there should have been three men, each distinguished in his own subject of research and teaching, and yet at the same time displaying outstanding talent in a quite different area of scientific or artistic competence.

The detailed preliminaries and processes of the election of a new Head of a College in Oxford or Cambridge are normally veiled in secrecy. But there can be little doubt that after the death of Norman McLean, Charles was one of the two most favoured candidates as his successor. So evenly were they supported, however, that *neither* was in fact chosen. A former mathematical lecturer at the College, Sir Charles Darwin, was appointed from outside and as he was slightly younger than Charles, it seemed that the latter's chances of ever becoming Master had vanished. Yet after only two years in office the new Master surprisingly resigned in order to become Director of the National Physical Laboratory. This time, it appears, there was little opposition to Charles's candidacy and the door which had seemed to be closed forever in 1936 now swung open. The high honour of being Master, the occupancy of a lovely residence, the possibility of one day becoming Vice-Chancellor—all these suddenly came to Charles at a time when, as we shall see, he was labouring under strain and disappointment and grave uncertainty about his future. To be Head of a College is never an easy task. Perhaps the period 1939–50, during which Charles reigned over Christ's, was unusually difficult. Nevertheless there can be little doubt that he brought great distinction to the College and served it devotedly. Caius had provided the settings for his early triumphs in the world of exact scholarship: Emmanuel had given him scope to mature as lecturer, preacher, researcher: Christ's gave him the opportunity to discharge successfully extensive responsibilities in College and University affairs.

Not unnaturally he found a particular source of satisfaction in his association with the life of the Chapel. While he was Canon of Ely he could only attend services and preach occasionally. But once he became Master he felt that he had regained a pulpit and an altar which in a peculiar way were his own. The Chaplain, of course, fulfilled many of the regular duties but Charles loved to celebrate the Communion Office and to preach. One who belonged to a far "higher" Church tradition than that with which Charles was generally identified has borne witness to the impressive dignity and reverence with which he celebrated the Eucharist. Even such details as the lighting of candles were to him important. Everything must be done decently and in order.

At the same time, when preaching in Chapel he needed freedom, though it was never a slack or disordered freedom. As the time for the sermon approached he became tense; in his preparatory prayer his bodily postures seemed like those of an animal about to spring. Then, while speaking to the congregation, he walked up and down the aisle between the pews (in a Chapel planned in Collegiate style this is easily possible) or, as one who regularly listened put it, he exercised a kind of dance as his body kept time with his words which flowed so rhythmically and under such perfect control. But above all it was his eyes which captivated his audience. Before he had uttered a word the compelling look seemed to challenge attention. Then his beautifully controlled and modulated voice, quite distinctive in quality and tone, cast a spell over his hearers even when the content of the sermon was unfamiliar or too demanding.

Though suspicious of many aspects of ecclesiastical tradition Charles had a proper regard for the past associations of a particular place. This

G

sense was quickened almost daily when he became Master of Christ's for in no College is the physical link between the Lodge and the Chapel more intimate. In Lady Margaret's time a small oratory was constructed upstairs in the Lodge and this contained a window through which she could observe the services in the Chapel below. A passageway leads directly from the Lodge to a stairway descending to the ante-Chapel and Charles, for whom the worship of a living fellowship had always been one of the most cherished of human experiences, valued as highly as any Master the opportunity which Christ's afforded of an easy and natural commerce between the life of the home and the worshipping life of the College community.

As Fellow of Christ's and later as Master, Charles found himself called upon to share in and uphold the traditional rituals of a common table which are possibly more complex than those of any other College in Oxford or Cambridge. To this, however, he in no way objected. At heart he was both a sacramentalist and a ritualist. What he could never accept was a narrowly defined and exclusively restricted sacramentalism. If a society was to hold together it needed rules and orders of procedure. But it had no right to claim that these were the only possible rules. The Spirit, both in nature and in human relationships, operates in ways whose regularity and orderliness can be observed but not in such a manner as to preclude the possibility of new adaptations and new manifestations within the ongoing adventure of creative life.

Such were some of Charles's interests in College. Outside, little more than a hundred yards away, was Holy Trinity Church which had become famous as a centre of Evangelical witness in the days of Charles Simeon early in the nineteenth century. In the twenties he had taken a mission in this Church and the Vicar in the thirties was one of his oldest friends, Edward Woods, a leading Liberal Evangelical who was later to become Bishop of Lichfield. He was later succeeded by Max Warren who drew Charles into a closer association with the Church than ever before. He was always welcome as a preacher and to a degree was able to continue the kind of ministry which he had found so congenial in the 8.30 Services at Liverpool Cathedral. The audience was intelligent but not strictly academic. Charles was at his best in mediating a positive approach to the Bible in the light of contemporary scholarship to those who were eager to discover a faith for living which was neither irrational nor simply based upon unquestioned dogma.

This kind of audience was to be found also in some of the Free Churches. Emmanuel Congregational Church had been noted as a centre of the best liberal theology early in the century. When Charles returned to Cambridge one of his valued friends, H. C. Carter, was its minister and although at that time it was comparatively rare for an Anglican to be found in a Free Church pulpit, Charles became a not infrequent preacher at Emmanuel Church. Similarly his relations with St. Columba's Presbyterian Church were of the happiest and he had no hesitation in offering his own services at a time when the charge was vacant and when there might have been difficulties about a regular pulpit supply. He had a profound regard for the brilliant group of scholars who were Professors at Westminster College (Presbyterian)— John Oman, Anderson Scott, Carnegie Simpson and later W. A. L. Elmslie and Herbert Farmer—while T. R. Glover the Baptist, noted classical scholar and public orator, author of best selling books on the Jesus of history and the life of prayer, was a man after his own heart. Charles refused to be circumscribed by any restrictive Anglican formalities. Fellowship in the Spirit he sensed immediately and he was ready —perhaps too ready—to ignore denominational differences so long as co-operation in the advancement of the Kingdom could be achieved.

With the two Anglican theological Colleges Charles enjoyed consistently good relationships throughout his period as Regius Professor. The Principal of Ridley Hall, Paul Gibson, was a leader amongst Liberal Evangelicals and an enthusiast for the missionary work of the Church; Charles become a member of the Council of the Hall, often preached in Chapel and at a later time conducted memorable Quiet Days for the students in the Long Vacation terms. All would go out to some rural setting and there in the Parish Church or walking in the surrounding countryside Charles would speak about the matters nearest to his heart —the life of the Spirit as manifested in the personality of Jesus, in the fellowship of believers and in the patterned continuities of the natural order. These days left an abiding impression upon successive generations of men trained at Ridley for the ministry of the Church.

By virtue of his office as Regius Professor, Charles automatically became Chairman of the Governing Body of Westcott House and this brought him into immediate touch with one of the most successful and most revered of all Anglican Principals of this century—Canon B. K. Cunningham. Each was a man of sharply independent mind but they worked together in complete harmony. Charles was never one to interfere. He was always happy to be consulted or to give assistance but never tried to dominate either in Committee or in the spheres of other men's responsibilities.

Perhaps his closest friendship, however, was with Kenneth Carey who was Principal of the House for fourteen years until he became Bishop of Edinburgh in 1961.

He has written:

"I have very good reason to remember Charles Raven with immense gratitude. He was very largely responsible for my appointment as Principal of Westcott House. There were various powerful members of the Westcott House Council at the time who, naturally enough, were very keen to get a scholar as Principal. Two or three people were in fact offered the job, but for various reasons had to turn it down and it then seemed to Charles Raven and one of the others that they had better settle for me. Sometime afterwards I read the Minutes of the Meeting and I know with what enormous patience and wisdom Charles guided the discussion. I did not know him at all well at the time, but from the moment of my appointment he gave me unswerving loyalty and the most delightful friendship until the end of his life. I tell you all this because I think there are some people who thought that Charles was an intellectual snob. Obviously, with his great brain, he had great respect for people with brains, but never at any time did he make me feel inferior or, as he might well have done, cast any doubts on my ability to be Principal of Westcott House at a very difficult time. I think this complete lack of intellectual snobbery was partly due to his great devotion to B. K. Cunningham.

With characteristic exaggeration, he was once heard to say: If I had a son who was going to be ordained I would rather send him to B. K. in his dotage than to any other Principal that I know of."

Other religious organisations in Cambridge to which Charles was always ready to give assistance and support were the varying mission-ary—oriented groups, those with some specific social concern, and above all the Student Christian Movement. Though, as we shall see later, he experienced one of his most bitter disappointments when in the mid-thirties he began to realise that his hold on the student mind generally was weakening, the S.C.M. in Cambridge (and particularly in Christ's) always regarded him as friend and counsellor and one who could enter with sympathy and insight into the problems which perplexed those with Christian ideals during the period preceding and following the Second World War.

Charles had found it desperately hard to make the break from Liver-pool. Certain features of his new way of life he found exceedingly irksome. But Cambridge was familiar to him and there were many old friends ready to welcome him back. His early impressions are well summarised in a letter written towards the end of his first term to Ethel Moors in Boston.

"The term has gone *very* well—far better than I dared to hope. My lectures have drawn and kept a big crowd—bigger I believe than any since Lightfoot's time—and there have been lots of opportunities for work in the Colleges. People have been quite amazingly generous: so far I've really not had an unfriendly word and as I get established there are going to be big opportunities. I'm sending a copy of my Inaugural Lecture—the big formal discourse that a new professor delivers and in which he has the chance of laying down the lines on which he proposes to work. I had to speak cautiously; for my success will depend upon holding people together at the start, and any sensationalism would have been fatal. But I think you'll see that I put internationalism, fellowship, and drastic reform in the front of my task. I had a huge crowd for its delivery.

So Charles was in good heart as he looked towards the future. But that future must inevitably now be concerned with a more academic approach to theology and with the duties of one of the leading professorships in the University. What in 1932 was the state of theology in the Western world? What particular contribution would Charles make to this discipline? His primary responsibility from now on was to lecture regularly on some aspects of theology and to promote the study of the subject in the University. How would he go about his task? What were some of the problems which he would soon encounter?

NOTES TO CHAPTER ELEVEN

1. p. 187: It is now occupied partly by a Housemaster of the Kings School and partly by boys under his care.

2. p. 190: There is no evidence that Milton actually planted it but it certainly dates from his period. "In the famous garden of Christ's three hundred mulberry trees were planted in 1608 because James 1st. wanted to encourage silkworm production. One of these trees is linked with the memory of Milton. Christ's also had seventeenth century archery butts, elms, limes, walls, alcoves, bowling green, tennis court, and summer house, 'beyond which is a cold bath, surrounded by a little Wilderness.' This pond, repaired in 1673, was one of Cambridge's few permitted swimming pools." Michael Grant. *Cambridge*, p. 106.

CHAPTER TWELVE

Towards a Coherent Theology

For a period of ten years Charles had been grasping the many opportunities offerred him in pulpits and conference centres all over the country to proclaim in vivid and untechnical language the Christian Gospel as it had come to be understood through the labours of Biblical scholars and church historians. He was renowned as preacher, writer and evangelist. In a sense both the United Kingdom and the United States had become his parish. He had wrestled with the problems of his time with the aid of the Christian revelation and his testimony had normally been received with acclaim.

But to be a University Professor in Cambridge was a very different matter. Perhaps John Gross is too sardonic when he describes the academic mind as "cautious, tightly organised, fault-finding, competitive and above all inordinately aware of other academic minds,"[1] but his words sufficiently indicate the contrast that Charles was to find in his new situation. It is true that his earlier academic record was impeccable and his book *Apollinarianism* was regarded as conforming to the best standards of traditional Cambridge scholarship. But what had he produced since? *The Creator Spirit* had wandered into what were then strange fields for a theologian to explore. Then just a year before his move to Cambridge a second substantial book had appeared—*Jesus and the Gospel of Love*. This, like *The Creator Spirit*, had been much concerned with the methods and categories of biology and psychology though it had also engaged in critical and historical investigations in order to demonstrate that the New Testament witness to the nature of Jesus's personality could be accepted wholeheartedly by anyone seeking to interpret his faith in terms of the modern scientific outlook. But the honoured names in Cambridge were those of men who had been *specialists* in some particular branch of Biblical study. What would be the programme of the new Professor who had striven for wholeness rather than for limited specialisation, for inter-disciplinary activities rather than for the careful observance of demarcation barriers between the various Faculties?

Some indication of the dangers lying ahead may be gathered from a letter written by a former Cambridge "character" after the news of Charles's appointment had been made public. F. J. Foakes-Jackson, still famous for his books on the history of early Christianity, had left Cambridge in 1916 to join the Faculty of the Union Theological Seminary in New York. But he remained very much a Cambridge man and was highly critical of many aspects of theological scholarship in the United States. In particular he abhorred what he called "slush" subjects, what in more respectful terms today would be called "inter-disciplinary activities." In a letter to an old friend in Cambridge he saw fit to comment on Raven's appointment in these caustic terms:

"If he has his way Cambridge will follow America. Men will cease studying, in order to promote disorder. The true way of education is to do one subject well (as Raven himself had done) and then to learn others through the experience of life," and concluded, "I have every hope he may become a Bishop and so have a larger sphere to play the fool in."

Another more serious indication of the suspicion felt by those occupying positions of theological leadership towards the "popularising" activities in which for some years Charles had indulged, may be found in the almost complete ignoring of *Jesus and the Gospel of Love* by the recognised scholarly journals. The Church weeklies reviewed it; the *Expository Times*, a monthly which mediated significant theological developments to the preacher, commented on it with enthusiasm; the more learned journals made no mention of it at all. Yet in some ways this book, more than any other which he wrote, expressed Charles's deepest understanding of and commitment to the Christian Faith. It could be called his *Apologia Pro Vita Sua* (he explicitily speaks of it as a work of Christian Apologetics) or a statement of his total philosophy of life. Yet when he began his work at Cambridge he knew that it had been dismissed as possessing no special significance for the student of academic theology.

Today this neglect seems extraordinary. The book shows an acquaintance with an amazing range of literature (the *Expository Times* wonders how amongst his many other activities he could possibly have found time to read so widely); it devotes its first major part to as balanced a discussion of the nature of *religious experience* as could have been available at that time; and in the central section the examination of the Christology of the New Testament is fresh, well-informed and designed to present a particular thesis which at least deserved a hearing within the contemporary debate. The last section may have tried to cover too wide an expanse of history in too limited a space but the final chapter which outlines a Christology for the twentieth century was certainly worthy of respectful attention.

Charles called *Jesus and the Gospel of Love* his "big book." It gathered up into an orderly, objective presentation the convictions about which he had written more subjectively and personally in *A Wanderer's Way*. In his autobiography he had tried to vindicate the reality of religious experience—but this subject needed to be treated in much greater detail; he had given his individual testimony to the centrality of the Christ—but this needed to be compared with the total witness of the New Testament writers; he had criticised certain aspects of the Christian tradition—this needed to be supported by reference to specific historical records. So the book sets forth a comprehensive defence of theological liberalism as held in England around 1930–31. It operates within an evolutionary framework, it accepts the theories then in vogue of the psychological development of the individual, it regards personality as the highest category imaginable and the attainment of personal maturity in the pattern manifested in the historic Jesus, as the *summum bonum* of human life. The goal of the universal process is the creation of a new order: sons of God who bear the likeness of the perfect Son, Jesus, Who is God for us.

Jesus and the Gospel of Love was published in September 1931. In

May of the same year a book which was destined more than any other to confirm Charles in the convictions expressed in his own volume had been completed. This was *The Natural and the Supernatural* by John Oman, the distinguished Principal of Westminster College, Cambridge. At the end of January 1932 Charles preached a notable University Sermon at Cambridge on The Kingdom of God in which he dealt with the question of transcendence and immanence and referred with enthusiasm to Oman's book. In his inaugural lecture in November he referred to it as a "contribution of outstanding and permanent importance." And to successive generations of students attending his lectures designed to introduce them to the study of theology, his counsel was to "sell their beds" and buy Dr. Oman's book. It is true that he had one reservation—he did not feel that the author did "full justice to the significance of a thorough going belief in evolution, to the organic connection between the natural and the supernatural, and to the sacramental character of the Universe." But it is fair to say that if there was one philosophy of religion, one philosophic framework which Charles was henceforward to make peculiarly his own, it was Oman's interpretation of the natural and the supernatural. Charles had the greater knowledge of scientific method and of the history and development of the biological sciences. Oman, an immensely learned man, had the greater knowledge of the history of philosophy, of German thought and of other world religions. Though the two men never became close friends (Oman died in 1936) Oman's successor in the Chair at Westminster College, Herbert H. Farmer, became Charles's associate in the teaching of theology and although in some matters they diverged, particularly on the question of pacifism, they shared a common devotion to Oman's memory and an abiding admiration for his work. Charles was essentially the natural historian and theologian of nature, Farmer the philosopher and theologian of personal relationships. Each, however, drew deeply upon the well of wisdom which Oman had supplied in his remarkable books.

An inaugural lecture is an event of exceptional significance in the life of any scholar. He normally tries to look at the present state of affairs in his own discipline and to give some indication of the direction in which he proposes to move in his own work. For Charles the occasion was perhaps even more demanding than for most. He had been away from academic life for twelve years. He was returning to the place where he had, as it were, grown up intellectually. Some of his former teachers would be present in the audience. There was a feeling of crisis abroad, in the political, economic, and to some extent in the intellectual worlds. There was the chance for the new Professor to make some kind of prophetic pronouncement. Such an occasion, though an ordeal, stimulated Charles in the way that a first night affects a great actor. His was to be no mere reading of a tidy manifesto. He would bring his pulpit and stage gifts into the service of his theological vision. He spoke without reference to notes. He paused dramatically for words which were already in the printed script. In fact the readers of this script "*Signs of the Times: Some reflections upon the scope and opportunity of Theology*" could find no discrepancy of any kind between the spoken and the printed word.

The pattern of the lecture was one which Charles often employed very effectively. First an analysis of the criticisms being currently levelled against theology; secondly at attempt to appraise these criticisms and to discover the inchoate needs and desires which they represented; thirdly a demonstration that in fact the Christian faith supplies the complete satisfaction of these needs; all that is required is that the leaders of the theological thought shall be quick to relate their heritage of traditional belief to the modern mind.

First the criticisms. Though professing to deal with ultimate reality, theology had been all too ready to take refuge in a supernatural region whose structures had little relation to the natural world of everyday experience; its concentration upon Biblical criticism and details of ecclesiastical order had prevented it from bearing a steady witness to Christ Himself and His gospel; its testimony to the secret sources of power which enabled man to live his life abundantly had been too often nullified by the obvious impotence characterising so much of the life of the Church.

Secondly, he claimed that as a result of his experience out in the wider world he had become aware of three noble and simple aspirations finding increasingly clamant expression. They were (a) The need for *unity*—a unity which could be achieved only partially through political changes, only partially through educational developments, but completely and finally through a common religion. (b) The need for a re-assertion of the worth of *personality* and of personal relationships, both in the sphere of commerce and industry and the realm of thought. (C) The need for *power* to transform desires into attainments, dreams into reality, hopes into fulfilment.

These, Charles said, were signs of the times. But what could be more significant than that they corresponded exactly to the age-long affirmations of the Christian Gospel, though negatively instead of positively. For were not the central tenets of this Gospel: "One God, the Father, in whom we live and move and have our being; one Lord Jesus Christ, Son of Man and Son of God, unique image of deity, supreme and effective symbol of the eternal; one Holy Spirit, Lord and life—giver, inspirer of the individual, creator of the fellowship"? Thus man's present quest, sometimes wistful, sometimes clamant, is for nothing other than that which the Christian evangelist seeks to proclaim and the Christian theologian to formulate.

If now the theologian is to perform his task adequately and relevantly he must relate himself to this threefold quest. First he must seek to construct a "coherent and synthetic system which shall do justice at once to our best knowledge of the natural world and to the highest experiences of religion." Secondly it is time to build upon the foundations laid by two generations of Biblical scholars who have studied history and analysed source materials; on this basis it is now possible to begin building the super-structure, interpreting the significance of the teaching and the person of Jesus Christ and above all displaying the true nature and highest possibilities of human personality in the light of the Incarnation of the Son of Man. Thirdly the time is over ripe for a new unfolding of the doctrine of the Spirit by the aid of our new knowledge of the history and psychology of religious experience. This could be expressed in a deeper concern for the spiritual life and the social activities of all who are engaged in the study of theology in the University.

The lecture ended on a more evangelical note than was common in this kind of academic exercise:

"If theology has for its function the intellectual aspect of religion, that function can only be fulfilled when the other elements of the personality are equally consecrated. If we are to teach the knowledge of God, it will be from an experience of His love revealed in Christ and in a life of ordered and active obedience. 'The acknowledgement of God in Christ' is our starting point; we ought to be able to validate the poet's words and so plan our teaching as to indicate that this acknowledgement

'Accepted by thy reason, solves for thee
All problems in the earth and out of it,
And has so far advanced thee to be wise.' "

So, with ringing assurance, the new Regius Professor launched out on his career in the Cambridge which he loved, the centre of advanced scientific research, the home of the best kind of liberal thought, to proclaim a theology appropriate to the new scientific age. He could play a part in the promotion of critical historical studies for which the Cambridge Divinity Faculty had become justly famous. The New Reformation for which he had lived and worked since the end of the War might still become a reality with theologians and scientists pooling their resources in the common cause.

But Cambridge itself was not exempt from tensions. Differences of opinion are natural and healthy in any University community but so far as Theology was concerned an issue was emerging which was to prove far more serious than any ordinary difference of opinion. How far Charles was aware of this before he took up his new appointment is uncertain. Probably he knew that his old teacher, Professor Bethune-Baker, had at times been the object of quite severe criticism but in any case he was a robust controversialist who was ready to defend himself against all attacks. What Charles was unlikely to have foreseen was that the Barthian influence, which he regarded as a growing menace, would establish its first major foothold on English soil through the

agency of a respected member of the Cambridge Faculty, now to be
one of his colleagues. In October 1932 Barth gave final approval to the
translation of his *Commentary on the Epistle to the Romans* which was to
appear in England in a sumptuous edition in 1933. The translator who
had performed this enormously difficult and demanding task was none
other than Sir Edwyn Hoskyns, Fellow of Corpus Christi College in
the University of Cambridge.

Students in any University are not slow to set up one teacher against
another. A battle of words can be great fun especially if some heat is
engendered. Not surprisingly, therefore, the story has gained wide
circulation that Charles and Hoskyns were at daggers drawn and that
the great theological debate at Cambridge in the Thirties was between
these two men. What seems true in retrospect is that the most important
theological issue at stake in that period can in fact be focussed by comparing their respective writings. What is not true is that there was any
sharp acrimony or public recrimination between the two. One of the
finest tributes to Hoskyns when he died at a comparatively early age in
1937 was that contributed to *The Times* by Charles himself. But the
conflict between the devotees of particular teachers is often far more
intense than that between their heroes themselves.

The debate, however, is of great importance as one tries to understand the sense of frustration that Charles increasingly felt as he tried to
give theological leadership in Cambridge during the years 1932–39.
His sermons and addresses to undergraduates who had no particular
training in theology and were often working in other disciplines were
exceedingly effective. Those who had recently come from school and
were bewildered by the many cross currents of thought in the University; those who were aware of the challenge of scientific methods and
discoveries to traditional forms of knowledge; those who had first
read some other subject and then hoped to find out how theology was
related to its concerns—all these heard Charles gladly.[2] But some of his
listeners, especially theological students, were unsatisfied. They did not
detect in his lectures any grappling at depth with the total Biblical
revelation; they did not hear the message of the Bible being related to
the alarming social issues which were demanding attention in the 1930s.

Hoskyns had studied in Germany; he still kept in close touch with friends who were beginning to feel the pressure of the rise of National Socialism; his approach to theology was almost dramatically opposed to that which had hitherto been taken for granted in Cambridge. His was a new voice. Charles, though absent from Cambridge for some twelve years, had returned to follow in the footsteps of his predecessors, hoping to advance and extend their work. Hoskyns, in contrast, tried to focus attention on startling new events in history rather than upon the slow evolutionary process of the universe. To those trained in history and languages, social problems and structures, Hoskyns's was the voice that they wanted to hear.

Some indication of the new approach to theology which was beginning at the time to find expression in England may be obtained by referring to a book which appeared in 1930 and to which Hoskyns made a major contribution. This was entitled *Mysterium Christi* and at first sight might have appeared to be entirely in line with that which had been Charles's major concern since the writing of his first book in 1916: "the elucidation of the greatest question which has been offered to the consideration of Christendom—'What think ye of Christ?'" (From the Preface). Cambridge was well represented amongst the contributors and Hoskyns occupied a leading role in grappling with the theme, Jesus the Messiah.

But the whole tenor of the book is different from the harmonious synthesis which had for so long been the object of Charles's search and indeed that of many other Cambridge scholars. The book had in fact come to birth as one outcome of the Stockholm Conference in 1925 which had focussed attention upon the great subject "the nature of the Kingdom of God and its relation to human society". A group of scholars, some English, some German, met subsequently for consultation and ultimately their labours found expression in this volume of essays. It is in many respects a disjointed and unco-ordinated collection in the editing of which little attempt was made to weave the parts into a unified pattern. Yet there is a recognisable unity of concern, an impressive consensus of faith in the living Christ whatever may be the difficulties of historical reconstruction, a common confidence that the

Church, if faithful to its Lord, will share His victory over the world.

But there is virtually no reference to modern science, no discussion of psychological problems, little attention to man's experience of the natural order—themes which had been at the centre of Charles's concern. Instead the unifying themes are revelation, history, atonement, eschatology. The Bible—not simply the New Testament—is the supreme witness to revelation; the task of the scholar is defined as learning the language of the Bible, listening to its words as they declare the activity of the living God, translating those words into terms which challenge man in his actual situation in the world of today.

The contrast may be sharpened by stating quite simply that whereas Charles's theological interests had been aroused as he became aware of the wonder of *the world*, most of the contributors to *Mysterium Christi* had begun, and sustained their theological concern, by responding to the wonder of cetain *words* and of the events to which the words bore witness. Charles was convinced that the world of his experience was God's world and that his task was to declare theologically—and that meant Christo-centrically—the detailed nature of that world. Hoskyns, a typical representative of the *Mysterium Christi* group, was convinced that *words* bore witness to crucial events in human history and that a particular collection of words, the Bible, testified to the central event through which all other events gain their true meaning. To observe, to record, to compare—these activities were as natural to Charles as eating and drinking. To wrestle with words, to relate words to events, to learn through words the meaning of events—these were the activities which commanded Hoskyns's energies unceasingly. Not that Charles was indifferent to language: language, naming in particular, was essential for the communication of his vision. And not that Hoskyns was indifferent to the world around him—he had for example an enthusiastic interest in rowing and farming: but his aim was to identify critical concerns in the life of humanity so that the words of one language might be translated and interpreted into those of another culture.

So in Cambridge, from 1932 until 1937 when Hoskyns died in the fulness of his powers, there was a remarkable polarisation of theological teaching between Charles at Christ's and Hoskyns at Corpus. They were almost exact contemporaries and their careers had been in many ways similar. One at school at Uppingham, the other at Haileybury; one at Caius, Cambridge, the other at Jesus; one gaining familiarity with the industrial north in 1908 in Liverpool, the other in the same year in Sunderland; each becoming a Chaplain in the First World War and winning recognition for distinguished service; one elected Dean of Emmanuel, the other Dean of Corpus. But in at least three respects they were poles apart. One had spent his earliest years in the relatively pleasant surroundings of the West End of London, in a family where the father had little regard for the Church and the mother a deep interest in the world of nature; the other had grown up in the grim surroundings of the East End of London where his father was a devoted parish priest and where the church was the one oasis in the midst of a social desert. Secondly, one had declined the offer of a period of study in Germany whereas the other had accepted and been deeply influenced by it; Charles had no bonds of friendship with German scholars whereas Hoskyns came to possess an unusual mastery of the language and music of Germany and counted some of its leading scholars amongst his intimate friends. And thirdly whereas, in the way that I have suggested, Charles, having gained vivid impressions through what he saw with his eyes, then proceeded to express them in appropriate language-forms, Hoskyns came to his ideas through the medium of words, words which he wrestled with, experimented with, played with; words which in certain contexts appeared to him disturbed, deflected, bent out of the straight but through which he tried to bear witness to the world of ultimate reality.

In summary Charles built up a system of theology in terms of his experience of *the world* in which he had found personality to be the highest category imaginable and in which he believed Jesus with his Gospel of Love to be the highest expression conceivable of the grandeur of the human person. Hoskyns, on the other hand, built up his theology in terms of his experience of *the church*, the community in which he had found the noblest manifestation of sacrifical love and whose pattern of life, he believed, had received its crucial and definitive symbolisation in the career of Jesus the Messiah. Charles came to Christ and the

Church through his experience of the world of nature and of individual persons; Hoskyns came to the world and its needs through his experience of the Church and the Christ in the Church. Each man exercised a powerful ministry in the Cambridge of the Thirties. Inevitably the two theologians were compared and contrasted and sides were taken. Disciples on one side or the other tended to glory in his Paul or his Apollos. But so far as the personal relations between the two men was concerned there was no open antagonism. Charles could not fail to associate Hoskyns with Barth; Hoskyns could not fail to associate Charles with Bethune-Baker. But each, I think, respected the other while seeking, to the best of his ability, to set forth in his own way the truth as he saw it in Jesus.

NOTES TO CHAPTER TWELVE

1. p. 199: *The Rise and Fall of the Man of Letters*, p. 297 f.
2. p. 206: C. A. Coulson, Professor, first of Mathematics, then of Theoretical Chemistry at Oxford, affirmed that when he was a student at Cambridge and the tension between his personal faith and his newly acquired scientific knowledge became acute, Charles was one of the three leaders of thought in the University (the others were a physicist and a mathematician) who helped him to retain his faith.

For Hoskyns cf W.O. Chadwick, Michael Ramsey, pp. 27-30.

CHAPTER THIRTEEN

The Consistent Pacifist

Why did Charles become a pacifist? Why did a man who had served with distinction in the trenches of Flanders and who never ceased to look back upon his war-time associations with fighting soldiers as amongst the most formative and inspiring of his life, come to the conclusion that any participation in war was unworthy of a Christian man? Why did he hold to this conviction through thick and thin, when many of those he most admired abandoned the way of pacifism while some whom he least admired attached themselves to pacifist organisations? How could he maintain his position without qualification during the darkest period of the Second World War when it seemed that the country which he loved was about to be overwhelmed by the nation to which he had for long felt so strong an antipathy?

There are no obvious answers to these questions. That he committed himself irrevocably in 1930, that he never wavered in his advocacy of pacifism as the only way which could bring about a radical change in human affairs—these facts are clear enough. He was never a fanatic in the sense of being a man who tried to force his views upon the consciousness of others at all times and in all seasons. Those who listened to him during the Second World War testify that he rarely if ever used the privilege of the pulpit to propagate his own distinctive pacifist message. Some have called him a "militant pacifist" but in fact there was no concern or interest which Charles took up which he did not pursue with enthusiasm mixed with occasional militancy! What is hardly open to question is that no leader of the pacifist cause in the period between 1930 and 1950 was more convinced that his crusade was inspired and directed by *theological* principles and by hard *reasoning* rather than by flabby sentiment or transient emotion. He was willing to admit that Christians might differ in their interpretation of what the way of Jesus implied. For himself the way of Jesus meant the way of the Cross and in the twentieth century world that for Charles meant the way of pacifism.

Numerous organisations whose general aim was to promote this way of life were active in the 1930s. The one to which Charles attached himself most devotedly and of which he was to become an acknowledged leader was the Fellowship of Reconciliation. In the 1920s his hope had been for a new reformation through a wide-spread spiritual renewal; in the 1930s the hope became directed towards a more limited objective—the achievement of reconciliation between races, classes and sexes. To this end it seemed essential to deal first with the major threat to all forms of reconciliation—namely the resort to war. He became convinced that unless war in its twentieth century form could be renounced or eliminated or nullified entirely no substantial progress towards reconciliation in its widest sense could possibly be made. So in 1930 he joined the F.O.R., in 1932 he became its Chairman, and from 1945 until his death he was its honoured President.

The F.O.R. came into formal existence at the beginning of 1915. Henry Hodgkin, the distinguished Quaker, called together a group of interested people to meet in Cambridge at the end of 1914 to consider the attitude of Christians to war. As a result of their consultations the name Fellowship of Reconciliation was adopted and five guiding principles were formulated to express the aims of the new movement. These affirmed that love as revealed in Jesus Christ is the only power by which evil can be overcome, that in order to establish a world order based on love those who believe in its power must accept and live by this conviction fully, that therefore they must not wage war but rather seek for the enthronement of love in personal, social, commercial and national life.

Amongst the early leaders of the Fellowship were George Lansbury, the Labour politician, and W. E. Orchard of King's Weigh House, together with Maude Royden and Lucy Gardner who was to be so closely associated with Charles in the organisation of Copec. Though its numbers remained small during the First World War interest in its aims spread to Holland and America and in 1919 the International Fellowship of Reconciliation came into being, an overall organisation of which the national Fellowships were constituent parts. All were agreed in refusing to participate in any war and in working for the realisation of the unity of the human family through love. It is significant that in the American Fellowship a leading member, who came to occupy a position on the Executive, was Mrs. Ethel Moors. And some time during the 1920s Reinhold Niebuhr joined the Fellowship, only to leave it at the end of 1933 when he became more fully aware of what was happening amongst the nations of central Europe. As early as 1927 Niebuhr had been critical of *absolute* pacifism but felt that some kind of pragmatic pacifism was viable. However this policy also seemed ultimately unworkable and he therefore resigned from the Fellowship. Henceforward he and Charles, though united in many common concerns, were to advocate very different policies for dealing with the world's evils.

Charles had been faced with the fearful question of participation in War in August 1914. He was never a man for half-measures and though already in Orders, felt it his duty either to enlist with others of his contemporaries or to take the consequences of being a complete conscientious objector. Four times he tried to enlist but on each occasion was rejected on medical grounds. At length, as we have seen, he accepted what he had regarded as a half-privileged position—that of a Chaplain—and thereby experienced many of the horrors of war at first-hand. These experiences obviously left a permanent scar but in the years immediately following the Armistice the question of ever again being called to participate in war did not seriously arise. Had it not been the war to end wars? The nations were too exhausted to plan another. Yet at Copec the subject was given a place on the agenda and in the final Report it was affirmed that "all war is contrary to the spirit and teaching of Jesus Christ." Was it not enough to leave the matter there, with the reasonable assurance that it would not again become a serious issue within the foreseeable future?

Ten years afterwards Charles declared that so far as his own convictions were concerned he had come to the conclusion as early as 1924 that the abolition of war was in fact the supreme issue of the time. The majority view of the Conference had been that housing and slum clearance constituted the most pressing social problems. But Charles's own view, as he confessed later, was that only the cause of peace was large enough, far-reaching enough, to be a worthy consequence of all the work and discussion that Copec had entailed. Of course education, health, unemployment, sex relations, missions were important but behind them all and threatening them all was the possibility of another war. Peace, he felt, was the *universal* issue. To focus attention upon this one over-arching moral problem was, he believed, the clear responsibility of the Christian Church.

But what immediate steps could be taken? For a while all his energies were directed towards the spiritual renewal of Christians and towards a theology which would do justice to the discoveries of modern science. By 1928, however, a change was beginning to appear in the general atmosphere of public life. There was a feeling of unease about Versailles and reparations; a recalling of the horrors of the Western Front in fiction and historical writing; a lessening confidence that those kinds of things could not happen again. By the time the Lambeth Conference met in 1930 war had become a live issue on which the Bishops felt bound to make some pronouncement. They affirmed in brief "that war as a method of settling international disputes is incompatible with the teaching and example of our Lord Jesus Christ." So from 1930 onwards the world moved steadily towards a division into three camps—those who seized every opportunity to advance their own ambitions by force of arms, those who used every means of diplomatic manoeuvre short of war to counter these ambitions and those who sought through some form of pacifism to influence the present and to prepare a programme for the future if the nations of the world should ever again become involved in a major war. To this third camp Charles committed himself in 1930 and soon came to be recognised as one of its outstanding leaders.

1933 was in many respects the crisis year. On January 30th, Hitler became Chancellor of the Reich. On February 9th, the motion for debate at the Oxford Union "That this House will in no circumstances fight for its King and Country" was carried by 275 votes to 153. In March the Baptist Union of Wales requested that a clear lead should be given within the whole denomination against future participation in war. At the Methodist Conference in July Henry Carter, an important figure within the Church's Secretariat, proclaimed his dedication to complete pacifism and his lead was followed by some six hundred ministers within the Methodist Peace Fellowship. In October, while the Disarmament Conference resumed its discussions, Hitler withdrew from the Conference table and thereby made clear that Germany would in no way be bound by considerations of collective security.

It was against this general background that Charles seized the opportunity, offered him by his election to the Sir Halley Stewart Lectureship, to deliver in 1934 a notable series which he entitled *Is War Obsolete?* Already, since the foundation of the lectureship in 1926, men of great distinction in public life had expressed their views on matters concerned with social, economic and international welfare—Sir Oliver Lodge, Gilbert Murray, R. H. Tawney, Wickham Steed. Now Charles was to address himself to the particular issue which he had increasingly come to feel overshadowed all others: how could a Christian reconcile the conflicting claims of religion and citizenship in the context of movements in the world which could so easily lead to war?

This was his first substantial contribution to pacifist literature[1] and it is probably his most impressive statement. It is balanced, well-argued, enlivened by personal memories, constructive in its presentation of alternatives to war. His later writings on the subject tended to repeat what he had stated better in this his first book and a note of petulance crept in because of the realisation that his views were being either resisted or ignored. But *Is War Obsolete?* is as good a defence of pacifism as could be fashioned in the light of *natural theology*. What it fails to take serious account of—and to this I shall return—is the witness of *social and historical theology*. And this was the real cause, it seems to me, of the disagreement between Charles and Reinhold Niebuhr. Charles was committed to a theology of evolutionary process and believed that this enabled him to make a universal judgment on the individual's relation to war. Niebuhr was engaged in working out a theology within the clash of warring social interests, of conflicting political pretensions, of rival economic policies. Wars between nations must be regarded as major outbreaks of deep-seated passions, brought to boiling point by oppression and injustice without, by greed and fear within. For Charles renunciation of war was for the individual the only way forward to a new order; for Niebuhr it could have no hope of dealing in any radical way with the ills of an immoral society.

In the book *Is War Obsolete?* Charles began by speaking frankly about his own searchings of conscience concerning peace and war ever since the conclusion of hostilities in 1918. In recent years these had become so tense that a decision for or against pacifism had to be made, one way or the other. On the one side he had felt highly uncomfortable when listening to certain forms of pacifist propaganda. For example, there was the recent book *Cry Havoc* by Mr. Beverley Nichols. "Believing as I do that his cause is right, eager as I am to see the world set ablaze for peace, there are far too many passages in his book which provoke in me a deep intuitive impulse to say with Mr. Yeats Brown, the mass of mankind, thank God, is not pacifist" (p. 40). On the other hand he had felt far more uncomfortable amongst the advocates of caution and compromise. "Better the nightmares of Mr. Nichols, better any sort of crazy pacifism, than "the wisdom of this world, earthly, sensual, devilish", than the caution which prides itself upon seeing both sides of a question and thinks that the function of a leader is to chair committees and see that they reach inoffensive results. "Go slow" may be a wise man's motto: it is exactly what the Pharisees must have said when Jesus appeared before the Sanhedrin" (41). And to show that he himself was not speaking out of ignorance of the real meaning of war he proceeded to give vivid examples of his experiences in the trenches at the time when gas was first used in modern warfare.

The full argument of the book is developed in five stages. First Charles spoke of the conflict of loyalties which is bound to be felt when any such issue arises. For himself, a determining factor had been the conviction that at a particular moment in history some supreme moral issue may present itself, calling men to critical decision and action. The example which sprang to mind and to which he often subsequently referred was that of Wilberforce and the abolition of slavery. In the first half of the nineteenth century the slave trade had revealed itself to be the most open and concentrated form of evil. Until this had been tackled by public protest and absolute renunciation no real moral progress could be made in other departments of life. So, in regard to war, the day of the middle road had passed. The possibilities of modern destructiveness were so fearsome that full scale war could achieve nothing but harm to all concerned. To decide for the absolute negative was therefore, in Charles's view, the only policy for sane persons to adopt.

A second chapter dealing with the way an individual could seek guidance on this issue was of a more personal kind. But then in the third chapter he reached the crux of the matter. How could a Christian be true to his own conscience and at the same time fulfil his obligations to the State of which he wished to be a responsible citizen? Here for the first time he registered his disagreement with Reinhold Niebuhr whose writings were just beginning to be read in England. *Moral Man and Immoral Society* had been published in 1932 and Charles had become aware of the distinction which its author had made between the demands of the ethic of love upon the individual and the possibilities which are open to him in his social relationships. "Human collectives," Niebuhr had written, "are less moral than the individuals which compose them"—but this judgment Charles entirely refused to accept. It was not, he held, true to human nature. Collective renunciation of war was, he believed, as open a possibility as individual renunciation. It was the duty of the Christian therefore to make his own decision and then do everything in his power to persuade his fellow citizens to follow his example in what he regarded as morally right. Fundamentally Charles believed *that human nature collectively* possessed potentialities for right corporate action which could be brought to fulfilment by means of example and persuasion. Niebuhr was entirely sceptical about such a possibility. He was too well aware of conflicting interests and selfish desires in large scale groups, of rationalisations and slogans swaying group behaviour, to be able to accept the possibility of any mass-movement towards absolute righteousness. From 1934 onwards

Charles had gradually to come to terms with the fact that in circles
such as the Student Christian Movement, where his own influence had
been paramount, the voice from America was gaining increasing attention and the approach to social and international ethics which Niebuhr
advocated was finding increasing support.

Charles, however, could never entertain the thought that a Christian
was called upon to live in *two* worlds. Whether he was confronting
those who claimed that there was a clear cut division between the sacred
and the secular, the supernatural and the natural *or* those who defined
two separate realms of ethical responsibility, the individual and the
social, his answer was always the same: God is One, Truth is One;
God's activity in creation, redemption and inspiration is One; God's
purpose for mankind is One. Any kind of dualism, dialectic or even
polarity was, he believed, a blurring of the call to decision, an
obfuscation of truth. Therefore once an issue had reached a stage of
clarification where it was seen to be of *universal* significance, there was
no alternative, Charles felt, but to make a firm decision on one side or
the other.

The fourth chapter took up in a surprisingly open and even moderate
way the question of the use of force in situations other than that of
international conflict. Was corporal punishment justifiable in a family
or school situation? Was the existence of a police force defensible for
the protection of society? Could a case even be made for using weapons
of modern warfare when dealing with guerillas or bandits in remote
uncivilised areas? At this stage of his thinking—some will feel incon-
sistently—Charles was prepared to sanction the use of physical force in
each of these situations. What he would not countenance was resort to
the full panoply of war for the settling of disputes between nations or
groups of nations in the world of the twentieth century. This he was
convinced would bring about either mass murder or mass suicide.
He therefore judged it possible to sanction the use of physical force for
the maintenance of order within a local and limited situation; there was
no justification for using it on a mass scale when the survival of the
whole of civilised society would be thereby threatened.

The final chapter dealt with a theme which Charles was always eager to keep before his readers' and hearers' attention: what is the positive alternative to War? Aggressive and pugnacious tendencies cannot simply be repressed. They must be transformed, channelled into policies which will deal constructively with the enemies of co-operation and peace—ignorance, prejudice, inequality, injustices of all kinds. He advocated whole hearted support of the League of Nations Union and of all government efforts to preserve peace. He spoke of co-operation in moral uplift and education, of the work of evangelism and relief of suffering. But in point of fact the alternatives tend to be somewhat vague, general and ill-defined. He admits himself that "without concrete and limited objectives discipleship becomes vague, ineffective, senti-mental" (p.70) but this leads to a concentration on the negative act of renunciation rather than upon positive measures of social and economic reform. It is arguable that this was the fundamental weakness in Charles's whole approach to social ethics once he had fully embraced the pacifist cause.

Through the Halley Stewart Lecture Charles had cleared his own mind, worked out an impressive apologia on behalf of pacifism and at least indirectly issued a challenge to his fellow Christians to enlist in the same crusade. But it seemed unlikely that his book would reach a wide audience and meanwhile events were moving fast in the world outside Britain. If there was to be any mass response to the call for peace, something simple and more direct was needed than the careful scholar-ship of *Is War Obsolete*? This was in fact forthcoming almost immediate-ly through the voice of Canon H. R. L. (Dick) Sheppard who, through his personal magnetism and use of the radio from St. Martin in the Fields, had become more widely known than any other Church leader in England. It was he who in October 1934 employed every available means of publicity to invite those of his own sex to write the following words on a postcard and send it to him: "I renounce war and never again will I support or sanction another and I will do all in my power to persuade others to do the same." The response was over-whelming. The Peace Pledge Union was formed with Charles as one of its sponsors,[2] and by June 1936 more than 100,000 men had enrolled themselves as members.

Sheppard's initiative was followed in June 1935 by an enormous Peace Ballot organised by the supporters of the League of Nations. A nation-wide house to house canvas was carried out and as a result some eleven and a half million votes were registered in favour of Peace. This Peace Ballot, Ronald Blythe has said "marked the pinnacle of thirties pacifism and at the same time revealed the limitations of the League of Nations. This nation-wide knocking on doors and beating of breasts quite drowned the sounds from German dockyards where the Scharn-horst, Gneisenau, Bismarck and Tirpitz were being laid down."[3]

This was the pinnacle. In October, at Brighton, a dramatic check to pacifist progress was registered when at the Labour Party Conference Ernest Bevin mercilessly attacked George Lansbury, the Socialist apostle of peace, and thereby began to change Labour's attitude to war. And when in 1935 Italy flouted all the standards of the League and indeed of Western civilisation by her behaviour in Abyssinia, it became clear that the cause of peace would not be guaranteed merely by writing postcards and registering votes. So far as the country at large was concerned the responsibility rested in the hands of Parliament. But meanwhile an intense debate had begun to take place through pamph-lets, through the press, through public meetings, to determine what were the possibilities, maybe the limits, of the pacifist programme and it is not surprising that one of the most vigorous defenders of the absolute negative was Charles himself.

An early salvo—and one which Charles must have found specially galling to receive from a man whom he so greatly loved and admired—appeared in an article written by Archbishop Temple for the York Diocesan Leaflet. Large sections were quoted in *The Times* of October 29th, 1935. In commenting on the League's inability to prevent Italian aggression, Temple has asked whether it could even now take action and so give a lead to "the greatest political enterprise ever undertaken—the curbing of national sovereignty by the representatives of the common interests of mankind." But in an earlier context he had referred to extreme pacifism as *heretical* and this accusation he now felt bound to explain more fully. He had not intended to imply that an individual who holds such a view is a heretic—unless he becomes completely aggresive about it. But he believed that extreme pacifism was heretical *in tendency* and this for three reasons. It tended to regard the New Testament as completely superseding the Old as Marcion had done; it tended to regard the material as incapable of being completely subordinated to the spiritual as had been the case with the Manichees; and it tended to regard man as a creature who was capable of directing and governing his life by love alone, a view associated in history with the name of Pelagius. The law of love, Temple concluded, cannot be said to apply to nations "consisting in large measure of unconverted or very imperfectly converted citizens."

Charles was an expert on the history of early heresies and to find himself judged guilty, at least in tendency, on three counts must have come to him as something of a shock! Two days later *The Times* printed his reply.

"To comment fully upon Dr. Temple's explanation of his views upon pacifism and heresy would require more space than you could give.

In effect he withdraws the charge by admitting that "heretical" is a term only appropriate to doctrines formally condemned by the Church. But his last sentence cannot pass unchallenged. He writes 'The law of love . . . imperfectly converted citizens."

If this be true the Apostolic Church was wholly mistaken in its missionary methods: the enforcement of law should have preceded the preaching of the Gospel. For Christian nations or Christian Archbishops to proclaim that "the law of love is not applicable" is not only heretical in tendency but definitely an act of apostasy."

The charge of apostasy seems to have disturbed the Archbishop less than had been the case with Charles and heresy. In a speech reported on November 4th, he pointed out that if all the world were to become Christian, truly and whole-heartedly, there would be no more war. "But if while that process of conversion is incomplete the Christian calls nations to act by love only when justice is still insecure he is likely to receive immediate applause but to produce no actual result. Love of neighbour is very hard for individuals; for nations it is much harder. The virtue that can be effectively established is justice." In other words, for Temple the Kingdom of Love was the ultimate ideal; the establishment of justice the proximate possibility. Whereas Charles longed for the dramatic gesture which would in his view bring about a radically new mutation in human affairs by eliminating once for all its most obvious evil, Temple advocated a policy of patient weighing up of values, balancing of possibilities, judging the course which would achieve the maximum of good within any given situation.

In the spring of the following year (1936) Charles found himself in the news once again. *The Times* of March 19th reported that Professor Raven had said at a public meeting in Birmingham that it was almost certainly true that nine out of ten of the most virile young men at Cambridge University would go to prison rather than go into the Army. Those in authority, he continued, seemed to have no conception of the young people's deep conviction on the subject of war. They thought that peace-lovers were queer, cranky, disappointed and effeminate people. That was untrue. (Obviously Charles laid himself open to the challenge that he must produce evidence for his figures and a definition of the term "virile"). This assertion, though not gaining as much publicity as the motion of the Oxford Union in 1933, was not forgotten and aroused considerable resentment in Cambridge as the menace of war became ever more serious.

Possibly the Birmingham speech would have attracted even more attention had it not been that within less than a week Charles's old friends in Liverpool suddenly stole the limelight. There the Dean and Chapter made it known that they could not in conscience say prayers for a Government with whose policy on the Rhineland they so strongly disagreed. This really roused the politicians! Now it was the turn of Mr. Duff Cooper, the Secretary of State for War, to speak in Birmingham. "Who," he cried, "are those ignorant clergymen who presume to give His Majesty's Government advice on foreign affairs?" After affirming his own loyal allegiance to the Church of England he went on to say: "Really the attitude of some of these clerics who barge in on the political arena makes me feel some sympathy with Henry II who in a moment of haste expressed an opinion which led to an unexpected vacancy at

Canterbury." Warming further to his subject he declared that the most dangerous, insidious and fatal enemy of recruiting for the Army was the kind of sloppy, irrational, nonsensical pacifism which induced people who should know better to argue that because war was a bad thing men should not be soldiers.

This outburst was followed the next day by a weighty letter to *The Times* from the leaders of the Churches of Britain (apart from the Roman Catholic Church) giving general support to the Government policy of rearmament. But this drew a protest from Charles and other leaders of Christian pacifist groups. They claimed that the pacifist position, which repudiated war altogether, had not been included in this communication. Mr. Duff Cooper on his part returned to the attack by challenging the leaders of the Church to denounce pacifists publicly as heretics.

The debate took a new turn when, towards the end of April, Dick Sheppard wrote to *The Times* on behalf of pacifists and pointed out that the Lambeth Conference of 1930 had condemned war as a method of settling international disputes. Hensley Henson, the Bishop of Durham, replied in characteristic fashion that the Lambeth resolution had been "unfortunate": "at best it is a platitude and at worst it encourages a very formidable error."[4] He appealed to the doctrine of the just war (the Latin version of the thirty seventh Article of Religion, he pointed out, refers to *justa bella*). "Would any," he asked, "maintain that a Christian citizen ought to refuse to serve in a war waged by his country in defence of international good faith and elementary justice? Does Christianity require the desertion of the Abyssinians? Pacifism in the present state of the world seems to me little less than a sacrifice of Christian principle to humanitarian sentiment. It is not for nothing that the cross is the symbol of Christ's religion." So the extraordinary paradox emerged that whereas Charles on his side passionately appealed to the Cross as providing the final justification for Pacifism, the Bishop of Durham on his side was appealing to the Cross to justify armed intervention on behalf of the plundered Abyssinians.

The Times of April 29th, 1936 is of unusual interest in regard to the pacifist debate. The historian G. M. Young examines the phrase *justa bella administrare* and claims that a Roman would certainly have read it as meaning to serve in wars undertaken and conducted by the sovereign in authority. Hence the Article means: "A Christian man may not go filibustering on his own account but when he is called to take part in his sovereign's wars, *ex mandato magistratus*, he may serve with a clear conscience." In another letter, however, signed by Charles and Dick Sheppard, all appeals to medieval theory concerning just wars are dismissed as out of date and irrelevant. It is high time, they claim, to think clearly about war in the present. "Is it a just war if fought in defence of a status quo established by an unjust treaty? Or if fought to restrain other people from doing what we have ourselves created a vast empire by doing—unless we first show signs of repentance? Or if it employs thermite and mustard gas against a defenceless civil population? Or if it involves the mass-suggestion and organised lying of modern propaganda?"

These questions could, they allowed, be subjects for debate. But "the pacifist will not be greatly concerned with it. He will wish to ask questions of a more searching character such as are suggested in the Bishop of Durham's last sentence. What does the Cross symbolise? If ever there could have been a just war it would surely have been fought to overthrow Roman oppression in defence of the nation of Israel or fought by the disciples that their Master might not be delivered to the Jews. In both cases Christ's answer is clear and decisive. That answer was endorsed by the unanimous voice of the Church in the first three centuries when Christianity and war were declared to be incompatible. The Church could not now accept the fantastic thesis that pacifism is heresy without wholly repudiating its claim to continuity with centuries held in special honour. Let us examine the significance of the cross and see whether the Early Church or the age which followed Constantine has the truer interpretation of it. Some of us have tried to do so and whatever the ecclesiastical authorities decide, have come to a conclusion. We have seen war and its results and with every respect for those who differ from us we say 'No'."

Further letters from such well-known figures as Aldous Huxley, Edwyn Bevan and Quintin Hogg raised detailed points of interest but the

Charles in student days.

Charles and Bee with their first-born.

The Raven family
outside their Liverpool home.

Chaplain in the First World War.

Bird-watching.

Regius Professor in 1938.

Charles participating in the Foundation of the Dean and Chapter Ceremony at Liverpool Cathedral in 1931.

Charles with the Rev. T. B. (Tubby) Clayton on his left in a group of Royal Chaplains.

Charles with student-ushers after the wedding of Ian Ramsey. On his right is Eric Heaton, later to become Dean of Durham.

Christ's College: The Master's Lodge.

Chancellor (Field Marshal J. C. Smuts) and Vice-Chancellor.

The Queen Mother with the Vice-Chancellor on the day when she
received the Honorary Degree.

The 'Mission' to Moscow in 1953.

The return visit by the Russian delegation in 1954.

Charles with Ethel.

The Degree Ceremony in New Delhi.

Charles with Ninette.

In the garden at 10 Madingley Road.

chief issue had been defined by leaders such as Temple and Henson on the one side, Raven and Sheppard on the other. The two sides started from different premises and reached different conclusions. But Charles had now to address himself to one of the most important papers that he was ever asked to write. The Oxford Conference on Church, Community and State, drawing together leaders of Christian thought from all over the world, was due to meet in July 1937. Charles had been invited to contribute an essay to one of the preparatory volumes and this was to be entitled *The Religious Basis of Pacifism*.

In his earlier book *Is War Obsolete?* Charles had obviously been concerned to give a reasoned apologia for his own commitment to the pacifist position. But in his paper for the Oxford Conference he moved away from the directly personal and attempted to show that a full Trinitarian theology necessarily implied commitment to pacifism by the Church as a whole. Only so could the Church be faithful to the creative purpose of God, the redeeming ministry of Christ and the continuing work of the Holy Spirit. Though Charles returned again and again to the actual example of Christ as revealed in His earthly career which ended on a Cross, he was more and more anxious to demonstrate that this historical drama was the outward and visible manifestation of that which was central in the very life of God Himself.

A summary passage taken from the Oxford essay makes this aim quite explicit:

"Why then do we claim," he writes, "that pacifism is the inevitable corollary of our theological and religious convictions? Because for us pacifism is involved in

(a) our concept of God and of His mode of creative activity
(b) our understanding of Jesus and the method of His redemptive and atoning work
(c) our apprehension of the Holy Spirit and of the Koinonia established by Him.

Put less technically these involve:

(a) a belief that in the nature of God, and therefore, in His dealings with

H

man and in man's true way of life, love is always primary and
justice derivative

(b) that in the teaching and atoning work of Jesus it is plain not only
     that those who take the sword perish by the sword but that the
     sole redemptive activity is the power of the love that gives and
     suffers, that is of the Cross;

(c) that worship and fellowship, the love of God and the love of men,
     are inseparably united; that what is wrong for the individual
     cannot be right for the community, that the fruit of the Spirit is
     love, joy, peace—a way of living of which modern warfare is a
     flagrant denial, and that it is only as this way of life is realised that
     the ministry of the Church can become creative, regenerative and
     inspirational."

This is a beautifully ordered statement. It expresses as succinctly as is
to be found anywhere in his writings what had come to be his total
philosophy of life. Nature, history and experience woven into a threefold cord—God, the world, and mankind are integrated within the one
evolutionary process. The key-words creation, regeneration, inspiration
are played as musical variations on the one basic theme of Love. It was a
lofty ideal. But how would it appear to Christians from central
Europe where armies were already marching or to those of a
different theological tradition for whom love, power and justice could
not simply be arranged on levels of priority but were seen as constantly
interacting in a never ceasing dialectical struggle? In the opinion of
those present at the Conference the commission which was concerned
with international relations and in particular with peace and war
engaged in the most lively debates and became in many ways the
focus of the whole meeting. And although it seemed for a while that
nothing constructive would emerge from the discussions, the final
resolutions set forth, as clearly as was practically possible, three positions
which were held to be tenable within a full Christian witness. These
were the commitment to complete pacifism, a readiness to participate
in "just wars,"[5] and the willingness to obey the commands of the State
unless the citizen is absolutely certain that the war is wrong. The

delegates would not commit themselves to any one of these three positions as representing the only possible Christian attitude to war, but they insisted that their own perplexity was itself a clear indication of the sin in which the followers of Christ were themselves implicated.

Charles could hardly have been satisfied with the final statement but at least the case for Christian pacifism had been clearly presented and accorded a place of legitimacy in the final report. He had, perhaps partly through the stimulus of the occasion, attained a firm conviction that his own position was *theologically* "inevitable." Whatever he might *feel* by reason of his experiences in the First World War or as an outcome of his loyalty to his own country, he believed that he was bound to follow his *mind's* understanding of the purpose of God for the future destiny of mankind. If God's purpose of love was that all men should be brought together to live as sons within His family then no individual feelings or lesser loyalties must be allowed to stand in the way of its fulfilment. Charles was convinced that his own theological reinterpretation was true to the New Testament and to the earliest theology of the Church. In the first three centuries of the Christian era theology had declared war to be incompatible with a life of Christian discipleship. Why then should things be different today? It could only be that perversions of the Church's original theological outlook had led and was leading to aberrations in individual and social behaviour.

Meanwhile the various pacifist organisations were increasing their efforts as the situation on the Continent grew more menacing and as the movement towards re-armament gathered strength in Britain. At the Cambridge Union in February 1937, the motion was passed (100–76) "That this House will refuse to be recruited or conscripted for any other purpose than the defence of the collective peace system." Through the agency of the F.O.R. Embassies of Reconciliation were organised, the most famous of which was that which went forth like lambs amongst wolves in April 1937: Lansbury and Percy Bartlett and Corder Catchpool travelling to Berchtesgarten to engage in peace talks with Hitler himself. The campaign for peace achieved its most spectacular success when Dick Sheppard was elected to the Lord Rectorship of Glasgow University in 1937. But almost immediately thereafter his sudden death deprived the movement of its outstanding popular leader. The situation in Britain became increasingly complex, with opposition to war motivated by a quite heterogeneous assortment of drives—towards religious integrity, towards working-class solidarity, towards individual safety, towards Utopian possibility. It was not easy for Charles to give his own distinctive witness in the midst of such a welter of conflicting interests.

Yet through his Chairmanship of the F.O.R., through his writing and speaking, and through his engagement, when it seemed opportune, in acts of public demonstration or protest,[6] he undoubtedly established himself as the leading Christian intellectual in the whole peace movement. Vera Brittain summarised his contribution during the period between 1932 and 1942 in this way:

> "His main concerns were, first, to replace the negative war-resistance policies of such bodies as the War Resisters' International and the Peace Pledge Union with a positive emphasis on reconciliation. Secondly, he sought to unify the denominational Christian peace societies and to keep closely in contact with such bodies as the League of Nations Union, Federal Union, and the Society of Friends. One consequence was the creation of the Christian Pacifist Groups Committee and for him the membership of many different societies in association with Percy Bartlett (Quaker), Henry Carter (Methodist), George McLeod (Church of Scotland), and H. R. L. Sheppard (Church of England). Thirdly he endeavoured to formulate a more coherent and wide ranging theology of Christian pacifism by both special lectures and books such as *Is War Obsolete?* (1934), *War and the Christian* (1938), and *Is Christ Divided?* (1943)."[7]

In addition to the books mentioned by Vera Brittain, Charles wrote *The Cross and the Crisis* (a series of lectures given at the Summer Conference of the F.O.R. in August 1940) *Lessons of the Prince of Peace* (the Bishop of London's Lent Book for 1942) and *The Theological Basis of Christian Pacifism* (The first series of Robert Treat Paine Lectures given in Boston, New York and Chiago in 1950). It is not unfair, I think, to comment that none of these add any thing substantial to the historical and theological justification of the pacifist position which he had presented in *Is War Obsolete?* and in his Oxford paper on *The Religious Basis of Pacifism*. Even *War and the Christian*, written especially for students in the critical year 1938, and designed to set out clearly both the pacifist and the non-pacifist positions, does not go beyond *Is War Obsolete?* except perhaps in its sense of urgency. What seems almost incredible today is that Charles could have written as late as May 1938: 'Assuming the worst that can be said of Mussolini or Hitler, it remains true that an intelligent psychology will approach them fearlessly and without parade of arms, will strive to understand and discuss their grievances and ambitions and will meet their advances with generosity and 'sweet reasonableness" (p. 156). Yet he had been willing to allow that when dealing with, for example, unruly tribes on the North West Frontier of India force and even armed force might be the only possible method to employ.

As war seemed ever more likely, pacifist leaders became increasingly concerned about what the consequences would be for those whose consciences forbade them to fight. In May 1939 a letter appeared in *The Times* signed by Charles, Henry Carter, Percy Bartlett and Leyton Richards (Congregationalist) urging that if war came it would not be right for Parliament to introduce general conscription. "War", they wrote "with all its futility and wastage, is a fundamentally unchristian thing and the compulsory training of men to slaughter their fellow-men is to us intolerable." Once war had been declared, the urgent questions for Charles and his associates were whether they could take any steps towards bringing about a negotiated peace and whether they could begin to think out plans for a more just and equitable society after the War. Amongst non-pacifists, the man who shared their concerns most deeply was in all probability Dr. G. K. A. Bell, the Bishop of Chichester, and a meeting was soon arranged with him to consider a common strategy. But Bell had to keep in touch with his continental friends and few if any of these favoured pacifist policies. Hitler had become too demonic a figure. The war, they believed, had to be fought and although Christians of every country and on both sides of the conflict would maintain their sense of brotherhood in

Christ, still the gross evil of Nazi-ism must be crushed if there were to be any hope of a better world.

By June 1940 the people of Britain were facing the possibility of invasion and the outlook for pacifists was bleak indeed. On the one hand their fellow citizens were bound to question whether they were taking a full share in the national emergency; on the other hand, if the enemy should succeed in his ambition, their own profession might be subject to the ultimate test. A communication was sent out to leaders of the Council of Christian Pacifist Groups instructing them in veiled language how they were to keep contact with one another and how they were to rally their members in case of critical emergency. Friends' Meeting Houses were designated as centres of obvious identification for mutual support.

In the more limited circle of the Church of England a deputation of three—Archdeacon Hartill, the Rev. R. H. Le Mesurier and Canon Raven—representing 371 Priests and 2,571 communicant members of the Church, waited upon the Archbishops to raise with them certain matters concerning pacifism in the period of crisis. Was the State to be regarded as the final authority on moral issues? Could priests be enrolled as members of the Defence Corps in defiance of Canon Law? At what point must the Church refuse to support the war-effort if methods came to be used which were abhorrent to the Christian conscience? Must the subject of pacifism be barred from thinking and discussion amongst priests of the Church? The Archbishops gave firm but moderate replies, making it clear that they could not themselves embrace the pacifist faith but that they entirely recognised the right of individual pacifists to hold and expound their views within the Church of England. In the printed report the Deputation expressed its gratitude to the Archbishops for their "courtesy and understanding in the treatment of a rather obscure minority."

In July 1940 Charles was called upon to perform a very different kind of task. Early in the month Reuters reported that Mr. Gandhi had issued an appeal from New Delhi to every Briton to accept the method of non-violence instead of the method of war.

"I appeal for the cessation of hostilities, not because you are too exhausted to fight but because war is bad in essence. You want to kill Nazism. You will never kill it by its indifferent adoption. You will have to be more ruthless than the Nazis. I suggest that the cause that demands the inhumanities that are being perpetrated today cannot be called just. This is no appeal made by a man who does not know his business. I have been practising, with scientific precision, non-violence and its possibilities for an unbroken period of over fifty years. I have applied it in every walk of life—domestic, institutional, economic and political. I know no single case in which it has failed.

My non-violence demands universal love and you are no small part of it. It is that love which prompted my appeal to you. May God give power to every word of mine. In his name I began to write this and in his name I close it. May your statesmen have wisdom and courage to respond to my appeal."

Sympathisers in Britain were to some degree hampered in making response because of uncertainty about the precise wording of the appeal: telegraph agencies differed in their versions. However the Council of Christian Pacifist Groups decided that a reply must be sent and Charles was asked to prepare a revision of a preliminary draft. This he did in the following terms—though whether the letter was finally sent and whether it ever reached its destination seems to be uncertain.

Dear Mr. Gandhi,

Your very impressive appeal to all Britons to abandon here and now the way of war in favour of the more excellent way of non-violent non-co-operation, to which you have dedicated yourself, has only been published by a very few newspapers and in a very abbreviated and misleading form. We have just received through Reuters Agency and Miss Harrison a fuller version of it, and believe that this will be sent at least to our statesmen if not to the people in general.

It is a deep disappointment to us that your very moving and timely words, endorsed as they are by the evidence of your own long experience, should not have reached those to whom they were addressed. It is a still deeper disappointment that we should have to acknowledge the conviction that if the appeal had been properly published it would have met with little response. Non-violence, involving as it does great spiritual resources, not only of fortitude but of forgiving love and faith, demands a consecration and a discipline which we have not been ready to accept. To most Britons the call to throw down their arms in the moment of supreme peril and in face of triumphant aggression would seem mere cowardice and treason—an invitation to save their lives by the surrender of those principles of liberty and justice which are dearer than life. Even those of us who share your knowledge that we cannot overcome evil and that war brutalises and degrades, are conscious of our own unfitness to display the full power of non-violence and of our failure to convince our fellow countrymen of its value and practicability. Our sorrow that your example and appeal have not met with a wider response, does not lessen our gratitude to you, our affectionate admiration for your witness, or our desire to make what reply we can to your challenge and warning.

If we are to attempt such a reply by a fresh dedication of ourselves to the way of non-violence, there is one matter which we must venture to lay before you.

As Christian Pacifists who share your faith in the power of non-violence (expressed for us supremely in the crucifixion of Jesus Christ), we have always felt that non-violent non-co-operation was only one part of a two-fold duty. During the past years we have tried to work for reconciliation, not only by denunciation and personal rejection of war and the consequent discipline of Satyagraha, but by active effort to remove the social, economic and political iniquities which are primary causes of war. We have felt that a passive resistance to evil by non-co-operation was of itself insufficient; that inherent in any true pacifism was the duty to work for a radical reform of society by the abolition of economic and imperialistic exploitation; and that only in a community in which the difference created by financial, cultural or racial inequality were wholly subordinated to the promotion of fulness of life for all humanity—a community personal in its values, co-operative in its activities and world-wide in its scope—could true peace be attained.

We believe that you fully share this double concept of our task. But we are aware that to many of our people the doctrine of non-violence seems a negative rather than a positive ethic, a cult of non-attachment, able to arm the individual agains the shocks of circumstances, but calculated to promote a Stoic "apathy" rather than a Christian redemption. The way of love as we understand it in Christ, though it involves a selfless refusal to meet evil by war or by flight, involves also an active forgiving of enemies and a ceaseless endeavour to maintain a relationship of sympathy and service with them.

It may be that in days as critical as these when power-politics and militarism dominate Europe, the only course open to us is that of passive non-violence. But we cannot dissociate this from the active endeavour to witness to a way of life in which the energies now devoted to destruction should be used for the abolition of poverty, the enrichment of man's social and cultural inheritance, and the achievement of world-unity. It may be that this present agony will convince us of the need and inspire us with the power to respond more worthily to your appeal. But it may also be that if you would address a further message to the spiritual leaders of mankind, a united word might yet be spoken by them which would initiate negotiations for a constructive settlement and put an end to this fratricidal conflict.

Assuring you of our gratitude and admiration,

We are,

Most sincerely yours,

As the threat of invasion receded, the attention of pacifists was directed towards two main issues—the nature of the methods of war which were being employed and the nature of the peace which could ultimately be established. Charles remained active in discussion wherever possible but, after the summer of 1940, his activities outside Cambridge had to be severely curtailed. Transport became increasingly difficult but in addition Heads of Colleges were officially warned to stay in Cambridge and particularly in relation to air-raids there were specific duties to perform. Whenever London or the Midlands were raided, Charles received a secret signal "Enemy aircraft overhead" and he therefore re-planned his life in order to make it possible to be regularly awake and alert between 10 p.m. and 3 a.m. during which time he was able, as he put it, to make "uninterrupted contact with the seventeenth century and one of the great men of our island" (John Ray whose biography he was now writing).

Further in March 1943 came his own serious heart attack and this was followed in the summer of 1944 by the shattering blow from which it was even harder to recover, the sudden death of Mrs. Raven. For varying reasons therefore his witness on behalf of pacifism during the actual war years was muted, though the whole question assumed a new intensity when the first atomic bomb was used in the attack on Japan in August 1945. The news was received while a Conference of the Fellowship of Reconciliation was actually in progress and Charles, who had prepared his speech, threw it aside and spoke in almost apocalyptic terms about the consequences of this new instrument of war. It was perhaps supremely painful to him that, having known and admired Rutherford, he should live to see the brilliant scientific discoveries of this great man being employed for the destruction of innocent victims.

This in fact was to become one of the two major matters of concern for pacifists in the period immediately after the War. The other was the question of ensuring that an adequate presentation of the pacifist faith should be made at the First Assembly of the World Council of Churches which it was planned to hold in the near future. The situation had changed out of all knowledge since the great meeting of Church representatives in Oxford in 1937 and, with the bitter memories of war remaining so personal and so poignant—especially in such a location as Amsterdam—it would be far from easy to gain a hearing for the cause of pacifism at all. Moreover there were tensions within the ranks of pacifists in Britain itself. In 1947 the Annual General Meeting of the Peace Pledge Union passed a motion asking the National Council of the Union to give active leadership to a campaign to destroy the National Service Act. When the Council met, it found itself sharply divided about the legitimacy of the motion and the policy of attempting to carry it out. Charles, Middleton Murry, Donald Soper, and the greatly honoured leader Alex Wood, resigned from the Council *en bloc* on the grounds that whereas an individual might feel compelled to make a decision of this kind, the Union could not be committed to such a policy as a whole.

Returning to the two major issues of the post-war period, the British Council of Churches acted with commendable speed in appointing a strong commission under the Chairmanship of Dr. J. H. Oldham to "consider the problems created by the discovery of atomic energy." It included some of the leading theologians and philosophers in the country, several of whom were close friends of Charles. But when the Report was published in May 1946, his first reaction was one of deep disappointment, which turned later to passionate indignation. He accused the Commission of "white washing" atomic war. He admitted that there was much that was good and finely expressed in the Report but still found the main conclusions "tragically depressing". Why was there no clear and absolute condemnation of atomic war in any shape or form? Why was every point of view represented except that of the "consistent pacifist?"

Having deplored the indecisive and intolerably "negative" character of the documents he summed up his criticisms in two final paragraphs:

"If it be thought unfair to judge the Report by what it fails to say, and to read its positive contents in the light of that failure, it must be remembered that the danger with us as with the German Christians is always that we may provide moral sedatives to lull to sleep the inconvenient protests of sensitive consciences. When the appointment of this Commission was announced there was inevitably a suspicion that its business was to allay the sense of guilt and stifle the protests of Christians. Most of us condemned this suspicion as cynical. The Report terrible as it is to say so, cannot but contradict this condemnation. To plead for "the exercise in the world of an active love for their fellow-men" (p. 80) after having stated that "some" (but only

some) "members of the Commission take the view that in no circumstances whatever should a Christian approve the use of the atomic
bomb" and having rejected this view, is surely "to make the Cross of
no effect."
This is indeed the weakness of the whole document, that it assumes
that the exercise of power is the only means for overcoming evil; that
it has no acknowledgment of Christ's refusal either to fight or to
flee; and that in consequence it has no clear faith in the victory of
love and no clear gospel as to the conditions of that victory."

Charles was not invited to attend the constituting assembly of the
World Council of Churches as a delegate and consequently had no
opportunity to speak there on behalf of pacifism. But he shared the
concern of his friends within the movement that the subject should not
be allowed to go by default. Steps were taken by the International
Fellowship of Reconciliation to produce a statement of the pacifist
position which could be submitted to the Assembly and it appears that
Charles was mainly responsible for the final draft. This was framed in
explicitly theological terms and pleaded for a complete renunciation of
war by the Church as a whole. "The true Church of Christ, the extension of the Incarnation, Atonement and Resurrection and the incarnation
of the Holy Spirit, cannot ever be at war. It must be the universal,
supranational fellowship which refuses to participate in violence and
war. It cannot do otherwise and yet remain Christian." All historical
relativisms were repudiated; the possibility of being guided by absolute
authority and absolute standards was upheld. This in fact was the key
to the whole debate on Christianity and War. Is it possible for those who
live within the *relativities* of history, both as individuals and in their
life in society, ever to formulate *absolute* standards and to follow them
absolutely?[8]

NOTES TO CHAPTER THIRTEEN

1. p. 215: In June 1931 Charles sounded the alarm which he felt through an article
in *The Liverpool Review*. There were, he recognised, conflicting claims
for a man's loyalties in the world of business as well as in the world of

politics. But whereas "we may not yet be able to contract out of our partnership in the evils of a competitive society . . . war can be isolated and outlawed; and a decisive step taken by the Churches to renounce it."

2. p. 219: Others included Lansbury, Middleton Murry, Donald Soper, Aldous Huxley.

3. p. 220: *The Age of Illusion*, p. 251.

4. p. 223: In a sermon at Cambridge in April 1937, Henson gave a neat definition of his own position: "The path of the Christian's duty seems to me to be a via media between the pacifist's prohibition and the erastian's insistence."

5. p. 226: *The Universal Church and the World of Nations*, p. 291 f. i.e. those justifiable by international law or those defending Christian principles.

6. p. 228: Late in 1938 he went with Lansbury and five other pacifist leaders to No. 10 Downing Street to plead for non-violent methods and the calling of a new peace conference.

7. p. 228: *The Rebel Passion*, p. 90 f.

8. p. 236: Charles's pacifist principles were put to a severe test when, not long before the outbreak of the Second World War, the worsening situation on the Continent caused the Royal Ordnance Depot authorities to write to him about the possibility of using Wicken Fen (of whose trustees he was Chairman) as a source of supply of buck-thorn. (The old name of buck-thorn was the gunpowder-tree; it grew freely in this particular fen.) The reason for the enquiry was that hitherto supplies had been imported from France and Czechoslovakia. By burning the buck-thorn, pure charcoal could be obtained and this was an essential ingredient of time-fuses. If anything should happen to interfere with supplies from the Continent the consequences could be extremely serious.

Charles gave his permission and Wicken Fen thereby played no small part in the war effort. If incendiary bombs had fallen upon it, the results again could have been disastrous for the manufacturers of gunpowder.

CHAPTER FOURTEEN

Towards a Synthetic Philosophy

In an impressive series of Riddell Lectures delivered in Newcastle-upon-Tyne in 1935 Charles presented an outline sketch of his re-inter-pretation of the doctrine of God as Creator, Redeemer, Sanctifier in the light of modern evolutionary theory. Seven years were to pass before he returned to the theme in any comprehensive way. Then the opportunity came to give the Open Lectures in his own University: they were deliberately planned to appeal to students of all faculties rather than simply to those engaged in formal theological studies. Already Dr. J. S. Whale and Professor C. H. Dodd had performed the task with great distinction, Whale through a consideration of basic Christian doctrines, Dodd through a fresh look at the Bible in the life of today. Not unnaturally Charles chose the theme of Science and its relation to Christian Faith. Published in 1943 under the title *Science, Religion and the Future* the book containing the lectures is probably the most impressive short treatment of the subject that he ever made.

In studying these lectures and comparing them with *The Creator Spirit* of 1927 and with *Evolution and the Christian Concept of God* of 1935 it is possible to detect a very important development in Charles's approach to the general subject. In the earlier two books he had been concerned to show that modern studies in biology and psychology were providing a convincing and coherent paradigm for the re-interpretation of Christian doctrine in the twentieth century. Evolution was the keyword, emergent its necessary qualifier. The Christian could not accept a doctrine of evolution which was simply a celebration of chance and blind force; on the other hand a doctrine which allowed for the emergence of successively higher stages of the organisation of life could be welcomed as explaining the way in which the universal divine activity had been working in creation, redemption and continuing sanctification.

But with the completion of the Riddell Lectures he began, it seems, to be increasingly preoccupied with problems of *history*. In a very real sense this was a return to his first love. Though he gave consistent and eloquent witness to the reality of Christian *experience*, he was unlikely ever to become a great philosopher of religion; he was an enthusiastic observer and recorder of natural phenomena but he was unlikely to become a great *experimental scientist;* the field in which he had been carefully trained and disciplined and in which he had performed work of originality and distinction was that of *historical* studies. He possessed an unusual command of Latin and this could be of special value in the study of the lives of earlier scientists. He already had a working knowledge of the historical development of the life-sciences. Could he not then make a real contribution to the history of science and thereby to the wider history of human ideas by undertaking a serious study of the way in which the discipline which had at first been comprehensive and concerned with the whole life of man had narrowed its vision and its field of enquiry by concentrating its attention on the physical universe and the nature of material substance? One almost feels the stirring of a new enthusiasm. Somehow the thirties had been a time of frustration and disillusionment. The Reformation of doctrine which he had advocated had gained little acceptance amongst his fellow theologians. The new concern for life and wholeness which he had hoped to promote in scientific circles was still largely neglected. Was there some more basic task that needed to be undertaken, some search for false assumptions and wrong ideas which could be exposed and corrected? Could he thus prepare the way for that better understanding between theologians and scientists which he still so ardently desired?

He was convinced that something had gone seriously wrong. The old excitement for historical studies gripped him again. The establishment of a settled home in Cambridge, followed so quickly by the outbreak of war and the consequent curtailment of outside activities as well as of teaching duties, made it possible to formulate a plan of historical research which would ultimately enable him to speak with greater authority on the relation between science and religion in the contemporary world. If he could discover to his own satisfaction how the alienation between his own two great loves had happened and then could set out the story in detailed and convincing fashion, was there not some hope that the folly and sadness of the alienation would be recognised and that an increasing number would join in the mission to draw together what ought never to have been allowed to drift apart?

So from the end of the thirties Charles gave his attention increasingly to the *history* of science. What he had already accomplished as a natural historian stood him in good stead when he began this more extensive task. The men he intended to study—pioneers in botany and zoology and anatomy—had shared his own enthusiasms and had been amongst the earliest practitioners of the methods of observation and classification which he had himself employed so diligently. Was there any single figure on whom his sights could be set—for he loved in his historical studies to focus attention on a particular man as he had done in the case of Apollinarius. A whole period of history could be illuminated by a careful exposition of the experience of a representative individual. Perhaps Linnaeus was the important pioneer? But no, there was a still more significant figure and that an Englishman. Charles determined to embark on an exciting though an arduous and long drawn out voyage. He would write a biography of 'our countryman, the excellent Mr. Ray'. "My son and I," Charles wrote, "had spent our spare time for some years on the plants of Cambridgeshire; the first county flora was John Ray's wonderful little book of 1660; a large-scale biography of the first, and perhaps greatest, British naturalist would be the best possible prelude for my new task." So the name of Ray and Raven, each in his turn a devoted son of Cambridge and an enthusiastic collector of the flora of Cambridgeshire, became linked together in an association which is unlikely ever to be broken or superseded.

The book itself was a monumental achievement. It involved the collating of every record of Ray's travel and research, the translating of his countless descriptions and identifications from the Latin, the collecting of "nearly all the plants, birds and insects that he records, and often in the same localities." As the reviewer of the biography in the *Times Literary Supplement* remarked: "If Dr. Raven feels in contemplating the first volume of Ray's *History of Plants* a sense of awe at its sheer mass and magnitude, his own readers will be not less impressed with the remarkable industry with which Dr. Raven has collated, annotated and explained, and in many cases followed Ray plant by plant and insect by insect in illustrating, identifying, checking and correcting the detailed descriptions of the master. Ray, in fact, is the father of the English field naturalist; and Dr. Raven, no less than Gilbert White, is in the true line of descent." Though the name of Keble Martin may have become familiar to a wider public there can be little doubt that Charles deserves to be regarded as the outstanding parson-naturalist of the twentieth century.

John Ray: Naturalist was beautifully produced by the Cambridge University Press. Extending to more than five hundred pages it contains indices of the Latin names of Flora and Fauna each of which contains some five hundred entries. It traces Ray's life as a botanist, his travels and adventures in Britain and other parts of Western Europe, quotes at length from his books and gathers together in separate chapters his contributions to the histories of birds, fishes, insects and mammals. Finally a chapter on Ray's best-known book *The Wisdom of God* celebrates his achievements as both a scientific genius and a devout Christian apologist. This book, Charles wrote, "supplied the background for the thought of Gilbert White and indeed for the naturalists of three generations; it was imitated, and extensively plagiarised, by Paley in his famous *Natural Theology;* and more than any other single book it initiated the true adventure of modern science, and is the ancestor of the *Origin of Species* or of *Evolution Créatrice*" (452)

The task could hardly have been carried through with such obvious zest had not Charles shared so deeply in the interests and ideals of Ray himself.

"It may be that others will not share my delight at the first discovery of the sulphur clover or the alpine bartsia, the mnax shearwater or the purple emperor. For them perhaps it strikes no chord that he too enjoyed the abundance of Jacob's ladder at Malham Cove or of Cornish heath at Goonhilly, or that he marvelled at the loop of the trachea in the whooper swan, and the sanitary habits of newly hatched hawks[1] and the presence of smelts in Rostherne Mere and the ammophila dealing with its caterpillar, and the assembling of male moths round a freshly emerged female. When he was confused by the defects of the books on which he relied, when he wrestled with the problems of local variation and plumage change, when he found himself compelled to question the orthodoxies of his day, when his friends reported to him impossible new species and fantastic new speculations, what naturalist will not remember his own experiences and feel a thrill of human sympathy?"

Charles lived for a period in Ray's world, read his records and translated his documents, shared his spirit and followed his methods and thereby provided for his contemporaries and bequeathed to his successors one of the great historical biographies of this century.

Its publication brought him international recognition. In spite of its size and complexity of detail and the difficult conditions of the war and post-war periods, the first edition sold out and a second was printed in 1950. There were enthusiastic reviews in British papers and it received a most favourable notice in the Archives Internationales d'Histoire des Sciences. An American biochemist wrote that "Dr. Raven has created the definitive biography of Ray and the immense labor which must have gone into his tribute to Ray will be at least partially repaid by the gratitude of later scholars." The Curator of the Botanical Institute in Florence wrote to seek further information about Ray's visits to the neighbourhood of Rome, particularly in relation to the genus Acer. A young English doctor in a letter to a friend declared after reading the biography that "if one dared to classify characters of men I would not be surprised to find Ray and Raven in the same genus and belonging to the same species!" From this time onwards Ray's and Charles's fame were intertwined. He had rediscovered the greatness of Ray and in trying to communicate it to his contemporaries had himself gained immensely in stature as a historian of nature, as a sensitive interpreter of a fellow human being and as a witness to the wonder of God's revelation through the works which He had created.

Encouraged by the reception accorded to *John Ray*, Charles set to work on a task to which he had been drawn while collecting material for the biography. Had he, in trying to do justice to Ray, perhaps underestimated the contributions of earlier naturalists? Equally the question arose whether historians of science, in dealing with the period before the seventeenth century, had concentrated their attention upon significant developments in mathematics and astronomy and mechanical devices and had failed to take into account the notable achievements of pioneers in the fields of botany and medicine. Charles determined to make a careful investigation of the records of English naturalists who had lived between the twelfth and the seventeenth centuries. Beginning with Alexander Neckam, who was born in 1157, he continued his study to the time of Sir Thomas Browne, who was one of the earliest leaders of the Royal Society and who died in 1682. In brief Charles wished to establish the thesis that whereas Neckam in the twelfth century and Bartholomaeus Anglicus in the thirteenth were still living in a world of fancy and legend and magic, with little reference to the actual behaviour of plants and living creatures, by the seventeenth century a new method had at least begun to be adopted—the method of observing and naming and describing the phenomena of nature, the method which was to gain increasing acceptance as the only proper scientific procedure, the method that has made possible the astonishing developments of the last three centuries.

An important point which Charles made in his book and one to which he returned later in his Gifford Lectures was that the real beginnings of modern zoological and botanical science are to be found in the work of late medieval *artists* rather than in the speculations and theories of *philosophers*. It is in carvings and paintings that we first encounter the labours of patient observers whereas poets and dramatists still accepted without serious question the kind of world-view presented in the writings of Bartholomew. But gradually men such as William Turner (b. 1508) (worthy to be called the first British biologist) who recorded observations of plants and birds in his native county of

Northumberland and then went on to read medicine in Cambridge and study the flora of the countryside; Thomas Penny born in Lancashire in 1530 who became in due course an excellent entomologist; John Caius (b. 1510) who edited the works of Galen and produced the first clinical account of the sweating sickness; men such as these observed the behaviour of *living* things, made drawings, kept records, and checked older accounts by the evidence of their own eyes rather than by trying to press the evidence into the mould of older theories.

From Neckam to Ray, published in 1948, was widely acclaimed. For example one reviewer in a scientific journal, declared that in modern times:

> "so great has our knowledge become and so specialised must the modern research worker be that few naturalists today capable of appraising the worth of say, Penny's contributions to zoology would be able with equal competence to assess Ray's contributions to botany. Professor Raven, eminent as a philosopher and all round field naturalist, has very successfully performed these formidable tasks of correlation and assessment and produced a work which must surely be placed among the classic histories of biology. That approaching a thousand names of persons are listed in the index indicates its thoroughness."[2]

By these two books Charles established himself as a leading pioneer in an area which had hitherto attracted little attention among historians. any confidence but since 1945 the subject has increased in importance. Few in fact had sufficient scientific knowledge to explore the field with His work on John Ray was definitive. *English Naturalists from Neckam to Ray* was more polemical and its judgments, particularly on the earlier period, have not gone unchallenged. Nevertheless the very fact that it was awarded the James Tait Black Prize for the best biography of the year is sufficient testimony to its quality and at least for the botanical and biological sciences Charles's work is worthy to be regarded as a contribution of the first order to their history.

The material which he ultimately used in the writing of this major work proved useful in two earlier contexts: the Herbert Spencer

Lecture which he had been invited to deliver in Oxford in 1945 and the L. T. Hobhouse Memorial Lecture which he gave at Bedford College in the University of London in 1946. The first he entitled *Synthetic Philosophy in the Seventeenth Century*, the second, *Religion and Science: A Diagnosis*. In both instances he took up the theme of the scientific obscurantism of the Middle Ages and the change which had taken place through the new ideas and aspirations of the Renaissance and the Reformation. Gradually, with the breakdown of the medieval system, a new synthesis between religion and science became possible and was almost achieved in the seventeeth century—but not quite. This in Charles's view was due on the one side to the pre-occupation of science with mathematics and mechanics to the detriment of biology and botany and medicine: on the other side to the failure of religion to break free from the mythological and authoritarian framework within which it still tried to organise its intellectual life. The Cambridge Platonists, he believed, had made a magnificent attempt to create a new synthesis in the seventeenth century. Could not a similar attempt be made in the twentieth century with theologians developing a truly authentic natural theology and with scientists abandoning the narrow confines of mechanism and behaviourism and providing instead a science of *life* in all its dynamism and wholeness?

Charles always regarded Oxford with respect but was a little suspicious of its philosophising. He opened his Herbert Spencer Lecture with the words: "For a Cambridge man to deliver a public lecture in the older University must always be an experience charged with emotion." He closed with a characteristic flourish: "It is indeed something of an irony that the scientific interpretation of nature should after four centuries have replaced the hieroglyphics of mediaeval Catholicism by the robots of modern Behaviourism. Is it more foolish to equate fable with fact or mechanism with meaninglessness? Such a question leads us directly to the chief problem of our time. But "that" as Rudyard Kipling taught us to say "is another story—a story for grown-ups"—a story not for a Cambridge historian but for an Oxford philosopher!" In point of fact though Charles had not attempted a philosophical analysis he had put forward a quite explicit interpretation of history. And it was that interpretation which was to come under question from historians of science who were not convinced that the pattern of development from the thirteenth to the twentieth centuries was quite as neat as Charles imagined it to be.

However, the opportunity was soon to come for his historical studies in the fields both of the development of Christian doctrine and of the advancement of scientific knowledge to be brought together into one major synthetic treatment which must be regarded as the crown of his literary work. No lectureship in Britain is more famous than the Gifford series and indeed it is hard to think of one which enjoys a comparable prestige in any part of the world. In 1949, while he was still Vice-Chancellor, the invitation came to him to deliver the lectures in Edinburgh in 1951–2. He would have preferred a longer time to prepare, expecially as his retirement from Professorship and Mastership was to come in 1950, involving him in the upheaval of moving to a new situation. However the invitation could not be declined and so in moments of leisure he began to draw out a sketch plan of the two series, one of which he had decided would be devoted to the history of science and natural theology, the other to Christian experience and interpretation.

From his extant papers it is evident that he quickly assembled the titles of the subjects to be covered in his twenty lectures and that the writing was completed in a single draft which needed only minor revisions. For ten years he had been giving his mind constantly to the subject of the progress of natural history in Western Europe since the Middle Ages and it was not difficult to return to his studies of the early Church and to describe the way in which the Fathers viewed the world of nature. Thus the first series was almost ready made; it provided the opportunity for him to bring together in orderly fashion the convictions about the changes in man's attitude to the natural world and above all to the world of living things which had become firmly established in his own mind. If he could persuade his audience to accept the view that organic and holistic categories were alone appropriate for the interpretation of nature, it would be less difficult to lead them on to an interpretation of religious experience in similar terms. And if it had once been accepted that a single framework of interpretation was valid and necessary, then the gulf between science and religion would have been bridged and a synthetic, unified view of man's total experience established.

The first volume of the Giffords consists of a series of tableaux, all concerned with the vision of Nature, drawn successively from the Bible, the early Church, and the writings of such worthies as Gesner and Cudworth, Linnaeus and Darwin. The second volume takes up the experience of the Holy within Nature and seeks to show how this attains its highest level of realisation in terms of Human Personality. It is as God Himself is revealed in and through the personality of the Christ that the highest conceivable manifestation of deity gains expression: it is as man responds to that revelation in and through a full self-commitment that he enters into a true communion with God and consequentially with all who share this unifying experience. A man becomes "intensely alive" as he lives in the knowledge and love of God: at the same time "every real communion with God is inevitably linked up with a new relatedness to our neighbours."[3] The consumimation towards which Charles never ceased to direct his gaze and his hopes was that which the Apostle had seen from afar and to which he bore testimony in the eighth chapter of the Epistle to the Romans: the glorious liberty of the children of God when all would dwell as one family within the Father's home.

As had for long been his custom Charles delivered the lectures virtually extempore with just a few scribbled notes as *aides-mémoire*, so retaining his hearers' attention from first to last. The Vice-Chancellorship at Cambridge gave Charles his finest hour in the world of public affairs; the Giffords gave him his finest hour in the world of academic distinction. His life's work on the reconcilation of religion and science reached its fullest expression.[4]

Any further exercises in this field would chiefly consist in giving particular applications from his system to specific problems which might arise as Christians sought to come to terms with the effects upon human life of the ever-accelerating advances of science and technology as they moved towards the control of the natural order.

Two further books—each in its way a considerable achievement—
were yet to come from within this general area of thought and investigation. Charles had a great affection for his doctor son-in-law and often
discussed medical matters with him. He therefore responded with
enthusiasm to the invitation extended to him to deliver the Markle
Lectures at the College of Medicine of the University of Cincinnati
in the spring of 1958. The lectures were recorded and subsequently
printed under the title *Science, Medicine and Morals* and they constitute
one of the earliest attempts to face the challenges to traditional tholog-
ical and ethical norms presented by modern medical science. If life
itself can now be generated and manipulated and controlled by
scientific techniques how can it still be claimed that the Spirit of God
is the "Lord and Giver of Life," how can standards and checks be
determined by which man's use of these techniques must be governed?
Though the words conservation and ecology had not at that time
entered the popular vocabulary, it was for the preservation of a balanced
and integrated natural environment that Charles appealed. And again,
although the emphasis in the field of psychotherapy at that time when
the lectures were delivered was still upon the individual, his needs,
his aberrations, his readjustment, Charles in a measure forestalled more
recent developments by his emphasis upon the necessity to view man
within his environment, natural and social. He saw that the days of the
lonely specialist were numbered. We are "cells or co-operative units
in the one body of mankind." (p. 182)

The visit to Cincinnati in 1958 not only led to the publication of the
book on Medicine but also contributed indirectly to Charles's final
full-scale book completed just two years before his death—the first
biography in English of the noted French Jesuit and palaeontologist,
Père Teilhard de Chardin. For while staying in Cincinnati Charles
seized the opportunity to consult with his friend, Dr. George Barbour,
who had worked with Teilhard in China and had known him intimately. His interest, which had been aroused through contacts in
Brussels and Paris with friends of Hélène Jeanty (whom Charles married
in 1956) who spoke enthusiastically of Teilhard, now became almost
an obsession and although his knowledge of French and of the Catholic

tradition had hitherto been relatively meagre, he determined to gather material for a life of Teilhard in the way that he had done for his earlier heroes of the scientific movement in England. At his age this was surely an astonishing achievement. He naturally derived immense help from his wife and from other friends in matters of language but the necessary reading of Teilhard's own works and of the considerable literature about him which already existed in French must have taxed his concentration and determination to the limit.

Yet in many respects the whole experience proved to be for him a rejuvenation. From 1925 onwards he had hoped and prayed for the coming of a New Reformation in which theology would embrace the modern scientific world-view and in which science would devote some of its best energies to the exploration and appreciation of man's religious experience. But by 1936 what Professor E. L. Allen in his book *Religion in Britain since* 1900 described as "the great blight" had infected the realm of thought, and with the coming of the Second World War the prospect of any creative unification of religion and science seemed to become increasingly remote. Now, however, this "Seer", as Charles called him, had suddenly captured the attention of educated people in France so that some three hundred thousand copies of his definitive book were soon circulated. And Charles quickly realised that Teilhard, who was roughly his own contemporary, (they were four years apart in age) had been captivated by the same vision of unity and continuity which he himself had seen and tried to communicate throughout most of his working career. By writing a biography of Teilhard and relating it to his scientific and theological ideas, Charles could in fact present yet another exposition of his own essential message. Perhaps the world which had refused to listen to him directly might listen indirectly as he unfolded the life-story of a French Catholic scientist.

It is, in fact, extraordinary that the whole conception of man and the universe which Charles had been trying to make vivid and convincing to his contemporaries for more than thirty years gained far more attention in England through the works of Teilhard than ever it had done through his own writings. A prophet is not without honour save

in his own country! A devoted scholar-priest, prevented by ecclesiastical authority from disseminating his own writings; a somewhat
mysterious figure who spent long and lonely years in China and finally
died in America far from his own native land; a terminology which
was unusual and which included certain neologisms soon to become
fashionable in influential sircles; all of these factors may have contributed to the international posthumous fame accorded to Teilhard,
a fame which gave Charles unalloyed pleasure. But it still remains true
that Charles had much earlier and quite independently reached views
very similar to those of Teilhard and had done so, it may be claimed,
through careful observation of a wider range of phenomena than had
been the specialised subject of study of the French palaeontologist.

Though two chapters are devoted to Teilhard's French background
and to the influence on his development of the years he spent in England
just before the First World War, the book proves to be in the main a
series of essays on various aspects of his thought—on human origins,
on emergent evolution, on the problem of evil and on Christology.
A chapter specially admired by reviewers was that entitled Teilhard
and St. Paul for in this Charles took the opportunity to demonstrate,
as far as he was able, that his own and Teilhard's view could be regarded
as a legitimate expansion of the essential insights of the great Apostle.
"Teilhard in his whole Christian vision of the process of Cosmogenesis
and Christification is actually and avowedly restating for us the
theology of St. Paul as this came to its fullest expression."[5]

Charles could never allow that the correct interpretation of St. Paul
for our time had been given by Karl Barth; Teilhard's realisation of
"the tragedy and evil of our humanity in war-time but also and
compellingly its fortitude and fellowship"—yes: but Barth's insistence
on "the depravity and helplessness of mankind as a whole and the sin
and folly of its individual components"—no! "We must recognise the
sincerity and the convictions of the Barthian message of God's "other-
ness" and man's impotence, even if we must deplore its theology and
much of its effects. What we find hardest to accept is that the Protestant
world enthroned Barth while the Vatican exiled and did its best to
silence Teilhard."[6]

The book was well received in Britain, in the U.S.A. and in the Dominions. It is true that a reviewer in England found it disconcerting to see Teilhard "admitted as it were to honorary membership of the Athenaeum in the company of Lloyd Morgan and Bishop Barnes"! This may have been unfair but there is no doubt that part of Charles's enthusiasm for Teilhard sprang from his conviction that the great English succession of Ray, Maurice, Lloyd Morgan, Whitehead, Oman had been signally confirmed and continued in and through the researches and writings of the distinguished French Jesuit.

All of these men, Charles held, had in their respective ways stood for convergence and complexification, for world unity, individual integration and universal community; for wholeness of experience, continuity of evolution, organic inter-relatedness. To find that Teilhard had expressed each of these categories so coherently and with such a wealth of circumstantial evidence caused Charles to welcome him into the long line of thinkers stretching back to Origen with what the Catholic reviewer already quoted described as an "apocalyptic enthusiasm".

But alas, there was one sour note in the encomium. Charles bitterly resented the fact that the most damaging attack on Teilhard had come from the pen of a distinguished English scientist, distinguished particularly in the realm of medical research which, as I have noted, Charles admired perhaps more than any other scientific discipline. The attack on Teilhard by Sir Peter Medawar in the pages of *Mind* has become famous: Charles's riposte is not so well-known but deserves to be set alongside that which caused it to be written.[7]

Few reviews in learned periodicals can ever have been more disdainful and even vicious than Medawar's assessment of *The Phenomenon of Man*. "The greater part of it is nonsense"; its language is "tipsy, euphoric, prose-poetry;" it is described as "philosophy-fiction, anti-scientific in temper;" it is the work of a man who "has no grasp of what makes a logical argument or of what makes for proof;" it produces in the reader (Medawar) "a feeling of suffocation, a gasping and flailing around for sense;" he has read and studied it with "real distress, even with despair." Charles who was ever quick to spring to the defence of anyone assaulted by words declared that the language of this review "can hardly be paralleled since the pontificial heresy-huntings of the fifth century. Let me recommend to Dr. Medawar the writings of St. Epiphanius. The high priests of scientism are following a bad example—but the saint though equally vituperative was a better critic."

However, that which moved Charles to real indignation was Medawar's use of the word "dishonest". The book, he claimed, was a "bag of tricks". "The author can be excused of dishonesty only on the grounds that before deceiving others, he has taken great pains to deceive himself." To charge such a man as Teilhard, whose humility and integrity had never been questioned by those who knew him intimately, with "dishonesty" seemed intolerable. Even when qualified by the strange explanation "taking great pains to deceive himself" the charge was serious enough. One man may be careless in his work and jump to illegitimate conclusions; another may through some oversight, misinterpret evidence; but it is not easy to imagine anyone deliberately, over a long period, taking great pains to deceive himself. Charles did not attempt to refute the charge. He was content to let the record of the man's career as set forth in his book speak for itself.

The biography of Teilhard was the last major book on Science and Religion that Charles wrote. It reveals clearly the way in which he sought to distinguish his own position from that of scientists such as Medawar on the one side, from anti-scientists such as Barth on the other. He may have been mistaken in his interpretation of the particular positions of those two men but they at least represented for him on the one side the attitude which seeks to interpret the universe solely in terms of physics and chemistry and mathematics, on the other side the attitude which seeks to interpret it solely in terms of the Word from a transcendent beyond which has no relation to the structures of the universe as already experienced by man. With these two negatives dismissed, Charles believed that the true and indeed the only possible way of interpretation was to see the universe as a single evolutionary process in which personality was the highest conceivable attainment and the establishment of a community of persons the noblest conceivable goal. What he seemed never able to entertain was the possibility that the universe could be interpreted in *two* ways, neither of which was reducible to or assimilable by the other. Continuity *and* discontinuity, unity *and* duality, the organic *and* the dialectical, progress through evolution *and* progress through resistance to evolution, steady growth *and* radical change, man co-operating with nature *and* man controlling nature; to attempt to hold dualities such as these together through the use of complementary models seemed to Charles to accept the possibility of final paradox which to him was a policy of despair. He hardly seemed to realise that a single scheme was always in danger of being identified as ultimate in itself—an idol, even though a moving, expanding idol.

That Charles made a great contribution to the healing of unhappy divisions, especially by his vivid expositions of the life-sciences and interpretations of religion to lay folk (as for example in his broadcast addresses published in 1952 under the title *Science and the Christian Man*) can hardly be denied. But that he spoke the final word not even his greatest admirers would claim. The very eloquence and persuasiveness with which he presented his unified interpretation of the universe may have hindered the expansiveness of outlook and openness to new conceptions of reality which are necessary if science and religion alike are to go forward to fuller and richer understandings of nature, man, and God.

NOTES TO CHAPTER FOURTEEN

1. p. 242: In a charming footnote on p. 470, Charles admits that when he himself first recorded these habits he thought that his observation was new!
2. p. 244: Journal of the Royal Horticultural Society 1948.
3. p. 247: *Natural Religion and Christian Theology*, 2, pp. 191, 199.
4. p. 247: One of the most appreciative and authoritative reviews of the Gifford Lectures was that which was written originally in *The Bishopric* by the then Bishop of Durham, A. M. Ramsey, and reprinted in the book *Durham Essays and Addresses* pp. 35–40. Dr. Ramsey begins: "It is a long time since I have read anything so fascinating, instructive and challenging as the two volumes of Dr. Raven's Gifford Lectures." Having described

the contents he offers three criticisms. (1) The confusion between dualism and duality. (2) The treatment of Israel's particularity. (3) The indiscriminating rejection of "neo-orthodoxy". But he expresses very great gratitude for the volumes and compares them with Hort's Hulseans. He concludes:" 'One day,' wrote William Temple, 'theology will take up again its larger and serener tasks and offer to a new Christendom its Christian map of life, its Christo-centric metaphysic. But that day will hardly dawn while any who are now concerned with theology are still alive.' Dr. Raven's Giffords are a promise that that day will come."

5. p. 250:   *Teilhard de Chardin*, p. 159.
6. p. 250:   Ibid. p. 29
7. p. 251:   Ibid. p. 211 ff.

CHAPTER FIFTEEN

The Ardent Feminist

Charles, who was once scornfully dismissed by Bishop Hensley Henson as an "ardent feminist", never lost the conviction that it was his advocacy of womens' rights within the Church of God that prevented the powers-that-be from ever offering him a bishopric. Whether or not this was so, there is little doubt that his was the voice which first pleaded eloquently that a completely new attitude should be adopted towards women in the Church. Actually he proved to be almost exactly half-a-century ahead of his time for whereas it was in 1922 that his revolutionary proposals appeared in *The Challenge*, it was not until 1972 that the Synod of the Church of England considered the question of Women in Holy Orders seriously with a view to action. In 1971 the Anglican Consultative Council had passed a motion to the effect that it "will be acceptable" if a bishop ordains women priests with the consent of his province and in November of that year the Bishop of Hong Kong and Macao took advantage of this sanction and ordained two women to the priesthood—the first official act of its kind within the Anglican Communion.[1] At last after fifty years of struggle in which, it might well be claimed, Charles was the pioneer and leading protagonist, the subject has been placed firmly on the agenda for Anglicanism as a whole and is likely to be debated in each of its several provinces in the coming decade.

From the year 1930 onwards, he strove with all his might to focus public attention upon the threat of war, to proclaim the way of pacifism as the only authentically Christian response to this menace. But although this issue was in the forefront of people's apprehensions and perplexities, it is possible that in Charles's scale of priorities the question of woman's place in society was even more important. In October

1945, for example, he wrote an article for *The Student Movement* in which he attempted to deal with the question which was bound to arise in the minds of the first post-war generation of freshmen at the Universities. "How has the coming of the age of atomic energy affected man's life on this earth?" He pointed out that the Second World War speeded up scientific developments and produced revolutionary social changes. The recent achievements of the atomic scientists had in a real sense ushered in a new age. But far-reaching changes had also taken place as a result of the First World War, though in less dramatic fashion.

"In the 1914–18 war the development was less noticeable: it effected the emancipation and enfranchisement of womanhood, made possible a new and equal comradeship between men and women, liberated for full service resources which had previously been confined to domestic channels, and, coinciding as it did with the universal knowledge of contraceptives, changed human life at its most intimate and critical point. Sex relationships are of course the most subtle and influential of all human affairs; and in 1918 we were confronted with the overthrow of the long-established (if not universal) convention of woman's subordination, and if we had been wise, would have concentrated massed efforts of study and planning in order to meet the situation. As it was, and with relatively few exceptions, we ignored it; tried to meet the new conditions by modifying the taboos and re-stating the conventions of the Victorian age; and have now seen the moral chaos that has resulted from our blindness. Unfortunately Christians who ought to have re-examined their presentation of moral standards and the case for monogamy were hardly less negligent and timid than the other sections of the community."

Some five years later in a sermon preached at a student service in Boston, Charles spoke again of the change in the attitude to woman and her place in society:

"I believe that religiously speaking it opens up to us the prospect of a really incarnational society because I am very sure that a human society dominated by the male sex only cannot reach the fullness of the stature of Christ. It is always dualistic, always ascetic, and always military. We in the churches must confess that we have been afraid and reactionary, slow to seize the tremendous possibilities which the emancipation and full education and full citizenship of womanhood make available for us."

Dualism, asceticism, militarism! Here indeed were three of Charles's bugbears. He longed for the one organic society, in which man and woman would be united as partners, each performing a particular function within the one ongoing life; in which nature would not be repressed or mutilated but honoured and sanctified; in which violence and destruction would be exorcised and the gentler virtues enthroned. He believed that the most notable humanising influence in the First World War had been the presence of women in hut and canteen and hospital, saving men from the perversions which an all-male society inevitably begets. He was convinced that the admission of women into other vocations had been altogether right and wholesome and he could see no just reason why a woman could function as a doctor and not as a priest. So after the ten years of intense activity of a general social and evangelistic character which occupied him during the twenties, Charles determined to concentrate more selectively first on the theological problems which had become acute through the development of modern science and then on the ethical problems which arose through the threat of a renewal of international conflicts and through the unwillingness of society at large, and the Church in particular, to accord woman the status, to which, according to any rational judgment, she is entitled. Whether or not Henson's description of Charles as an "ardent feminist" was justified he was certainly a feminist in the sense that he championed the cause of womanhood, was constantly sustained and renewed by wife and daughter, mother and sister within his own family circle, and, generally speaking, enjoyed deeper friendships with women than with men in public life.

I have already referred to his close association with Lucy Gardner in the organisation of Copec. The friendship with Ethel Moors which

J

began in 1927 grew deeper over the years until it ripened into marriage in 1953. Naturally he was attracted to women who shared his concern for the interpretation of mystical experience and of these, two were outstanding in the 1920s. Mrs. Herman's book *Creative Prayer* became something of a classic; Evelyn Underhill's *Worship* was one of the most successful in the Library of Constructive Theology. Charles enjoyed the friendship of both and wrote about the latter:

> "Evelyn Underhill was, in her dealings with human souls, in her insight into the deeps of God, in her exposition of spiritual experience and in her prayer, greater even than in her writings. It was my privilege to invite her to take a retreat for clergy: I can never forget the speed with which their resentment was turned into gratitude, as she opened to them the mystery. No man has in that respect given me so much."[2]

Equally he admired the most celebrated woman preacher of her time—Dr. Maude Royden.

> "When on a summer afternoon she spoke in the great tent at Swanwick to the hundreds of young men and women fresh from their games on their relationship one to another and on the meaning and splendour of sex, she did what no man could have done, and for her male hearers at least lifted the whole subject on to a new level."

And through Copec he became acquainted with one who was already making her mark in the theatrical world—Sybil Thorndike, one of the best-loved characters of this century.

When after 1932 he began to take a full share in the University life of Cambridge he enjoyed a close friendship with the medieval historian Helen Cam who was his exact contemporary and who, after a distinguished career at Girton College became, in 1948, the first woman professor at Harvard. She and Charles shared many interests—natural history, the life of New England, the Chantry community—and each gained strength through friendship with the other.[3] Late in the 30s Charles also became acquainted with a remarkable Russian exile,

Julia de Beausobre, whose book *The Woman who could not die* made a deep impression when published in 1938. In a University sermon Charles referred particularly to her treatment of *Creative Suffering*— a theme so central to his own philosophy of life. Her life itself constitutes one of the most extraordinary records of the twentieth century, beginning as it did in the luxurious surroundings of Russian court circles, issuing in a devoted marriage from which she was torn away and subjected to almost incredible suffering with no news of her husband's fate, finally learning of his death, and then discovering a way to emigrate to England, meeting and marrying Sir Lewis Namier and ultimately writing his biography in brilliant fashion—this was another woman whose story made an instant appeal to Charles and whose friendship enriched his life.[4]

But much as he valued and depended upon the friendship of other women it was the complete security of his own home and the complete devotion of his wife Bee that sustained him through the hectic journeyings hither and thither during the 20s and through the stresses and strains of academic life in the 30s. It seemed that whatever happened to him—the rise and fall of student acclaim, the approval and disapproval of ecclesiastical authorities, the popularity or unpopularity of the theological position which he advocated—Bee was always there to listen, to understand and to sustain. She felt unable to give him direct mental stimulus for whereas her own brain worked by ordered stages Charles leapt ahead at almost lightning speed. Yet she had an amazing capacity to bring calm to anyone who was emotionally disturbed; her own serenity somehow communicated itself to everyone within her immediate circle.

She was a typical lady of senior Cambridge: a gracious hostess, traditional in her ways, with no trace of self-concern. She was tall and very thin but never complained of exhaustion though in about 1940 she became unwell and had to consult specialists. No clear diagnosis was made of her trouble and soon Charles's own breakdown in 1943 claimed her special attention. All through she had watched over him and prevented him from running himself to death, giving him the demonstrative affection which he seemed so constantly to need. Now in a special way she supported him, restrained him when necessary during the days of convalescence and rejoiced with him in the consciousness of his steady recovery of health and vigour. But as she poured out her care and concern towards him she hardly perhaps realised—it is clear that Charles did not—how great demands were being made upon her own resources. Even when in 1944 she became ill and had to rest completely there seemed no obvious cause for alarm. And then suddenly the devastating blow came. While Charles and Bee were on holiday near Anglesey she was stricken, rushed to hospital but collapsed and died.

All had come so unexpectedly that Charles seems to have been for a while completely stunned. He admitted afterwards to a friend that he almost despaired of going on living. His own heart condition was still to a degree precarious yet he was seized with the idea of struggling up a hill-side as fast as he could and welcoming the probable outcome. To whom could he turn to support him and take charge of affairs in the Master's Lodge? Mary, his eldest daughter, had through many years before the war given him secretarial help and had constantly driven him to and fro between Ely and Cambridge. But she was now serving in the Wrens. Could she perhaps be released? It was not easy but with the war moving towards its close there was some relaxation of regulations and ultimately she was able to take her mother's place as hostess first in the regular life of the College, and then, far more demandingly and almost without warning, as partner to the Vice-Chancellor in the exacting duties of University hospitality. So father and daughter worked together in the Lodge until retirement brought the years of Mastership to an end in 1950. It was then that the College expressed in full measure its recognition of the magnificient service that Mary had rendered to her father in his hour of great need and to College and University as a charming and efficient hostess.

As early as 1928 Charles wrote a careful and considered statement on the admission of women to Holy Orders and it is doubtful if the innumerable pamphlets and articles and reports which have appeared since that time have added anything substantial to the main arguments which he advanced or to the main policies which he advocated. The book was written between the two Lambeth Conferences which brought such an extraordinary volte-face on the whole question, Lambeth 1920 having resolved that the "ordination of a deaconess confers on her holy orders" while Lambeth 1930 proceeded to withdraw this assertion. Charles of course did not know that Lambeth 1930 would behave in this way but he was well aware that his own crusade was unlikely to commend itself to the authorities of the Church. In his preface he wrote:

"It would obviously be easier for me not to publish a book which will arouse fierce and prejudiced criticism. I can only say that there is a constraint upon me which brooks no refusal and that I have not given away to it hastily. I am not a feminist and I have no desire to be a revolutionary. But for some years the conviction has grown in me that the admission of women to Holy Orders on an equality with men is inherent in the teaching of Jesus and necessitated by a true understanding of the nature of the Church; and my experience of their spiritual fitness and of the needs of the time confirms this conclusion."

Amidst all the changes which had been taking place in the first quarter of the twentieth century none, he considered, had been more far-reaching in its possibilities than that which had brought about the new pattern of relationships between men and women—a change comparable to those which took place when man first learned to domesticate animals, when he built his first city or designed his first boat. Yet although women were now discharging the duties of doctor, lawyer, politician, and journalist, few in the Church seemed to have realised the wider implications of this new development. As an illustration he pointed out that in the essay which he had contributed the previous year to the composite volume *The Future of Christianity* he had devoted two lines to the statement that room would have to be found for the ministry of women. Yet the Bishop who wrote the introduction had castigated him for the "emphasis given to the ministry of women" which "will seem to most people disproportionate and to many offensive!"

Having touched briefly on freer sex relationships, on educational problems and on equal pay in industry, he proceeded to ask what the emancipation of women meant within the context of the life of the Church. The new freedom had produced great benefits; it had also opened the door to new forms of temptation—for example those surrounding business girls who could now be found living in lonely lodgings in our great cities. Must not the Church seek to minister to the tempted and fallen? And are not women fit to share in this ministry, not just as subordinate but as equals? Having served for years as an Examining Chaplain Charles was convinced that literally dozens of women within his acquaintance were far nore fit for ordination than the majority of men then being accepted. Yet all that was open to them was a quite limited and routine form of parochial service with no prospect of more responsible or more creative ministries to match growth in experience. ("It is waste and wickedness to turn a race-horse into a pit-pony".)

What then, he went on to ask, are the theological principles involved when considering the possible ordination of women? All depends on the nature of the Church itself and its ministry. Is not the Church "the expression and instrument by which the Spirit of Christ operates in the world, His body, an organism not an organisation?" It is His life that animates the whole and operates through each of its members. This is elementary New Testament teaching which most Christians would readily accept. But the analogy of the body naturally made a special appeal to Charles the biologist and he proceeded to draw out its implications in considerable detail. In nature structure is modified in correspondence with environment, form with function. So in the life of the Church. At the beginning, form was direct and simple. But in relation to new situations, appropriate instruments must emerge.

"To develop its ministerial system by admitting women to the priesthood would only be to continue the process by which the whole of the institutional structure of the Church has come into being."

It would be to authorise sacramentally what had already become a necessity for the proper functioning of the Church. And, moreover, when women are so obviously manifesting the operations of the Spirit in their preaching, their pastoral care, their sensitive ministry to individual needs, who is to deny them the sacramental authorisation which ordination provides? Even in the Church of Rome a woman is allowed to baptise in a case of dire emergency. Cannot women perform wider sacramental ministries without any sense of incongruity?

> "Is it really worthy of the Church of Christ to spend years of effort in devising means by which it can give authorisation to the need of the sick for the reserved sacrament and to dismiss inconsidered the vastly greater spiritual change which the Women's Movement represents?"

In considering objections in detail he focussed attention on those arising out of traditional principles (or prejudices) concerning womanhood in general; those based on Scripture; and those derived from Catholic authority. On womanhood in general he dismissed objections concerned with physical or temperamental characteristics as absurd but allowed more weight to those which are concerned with the difficulty of combining ministerial duties with those of the home and family. He suggested that just as men can be "seconded" for periods to serve e.g. as a travelling secretary, so a woman could be given extended leave to fulfil her task of child-rearing. In regard to the Bible he urged that Old Testament regulations were only valid for a particular culture. The attitude of our Lord he judged to be unequivocal. There was no discrimination in his treatment of men and women. In choosing apostles for mission-preaching it was inevitable that he should have confined the office to men seeing that the conditions of the world at the time would have made it impossible for women to undertake that particular task. St Paul's practical regulations he again regarded as conditioned by the social situation in which he lived but there can be no doubt that in principle he saw all distinctions of sex, race and class as having been transcended through the coming of Christ.

When considering the appeal to tradition and Church authority Charles had no difficulty in showing that the claim that certain elements in the constitution of the Church are fixed and unalterable is really untenable. But he knew that there were those in his own Church who were using the biological analogy to support their view that certain well-defined structures were necessary to preserve continuity in any organism and that it was possible to identify what were the *essential* structures in the continuing life of the Body of Christ, His Church. But he was unwilling to limit the plasticity of structures in this way. For him the characteristic notes of any living organism were adaptation to environment, growth through sensitive adjustment, survival through changes of form. "Anyone who traces the development of gill-slits into eustachian tubes or the various functions served by the front pair of limbs will hesitate to speak of any organ in the body as unalterable." And this is the true parallel for the life of the Church. While women were in subjection in society generally, no thought of ordination could arise. But now "quite certainly the appearance of educated and qualified women is in accordance with the Spirit of Christ; it creates a new opportunity for the improvement of the structure of the Church; indeed it constitutes an environment to which the Church must if it is to survive adjust itself."

After making a further plea that Christianity is a religion of freedom and not of obedience to a set of unchangeable laws, Charles concluded by considering the objections that the time for change is not ripe, that there is no strong demand for change (An argument appearing it may be observed in *The Spectator* of November 18th. 1972), that to ordain women will impair relations with the Roman Catholic and Eastern Orthodox Churches. Such plausible defences of delay and inaction he regarded as utterly flimsy when the urgent needs of the time are given proper weight. The church is being challenged to take its part in a new age in which women will become increasingly active and responsible in every walk of life. Will the Church become the one department in which woman remains in subjection and her gifts are allowed to fulfil no function in the process of the upbuilding of the Body of Christ?

There is little evidence that Charles's prophetic outburst made any marked impact upon the thinking and planning of the Church at large. In fact from Lambeth 1930 came the call to retreat rather than advance on this particular issue. In course of time Charles gained the support of his fellow Regius Professor of Divinity in the University of Oxford, Dr. Leonard Hodgson, and in 1935 a commission on the ministry of women appointed by the Convocations of Canterbury and York found no compelling theological reasons for or against the ordination of women—but still affirmed that the male priesthood was the appropriate ministry for the Church today. Charles became one of the two joint Presidents of the interdenominational Society for the equal ministry of men and women in the Church and continued whenever possible to stress the importance of this cause. But ironically it was not until two years after his death that a new attitude revealed itself in Anglicanism through the publication of the report *Women in Holy Orders* by the commission appointed by the Archbishops to study the question of the ordination of women in preparation for Lambeth 1968. Charles did not live to see the first implementation of the policy for which he strove for more than forty years. Though his own theological and sociological arguments may have been defective in certain respects (for example he almost certainly tried to make the organic model as regulative for the life of his own day as others had, in former ages, tried, in a way which he deprecated, to impose some other strictly defined model upon their own ecclesiastical theory and practice) he saw clearly that a new era had dawned in the normative relationships between men and women and that it would be impossible for the Churches of Christendom to continue indefinitely with their assumptions of male supremacy in society generally and of male monopoly of all essential functions in the life of the Christian community in particular. He gained little attention and little outward success in the advocacy of these reforms. But he never ceased to give freely of his time, his energies and his counsel to particular enterprises in which women were devoting their talents to the service of Christ in creative ways.

Of these the one which captured his imagination and commanded his complete loyalty from the days of his Blechingley incumbency to the and of his life was the "Chantry" family at Sevenoaks, whose women members came to be called the Blue Pilgrims. Probably much of the appeal of this particular community he found in its completely non-monastic character: there were no codified rules, no formal status within the Church of England, no fixed and limited objective which the members all sought to achieve. The foundress, Beatrice Hankey, was born in 1858 and towards the end of the nineteenth century became active in mission work at Walmer (where she lived) and in other towns of eastern Kent. Then in 1902 she began to see a new vision—a vision of young women from the more sheltered and leisured classes who, at that period, often had little opportunity to pursue a vocation, banded together as disciples in the service of Christ and committed to undertake special missions of help in response to particular needs.

All began as a family concern with Beatrice inviting a few younger relatives to spend four days with herself and her sister in the home of the Bishop of Dover in Canterbury. It so happened that this was an ancient house and over the doors of the rooms names such as Charity, Hope and Rest were inscribed; during the house party everyone took for the time being the name of the room in which she was staying. So valuable did the "retreat" prove to be that it was repeated in much the same form in the next two years and in 1904 the house-mother (Beatrice) read to her guests long sections from the *Idylls of the King*. So from the ancient room-names in the Bishop's House, coupled with the names of Tennyson's Knights and Bunyan's Pilgrims, an order of Christian chivalry emerged. Under the leadership of Miss Hankey who took the name Help (her sister had pinned over her door the title "One called Help" from *Pilgrim's Progress*) the family or movement or order took shape and by the time that Charles was introduced to it, had acquired as its permanent home the beautiful house called The Chantry almost adjoining the ancient church of St Nicholas at Sevenoaks.

I have described in some detail the origin of the names adopted by the "Knights" because this feature has to the outsider seemed perhaps the most artificial, even bizarre, element in the life of the community. As the membership grew, time-honoured names from Tennyson and Bunyan ran out and such titles as Jewel and Eager Heart, Unbound and

Rainbow, Windflower and Zephyr were adopted. The annual gathering of the community for consultation and renewal was always known as Camelot and the ideals of Knighthood (re-interpreted in line with an early English version of St Mark's Gospel in which "disciple" is translated as "learning Knight") governed its structure and its activities. Personal friendship, personal dedication, personal service have been the key-notes of its life from the beginning and this undoubtedly commended it to Charles who was always irked by committees and constitutions. Originating as a company of young women whose roots were in the Church of England, it gradually expanded to include men, members of other denominations, and ultimately small groups in other countries such as Germany and Holland. It has never become a large movement; it has never gained wide publicity. But the very fact that the Knighthood is now roughly seventy years old and includes some three hundred members, bound together by strongly personal ties, witnesses to the power of its appeal and to the value of the work which the Knights have done in depressed areas between the wars, in huts and shelters during the Second World War and in missions of reconciliation after the war. The Chantry remains a house for prayer, for hospitality, for conferences. The Knights continue to fulfil the responsibilities laid upon them by their Charter—to learn, to love, and to serve.

Into this knightly company Charles himself was admitted, as he later wrote, "by a woman; and I know that in bestowing upon me the token of membership she gave also the grace of an ordination as truly as any bishop." He was given the name Uplifter and from this time forward became the theological guide, the counsellor and above all the friend of all members of the Chantry family. He was often present at Camelot and his addresses were often recorded in the Signaller, the annual record of the community. He greatly admired the way in which, in 1928, when unemployment was at its worst, Miss Hankey and some of the Knights went down to South Wales and lived quite simply amonst the mining families, seeking to bring rays of hope into the dark situation by whatever expressions of friendship and service were possible. He himself joined them from time to time and on a memorable occasion bore witness to the value of their work.

This was at the Cromer Convention in 1932, (a summer gathering for instruction and encouragement in the life of the Spirit on whose platform of speakers Charles often appeared; his combination of theological competence and evangelistic zeal was exactly suited to such an occasion and his addresses were long remembered) Miss Hankey was suddenly stricken down and lay dangerously ill at the very time when Charles was speaking on the subject which had been allotted to him: *The Spirit Energising Fellowship.* Few themes were nearer to the heart of his whole philosophy of life. And the term which came nearest to expressing the secret of the vital continuity was "sensibility". "Sensibility, quickness of intuition, quickness of response, immediate and spontaneous vitality, that which, when it sees, is instant to put into effect that which has been seen. That which does not shirk the world's pain, nor blind itself to the appeal of the world's tears, but is exquisitely sensitive and speedy to have pity. Such sensibility is not only the supremely vital product of the human evolutionary process, but is the hall-mark of the energy of the Spirit of God."

He then went on to speak of one:

"who more than any that many of us have known possessed just that quality of immediate, spontaneous discipleship. Some months ago, I went down, not for the first time, into the distressed areas in South Wales and there I was able to see the first-fruits of one woman's adventuring. She had gone there, quick to perceive the appeal of suffering, gone there with nothing to give except God and His love, Christ and His sympathy, Christ and His trust in human beings, the fellowship of the Holy Spirit. She and others with her had remade the lives of men and women by the gift of the Spirit of Christ among them, working miracles in places otherwise dismal, depressed, degenerate, bringing health and newness of life, as Christ's ambassadors, if they be Christ's, can bring it."

Perhaps this was too romantic an account of what the Blue Pilgrims actually achieved but in days before the welfare state and its social services these women gave the best they had in sympathy, in trust, in service, trying to act as channels of the Spirit in personal ways until such time as new resources for material betterment might become available.

Miss Hankey made a temporary recovery during the weeks following the Convention but early in 1933 she died. It must have seemed almost impossible for Charles to add to his writing activities at that time, but he was evidently prevailed upon to assist in preparing a biography of the foundress of the Knighthood and this was published in 1937 under the title *One Called Help*.

Miss Hankey was one of the notable band of woman pioneers of this century and her influence upon Charles himself is reflected in the one passage of the book where his own association with the Knighthood comes fully into view. The words quoted are attributed to "One of the Anglican clergy who joined the Knighthood" but they can hardly be other than those of Charles himself. They reveal so much of the forces in life which moved him deeply that they deserve to be quoted at length:

"I had been asked to speak at Heathfield and came knowing nothing of Help and very little of the character or purpose of the gathering. It was literally a revelation—one of the few unforgettable experiences of my life.[5] For a moment, only a moment, the symbolism, the names, the seeming lack of ordered programme were rather daunting. Then one was caught up into the friendship and freedom of it. Here were folks with whom one could not pose or be shy, folks with whom one was at once at home. Here was the authentic community, the fellowship that one had seen in glimpses under fire, the spontaneity of childhood combined with the sympathy of maturity, the integration of personality of which one had dreamed and argued, the welding of individuals into an organic unity of which Pentecost was the pattern. Does that sound exaggerated? It happened and I can never forget the joy of it."

After this introduction his first Camelot

"came as an amazing discovery. For years and years I had felt something of what a Christian means by his discipleship. I had tried to tell others the good news of the Kingdom of God. But all the time

I had been aware that I was, as it were, standing outside the doors of the King's palace. Sometimes great and generous spirits opened the door and showed me what lay within it so that I could try to tell of it, sometimes they even beckoned me to come in. But I was afraid. I know I was really living in the world and not in the family of God. And then suddenly through a revelation of the power of fellowship I was gripped and held and lifted. I was inside the door, seized of the freedom of my home, a child of the house."

Beatrice Hankey symbolised for Charles the utter absurdity of exluding women from full recognition and ministry in the life of the Church. She

"the most integrated and luminous Christian I have known, was to me and to very many others both men and women far more a bishop, a mother in God, than any ordained or consecrated Churchman. She was all of a piece, swift to put into the appropriate act what she felt and saw; able to create out of a crowd of individuals a fellowship united organically by the Spirit of God.[6] Her work, her personality, live on.

To deny to such Christians the outward and visible sign and acknowledgment of their ministry is not only to be false to the example of St Peter and Cornelius; it is to make unreal the whole sacramental ordering of the Church. Where God's gifts are manifest and effective, the failure to authorise them is not merely a wastage but a denial of the true character of Christian organisation.

But there is a further principle involved. The Church if it is the body of Christ, fully expressing His fulness of life, cannot do so while it is representative of and controlled by one sex alone. There is in Jesus the perfect quality of man and of woman alike, the paradox of diastole and systole, of individuality and community, of adventurousness and of home-making. An embodiment of the Divine can only be fulfilled in the complete humanity of a man-woman partnership. Until the Church gives true status and scope to both alike, it will not reach a fully Christian level of being; it will remain power-ridden, dualistic, unstable. When at last after aeons a real partnership in secular affairs has become possible, it is a tragedy that the Church, in which as in Christ there should be neither male nor female, allows itself to be enslaved by its own traditions (and by less worthy motives) and to reject the opportunity now for the first time presented to it."

A visit to the Chantry always brought Charles refreshment; it was a place where a gracious mother-figure presided, where the beautiful garden with its ancient mulberry-tree (probably planted at the same time as the famous specimen in the Fellows' Garden at Christ's) provided constant interest and delight, where his own voice was listened to with rapt attention, where he was ever conscious of being appreciated rather than criticised—it became to him a kind of Bethany-home where he could entirely relax and enjoy its spirit of fellowship. Every experience of this kind was a sacrament of the life of the family of God. True religion for him consisted not in celebrating a powerful God's dominance over nature and in exercising a male priesthood's primacy in the ecclesiastical organism but rather in recognising with joy the coherence of all nature in God and the equal status of men and women as they performed their respective functions within the total divine society. Androcentrism was to him intolerable, especially when it was clothed in ecclesiastical garments. "In Christ, neither male nor female" became one of his most oft-quoted texts.

But his convictions concerning man—woman relations were not only theologically grounded; they also corresponded to a deep personal need. D. H. Lawrence once wrote in a letter: "It is hopeless for me to try to do anything without I have a woman at the back of me"—a confession that Charles could well have echoed. More surprisingly it was not Lawrence but the celibate Teilhard de Chardin who wrote: "Through woman and only woman can man escape the isolation in which his very perfection may too easily imprison him." Charles was fortunate in possessing or in gaining the love of a succession of women who stood at the back of him and helped him escape from his isolation. But the greatest of these, of whom we hear comparatively little, but from whom through more than thirty years he received unceasing sympathy and unswerving support, was the one about whom he spoke to a gathering of students in 1955 in this way:

"I suppose that the most wonderful moment that has ever come to me, was the moment on the morning after my greatest bereavement. I had spent the night with my dead, and a friend came and took me out from the death chamber, into a morning of gold and sapphire in one of the most lovely places I've ever been in. And sitting there, suddenly what Shelley called the "dome of many-coloured glass", this wonderland of radiance and sunlight and sea, splintered—smashed—dissolved; and I knew that this world and all the wonder of it, the birds and flowers which I had loved since I was a child, and the beautiful, beautiful people who ministered to me so generously, so unselfishly, so divinely—that all that, all this surface world is only the medium in and through which we children of God work out our contact with the eternal and communicate our knowledge, our little knowledge, our glimpses of the eternal, and learn a citizenship which is not of the earth and does not pass away."[7]

NOTES TO CHAPTER FIFTEEN

1. p. 255: The ordination performed by Bishop R. O. Hall of Hong Kong in 1944 during a critical period of the Second World War was regarded as irregular and after it had been repudiated by the Convocations of Canterbury and York the woman "priest" resigned her orders.

2. p. 258: *Natural Religion and Christian Theology*, II p. 206 f. "Her letters, more than any other influence, made me aware of the reality and depth of Catholic devotion."

3. p. 258: Charles was delighted whenever a woman of his acquaintance gained academic distinction. He used to speak of Dorothy Emmet, the only woman to have been offered a Chair both at Oxford and Cambridge—and she declined them both: Had she accepted Charles, said, I should have sung *Nunc Dimittis*.

4. p. 259: "The accounts of suffering that have helped me most are a lecture on Creative Suffering by Julia de Beausobre and her book *The Woman who could not Die*." op. cit., p. 115.

5. p. 269: Charles referred to it again in glowing terms in the course of the addresses which he gave to students at McGill University in 1955.

6. p. 270: "She and the community which she had formed represented what Christendom in the twentieth century might be, and disclosed a way of life authentically reflecting the quality of the New Testament." (Charles in an unpublished paper.)

7. p. 272: It is not without interest that J. C. Smuts, for whom Charles had an unbounded admiration, included many women amongst his regular correspondents. "He confessed once to 'a weakness for women, not in the sexual sense, but from some inner affinity and appeal,' the attraction of opposites, he thought, as in electro-magnetism." *T. L. S.* November 9th 1973.

CHAPTER SIXTEEN

The Unrepentant Liberal

Early in November 1948 Charles addressed a meeting at Westminster College, Cambridge. In the course of it he referred to his friend, Dr. J. H. Oldham, the Editor of the *Christian News-Letter*, who was present, as one who had regarded his own theological views as "superficial and optimistic". Dr. Oldham was deaf and only when he later read the notes of the addresses did he realise what had been said. He thereupon wrote to Charles to express surprise that he could ever have given such an impression. "I have been too much aware of the place which the Cross holds in your thinking to be tempted ever to apply to it the adjectives in question." He admitted that in some respects their outlooks may have differed but this only increased his desire "to get more deeply into the heart of your thinking." Charles replied at length and in so doing revealed a great deal about his own inner struggles ever since the mid 1930s when it gradually became clear to him that the "liberalism" for which he had crusaded in the Church, in student circles and in ecumenical discussions was no longer in the ascendant but that views which appeared to him reactionary or obscurantist were gaining increasing support—and this not only amongst the ill-informed but also amongst those whom he was bound to regard as amongst the leading thinkers of his time.

This is his reply to Dr. Oldham:

Mr dear Joe,
I am very sorry if my allusion to your criticism of my views is unfair or unkind. I said it half jestingly in order to warn my hearers that I had been and am an unrepentant liberal in theology.
Your letter gives me opportunity to explain the source of the

impression which I reported at Westminster. In the volume which you prepared before the Oxford conference, called, I think, *The Churches Survey their Task*, my theological position was reviewed and condemned as optimistic and superficial. No names were mentioned and perhaps I was wrong in reading a personal reference into the comment. But it came at a time when I was religiously very lonely. I had been dropped out of almost all ecumenical work in spite of my share in Copec and the Jerusalem conference. I had also no position at all in my own Church except a nominal connection with Ely. I had a very difficult piece of work in Cambridge trying to unite a Faculty which was deeply divided and a College which was under peculiarly trying leadership. Consequently the criticism hurt me far more than it should have done, and coming from you whom I have always loved and admired, it was more difficult to accept.

It is an old story now and I can write of it with detachment. I think you will realise how hard it then was for me to find myself almost entirely alone and unwanted by the movements in the Church in which I was peculiarly interested. Obviously no sort of blame attaches to you or anyone else. In fact, the discipline of it was probably of enormous value to me, especially in view of the amount of pain that I have had since. But it left a deep mark and has made me feel scarred ever since.

Forgive me for unburdening myself so intimately. But your letter touches me very deeply and I have recently hoped that some day I might be able to explain the matter to you.

For more than ten years Charles had felt rejected by the Church.[1] He had not been consulted about any vacancy in the Church's leadership. He knew that representations had been made on his behalf by well-wishing supporters when the see of St. Edmundsbury and Ipswich had fallen vacant in 1940 and again when Bishop David of Liverpool retired in 1944. (How happy he would have been to return to his old associations on Merseyside.) But nothing came of them. He felt that the Prime Minister's Secretary for Appointments had a prejudice against Cambridge in general and perhaps against himself in particular

When opportunity arose he wrote frankly to his friend Wilson Harris, the University Member of Parliament, to the effect that some kind of discrimination was being exercised against Cambridge. He had never been asked whether any member of the Faculty of Theology might be suitable for high office. He ventured to mention in his letter the name of Launcelot Fleming, the Dean of Trinity Hall, as eminently qualified to bear some higher responsibility, and at least had the satisfaction of learning shortly afterwards that his friend had in fact been offered and had accepted the Bishopric of Portsmouth. But from 1937 onwards Charles felt "out of it". He had no pulpit in which he could minister regularly, no kind of ongoing pastoral responsibility. He even considered the possibility of combining the incumbency of St. Edward's Church in Cambridge when it fell vacant in 1939 with his Regius Professorship. But before a final decision needed to be taken he was elected to the Mastership of Christ's and this brought him the prospect of pastoral work and preaching in his own College which to some extent supplied the need of which he had grown increasingly conscious. Still, when all was said and done, it was difficult not to feel that the authorities of the Church had rejected him as a potential leader. Was it the case that there was no longer a place for liberals in the Church of which he was an ordained minister?

Then in regard to ecumenical movements within Christendom at large: at Jerusalem in 1928 Charles had gained international recognition; at Oxford in 1937 he had prepared one paper and served on one of the Commissions but had by no means played a leading part; at the Edinburgh Conference on Faith and Order in 1937, at the International Missionary Conference at Madras in 1938, he had figured not at all. Yet no one had been more eager than he to break down the barriers which divided Christendom into mutually exclusive denominations. He had preached in Churches of other communions in Britain and in America at a time when such action lacked official approval. He strongly advocated the practice of united communion as a means towards achieving unity. He rejoiced in his relationships with the leaders of the Free Churches in Cambridge. He greatly admired the Presbyterian tradition and welcomed any opportunity to minister in the Church of Scotland. Yet it seemed that within the growing organisation of the ecumenical movement and its official meetings his own contribution was no longer valued. Was it again the case that the kind of liberal theology which he represented and advocated had lost all its former appeal and that his would become increasingly a voice crying in the wilderness?

Perhaps most bitter of all was the realisation that he could no longer arouse the enthusiam of the young and rally them to the cause of liberalism in the way that he had previously succeeded in doing. Up until about 1935 he had been constantly in demand for student conferences; his books and articles had been widely read by students; he had seemed to express symbolically the theological outlook of the Student Christian Movement and had counted its younger scholars as amongst his most devoted friends and supporters. But slowly and subtly the climate was changing. He was still in demand in his own University and as preacher, for example, at the late Sunday evening services in St. Mary's, Oxford, But at student conferences continental theologians were gaining a respectful hearing, Reinhold Niebuhr was being lionised, the *Student World* (the magazine of the International Student Christian Federation) was giving a strong lead in the direction of the theology of crisis and even the organ of the British Student Christian Movement was, it seemed, less hospitable to "liberal" views than had for long been its tradition. In fact Liberalism was no longer the *popular* movement. Yet half bitterly, half defiantly, Charles still claimed that he was an "unrepentant liberal".

By the time that he came to give his Gifford Lectures in 1951-2, he had perhaps reached a stage when he could look back on the progress of events rather more dispassionately. In an appendix to the First Series he does indeed refer to an "anti-liberal crusade" which had been waged in the Church and which had been given detailed historical documentation in the two volumes of Canon Roger Lloyd's *History of the Church of England in the Twentieth Century*. But at the beginning of the Second Series he speaks in cooler terms of the "liberal" and "modernist" movements in British Christianity and describes how the term "liberal" in England has been used in a different sense from that common in

Continental Protestantism, how the term "modernist" has represented something other than Roman Catholic "Modernism". He traces liberalism in Britain back to the Cambridge Platonists whose desire was to avoid the extremes of Puritanism on the one side, the Catholicism of Archbishop Laud on the other and brings it forward through Coleridge and Maurice to the Cambridge trio who remained in many respects his heroes—Lightfoot, Westcott and Hort (and of these Hort occupied a special place in his affections because of his wide-ranging scientific interests). Charles, though often appearing on the platform of the Modern Churchmen's Union, did not identify himself with its more controversial activities. He wanted to be in the fullest sense of the word a liberal, a man concerned for a reasonable faith, with a proper regard for the contributions of scientific and historical studies, and with a tolerance towards other's opinions which it was assumed they would show towards his own.

Standing as he did however for this kind of liberalism, Charles found himself threatened on the one side by what in the broadest terms can be designated "neo-orthodoxy", on the other side by what can perhaps best be described as "neo-catholicism". From roughly the year 1930 onwards the Western world began to close in on itself. The days of free expansiveness in which the individual could move hither and thither, making fresh discoveries and establishing fresh conquests, were drawing to an end. New methods of rapid communication were bringing the peoples of the world closer to one another. New weapons of war were reducing the ranges of isolation from areas of conflict. In face of aggression and threats to one's own personal safety or identity or integrity the natural instinct is to turn to others for support and reassurance. As the world closed in, the Church also closed in to become the Church of the authoritative Word or the Church of the authoritative Order. The times were becoming too serious, it seemed, for every man to do what was right in his own eyes. The call was for a new obedience to God's Word, a new discipline within God's Order—a closing of the ranks, a rediscovery of the distinctiveness of the Christian Gospel, a determination to stand for the faith against all assaults of the enemy in whatever guise he might come.

But all this appeared to Charles, living it must be admitted in a peculiarly sheltered part of a peculiarly sheltered island, to be a policy of retreat based either on fear or despair. To him the most serious challenge was that which sprang from the seemingly omnicompetent power of Science to control nature and human life. It was of little use to close the ranks around the Bible or the Hierarchy if thereby Christians cut themselves off from the great tasks confronting them (those of relating the Christian faith to the natural sciences and the human sciences, those of studying "God and everything else together") and allowed the world at large to blunder on towards destruction. So he continued to champion the cause of liberalism as he conceived it against every form of what he regarded as a deliberate anti-liberal crusade. But this inevitably brought him into conflict—sometimes unhappy conflict—with many other Christians during those critical years.

First there was his liberal attitude to questions of Church *Order*. He had little interest in the detailed examinations of episcopacy and its relation to apostolic succession which occupied the minds of so many Anglican theologians during the 1930s. Strangely enough he agreed with them in regarding the Church as a living *organism* rather than as a planned organisation. But he drew from this conception very different conclusions from those of his Anglo-Catholic contemporaries. For them it implied that there must be a continuing skeleton *structure* in the Church; for him that there must always be adaptation of *function* to emerging needs and circumstances. Charles was not amused when a young Anglo-Catholic reviewer of his book *The Gospel and the Church* referred to "his defective theology", exhorted him to study "the doctrine of the mystical body" and declared that the Church's "hierarchical organisation, so far from being the negation of organic community, provides the structure which every complex organism must have."[2] Thus whereas the Catholic looked at an organism and saw its bony structure, Charles the liberal looked as it and saw its amazingly dynamic sensitivity and adaptability to new conditions. It was this that he wanted above all to see in the Church of his own day.

On the theological level this difference did not trouble Charles unduly: he was quite convinced of the rightness of his own position. But on the level of practical policies the matter could be more serious. For years he had preached in churches and chapels of other denominations when invited to do so and no formal protest seems ever to have been made. From South Wales came a pained protest from a Rector when he learned that Charles was to be preaching in the Salem Baptist Chapel on the evening when his own Harvest Festival was to be celebrated. But in England there had been no restraint on his interdenominational activities. It was in Scotland, however, that the storm broke and Charles found himself involved in a situation which would fortunately have been almost unthinkable a quarter of a century later.

Some time in 1939 Dr. W. A. Smellie, the Minister of the ancient and beautiful St. John's Kirk in Perth, invited Charles to conduct a series of Holy Week services in his Church the following year. This notice however was too short but Charles agreed to go in 1941. It so happened that the Bishop of St. Andrew's was visiting St. John's Manse in the spring of 1940 and was told that this arrangement had been made. His reaction was one of mingled indignation and dismay. He expressed his determination to prevent such a breach of Anglican order in every way possible. Smellie relayed news of this encounter to Charles who replied immediately in the following terms:

"I am *very* sorry and ashamed that you should meet this sort of behaviour on the part of a bishop. But please do not think that it will in any way affect me.

As Professor here I am under no ecclesiastical authority but the Crown; and in Scotland the Crown is presbyterian not episcopalian! Furthermore I have by persistent refusal to confine myself to Anglican pulpits secured a certain liberty. No bishop has for many years past tried to prevent me from preaching in the churches of other denominations and I have long ceased to ask permission to do so. If a Scottish bishop tried to stop me from preaching for you, I should deny his authority to do so: but honestly I dont think he would be so foolish as to try.

Nothing more transpired for some months and it appeared that the Bishop had decided to take no action. But in point of fact he had mistaken the proposed date of Charles's visit. He thought it had been arranged for 1940 and it evidently came as a shock to him when in March 1941 he learned that Charles was actually being announced as the preacher for Holy Week at St. John's Kirk that year. He wrote at once to his friend, Eric Graham, the Principal of Cuddesdon College, to enquire whether at this eleventh hour he would intercede with Charles to cancel this ill-advised commitment.

Graham wrote on March 12th, evidently with some embarrassment, about what he admitted was no business of his. He testified to the fine Christian qualities of the Bishop—gentle and humble and the most lovable of men but firm on principles which he believed himself called to defend. If Charles went to Perth it would seem to be part of a deliberate attempt to expose the Bishop as an unreasonable and bigoted man. No such appeal, however, would induce Charles to change his mind and a somewhat painful correspondence ensued.

Though an appeal was made to the Archbishop of Canterbury his letter *to* Charles did not reach him until Tuesday in Holy Week, after the series had begun. He replied with respect that even if the letter had arrived in time it would not have in any way affected his conduct.

For the moment the issue in Scotland seemed to have been settled. Charles gave his addresses in Perth and no dire consequences followed. But the incident was not forgotten by the Bishops of the Episcopal Church and in 1949 he found himself in conflict with them on another issue. In October of that year he was invited by the Chairman of the Committee of Council of Trinity College, Glenalmond (whose Warden was a friend of Charles) to allow his name to be submitted for election to the Council at its next meeting. The proposal had the support both of the Warden and of the Bishop of Edinburgh and Charles, who had long been interested in the College, had no hesitation in accepting the invitation to serve if elected. (One can suspect that the prospect of a journey to his well-loved Scotland twice a year, with all expenses paid, especially to the highlands of Perthshire which had been one of his happy hunting grounds for birds and plants, made a ready appeal to him!) But three weeks later a letter arrived from an old friend of Liverpool days, John C. H. How, who had gone from the Rectory of Liverpool to become Bishop of Glasgow and Galloway and was later elected Primus of the Scottish (Episcopal) Church, to say that at a meeting of the Bishops in Edinburgh "no little consternation" had been aroused when they learned that Charles's name was to be proposed as a member of the Council; they would have strong hesitations about voting in his favour. Would he really find himself in sympathy with the peculiar position of an Episcopalian School in the heart of Presbyterian country?

The letter was most cordial and the Primus expressed his own pleasure at the prospect of being associated in a piece of service with Charles once again. But he felt bound to ask for some reassurance that Charles would appreciate the definite Episcopalian status of the School and be in sympathy with its specific aims and objects. This assurance, however, Charles flatly refused to give. The initial letters which had come to him had mentioned nothing of the kind. He would certainly promise loyalty to the College as a member of the Council but if the Bishops were now suggesting that he should, as a condition of membership, promise to abstain from ever again preaching in Presbyterian Churches or in the Scottish University Chapels then it was clear to him that he could give no such pledge without violating his conscience. The Primus replied at length, pointing out that University Chapels were regarded as extra-ecclesiastical and that he was not asking for a pledge—only that Charles would respect the sensitivities of Episcopal Bishops who were seeking to uphold the principles of the Church they were serving.

With Charles still refusing to capitulate, it looked as if the meeting of the Council on December 7th would be an exceedingly awkward one. But instead it proved to be a complete anti-climax. Before any ecclesiastical questions were raised a layman, Admiral James, objected to the nomination on account of Charles's age—the Council needed younger men seeing that nearly all its members were relatively advanced in years. The point was taken and Charles was not invited. The Primus and the Chairman of the Committee of Council wrote handsome letters of apology that he should have been troubled in the first place. Obviously the Primus, though embarrassed, was enormously relieved that the question of Church loyalties had never been raised and that the candidature had never needed to be debated on these grounds. It was doubtless a disappointment to Charles—but the Gifford Lectureship which he was soon to undertake would yield far greater satisfaction than anything that might have come to him through meetings of a Council which at least at that time would have been sharply divided in their attitudes to this liberal Churchman who might prove to be a cuckoo in their nest.

With all his love for the Church of Scotland Charles fully realised that it too had not been immune from the spirit of anti-liberalism, especially in matters of Biblical criticism and doctrinal formulation. This was brought vividly home to him when he engaged in a close study of the life of W. Robertson Smith in preparation for the Oration which he had been invited to give at the celebrations in Aberdeen on November 8th, 1946 of the centenary of his birth. This utterly brilliant student of Semitic languages and literature had been deprived of his Chair in Scotland because of what were regarded as his heretical views on Biblical criticism but had subsequently received honour and hospitality as a Fellow of Christ's in Cambridge. It was natural that the Master of his old College should point out how great had been Cambridge's gain through Edinburgh's loss. He did not hesitate to criticise Principal Rainy who had to some extent been exonerated from blame by his biographer, Carnegie Simpson.[3]

Whatever may have been the demands of ecclesiastical order and expediency this did not in Charles's view excuse the veiled persecution of a man whose only concern was for truth and honest scholarship. At Aberdeen he reminded his audience that Christ's had been praised in a history of the University of Cambridge for its "large-minded comprehensiveness" where "men of all creeds and parties enjoy harmonious College intercourse." In such a setting Robertson Smith had found himself completely at home. His near-omniscience had become proverbial and yet all his knowledge had been integrated as his life's offering to God. Scripture and history, Judaism and Christianity, worship and morality—Robertson Smith had gained eminence in one field after another and although he had died at a comparatively early age his name would live as that of a daring pioneer who never sought fame for himself but only that truth might prevail and a fuller integration of knowledge be established.

This was Charles's one attempt to explore Scottish church history in any detail though he was happy in his Gifford's to celebrate the achievements of such "liberal" thinkers as Thomas Erskine of Linlathen, Henry Drummond (whose writings on natural law in the spiritual world were in some respects an anticipation of Teilhard de Chardin and of Charles himself), Archibald Allan Bowman the Glasgow philosopher, "greatest of our prophets after the First World War", and of course in particular "the great teachers and leaders whom Scotland sent to us" (i.e. to Cambridge)—James Adam, Peter Giles, John Oman and Alexander Wood. To these Scotsmen of an earlier generation Charles owed an incalculable debt. But amongst those of his own contemporaries none became closer to him in mind and outlook than the Founder of the Iona Community, George MacLeod and his associate in the enterprise, Garth Macgregor, the distinguished Professor of New Testament in the University of Glasgow. Both were pacifists, both were deeply concerned about new experiments in Christian life and witness.

From the earliest days of the Iona Community in 1938 Charles became an eager supporter of the enterprise and a frequent visitor to the island. In May 1939 MacLeod was corresponding with him about possible dates of his coming to lecture or conduct retreats and concluded his letter. "You have no idea what an encouragement it is to me to feel that you are with me in this thing." In January 1944 he offered him the prospect of bringing Mrs. Raven so that after a week of lectures the two might holiday together on the island for the rest of the time— an arrangement tragically disrupted by Bee's sudden death in June. In spite of this Charles fulfilled the engagement in August and on his return home received a letter which reveals how close a bond had been established between the two men.

"I suspect that the return home has a sweetness but also an agony when there is not, as of yore, someone to relate all to and to give you the news. Prevenience is of the essence of Grace and I want you to know how grateful we are before you are settled in. To travel a thousand miles to address a couple of handfuls of distraught Presbyterians is no obligation on a Regius Professor, least of all when he should be going gently; and to live in a cell 6 ft. by 2 ft. is no catch for anyone who knows the Master's House at Christ's College. But I hope the oyster plant and the birds were partial compensation.

Your words and understanding were an enormous encouragement to me: especially your sharing of the agony that you have something to get across but fear the rope you throw only slithers on the other deck and falls back to you.

So Charles gave time and energy to serve whenever possible and received from Iona the friendship and inspiration which he specially valued through the trying years 1939–47. Both Iona and the Chantry appealed to Charles's sense of the romantic, to his love of nature and to his readiness to respond to manifestations of the Spirit in intimate fellowship wherever found. In both settings he could speak with complete freedom and with the assurance of a whole-hearted response. Dr. Archibald Craig, who was for a short time Assistant Leader of the Iona Community and knew Charles well, has pictured him in action at one of the summer conferences on the Island.

"One treasured memory of Raven concerns a course of talks he gave in Iona under the auspices of the Iona Community. Standing in front of us without any kind of desk or notes, sometimes leaning, indeed lounging, against the mantelpiece of the conference-room fireplace, he spoke on each occasion for the best part of an hour in a fascinating way: syntax clear and crisp, diction attractive; the flow of thought never losing continuity but changing direction or pace from time to time in leisurely loops or exciting leaps; and all so full-fed and effortless. His theme—the developing relationships between religion and science in the history of the West—had been a lifelong interest and was presently to appear as an ingredient in his Gifford Lectures, so that his mind was doubtless saturated with it. Yet not

all scholars, let alone Gifford lectures, can speak with such easy
mastery of their subject-matter or present it with such skill to a given
audience in extempore speech as Raven did on that occasion.

> They that in play can do the thing they would,
> Having an instinct throned in reason's place,
> —And every perfect action hath the grace
> Of indolence or thoughtless hardihood—
> These are the best . . ."

All these are happy recollections of Iona and Charles's friendships
with senior member of the Community. But amongst the younger
members some were critical of Charles's "liberal" theology. Of these
the most outspoken was Alex Miller, a young New Zealander who
had been prominent in S.C.M. circles in his own country and after
coming to Britain had launched, with Daniel Jenkins as co-Editor,
a new "Journal of Confessional and Catholic Churchmanship"
entitled *The Presbyter*. To the March 1943 number Charles contributed
an article criticising what the leaders called "the new expression of the
Reformed Faith" in no uncertain terms. Confessing himself un-
ashamedly a liberal of the older generation he described the theology
expounded in an earlier article by Daniel Jenkins as "reactionary, ill-
founded, and if not itself transformed, disastrous". He accused the new
theologians of the younger generation of "arrogance and contempt"
and in particular deprecated their uncritical approach to the New
Testament writings, their indifference to the facts of history and their
Apollinarian Christology. He regarded their emphasis on the Reformation, rather than on the rise of the modern Scientific Movement, as a
misjudgment of the most significant factor relating to our own time
and their neglect of the doctrine of the Holy Spirit as an index of their
inability to understand the nature of true immanentism and of the way
in which the Divine life is manifested in humanity and in the universe
at large.

"That a 'new Reformation' as T. H. Huxley called it is sorely
needed, "he concluded "I should be the last to deny. My whole life

has been an effort to promote its coming. But it is a Reformation not in terms of Chalcedon, Luther and Dr. Barth, but in those of the twentieth century, of Christ as the consummation of the creative process, of the scientific method and outlook applied to the whole range of experience, and of an interpretation covering every aspect of life, individual and corporate. It will in fact preserve that "proportion of the faith" which the Apostles were inspired to reveal but which the "new theology" seems at present to impair."

Daniel Jenkins, a young Congregationalist who had gained wide acclaim through his book *The Nature of Catholicity*, replied to Charles in the April number in an article entitled *Do Liberals Understand It?* (i.e. the Reformed Faith). As regards the charge of seeming arrogance he suggested that this may be due to the quite different conception of the nature of theological truth which "reformed" theologians hold in contrast to "liberals".

"As we understand them, they are not as concerned as we are to assert the absolute once-for-all character of the Gospel revelation and the necessity for marking off its truth from that of the world. They are more at home in approaching truth through probabilities and relativities, which approach they may think is the more humble and reverent one. We do not, and give reasons for our position."

On the matter of the appeal to history he suggests that it is Dr. Raven who is unhistorical in that he tries to recreate a "Jesus of history" in harmony with modern ideas instead of allowing full weight to the faith and witness of His earliest interpreters. And so far as the appeal to scientific method is concerned Jenkins asserts that "the methods of the scientist are not those of the theologian": the latter is concerned with man's fundamental relation to God and God's ordinance for his world which have not been changed by the rise of the scientific movement. Finally in rebutting the charge that the Reformed theologians neglect the doctrine of the Holy Spirit Jenkins contrasts their own emphasis on the Spirit Who is received only when the Father is known through His Son, Jesus Christ, with Dr. Raven's "diffused world-spirit, manifesting itself everywhere with large-hearted comprehensiveness", "like a sign-post pointing in all directions and therefore giving no guidance at all."

"We need a new Reformation in terms of the twentieth century. We are agreed. But these are the terms of a civilisation hopelessly adrift from its moorings in God, and moving blindly to destruction. The whole purpose of the revival of Reformed theology is to safeguard and illumine and confirm the truth of that message, in a time when on every hand it is distorted and denied."

The exchange was restrained and useful. It showed how wide the gulf had become between the "liberal" whose eyes rejoiced to see the wonderful works of God manifested in nature and human personality, and the "Reformed" who looked out on the world and saw God's judgments at work in the history of an apostate civilisation (though in the midst of human history could also be seen the once-for-all manifestation of His grace and mercy in the revelation of His Son). Charles was particularly distressed by the fact that the Student Christian Movement, which he had for more than twenty years regarded as the advance guard of the New Reformation, seemed to be selling out completely to continental influences and to reactionary theology. He deplored the way in which the magazine *The Student Movement*, under the editorship of Alan Richardson, had swung far over towards the neo-orthodox or anti-liberal position.[4] In fact he had become so disillusioned with the outlook of the theological leaders of the S.C.M. that in 1943 he was seriously suggesting that the Cambridge Branch might hive off from the main Movement and set up its own alternative organisation of a more liberal character. At least he was disposed to withdraw his own support—though as it turned out he became to some degree involved again in S.C.M. activities in the years after the War.

Though the exchanges in *The Presbyter* in 1943 had been comparatively mild, an article by Alex Miller in February 1944 stirred Charles to indignation and anger. It was the more painful to him in that Miller had become closely associated with the Iona Community whose fellowship had already come to mean so much to Charles himself.

Miller entitled his article, *Theological Counter-Revolution: Dr. Raven's last Two Books*,[5] and proceeded to attack him and them with no holds barred. Charles had dubbed the movement towards the medieval and Catholic which emerged in Anglicanism after the First World War and that towards Continental Protestantism which was associated with the crisis of the late Thirties as both "plainly pathological"; Miller turns the argument and suggests that the label may apply to Charles's own books, written as the author admits in a time of emotional and physical strain. Dr. Raven had questioned the "sincerity" of certain preachers of neo-orthodoxy: this Miller declared can only be called "unscrupulous controversy" and unworthy of serious debate.

Miller went on to deprecate passages which he described as "unregulated and undocumented abuse": "if Dr. Raven is to convince us—he must give us an orderly treatment of what Reformation theology says, rather than his own personal opinion of ill-defined trends which he happens to dislike."

He readily allowed that Dr. Raven had some very great things to say about a proper reverence for the created world and a regard for sound scientific work as true service of God: that he also had included in his commentary on the Epistle to the Romans "some very great expository writing". But the fact remained that younger Reformed theologians could no longer find the guidance they needed in the works of the theological masters of a former generation which had been "mapped in the placid colours of the nineteenth century;" they looked instead to the theologians of crisis to provide them with an ordnance map to direct them forward step by step in the dark and dangerous times in which they were living.

This was perhaps the severest treatment that Charles ever received and he resented it deeply. Miller invited him to reply so that a clearer understanding of the important issues might be gained. But Charles declined, saying that no useful purpose would be served by simply repeating the substance of his books which he had no intention of withdrawing. He was particularly incensed at the way Miller had dismissed Oman as no longer speaking to his generation.[6] But so far as *The Presbyter* was concerned he preferred to make no comment. In

K

spite of Miller's protest that it was "a plain matter of public and church responsibility" for Charles to offer some kind of response to the charges made against him, he refused to be drawn. He wrote a curt and almost brutally frank reply which he first submitted to George MacLeod as Miller was then staying in the Glasgow community-house. George's advice was to tear it up and leave things in a dignified silence. He regarded the reply as entirely justified but to drag out a correspondence of this kind would do no one any good. So the affair ended and Charles soon became busy with other things. It was not until he came to prepare the Gifford Lectures that he returned to a further consideration of Liberal Theology and its contribution to twentieth century thought. This proved to be a far more balanced exposition and revealed a more sympathetic understanding of what the young "Reformers" had been trying to do. Nevertheless Charles's self-chosen title "An Unrepentant Liberal" remained an apt description of the particular role which he tried to play out to the very end of his life.

That Charles was over-sensitive to criticism there can, I think, be little doubt. One harsh and one mildly critical review in the periodical *Theology* were enough to convince him that its Editor, Alec Vidler, bore some personal hostility towards him—a conviction which subsequent correspondence showed was entirely without foundation. He wrote to a friend about the hurt which he had received from reviews which he regarded as evidence of "a bitter and personal contempt". "I have had all my life pretty savage treatment from a large section of my own Church" (His treatment of Dr. Barth had not been particularly gentle!) The Church Times at one period was prepared "to slash anything of mine". His historical judgments he felt, had not been controverted—they had simply been ignored!

Yet he realised that it was all too easy to be guilty of "a sort of subtle self-pity". to "look for opposition where it was never intended". to be "unduly sensitive and ready to expect kicks instead of ha'pence," Partly this was due, he believed, to the fact that as a pacifist he had experienced "a lot of loneliness and of hostility" in the opening years of the Second World War. "Banned from the B.B.C., dropped by almost all the leaders of the Churches" he could hardly help feeling hurt and frustrated. And when physical pain and sickness in 1943 were added to the mental burden which he was already bearing the strain became almost intolerable. It was out of this increasing strain that Charles erupted, as it were, into a stream of written and dictated letters which include some of the most beautiful as well as some of the most deplorable passages that he ever allowed to appear in print.

NOTES TO CHAPTER SIXTEEN

1. p. 275: Someone composed the lines:
   Charles Raven
   Has no haven
   But he has a perch
   In the Anglican Church.
2. p. 279: *Theology*, XL p. 155 f.
3. p. 283: Professor at Westminster College, Cambridge and a friend of Charles.
4. p. 288: Charles had known Alan well in Liverpool in 1930 when he was attached to the Cathedral while acting as S.C.M. Secretary in the University. Charles could never understand Alan's view of history which he began to work out in about 1940 and which came to full expression in his Bampton Lectures in 1964.
5. p. 289: *Science, Religion and the Future* to which I have referred in Chap. 14.
6. p. 289: This drew from Miller the interesting reply that the man who first introduced him to Karl Barth said in doing so that Barth was simply the mountain torrent running down from the towering peak whose name was Oman.

PART FOUR

1939–1965

HISTORIAN, ADMINISTRATOR,
TRAVELLER

CHAPTER SEVENTEEN

Out of the Depths

Interest in his Open Lectures *Science, Religion and The Future* was sustained from beginning to end and when the lectures appeared in print *The Times Literary Supplement* not only gave one of its centre pages to a portrait of the author and a laudatory review of the book but also devoted its leading article to a consideration of the issues which Charles had raised. The review was entitled *The Two World Visions: An Essay on Conciliation*—an apt description of the goal towards which all Charles's labours were directed.

But having sent the manuscript to the Press in February 1943,[1] Charles seems to have become oppressed by the feeling that he was fighting against odds which were too powerful to be disposed of through reasonable argument or through any direct appeal to the lessons of history. In the Lent Term a series of University Sermons dealt with the general theme of the Incarnation and in some of these, particularly in one instance, the notion that man must seek to come to terms with *two worlds* received renewed emphasis, the Incarnation being viewed as an intrusion from without rather than as an evolution within. Now it so happened that in the previous year a book had appeared which had made an immediate appeal, both on account of its penetrating wit and by reason of its unusual form. This was C. S. Lewis's *Screwtape Letters*, an interpretation of the contemporary religious situation with which Charles may not have been in full agreement but whose epistolary form may have seemed capable of imitation. He had a close friend in Cambridge, the son of his own much revered former tutor. He was the Rev. Henry St. John Hart, the Dean of Queen's College, a man who shared to an unusual degree his own interests in natural history. Charles determined to write him a series of *letters*, based on the first eight chapters of the Epistle to the Romans and designed to speak as forthrightly as possible to those responsible for the direction of the policies of the Church at this critical time in world history.

The letters began to be written on March 10th: in August a book of more than a hundred pages entitled *Good News of God* appeared in print. Most of it had been written within ten days of its inception. Then came a sudden and serious heart attack bringing severe pain and an immediate check on all his activities. But he was labouring under a compelling constraint. As soon as it was humanly possible he began to dictate the concluding portions to Bee his wife and when the book appeared it was well-ordered, it bore striking chapter titles, and it related in an easy and natural way to the New Testament text which it was intended to expound.

But in character it was unlike anything else which he ever wrote. Reviews described it as "a passionate and violent challenge", as "breath-less argument", as a "prophet's exaggeration". One voice welcomed it as "a breath of sea air". Another, that of a near relation, has since condemned it as "a nasty book". In fact it is a curious mixture of eloquent and beautiful passages on the one hand, of embarrassingly personal and vindictive references on the other. It proclaims the good news of God's salvation exultantly. At the same time it indulges in querulous self-pity and in petulant criticisms of others.

The Preface gives due warning of what is to come. "Urgency", "violence", "insolent", "pathological", "obscurantism", "dogmatism" are samples of its vocabulary. Charles boils over with indignation as he contemplates the arrogance of some of the younger theologians of his day as they serve up their "hotch potch of second-hand scraps from the continent", and dismiss the whole massive achievement of British theological learning as shallow, optimistic and Pelagian. Worse than this, however, he allows himself to sit like Elijah under the juniper tree, lamenting the success of the enemies of true religion and regarding himself as an isolated martyr in the cause of righteousness and integrity.

"I have been for thirty-three years in Anglican orders, and have (I imagine and, from Crockford, can indicate) had as wide an experience of varied service as any living theologian. Perhaps on that account I am now entirely without any official status, benefice or other position in the ecclesiastical world—except that my University insisted upon my representing it in Convocation and my friend, the Bishop of Lichfield, pitying my solitude, has lately made me one of his Examining Chaplains. To my mind, this lack of status is not an excuse for silence, but a constraint to speech. I am that rare thing, an Anglican priest under legal obligation to no Bishop and for all practical purposes to no Archbishop. I can commit no one by my utterances and can be disowned by all. It ought to be possible, in such happy circumstances, to speak without fear or favour, for God and not for man."

"In such happy circumstances!" He had been banned from the wireless because of his pacifism, he had been rejected by many of the leaders in the student world because of his natural theology, he had been quietly forgotten by ecumenical organisers whose major interest was in continental theological developments, he had been left alone in Cambridge while his contemporaries, particularly those fortunate enough to possess an Oxford background, were being advanced to the episcopate! He was obviously labouring under severe strain, partly physical for he had pushed himself to the limit in writing the biography of John Ray, partly emotional, as he lived in the midst of the war-situation and yet tried to live apart from it, partly intellectual as he felt himself completely unable to accept the theological dualism, as it appeared to him, of continental scholars. And the strain caused him suddenly to erupt into what he admits could be regarded as a violent book. All this is understandable. What however is less easy to understand is how, when it came to revising and correcting proofs, he could have allowed to go forward into printed form certain passages which seem to be merely self-pitying, self-justifying and even self-applauding! Some portions are as moving as anything he ever wrote; some, one could wish, might never have appeared under the title *Good News of God*.

Yet in spite of its obvious defects the book, though little known today, remains extraordinarily readable. It has the character of rapid, ad hoc, theological journalism by a man who really knew his stuff and was prepared to express his criticisms without fear or favour! It draws upon thirty years of careful study of the Epistle to the Romans; yet the applications to modern problems are fresh and incisive. It presents the Christian doctrines of the Spirit, the Church and the Sacraments in terms which are readily understandable because of their relationship to phenomena which fall within our experiences of the natural world. Above all it glorifies the living Christ and reveals its author as a man utterly devoted to the Master whose way of life he was constantly "learning, contemplating and striving to follow."

Perhaps the most memorable section of the book is that in which Charles looks back upon momentary experiences of ecstasy when, as it were, he entered into the very presence chamber of God Himself. It is worth quoting in full for it reveals the memories which meant most to him at a time when he was oppressed by the darkness of a world at war and by the apparent inability of the Church to illuminate that darkness in any appreciable way. These are the memories to which he returns and thereby regains encouragement and hope.

"The first and, as I now see it, the beginning of my consciousness of God, in my first summer term at Uppingham. Three small boys, two Scottish twins and myself, out for a walk on a Sunday afternoon. We had gone down the Leicester road past the mile post, struck left over the fields towards Wardley and the Eye Brook; and suddenly— I can see that scene with the inward eye as clearly as the view from my study window now; the fall of the hill, the drift of woodland in all the glory of June across the middle distance, the water meadows and slopes beyond fading into a dim blue haze where earth and sky met and mingled; and close at hand the hedgerow and a red squirrel racing up a little oak, and the blue butterflies dancing over the buttercups. I can see it, and catch the scents of it, and feel the play of wind and sun on my cheek, and experience again the sense of wholeness and goodness, of pulsing and sustaining and integrating life.

Or, again, and this was my coming of age, the day at the end of our summer holiday at Bassenthwaite when I had finished my freshman's year, the day when I set out alone on a bicycle, meaning to go by Keswick and Crosthwaite and Seatoller over the Styehead to Wastdale and back by the coast and Cockermouth, and discovered that the long carry over the pass was too much for me, and felt the pull of Great Gable, and spent timeless hours on its cairn facing what Ruskin had called the finest view in Europe. I have described that view (*Musings and Memories*, p. 147) and even tried to paint it; but no words, no pigments can tell the wonder of it for a youngster then first initiated into the presence-chamber of the hills and discovering his "Mount of God". I went up a boy, a boy who out of solitariness and great unhappiness was finding joy. I came down a man, ready for a man's adventuring. How can I select from a hundred moments, which could then be multiplied a hundredfold?

The day in the summer of 1917 in the trenches on the La Bassée front, those old trenches which were a museum full of the mixed evidence of three years of war. I had been gassed—forbidden to do duty, but allowed to hang about in the line. There was a corner of Old-Boots Trench where the naked chalk was bedight with a robe of popppies and cornflowers and marguerites—the tricolour of France—and where a swallow-tail butterfly and then a big queen hornet thrilled my entomological soul. I sat on the rough revetment and made a pencil-sketch of it—the peace of God in a land at war. And down the trench came a stretcher-party and a shapeless bundle that an hour before had been a laughing boy. And the presence enfolded him— plants and insects, the dead and the living were all ablaze with the Shechinah of God.

Or the day in 1927 which was (I suspect) the real birthday of my book, *The Creator Spirit*, the day when the pulling together of my scientific and religious interests was accomplished and I first achieved intellectual integration and a coherent outlook. It was in the Isle of Man on Clay Head overlooking Laxey Bay, where a single rock lies off the coast and a greater blackback nesting on it was being mobbed by Herring Gulls, and further off a party of black guillemots were courting on the smiling waves. I had been photographing the gulls and making notes of the antics of the auks when again the mystery was enacted. The scene, there as always, remains indelible in my memory. But it was charged with meaning. Hitherto I had exploited nature, collecting pictures and observations, using its resources for the satisfaction of my own curiosity and possessiveness. Now I knew that there was more in it than a playground for the children of men or a training-school for artist or scientist. Here was a world alive, transparent, sacramental; the work of God, the object of His love, the body of His indwelling. It was for me to enjoy. "And God saw that it was good"—that is how its story begins; "So God loved the world" is the secret of its suffering and its redemption. Or (and I must bring my recital to an end) the day in 1933, when the collapse of work in which I had spent eight years, the breakdown of friendships, and the sense of helplessness and frustration drove me out to a pursuit which I had forgotten for twenty years, to an evening's moth-collecting in Roswell pits. Lamp, net, treacle-tin, pill boxes were dug out from their cupboard, and after supper I started off shamefacedly to renew my youth. It was in fact renewed. The eye that can discriminate one species from another—in this case, *Leucania straminea* and *L. obsoleta* from *L. impura*—had not grown dim; the trick of boxing the desired specimen out of a multitude of others on the sugarpatch—a sleight of hand only acquired by years of practice—had not been forgotten: the ancient fascination of that most thrilling hobby resumed its power. But these did nothing but provide a temporary escape. The healing came when with the sudden closing in of darkness the perspective became a silhouette, and the wide horizon of the fenland narrowed down to the small circle of the lamp. You know how in that little world every leaf and reed-blade takes on value; how one becomes aware of ranges of beauty and interest normally ignored. So it was then. But out of the wealth of detail there was for me a drop of water in the axil of a teazle-leaf—a drop of water, and in it all the fullness of God. Our little lives, our fret and pain, so tiny and yet so tremendous. A drop of water and the presence of God."[2]

But not all of his memories were of this kind. There are caustic and almost bitter sections, referring to ways in which friends had "let him down". And the concluding paragraphs of the book are the saddest of all, showing that something had happened which had hurt him so deeply that the pain could never be forgotten. The new Reformation which he hoped was on its way, the new Pentecost with the Spirit of God reviving the whole Church, had been resisted and blocked by men of little faith and less imagination. Could there even yet be a reversal of this failure, a discovery or recovery of the experience of life in the Spirit and the outlook upon the universe which that life implied?

"Eighteen years ago I made a first attempt at such a recovery. I was in Liverpool with a bishop deeply concerned to bring unity and inspiration to his clergy in order to prepare them for evangelism. I wrote and lectured and preached on the subject continuously. Then we planned a course of studies centred upon the work of the Spirit in nature and history, in Scripture and the Church. We explored the whole field in the programme of the Church Congress held at Southport in 1926. We followed it up by the plans which led to the movement called the Way of Renewal, a movement whose object was to gather and instruct the clergy both by schools of study and by carefully prepared literature. We carried the work all over the dioceses of England. And we saw enough to be very sure that, where a living faith in the Spirit was given, great results did in fact follow. I shall never forget those schools—for the penitence and the wonder and the joy that they brought. To see men who had lost all hope beginning to discover afresh their faith in God and to find that He had need of them for His great adventure, and to believe that even in Little Puddlington they could fit themselves for His service. I can never forget the beauty of it—or the sure hope that it inspired.

They took the work from me—no doubt for adequate cause. They handed it over to persons, older, more cautious, more respectable. And in a few months it was dead. Then they dressed up a changeling in its place—one of those evangelistic campaigns on the lines of the eight-day missions which have become so heavily familiar.

They killed the baby then. But the life that was in it can be re-embodied; and perhaps the time for its revival is near. At least for myself I am sure of this, that as we can enter into that vision of the creative purpose of God which came to fill and dominate the thought of St. Paul; as we can recover the passion and work for the unity of the early Christians; as we can feel and respond to "the gift of the Holy Spirit," so even now we can in our measure be used to redeem the time."

Through this series of eight urgent, passionate, outspoken letters Charles had thrown down a challenge both to the scientists of his day who often seemed indifferent to questions of social morality and to the ecclesiastics who often seemed obsessed with the trivia of rank and ceremony. In addition he had poured scorn on the youthful devotees of Continental theology and in particular had seized every opportunity to express his antagonism to Barth and to the whole theological outlook which he represented. What reactions would there be to this onslaught?

At first it seemed that there would be very little. It was war time and scientists had other things to think about. In the Church papers allowances were made for exaggeration and exasperation expressed in some of the purple passages, while the concern for a deepening of personal spiritual experience was genuinely welcomed. The Church of England has, at least in modern times, dealt gently with its rebellious sons and it was not likely to be unduly disturbed by this outburst from a Regius Professor of Divinity at Cambridge.

But the sharpest response to the challenge, which was in fact a counter challenge, came from an unexpected quarter: from one who had in very real measure been adopted into his own intimate family circle. That a man to whom he had given himself so fully should dare to question his interpretation of the Christian Gospel and to rebut point by point many of the charges made in *Good News of God*, constituted one of the most painful experiences of Charles's life. For years he had been sniping at Barth and decrying the theology of Continental Protestantism. In *Good News of God* minor criticisms had exploded into an all out condemnation. And now a man whose scholarship he admired and whose friendship he valued sprang to the defence of those under attack and tried to show that truth was by no means all on one side. To appreciate the poignancy of the situation which arose when in 1945 Franz Hildebrandt's book *This is the Message: A Continental Reply to Charles Raven* appeared, it is necessary to go back a little in history and to describe how this young German pastor came to Cambridge and formed so close an association with Charles at Christ's.

Franz Hildebrandt, who was born in 1909, grew up in Germany and after a distinguished career in university was ordained into the ministry of the Lutheran Church in 1933. He was three years junior to Dietrich Bonhoeffer and in the great Church conflict of the 1930s became his closest friend and associate. But although they shared so much in common intellectually, artistically, and spiritually they were separated from one another by that which under the Nazi regime was a fateful barrier: whereas Bonhoeffer was the son of an eminent Berlin physician about whose Aryan background there could be no question, Hildebrandt's mother was of Jewish extraction. This meant that his situation became increasingly precarious as anti-Semitic regulations became more and more stringent. Yet for a period the two friends were able to work together wholeheartedly in the service of the Confessing Church and all that it represented in contrast to the German Christian movement which had capitulated to the Nazi ideology.[3]

The most dramatic development for Hildebrandt occurred when Martin Niemoeller, to whose Church at Dahlem he had been called as assistant, was arrested by the Gestapo in July 1937. Hildebrandt thereupon assumed the responsibility for the conduct of services in this famous Church but was allowed to preach only on two Sundays before he was himself arrested and imprisoned. However, after four weeks, largely through the influence of the Bonhoeffer family, he was released. Yet his friends knew that the lot of any one with Jewish blood in his veins would become hazardous in the extreme and they persuaded him, therefore, to emigrate to England. Mercifully he had retained his passport and this enabled him to travel to London and take up an appointment as Assistant at St. George's Lutheran Church. There he kept in close touch with Bonhoeffer and with the progress of events in Germany. He welcome the results of the Chamberlain mission and still hoped that peace could be preserved.

It was unthinkable, however, that he could return to Germany while Hitler remained in power. Early in 1939 he took charge of the Lutheran congregation in Cambridge and this gave him a good opportunity to engage in study with a view to obtaining an English academic qualfication.

He enrolled for the Ph.D. degree and Christ's provided him with the necessary College affiliation. In this way, both through the Faculty of Divinity and through College contacts, Charles became associated with this brilliant young German pastor and did every thing possible to support him in his academic work and in his pastoral duties at a time of growing tension. Already in the spring of 1939 they were joint speakers at a Conference and Charles was referring to Franz as "my friend".

Few men in England did more for refugees from the Continent in the years between 1938 and 1948 than did Charles. This was specially true of academics who often found it desperately hard to find employment of any kind in Britain, let alone a position matching their qualifications. Charles did everything in his power to find openings in Universities and when war broke out tried to make cultural facilities available for those held in detention. When for example in 1948 the Prisoner of War Camp at Trumpington, near Cambridge, was closed, the prisoners' representatives sent a special message of gratitude to Charles for all that he had done for their welfare. And in the case of Paul Roubiczek, who had been a prosperous book publisher in Berlin, Vienna and finally Prague, and who escaped to Cambridge in June 1939 holding a Czech passport and hoping for a visa to travel to the U.S.A.: when it became evident that the visa could not be obtained, Charles and Professor H. H. Farmer stood by him and his wife and even though for a period Roubiczek had to engage in manual work and his wife in domestic service, ultimately opportunities to teach German and to lecture on philosophy became available and Charles's support and encouragement were amply rewarded by the works of distinguished scholarship which Roubiczek in due time produced. There is a moving letter from Roubiczek to Charles written in August 1949 and saying in part: "You should be among the first to know that I have finished my book. It is indeed a relief—and I remember with great gratitude that this moment would have hardly ever come without your constant help and encouragement."

Unhappily Charles's efforts were not always crowned with success. A German doctor who had marched from Auschwitz to Buchenwald and had come out of the second camp alive, tried to gain permission to practise in England. But although Charles pleaded his case through correspondence with Lord Horder, the appeal was refused and the doctor was forced to emigrate to America. Such were some of the special cases. But in a more general way, the very challenge of exile and dispossession and war made Charles the more eager to labour for hospitality and recognition and reconciliation. He welcomed Hildebrandt to Cambridge and when war broke out gave enthusiastic support to his friend Max Warren who, with the help of Hildebrandt, inaugurated joint services at Holy Trinity Church for English and Germans to worship together. After the services many of the participants would cross the road to Christ's for a reception and later on services of a similar kind were held in Christ's Chapel itself.

In spite of these apparent rapprochements, Charles retained his deep antipathy towards Continental theology in general and to Barth in particular. But now a young man schooled in the best German academic disciplines but exiled from his own country, a man who had proved his courage and independence of mind by the part he had played in the drama of the Confessing Church, had come into the Cambridge circle to learn and at the same time to share with others the story of the struggles in which he and many others had been involved for the sake of conscience; was there not now the chance of establishing new understanding and a real reconciliation between German and English theology? Could not Charles and his friend Franz stand together as witnesses to the Gospel in a time when darkness was again descending upon the whole of civilised Europe?

When the Camelot of the Chantry community took place at High Leigh, Hoddesdon in May 1939 Charles took Franz Hildebrandt with him as a fellow-speaker. The latter spoke first and showed how the experiences of the past six years had resulted in the emergence in Germany of the Confessing Church, standing over against National Socialism and calling for personal courage and sacrifice from all its members. Guidance and comfort came to them through the words of the Bible, not through the voice of Hitler. Following Luther's definition of Christian living they were seeking to teach truly, to pray eagerly, to suffer seriously. There could be no compromise with National Socialism. Only by teaching, praying and suffering in accordance with Christ's commands could the Church be faithful to its constitution and assured of ultimate victory.

Charles followed and in characteristic fashion took up the theme of suffering, as the only pathway to fuller life. But for him suffering was pre-eminently associated with passive resistance, with the stripping away of self-interest and self-seeking, with a purgation of motive and desire. It was concerned with keeping faith when evil in its many forms was infecting the life of the total society in which we live and to which we belong. For Hildebrandt suffering was bound to be the result of witnessing to the truth of Christ in face of demonic forces of paganism, witnessing openly, even aggressively, against such policies as anti-Semitism which is the first step leading to anti-Christ.

There were other occasions when the two men stood together and bore their witness to a faith which transcends all natural divisions. There was a notable service in Christ's Chapel on Whit Sunday 1940. The rape of Rotterdam had just taken place. Hildebrandt who had been due to preach in German, had been put under detention. At Charles's urgent request the police agreed to release him for two hours so that he might take part in the Service which proceeded with alternate lessons and prayers in English and German respectively and with Charles preaching in English, Franz in German.

Charles spoke passionately, eloquently; Franz quietly, as if nothing unusual had happened. Again in the autumn of 1942 the two men shared the addresses at a Service School and agreed to speak in turn on themes from Romans 1–8. It was then, apparently that Charles conceived his plan for *Good News of God*, though as it took shape in his mind he warned his friend that some of it would greatly annoy him. They had often talked together in the Master's Lodge, and debated theological issues; they had still maintained friendship even when it was evident that their ways of doing theology were in many respects radically different. The gulf widened when Hildebrandt preached a University Sermon in February 1943, which, though masterly in its presentation, was obviously Lutheran rather than Anglican in its basic approach and again when Charles, through *Good News of God*, revealed afresh how strongly he repudiated the theological stance of Barth and of those who made the Word of direct revelation normative for their theology.

Yet the friendship held and in September 1943 Hildebrandt's marriage was solemnised in Christ's Chapel. Writing to Charles afterwards he expressed heartfelt thanks to "both of you" for "making our wedding-day so beautiful for us." But *Good News of God* had been written as a challenge "without fear or favour." Charles confessed to a friend that when he wrote it he thought that in any case he would be dead before it appeared in print so did not mind what he said. Was it to go unanswered? Was this to be the final assessment of continental theology, a theology in which Hildebrandt had been nurtured and equipped for a life-and-death struggle and which he could now never repudiate? Could he not put his own case forward as an exercise in dialectic, discussing and debating the issues in public so that a fuller understanding of the differences between the British and German outlook could be appreciated? So with almost equal speed Hildebrandt composed ten letters between December 13th, 1943 and February 17th, 1944 in the form of a commentary on the First Epistle of John and these appeared in book form, nearly two years after *Good News of God* with the title: *This is the Message.*

Whereas Charles had been passionate and urgent, Hildebrandt remained cool and temperate, often witty, yet uncompromising in his dependence upon Scripture and Scripture alone.

His introduction is courteous and disarming. He had in fact been quite uncertain about the wisdom of replying publicly to Charles. He submitted the manuscript to Mrs. Raven privately and she upheld his right to dissent. When subsequently her sudden death occurred while the printing of the book was actually in process, he offered to stop publication but was persuaded by certain of Charles's close friends to go on. These are his opening sentences:

"When Pastor Niemoeller, as happened very frequently, had an outburst of impatience at a Pastors' meeting against the advisers of a more moderate course, Praeses Koch gave him a grave look out of his deep blue eyes and asked 'Must you just put it this way, Brother Niemoeller?'

The question, soon used as a proverb in the vicarage of Dahlem, may well be asked here when a mere newcomer and infant in the Spirit ventures to publish ten naughty letters addressed to one who in more than one sense is his Master. Enjoying the privilege of friendship and close daily contact with a great man may make a youngster lose his head and his sense of proportion; the diatribe may look, as I believe Bernard Shaw has once said of a similar undertaking, as if a puppy was barking at an elephant. Worse than that, in this case, the Continental guest, so generously received and nursed, may suddenly turn out to be a nasty fifth columnist at heart. Why should he, of all people, come forward with a reply to *Good News of God*?"

In essence *Good News of God* had been the cry of a disappointed and disillusioned man, a man who had hoped for so great things in the twenties, had seen the possibilities of realisation slipping away in the thirties and now felt lonely and rejected at a time when the majority of men were involved in the final blasphemy of war.[4] *This is the Message*, on the other hand, was the battle-cry of a younger man who, though he had been stripped of earthly attachments and possessions, had found strength to endure and confidence to overcome simply through hearing again and again the message of eternal life in Jesus Christ, the Lord and Saviour of men. The chapter headings are variations on the one theme of the Gospel: this is the message, the promise, the commandment, the record, the victory, the confidence. The text is concerned with that which makes man strong to face and overcome all the powers of evil; it is the Word of God bearing witness to Christ, His Death and Resurrection, His Mediation and Victory on man's behalf. Hildebrandt in the thirties had wrestled with the powers of darkness in high places, had confronted what he believed to be the very incarnation of Anti-Christ. Like Luther, therefore, he had become utterly dependent upon the Word from beyond, bringing the message of grace and hope and eternal life. To proclaim that message "without fear or favour" seemed to him his plain and over riding obligation as a Christian man.

Whereas, then, Charles was ever seeking to identify himself with the world around him, to sympathise with its defects and failures and to draw it back towards its only possibility of unity and peace in the purpose of God in Christ, Hildebrandt had been almost compelled to stand over against the world, to listen to its threats and blasphemies and to defy it through reliance upon the Word of God alone. In his experience he had found nothing to rely upon in the natural order. "You love your birds," he writes; "I love Tinkle our black Persian kitten. Both I believe are lovely gifts of God, delightful for us humans to play with; but one day Tinkle will grow into a big fat cat and neither your nor my pacifism will be strong enough to prevent him running away and killing one of your little birds. On which side is God? What do our animals tell us of His nature?" (p. 24). Again he had known nothing comparable to Charles's moments of ecstasy on which he laid so much store. So far as the record of history is concerned how can its puzzles and ambiguities be interpreted except in terms of Christ and Anti-Christ? And as for the sacraments of nature which Charles valued as channels of grace, how could they be distinguished from the sacraments for which the Nazis claimed a divine sanction? Luther's criterion "We know not of God except through Christ and we know not of Christ except through the Holy Spirit" had been the touch stone for those who were tempted to worship false gods in the Germany of the thirties. How could Hildebrandt abandon in his new context what had been his salvation in the old? He could not forget the way in which so many of his compatriots had heard what they imagined was the voice of God, through the words of Adolf Hitler. England was hardly likely to be immune to the blandishments of secular "revelations."

In a crucial passage Hildebrandt defines the fundamental difference between himself and the Master.

"The one thing I find missing in your interpretation of the Good News of God is the fact that the Good News is His revelation not our conception, His own Word coming down to us from heaven, carried by His messengers, the prophets and apostles, and embodied in the scriptures of the Old and New Testaments. Without these instruments we could not hear His voice: without these documents we could not read the Good News."

Not the immediacy of mystical experience but the mediation of a Divine message. Not the wonders of this world but the amazing incursions from another world. Not the search for an interpretation of life's meaning through ecstatic visions but the humble reception of the message of eternal life through the Son.

Here were the contrasts. Charles had his conception of unity: the summing up of the total cosmic process in Christ. Hildebrandt had his: the reference of all things to the one criterion of judgment, God's revelation in Christ. Charles had his trinity: the one creative process, the emergence of the perfect personality, the continuing energy of the Spirit. Hildebrandt had his: Propter Christum, per fidem, sola gratia. The two men found their bond of union in the God-Man, the living Christ. Their interpretations of the way in which God was related to man and the world through Christ were still radically different.

Before submitting his manuscript to the printer Hildebrandt sent a copy to Charles who first jotted down certain lines of defence and then wrote a considered reply.

"Lines of defence against F. H.

1. Whatever be the case in Germany the alternative for this country is not between Nazism and bibliolatry.
2. For one who confesses to a complete insensitiveness to natural beauty, a total ignorance of nature and of science, to deny that others can get from these things a "Word of God" is as presumptuous as

it would be for me to deny all significance to music because to me it is meaningless.

3. The treatment of Wesley's Arminianism is very onesided. He like me would deny that man can save himself: but he made his missionaries read his version of Ray's Wisdom of God in the works of creation.

4. The refusal to admit the goodness of the unconverted as in Article XIII Lutheranly interpreted is to me very near the blasphemy against the Holy Ghost of the Beelzebub story.

5. Christ though uniquely sacred is so in a representative not an exclusive sense—the consummation of all things not only of the Old Testament.

6. I have been usually attacked as a pantheist, that is as one who has no room for anything except God: it is interesting to be attacked now as a secularist, that is as one who has no room for God."

The first and last sentences in his letter were:

This seems to me a very clear, able and telling criticism which makes your position lucid and presents it attractively.

My only criticism is that I think the book would gain if it recognised (even if only here and there) that I am not always and everywhere to be trounced, and that (no doubt mistakenly) I too claim to be a Christian—not merely a Pelagian, Nestorian etc. etc. etc.

Though appearing to accept the criticism in good part, Charles felt that he had been wounded by a friend. Further the hurt was made the more painful by the very fact that his own book was the last product of that joyful co-operation between Bee and himself which ended so suddenly at the very time that *This is the Message* was in the press. From 1945 onwards contacts between the two men became infrequent and after Charles's retirement they did not meet again. It was a sad conclusion to a friendship which had promised to provide Charles with the best opportunity ever of entering more sympathetically into the continental outlook and recognising that there was more than one way of doing theology. But he was unable to surmount his antipathy to any kind of duality, dialectic, extended debate. His passionate concern was for *unity*, for the one comprehensive expression of truth, for reconciliation and synthesis rather than for the continuing struggle and the creative clash of contraries.

In what was virtually the final exchange of correspondence in 1948 Hildebrandt wrote:

> "When the signs of the times seemed to favour ecumenical work and outlook, my hopes rose high. But when I had written *This is the Message* and felt the pain which I had caused you, I knew that I had made my first mistake, and that "confessions" of this kind, however laudable in the German situation, were really not wanted here . . .
>
> That one could ever act as a bridge-builder, that another point of view but that of the Cambridge tradition could even find a hearing in the university, was a hope, which I have once had, but have buried long since."

Luther's maxim that only fighting made him productive was one which Charles could never have accepted for himself in theory, even though it could be claimed that the polemical passages in his own books are some of the liveliest and most memorable that he ever wrote.

NOTES TO CHAPTER SEVENTEEN

1. p. 295: The review in *The T.L.S.* appeared on May 22nd, 1943.
2. p. 300: *Good News of God*, p. 47 f.
3. p. 303: "Hildebrandt's father was the Professor of the History of Art in Berlin University, and his mother was of Jewish origin. Hildebrandt, who was Bonhoeffer's junior by three years, was working on a thesis on the Lutheran *est*. The two had first met at Seeberg's seminar on the morning of the day before Bonhoeffer defended his graduation thesis. Now on Good Friday 1929, they met again by chance at a performance of the St. Matthew Passion at the Berlin Choral Society.

   Hildebrandt influenced Bonhoeffer's imminent conversion to an ever-increasing Biblicism, and from his immense memory often supplied him with vital quotations from the Bible or from Luther. He soon became a welcome guest in the Wangenheimstrasse (the Bonhoeffer family home) and deputised worthily for Dietrich at the piano when the latter could not attend the family musical evenings. This was Bonhoeffer's first really close friendship, which survived the painful separation when Hildebrandt was forced to emigrate in 1937." Eberhard Bethge. *Dietrich Bonhoeffer. A Biography*, p. 101 f.

4. p. 308:   "In the past four years—since friends and hopes and work went to smash in the cataclysm of war—there has hardly been a single night during which I have not spent at least an hour, generally between 3 and 4 a.m. in hell. That is no figure of speech, if hell means a consciousness of total estrangement from God, of utter dereliction, in which one's eyes are open to the vast selfishness and consequent hurtfulness of one's life, to the multitude of opportunities misused, loyalties betrayed and relationships perverted." *Good News of God*, p. 81.

CHAPTER EIGHTEEN

Light Riseth Up in the Darkness

Towards the end of August 1944 Charles confessed in a letter to his friend Launcelot Fleming:

"Bee's gifts of hospitality and insight, of calmness and integrity, were the basis of all that we tried to do in College and I don't see how to carry it on alone."

In November when writing to his friend Leslie Hunter, the Bishop of Sheffield, about a visit he was planning to make to his home he said:

"Term goes along very well; and my Mary is doing excellently. But it is a bit grim—I get tired out after about half a normal day's work—and the colour and savour have gone out of things. However we carry on."

Things were indeed at a low ebb. Charles was still feeling the severe effects of his coronary; Bee's death had left him utterly bereft; his position as a pacifist in war-time had been one of constant strain—so many of his friends were on the other side and some had actually given their lives in the course of the conflict. When in August 1945 the atom bomb was dropped it seemed that Science itself, whose progress he had hoped would bring so great benefits to mankind, had been prostituted to serve the cause of evil and to threaten the whole future of the human race. Moreover his own time was running out. The College Statutes required him to retire from the Mastership in 1950. By the time things were restored to anything like normality in the life of the University he would find himself near the end of his tenure of both of his official positions.

Yet he must carry on. And there were some redeeming features in the total situation. His request that Mary should be released from her war-time work might well have been refused; in fact it was surprising that the obstacles had been overcome so easily. In the College he had the support of a young Chaplain of almost unparalleled brilliance and promise: Ian Ramsey, a former Scholar of Christ's who had been appointed Chaplain in 1943 and then, in 1944, had been elected to a Fellowship. His own work on the history of science was continuing steadily and was to result in a worthy successor to the John Ray bio-graphy—*English Naturalists from Neckam to Ray* which was published in 1947. And with the war ended there was bound to be an influx of men of unusual calibre—men who had passed through all kinds of challenging and often harrowing experiences and now were trying to prepare themselves academically for a return to civilian life.

So in spite of the depression of spirit from which it was desperately hard to break free, Charles took up his responsibilities again, giving his regular lectures in the Divinity Faculty and presiding over the affairs of the College as the Governing Body began to plan for the future. Many Christ's men had fallen in battle or through enemy action and it was hoped that as soon as possible a new building could arise in their honour. In addition it so happened that two of the most distinguished of all the war leaders had once been undergraduates in the College and there was not a little irony in the fact that a pacifist Master was destined to act as the intermediary through whom both of these men of action would be granted signal honours in their old University.

The first was Admiral Lord Louis (later Earl) Mountbatten who in 1946 was still Supreme Allied Commander in South East Asia. In May of that year the Governing Body of Christ's bestowed upon him its highest honour by electing him into an Honorary Fellowship. This he accepted and dined with the Fellows in Hall in the following month before going on with his wife and daughters to the May Ball. As a token of his appreciation he offered the College a Japanese sword and we find Charles writing to him on January 22nd, 1947.

"Yesterday we had our first meeting of the Governing Body since your visit. I presented your magnificent Japanese sword. It lay on the table before me like the Speaker's Mace. I was asked to express to you our gratitude and apppreciation."

In March Lord Mountbatten assumed office as Viceroy of India and before long Charles was corresponding with him again.

The second distinguished war leader was Field Marshal J. C. Smuts. Over a long period Charles had admired him as a man and had warmly approved of his holistic philosophy. Probably he was present when Smuts, preaching in Christ's Chapel in October 1934, said in the course of his sermon:

"It is the sense of isolation, of utter loneliness and apartness which creates fear and despair. But in fact there is no actual isolation in this universe. There are no isolated atoms or individuals or souls in this holistic universe. On the contrary it is all a great society of companion-ship, of mutual influence—The strength of the whole is behind each individual item in its striving towards expression."

Such doctrine Charles found immensely congenial and enheartening and it must have been a special pleasure for him to welcome Smuts to the Master's Lodge in October 1942 and later to secure his portrait for the College "as a permanent token of our pride in his connection with us." In the academic year 1947–8 Charles was to correspond with him on another matter of unusual importance.

The circumstance which brought both of these men into a unique relationship with Charles was a dramatic turn of events which meant that instead of carrying through the normal duties of Professor and Master from 1946 until the time of his retirement, he was for two of these years, 1947–9, to hold the high responsibility of Vice-Chancellor in the University and to spend a considerable part of 1946–7 in learning the job. It was dramatic because the expectation (which was in due course officially confirmed) was that the Vice-Chancellorship, during the two years I have mentioned, would be offered to Mr. Knox-Shaw, the Master of Sidney Sussex, and of course Charles could not have succeeded him in the office seeing that only one year of his own tenure would have then remained to be fulfilled. The Council of the Senate duly elected Mr. Knox-Shaw but in the words of *The Times* obituary notice in 1972: "Naturally shy and self-effacing, he regarded himself, despite all his administrative gifts, as unsuited for the very demanding tasks of the Vice-Chancellorship and felt obliged to refuse its offer."

It is believed that some members of Council were hesitant to nominate Charles so soon after the War during which his pacifist position had been well known; some also considered him too volatile! Nevertheless the offer was made, Charles accepted, and thereby came to enjoy what, outwardly at least, was his "finest hour". Throughout his career he had attracted criticisms of one kind or another. Friend and foe alike however have agreed that he fulfilled the duties and responsibilities of Vice-Chancellor with immense dignity, with extraordinary efficiency and with obvious enjoyment. He showed himself to be an excellent chairman, patient in listening yet decisive in summing-up, not attempting to dominate in the way that he sometimes tended to do in other situations. Boring and tedious chores he undertook without complaint, doing the necessary home work and mastering detail with apparent ease.

When he was first approached about the possibility of his accepting the office, his daughter Mary insisted that he should undergo a complete medical check-up, for there were still lingering doubts about the after effects of his coronary. The report was unexpectedly re-assuring. In fact his own Doctor said that he was fit enough to row in the College boat. So the decision was made and he set himself to work with characteristic thoroughness to learn as much as possible about the Vice-Chancellor's duties in the year that remained before he assumed office. There were bound to be important changes and developments in the University life of the post-war period, not least in matters of finance as inflation played havoc with professorial and other academic stipends. It was to be one of Charles's major achievements to guide negotiations about medical stipends in particular forward to a satisfactory conclusion.

The formal election did not take place until the summer of 1947. The official announcement was then reported in New Delhi and brought a cordial letter from Lord Mountbatten, who by this time had assumed the Vice-Royalty. He referred to the fact that when he had himself been at Christ's the then Master, Shipley, served as Vice-Chancellor. It was good to know that the honour had now come back to the College. Charles replied, inviting him to consider being the Rede Lecturer in 1948 and this was followed in September by an even more significant suggestion. Earl Baldwin, the Chancellor, was obviously failing in health and Charles would be intimately concerned in the search for a worthy successor. Would Mountbatten allow friends in Cambridge to nominate him for the office when the time came?

The Viceroy replied, accepting the invitation to deliver the Rede Lecture (though subsequently he felt compelled to withdraw) and indicating his willingness to consider favourably any approach which might be made to him about the Chancellorship. Much however would depend upon the relation of his own future to the duties which a Chancellor would be expected to perform. Charles assured him that the duties would be very light.

But a letter from the Viceroy, written at the end of November, made it clear that his hopes of resuming an active career in the Royal Navy when his term of office as Viceroy had come to an end really prevented him from allowing his name to be considered for this unique position in the life of the University. He was likely to be abroad for considerable periods in the next few years and would therefore be unable to visit Cambridge and its Colleges except on rare occasions. While deeply appreciating the suggestion he felt bound to decline the honour.

In the middle of December Earl Baldwin died and the question of his successor became a matter of immediate concern. As Charles's correspondence reveals, Mountbatten's refusal of the honour opened the way for Field Marshal Smuts to be elected instead.

The installation of the Chancellor was to be the most notable event of Charles's first year of office; the conferring of an honorary Doctorate upon the Queen would be the outstanding occasion in his second year. On March 4th, 1948, the Queen's Secretary wrote to express her Majesty's readiness to accept this distinction and made particular reference to the fact that the last Honorary Degree which her Majesty received was at the University of Cape Town where it was bestowed by the Chancellor, Field Marshal Smuts. As it proved, however, the Field Marshal was unable to come to Cambridge in October and nothing could have been more appropriate than that the man who had been dubbed an "ardent feminist" should have been the one to bestow the Degree upon the first woman honorand of the University and this in the academic year when women were for the first time granted full status within the official life of Cambridge.

Charles and the Registrary, Mr. W. W. Grave, worked in the happiest co-operation as they prepared for the great event of the installation of the Chancellor: everything appears to have gone without a hitch. Part of the proceedings were broadcast and for a period Cambridge enjoyed something of its former glory after the austerities of war. For Christ's College it was a week of unparalleled splendour for not only were the Chancellor and Vice-Chancellor Fellows of the College but the year marked the Quincentenary of God's-house. A Feast to mark the occasion followed on the day after the Installation while on the day itself the beautiful College gardens formed a perfect setting for the traditional Garden Party.

At the ceremony in the Senate-House Charles, as Vice-Chancellor, delivered the opening address to welcome the Chancellor-elect. Felicitous in expression it included a section which revealed how closely his own interests were related to those of Smuts himself.

"Your range of interests, as statesman and soldier, lawyer and philosopher, man of action, man of letters and man of science, typifies the vast extent and recent expansion of the field of knowledge and demonstrates that the expert need not necessarily be the specialist nor the scholar confine himself wholly to the library or the laboratory.

Your great book, of which we hope soon to see a new and enlarged edition, tells the same story more explicitly. Its exposition of the principle of integration assures us that even in these days a University need not become a mere aggregate of Technical Colleges nor abandon a holistic outlook but can still remain what we declare it to be, a home of education, religion, learning and research."

In an impressive reply the Chancellor made it abundantly clear that of all the honours that had come to him in life this was the one that he treasured most. He described it as an Order not of Merit but of Grace. Recalling how fifty-seven years previously he had come to Cambridge a young "barbarian" and had been given hospitality, friendship, an atmosphere of culture and a spiritual home and had then returned to South Africa and within two years found himself and his people at war with the British people, he went on to make reconciliation and the establishment of peace the main themes of his address. With all his regard and affection for Charles he did not hesitate to denounce pacifism and unpreparedness as direct incentives to aggression. But his main emphasis was positive—on the need to create an open world and open conditions for the free movement of life and thought and speech. This, he claimed, was the great adventure of civilisation and of its teaching and research laboratory—the University.

In the afternoon at the conferment of honorary degrees the Chancellor and the Vice-Chancellor occupied central seats on the dais with the latter sitting on the Chancellor's left. The first recipient was the Archbishop of York, the second Winston Churchill who (the Archbishop being already seated next to the Chancellor) found himself, when duly admitted to the degree, placed next to Charles. In this way England's leading pacifist faced the great audience with a famous war-leader on either side!

Earlier in the day Winston had been thoroughly disgruntled. A summons had been sent to all participants in the Installation Ceremony asking them to arrive in Cambridge not later then 10.30 a.m. The majority arrived on the previous day and stayed overnight but Winston decided to come up in the morning and had a message telephoned to Charles to say that he would be arriving at 11.30 a.m. Charles firmly retorted that this was quite unacceptable as the proceedings were to begin at 11.15 a.m. Winston therefore had to leave his bed much earlier than usual and when he arrived at Christ's he settled himself down in a corner of the drawing-room where the distinguished guests were drinking sherry and sat gloomily, making no effort to communicate with anybody. Smuts came down to greet him and he recovered momentarily but his displeasure increased when he found that the police had decided to take him to the Senate House by a circuitous route, bringing him in through Caius College to a back door. However he finally recovered his spirits and told Lord Tedder a few days later that the honour had meant a very great deal to him; in fact that the events of the day had moved him deeply.

It is hard to think of an occasion when so distinguished and so widely representative a group of men were brought together within a University context. By general consent Charles's arrangements beforehand and the discharge of his responsibilities in the proceedings themselves (not forgetting also his daughter Mary's superb performance of the duties of hostess) were of the highest possible order. Letters of congratulation flowed in. "It was history in the making". "It was a great triumph for you personally". The Archbishop of York wrote that he knew "it must have been very largely due to your generosity and kindness" that the D. D. had been given him. And the Vice-Chancellor of Oxford, not a great lover of clerics nor given to easy praise, wrote of "the inestimable privilege of staying with you while he (i.e. Smuts) was there. I have always been a devoted admirer of Smuts but I came away from Cambridge much more than that. I concur in the view of Tedder that he is the greatest living man. It was enormously good of you to let me share the privilege of his company."

Finally—a more domestic touch—Charles's brother Ted[1] sent this note:

"As you know I am not a great hand at writing and I hope I am not unduly sentimental but I really feel I cannot let yesterday pass without just saying how exceedingly proud I was to be in the family. As I listened to you in the morning (and again at 8.0 p.m. on the wireless) and saw my niece Mary sitting between Churchill and Stafford Cripps and looking absolutely born to it, I felt that I had all the glory and none of the responsibility! It was just grand—and thank you."

Just over three years later he was writing in a very different vein to tell Charles that the doctors had diagnosed an inoperable cancer. But

L

even this was a letter of enormous courage and faith, a seal upon the close relationship which had existed between the two brothers, one of whom seemed always to be in the limelight, for better or for worse, the other pursuing his steady path of devotion and duty, little known outside his own College but a man to whom a long succession of Johnians owed an immeasurable debt.

Smuts's tenure of the Chancellorship was comparatively short—he died in September 1950. But his election to the office had been an inspired one—and there is no doubt that Charles was originally the moving spirit in suggesting his name. Between the two men a remarkably close bond had been forged. They shared the same philosophical outlook, they were both lovers of nature, they were both Christ's men, in a very real sense they were both born to rule. Charles repeatedly expressed his indebtedness to Smuts' book *Holism and Evolution;* Smuts on his part could find time, in the midst of the almost overwhelming responsibilities of the war years when leisure was at a minimum, to read Charles's biography of John Ray. Charles often referred to the occasion when he startled Smuts by telling him that he had come to the conclusion that his (i.e. Smuts's) interpretation of the theory of relativity must be wrong. When asked why this was so, Charles replied that it must be wrong somewhere because it was the only explanation of the great mystery that he had ever been able to understand!

There are charming references in Sir Keith Hancock's fine biography to the association of the two men in relation to the hanging of Smuts's portrait in Christ's and to his installation as Chancellor.[2] But probably the most significant link was their common concern about what another Fellow of Christ's was later to describe as the problem of the two cultures. Lord Snow in a famous essay published in 1955 drew attention to the gap between the arts and the sciences. Already however in 1945 Smuts was wrestling with what at base was the same issue:

"As he put it in a letter to the Master of his old College, science was the great revelation of the modern world but it was not the only revelation and the time had surely come for trying to bridge the chasm which now separated the different revelations and thus to restore unity in the higher life of mankind."

In a letter to another friend he expressed his concern more specifically:

"Science so far has had far too much to do with the things of sense and of matter, and the things of the spirit have been by-passed. But can it be said that atoms are more real than souls? And souls we have left to the novelists, while atoms have been tackled by the highest brains which our century has produced—Did I say novelists? I should have said parsons—and mostly such parsons![3]

Science and the arts, science and literature, science and religion—the fundamental issue is the same. Like Charles, Smuts was convinced that Personality was the key-stone of the arch which could unite any of these pairs.

"Personality to him was a phenomenon both of the natural world, with which science was concerned, and also of the spiritual world, with which religion, literature and art were concerned, it was the climax so far of evolution; it was also 'the point' of departure in human regeneratio. In his endeavour to understand what Personality meant he accepted Jesus as supreme evidence."[4]

With so much in common the two friends rejoiced when occasions for meeting became possible. Smuts could be absent from South Africa for only brief periods but he stayed at the Lodge twice at least after his Installation. Mary Raven found him an altogether charming and considerate guest and he on his part found these brief interludes a great refreshment at a time when the political scene in South Africa was full of menace. Smuts declared after the Installation that Cambridge had done him good and had made him feel once again that he was a man and not a worm.[5]

The Installation of the Chancellor and the honouring of the Queen were the most notable positive events during Charles's term of office. On the negative side, there were also two major events which brought him into some unfavourable publicity though in the end no serious damage was done. The first occurred soon after the Queen's visit. Traditionally November 5th has been, at least until recently, a night when undergraduates, both at Oxford and Cambridge, have let off steam by rowdy behaviour and by occasional skirmishes with the police. But for some reason on November 5th, 1948 Cambridge went berserk and the University, in the words of the Vice-Chancellor, reached new depths of hooliganism and destruction. Two weeks later a letter carrying his signature was circulated to all junior members of the University in the hope that when the serious character of the disturbances had been generally realised, they would be deplored by the great majority of resident members. The letter quoted a section from the Senior Proctor's report of the evening's events which gave details of damage to cars, glass and in particular the windows of the Senate House. What happened must pass into University history as a "shameful episode."

When the time came for Charles to make his final Vice-Chancellor's report to the University he could not refrain from referring to this outburst which had been the only serious incident to mar his period in office. Commenting on the general condition of the University and specially its undergraduate members he said:

"Those who suffered from or even read of the outbreak of hooliganism last November when more damage was done to University buildings than in all the years of war and decent citizens were brutally assaulted by groups of undergraduates may well have inferred that a period of moral and intellectual decline such as took place in Oxford and Cambridge between 1921 and 1925 was similarly following the second world-war. Many of us have expected that this might in fact happen; and for a year or two conditions in occupied Germany seemed to make it inevitable. There has been a small amount of evidence to suggest such a collapse; there is a small percentage of men with whom the University could well dispense, men vicious and ill-disciplined—perhaps a couple of hundred in all. But there has been no sign at all of any general or widespread falling off; the vast majority work hard—are keen and versatile, and responsive to the best traditions of the place, and in their friendliness and breadth of sympathies make College life happy and easy."

There the matter might well have ended had not Charles returned to his condemnation of the two hundred evil young men in an address which he gave a few days later to a meeting of the Workers' Educational Association in Cambridge. At this he declared. "I should estimate that in the University as a whole there were somewhere about two hundred young men who had better not be there; who seemed to be vicious and ill-disciplined—the kind of young men responsible for the hooliganism of November 5th last year." And he added: "They were nearly all in the Army of Occupation in Germany in the first two years after the War." Such statements were meat and drink for the Sunday newspapers. The editions of October 30th were full of this judgment on life in Cambridge, a form of publicity which was greatly resented in the University itself. Succeeding issues of *Varsity* printed protests, including a letter recalling that in 1590 Henry Barrow had written: "It appeareth unto all men what kind of fellowships the University colleges are, what kind of cages full of unclean birds, of foul and hateful spirits." Why, it was asked, if there were two hundred "gangsters" in residence—why had they not been sent down?

These adverse comments at the end of his period of office may have received more attention than would otherwise have been the case because of the fact that in the previous December he had stirred up a hornet's nest by some remarks made at a school prize-giving. In Newport (Essex) he had said (as reported in the Press) "Sending an ordinary youngster of eighteen into occupied Germany is just devilry and absolutely corrupting." Ironically on the very same day Archbishop Fisher, having just returned from a visit to the troops on the Rhine had declared publicly: "There is less likelihood of a young men going off the rails in Germany than if he were here. I am very well aware of the fears about the moral welfare of our troops in Germany which have been felt but my visit dispelled those fears for me."

Charles was now under attack from two sides. First there came a moderate and well-argued letter from Lt. Col. Bernard Fergusson of the Black Watch whose battalion had been the first to receive National Service soldiers. After exactly a year he had found the boys "happy, fit, cheerful, busy, well-behaved and well-conducted." He and his chaplain were at a loss to know whence Charles had obtained his information. Could he not come out on a visit and see for himself the conditions under which the young men were living and the effects for good or evil on their conduct?

To this Charles replied at length, detailing evidence which had come to him from three sources and excusing himself from visiting Germany because of the great pressure of business in the University.

Colonel Fergusson, (who later became Governor-General of New Zealand) took pains to reply through two further good-humoured and carefully documented letters and although Charles held fast to his conviction that the sending of conscript boys to the Army of Occupation was to be deplored, the correspondence closed in a perfectly friendly manner. In the case of the Archbishop, the interchange was less cordial. Dr. Fisher had written:

"It was of course pure accident that on the same day the papers had an account of what I had said about young soldiers in Germany and your quite different statement on the same subject. I wonder whether the difference is due to the fact that I am more up-to-date than you are in this matter. What you said was I think perfectly true twelve or eighteen months ago. I am convinced that a quite remarkable change has taken place in the interval. This is certainly so in the handling of our young soldiers. There is also I think a change in German behaviour and a groping towards hope and honest living. Anyhow, I hope you will get a copy of the Free Churchmen's Report. It is significant that they arrived at exactly the same conclusions as I did, and their Report details the kind of evidence which I also saw and which convinced me."

and to this Charles replied:

Yes, I had of course no idea you had spoken to the Press on the same day—nor had I any reason to believe that my few sentences on the subject in a prize-giving speech would attract any attention. But in fact I had, two days previously, discussed the matter with one of your colleagues who knows service conditions intimately and who has been recently in Germany; and his picture differed widely from yours. There has, I know, been a real effort to improve things, but with what success is not, to me at least, very evident.

The whole position seems to me inevitably corrupting—just as it was with young Americans over here. An occupying army, in a demoralised country, with money to spend, and living on a different scale of resources, is no place for boys of eighteen. It may not always lead to sexual troubles; it is subtly perversive of decent human relationships: the better the lad the more he is disgusted and damaged. Nor is it effective to provide more occupations and less freedom; even if officers and padres of the best kind were available, their task would still be impossible.

Charles's tone is obviously cool and would have appeared even more so if he had allowed a final sentence included in his first draft to stand. In this after "a large number of youngsters who have served in Germany" he wrote "and that I was frankly dismayed at your complacency." On second thoughts this was omitted but it reveals something of Charles's attitude to the Archbishop. After the loss of William Temple he felt that he no longer had any close relation with those occupying the positions of highest authority in the Church.

By commenting publicly on the morals of the young, Charles inevitably aroused controversy but in normal circumstances he could have debated with his critics without undue hurt on either side. Yet both at Newport and in his final speech in the Senate House he had spoken as Vice-Chancellor and therefore, in the eyes of the outside world, as representing the University as well as himself. So *Varsity* made the acid comment that "Indiscretion or irresponsibility may be provocative, quaint and rather charming when exhibited by an undergraduate. It is not quite so charming when found in a man who holds a position of dignity and responsibility." Charles felt he had been misrepresented by the press, quoted out of context and so on. But it was at least unfortunate that he should have used language which was bound to stir resentment and made assertions which were incapable of being checked one way or the other. However a dispassionate judgment would regard his indiscretions as of minor consequence compared with his outstanding achievements in ceremonial, in chairmanship, in despatch of business and in his real understanding of the needs and the opportunities of the University in a rapidly changing world.

So the period of the occupancy of the University's highest working office drew to its end in October 1949 and Charles took up the reins for a final year as Master of his College. The Master of Trinity Hall expressed the thoughts of many when he wrote of his admiration for the way "in which you have upheld the dignity and carried the burden of the high office which yesterday you laid down." Perhaps Charles valued as much as any the message which came from Wilson Harris, the University Member of Parliament. He wrote from the House of Commons:

My dear Raven,
I can't let you lay down an office which you have so brilliantly adorned without saying how intensely fortunate I think myself to have had the opportunity of collaborating with you so far as opportunity offered in these past two years. (And after all we did make one Bishop between us.) You must be glad to be free, and Mary too, I imagine, in spite of the zest and incredible competence with which she did her part. But I know you enjoyed the Vice-Chancellorship and no doubt you may sometimes wish it went on for four years instead of two.
I write, of course, with barely the top of my own head above water; the waves may close over it at any moment. But nothing in my life has given me so much satisfaction as being able to call myself a Burgess (albeit Junior) for Cambridge.

But his closest relationship in the actual work of Vice-Chancellor had been with the Registrary, Mr. W. W. Grave, and their regard for one another grew enormously during the two years of their collaboration.

Grave has since declared that of all Vice-Chancellors under whom he served Charles had the quickest mind. Whereas in some cases it had been necessary to spend most of a morning going over the business for a meeting of Senate, Charles would grasp the essential points in twenty minutes and be perfectly prepared when the meeting convened. At the same time Charles on his part knew how much he owed to the Registrary and significantly, when saying good-bye to him at the end of his period of office, said: "If you had only been with me longer, I should have been made a Bishop."

In retrospect it seems strange that a man who had enjoyed the highest honours that the University could bestow, who was in demand on all sides to lecture and to serve on committees of worthy causes, should still be hankering after some position of major responsibility in the Church—in particular a bishopric. He continued to be a key figure in the Fellowship of Reconciliation, he was involved in the work of the Council of Christians and Jews and became Chairman of its Executive Committee in 1951, he became a Trustee of the British Museum in 1949 and he kept close touch with Westcott House and Ridley Hall, the Anglican Theological Colleges in Cambridge and with St. Luke's, Pampisford an experimental College in the near neighbourhood. Yet no single job that would really stretch him seemed to be in sight after his sixty-fifth birthday when he would necessarily retire from the Mastership of Christ's. And he would be homeless too. Though he loved to travel, he depended much upon a stable base to which he could return for security and renewal. After July 1950—what?

It might have been expected that the Fellows would extend the tenure of office for a period seeing that Charles's Vice-Chancellorship had been so successful and that he was obviously still in full command of his powers. But a recent experience was still fresh in their minds. Maclean, who was Master until 1935, had held on to his office even when bed-ridden and after his death a statute had been promulgated to make sixty-five the retiring age. Darwin who succeeded Maclean held office for only three years and then resigned. Charles was thus the first holder to whom the new statute applied and it would have been a strange volte face if it had at once been amended or repealed. Moreover the retiring age for Professors was still sixty-five. There seemed no alternative therefore to laying down his University and College responsibilities in 1950 and looking elsewhere for a sphere of further activity.

Just when the matter was becoming urgent a new prospect opened up which seemed in many ways to provide an ideal solution. In 1948 the University acquired most of the parish of Madingley and with it the historic residence Madingley Hall. Situated about four miles out from Cambridge in a north-westerly direction, it stands in the midst of beautifully laid out gardens and well-preserved woods and contains carvings, panellings and tapestries of great historic interest as well as treasures of furnishing gathered from all parts of the world. Seeing that the Hall had been acquired during Charles's Vice-Chancellorship, he had naturally been much involved in the discussions on the use to which it was to be put. Clearly it was too far out to become a College in the ordinary sense of the word. Yet post-graduate studies and pro-grammes of adult education were becoming more and more popular and facilities for residence were increasingly in demand. To concentrate on the needs of graduate students in term-time and on courses of an extra-mural kind in vacations would mean that the Hall was being used to the full extent of its capacity both as regards space and time.

By the summer of 1949 the general picture of the future use of the Hall was taking shape and in October the Report of the Committee which Council had appointed to advise on possible plans was ready for discussion. There would obviously need to be a responsible Warden in charge of the new enterprise and the Committee recommended that he should be "a senior member of the University, well-known both in the University and outside it, with some acquaintance of adult educa-tion and in sympathy with extra-mural work." and that the initial experimental period of appointment should be for five years. Who could possibly fill the bill better than Charles himself? He had over many years been deeply concerned about possible forms of adult education; he was widely known inside and outside the University. Consequently, in spite of minor criticisms from those who felt doubts about the appointment of a man *so* senior in age and of one who had been so involved in the discussions about the future of the Hall, Council recommended that they be given authority to appoint Charles for five years from 1st October, 1950 or from a date as early as possible thereafter, and in January, 1950 the announcement was made public. In this way the uncertainties about the future were resolved, at least for the time being, and the prospect lay before him of residence in one of England's loveliest stately homes in a woodland area which could provide unlimited delight for the natural historian. Unhappily the outcome of what seemed to be an almost ideal arrangement fell far short of what was so confidently anticipated.

For nearly eighteen years he had been Fellow of Christ's, for nearly eleven years its Master. The place was full of memories. The day in 1936 when he was so nearly elected: the disappointment that followed and then the awkwardness of living in a close society by which he had, in a sense, been rejected: the reversal in 1939 and the satisfaction of occupying so lovely a house and enjoying its garden.[6] The many family memories: Bee the perfect hostess whom everybody loved: the grand-children in the Lodge, away from the bombed area of their own home: the awful emptiness after Bee's death: the heroic way in which Mary had taken her mother's place. The range of interests associated with the Senior Combination Room and the pleasure of entertaining guests from many varied backgrounds, especially during his reign as Vice-Chancellor. The strange experiences of war-time: his own name on a special list of those to be arrested when Hitler's men arrived in Cambridge: the hiding of the College plate in a hole dug in his own garden with the only clue to its position the word Hermaphrodite (between man and woman i.e. between the buildings marked Gents and Ladies): the nights when *John Ray* was written in intervals of fire-watching.

But his chief reponsibility in terms of vocation had been the care of the undergraduate members of the College. Amongst these he had somehow formed a special link with the Boat Club. He followed them faithfully on the tow-path, attended Bump Suppers without embarrass-ment and was thrilled at their successes. When one of his men gained his Blue and rowed in three successive winning crews, the last time as

President, Charles felt that the College had achieved one of its highest distinctions. Almost to the end of his life he remained an ardent supporter of College crews and teams, trying to arrange his engagements so that he could be present in person to watch the contest whatever it might be.

But of course he was equally excited at College successes in academic fields. By a happy coincidence two of the most brilliant undergraduates of his time came from overseas—one an African, one an Asian. The former was Davidson Nicol, the first African to become a scholar and later a Fellow of Christ's: outstanding in medical science, the first African at Oxford or Cambridge to be elected President of his J.C.R. and later to achieve distinction in University administration and as representative of Sierra Leone at the United Nations and in London. When asked if his son, Charles, had been named after the Prince of Wales, he replied, "No! after Charles Raven." The Asian, C. J. Eliezer, was a brilliant mathematician who, when Dirac was absent from Cambridge, acted as his substitute in the Faculty Lecture programme and was later to occupy a Chair of Mathematics first in Malaya and then in Australia. Of English undergraduates a young man, Anthony Caro, who was to become one of England's most distinguished sculptors, gained early experience by working on a reproduction of the Master's head. And in theology Christ's in the forties was a veritable nest of fledgling scholars: Ian Ramsey, former scholar of the College and now its Chaplain, who was to become Nolloth Professor of the Philosophy of the Christian Religion at Oxford; Maurice Wiles and Peter Baelz, still undergraduates, who were to become Regius Professor of Divinity and Regius Professor of Moral and Pastoral Theology respectively in Oxford in the early 1970s.

Charles used a study over the ante-chapel in the College and was easily accessible. Undergraduates found him somewhat awe-inspiring at first with his beetling eyebrows and his piercing looks. But after the first year they felt more confidence and, though he always maintained a certain distance, he managed to establish communication to a surprising degree. At the time of the November episode, though Charles reacted strongly, even severely, the majority of undergraduates supported him. His rule was more authoritarian than would be easily accepted today—for instance he believed that as Master he had the right to enter any man's room in College without warning—but the general opinion was that he was a big man, worthy of respect, whose mannerisms made him the more interesting and whose occasional haughtiness could be allowed for and forgiven. They laughed at him sometimes but recognised his proper right to the title *Master*. In fact neither of his other titles—Professor, Canon—seemed so apt to apply to a man whose whole appearance was magisterial and who in so many fields of knowledge had established a mastery of detail which few could emulate.

The College bade Charles and his daughter Mary its official farewell on June 9th, 1950. Of his speech the College magazine later reported that if one occasion could be singled out when his great gifts of oratory, both on public and domestic occasions, reached peak expression it was on this particular night, The speech by Mr. Paul Bircher, President of the C.U.B.C. was however printed in full. Having dwelt upon Charles's "fairness and wisdom" and the way in which he had widened the horizons of the College after the war, the speaker concluded with these words:

"The wit has said that we are governed by Master and by Maid. It has, however—fortunately for us—been that sort of rule in which we feel that Mary is a friend of ours who might even at times reiterate to you, Sir, the words of our Foundress when she instructed a Master of her day to deal with a student "gently, gently, gently." This presentation then we admit is to a team; a team of the Rev. Professor Charles Earle Raven, Doctor of Divinity, more commonly known as "the Old Man" and Miss Raven, more happily known as Mary. It is a presentation made by a group of men of diverse opinions and views, who have found a point of unity in the deep affection which we all have for you both. With wishes of God-speed in your new sphere and as a mark of genuine affection and gratitude, I ask you to accept from the Junior Members of Christ's College this table silver."

In three typical sentences he said good-bye to the undergraduates by telling them that they were a body of men of whom he was inordinately proud, for whom he had an almost senile affection and with whom he could profitably spend the rest of his life—if only that were possible! But forth from Christ's he must go, first to the other end of the world and then to what unhappily he came to regard as a "backwater," Madingley Hall.

NOTES TO CHAPTER EIGHTEEN

1. p. 321: Dean of St. John's College.
2. p. 322: W. K. Hancock. *Smuts. The Fields of Force 1919–1950*, p. 408, p. 507 f.
3. p. 322: Ibid. p. 395.
4. p. 323: Ibid. p. 401.
5. p. 323: Ibid. p. 508.
6. p. 331: In the inner court behind the Master's Lodge there is a lovely water-garden. The story is told that after a stormy College meeting, Charles, who was then Master, decided to resign. He returned to the Lodge, hurriedly wrote his letter and went out through the garden to deliver it by hand to the Senior Tutor. But it was dark and he stumbled into the pool. Compelled to go back to bath and change his clothes he lost the sense of urgency and the letter never, in fact, reached its destination. On a later occasion his grandson accidently fell into the water, fortunately with no untoward results.

CHAPTER NINETEEN

In the Class-Room and on the Air

In the eighteen years during which Charles occupied his official positions in Cambridge two forms of communication gained increasing prominence and importance in the life of the nation. It was a time of expansion in *higher education:* sixth forms in schools exercised a critical influence in the development of boys and girls who hoped to gain entrance to universities. Equally it was a time of enormous expansion in *mass-communications:* first the radio and then television began to change the whole process by which the nation at large received its information and its impressions. It was one of Charles's most notable achievements that he succeeded to an astonishing degree in breaking through the barrier of suspicion which the best minds among adolescents were beginning to feel towards religion in general and institutional Christianity in particular, and in showing that a full acceptance of the outlook of modern science need not involve abandonment of Christian faith. A second remarkable achievement was his rapid adaptation of style and method to the demands of the peculiar medium of broadcasting. He moved to and fro between pulpit and studio in a way that very few of his contemporaries found themselves able to do.

I

A man now prominent as theologian and educator has recalled his own days in a sixth-form in a northern Grammar-school. Charles, of whom he had never previously heard, came to speak to the boys about science and religion. The substance of the talk left no lasting impression but what was unforgettable was that a man who was obviously highly competent in the world of science spoke of his faith in such a way that it became clear to all that to him *Christianity really mattered*. Charles's friend, Henry Hart, for many years Dean of Queen's College, Cambridge, has testified that again and again when he had occasion to ask a boy what led him to read Theology in his University course he would answer; "Professor Raven came to my school for the week-end. He spoke to us first about some scientific subject and then on Sunday evening in Chapel he talked about Christ and faith." He showed in fact that theology like science could be a valid subject of study and that there need be no irreconcilable conflict between the two.

What exactly was the secret of his influence it is not easy to determine. He never talked down to boys. He invited them to look again at phenomena in the natural world with which they were familiar—birds or plants or butterflies—and then went on to speak of the relation of living organisms to their environment. This led naturally to a consideration of the whole mystery of *Life* and to the fact that the Life-process far transcends anything that can be weighed and measured and expressed in a formula. Finally he often appealed to his favourite passage in the eighth chapter of the Epistle to the Romans and described creation as a process still in the making, a process of self-giving and suffering in which God Himself is involved. The wonder of human existence is that the Spirit of God is alongside us and within us, sharing our struggle and ensuring that out of the mighty travail of the whole universe a noble and worthy end will be achieved.

Charles preserved many of the letters written to him by busy Head Masters after visits of this kind. He preferred not to go just to preach at a Chapel service. He would gladly spend two or three days, first winning the boys' confidence by talking about some theme in biology or natural history and answering their questions—and only then giving a direct message in Chapel about the fulness of life in and through the Christ. The letters must constitute an almost unique collection. They come from Winchester (four visits), Oundle (where he spent a whole week), his old school Uppingham, the Methodist foundation of Kingswood, Bath, the Quaker foundation at Leighton Park (a visit of three days duration), Cheltenham (speaking to boys and staff) Raynes

Park County School, William Hulme's Grammar School, Harrow and Rugby, Marlborough and St. Paul's, Canford and Cranleigh, and Bristol Grammar School whose Headmaster was a close friend and where a "C. E. Raven Prize for field work in Biology"[1] was established.

Headmasters are not normally gushing or effusive. Yet some of the letters were almost lyrical in their expressions of thanks.

"It isn't often that we have a man here who brings the whole place from its heels on to its toes: but that is exactly what you did and we are all more grateful than I can say." (1948)

"You really have been to some boys the first touch of Spring. I am thinking of two very tough biologists who, before you came, resented so much time being "wasted" but who are now glad to tell people how you opened their eyes. The boys' appreciation is universal." (1955)

"It is quite impossible thank you for all that you did for us last week-end. It was quite the most memorable and inspiring and exciting week-end I can remember since we came to . . . I am sure you would be encouraged and pleased to know how much it has been talked about. (A co-educational school) (1951)

"I asked one of the most intelligent members of my sixth form, what he thought of your sermon in the morning. "First rate sir! The best sermon I've ever heard, I think!" I put it myself alongside one of Gore's and one of Studdert Kennedy's that I heard at Rugby, the few that have really remained." (1941)

"It hardly seems a week last Saturday that you were with us because we are all, Masters and boys, still talking about it. You opened so large a new vision to us that in our discussions—and I have discussed it with many boys and colleagues—we all can contribute that part we saw most closely." (1951)

"I learnt more myself, not simply about birds but about what science is and ought to be after, than I can ever remember understanding in a single hour before; and one saw what it must have been like to sit at the feet of one of the great observers like Aristotle." (1934)

"I find I can't really express adequately how deeply grateful we all are to you for what you have done for . . . this week. I can honestly say without exaggeration that I believe it has been the most important week of my seventeen terms as Headmaster and the success of it is entirely due to you." (1951)

"Your address moved us all—even quite small boys felt power—and to me at least it gave a new inspiration and the determination to do for these boys the most that is in me to do during the time that remains to me." (1948)

He was tireless in visiting Schools during vacation time. In July 1949 we find him writing to the Headmaster of Cheltenham about the following March when he was pledged to Rugby for the first Sunday in Lent and, after his own term had ended on March 17th, would be visiting Taunton School on March 19th and Charterhouse on March 26th. He would be ready to give three days to Cheltenham in the week between. Naturally some of the enthusiastic responses on the part of boys were ephemeral but in many cases a lasting impression was made. Nearly twenty years after the event a Wykehamist could still recall three evenings in Chapel in Lent 1952 when a striking figure in scarlet cassock had spoken to some sixty boys who had come voluntarily to the services; and the mornings when the preacher had lectured to the sixth form, dealing first with Aristotle as a biologist and secondly with John Ray whom he claimed to be more significant in the history of scientific development than the greatly honoured Sir Isaac Newton. He remembered too the sense of confidence that Charles had inspired by showing that theology was just as rigorous an intellectual discipline as science. Whether delivering the Gifford Lectures or talking to sixth form boys the main themes were the same. And by his command of historical detail and his apt illustrations from the natural order he could hold the attention of boys through forms of presentation which were not very different in Rugby or Winchester from what they were in special Lectureships in Oxford or Edinburgh Universities.

Some might say, it is true, that it was easy enough for Charles to travel round as the distinguished guest, repeating virtually the same act wherever he went. Science and Religion was the title of the mono-logue which he presented with only slight variations in innumerable school contexts. Yet as the Headmaster of Harrow wrote: "To me it is a wonderful thing to find contact with a mind equally aware of the claims of the humanities and science; one of the great hopes for the future, it seems to me, is that we should heal the schism between the two produced at the Renaissance." And it must be added that a note constantly recurring in the letters of thanks is that of gratitude and admiration for the obvious output of vital energy which each address and sermon involved. Though his delivery appeared to be smooth and unconstrained, he never in fact approached an occasion without some apprehension and even nervousness; and although he repeated the same general theme over and over again, he was always trying to keep in touch with the most recent developments both in theology and science and to incorporate some new discovery or insight into his talks.

The substance of a letter from Mr. Hugh Lyon, for seventeen years Headmaster of Rugby and later Director of the Public Schools Appointments Bureau, provides an admirable summing up of Charles's contribution to education through his schools visits.

"I had an intense affection and admiration for Charles Raven, and I brought him to Rugby as often as I decently could, either to preach or to take our Holy Week addresses and/or to talk to the sixth. I remember once, during the war, when he was not altogether *persona grata* with the authorities, he said, "I hope you won't get into trouble for asking me to preach." It almost made me weep.

Beside the limpid clarity of his reasoning, I think the impression he made, whether in the pulpit or the class room, was due to his burning sincerity. He was all the time putting the whole of himself into what he said, and as he came away was obviously spent. The Power had taken and shaken him, and through him spoken to us all.

I have, I am afraid, no very detailed memory of his talk on 'Science and Religion', though I can see him now, winding his long legs round the lectern (to the boys' delight) as he struggled for the exact word. He usually started giving us some insight into the tiniest of nature's lovely things—a snowflake or a shell or a pimpernel—and from there built up a vision of the world, and of the message it gave us of a loving Creator. It always sounded so fresh, as if the thoughts were new-minted as he spoke them. And I think they often were, as he spoke straight out, without script or notes, and I doubt whether the groups he spoke to ever heard just the same address. But it was always a joy to hear, neither a cleric being polite to the scientist, nor a scientist paying lip-service to religion, but someone with real knowledge of both subjects searching for and discovering and revealing the truth which linked them."

Charles's ministry to Sixth-formers may well have been the most widely influential of his whole career.

II

Only rarely does a gifted orator become a good broadcaster. A man who is dependent upon seeing his audience and feeling its response often becomes inhibited when faced by a naked microphone in an enclosed studio. But at least two men in Britain became masters in both arts. They were Winston Churchill, the warrior, and Charles Raven, the pacifist. Both men could sway the feelings of vast audiences as they employed every artifice of looks and speech and gesture; at the same time each succeeded in projecting his distinctive personality and message through the medium of radio in the period before television became a serious rival. But whereas Churchill's finest hour was in the years between 1940 and 1945, Charles in contrast was forced to remain silent during that time. His period of fulfilment in sound broadcasting was from 1949 onwards. Though holding no position of eminence in public affairs his voice became known to thousands, both at home and overseas, through his ability to adapt himself to a form of presentation which was in so many ways different from that to which he had so long been used.

Not that he found it easy. His remarkable memory and his inborn sense of timing were a great help. His ability to paint vivid pen-portraits of men distinguished in learning or action, his facility in providing apt illustrations from the world of nature with which his hearers were familiar—these also were a great asset. But radio technique is very different from that of the pulpit or lecture—room. Charles had always been used to free movement and extempore speaking. Now he had to remain in one place and stay reasonably closely to a script. One of his producers has told how difficult it was to keep him standing still. The microphone had to pick him up from all directions and experience proved that he spoke more effectively from his own College settings than from a studio.

Charles saw clearly that one of the chief functions of religious broadcasting was to try to narrow the gap between the scholar in his study and the ordinary man or woman in the pew. So the advent of the Third Programme seemed exactly suited to his particular talents and he was the obvious person to speak on the subject of religion and science.[2] His experience with Sixth Forms also qualified him to take part in Schools Programmes: he could speak with enthusiasm, as well as detailed knowledge, about pioneers such as John Ray and Charles Darwin, making contact with his hearers by encouraging them to study the growth of plants and the behaviour of animals and by showing, for example, the important scientific data that Ray was able to record simply by careful observation of the stages in the development of an ordinary sowing of mustard and cress. Time and again the point was emphasised that God as Creator was to be conceived not as a Divine engineer or carpenter but rather as the Lord of life and of living processes, generating, sustaining, directing, making whole.

In the 1950s Charles worked in close harmony with Edwin Robertson of the B.B.C.'s Third Programme Department and spoke on a number of themes connected with the history and philosophy of science. He contributed to the notable series *Ideas and Beliefs of the Victorians:* to the series *The Making of Modern Science:* and to a more specifically religious series entitled, *The Christian Hope and Physical Evil.* An hour's lecture to the Royal Institution on *Some neglected aspects of the History of Science* was transmitted in full and surprisingly stirred the editor of Radio Review in one of the more popular newspapers to write with enthusiasm about the performance of the "Delightful Don". He described it as "the best entertainment I have had from radio and television this week."

"He had novel things to say and said them with the civil arrogance of
the humane scholar speaking authoritatively of matters of weight.
His language was clear and vigorous, precise without pedantry and
familiar without being slipshod.

Most talks are crammed too tight and spoken to the empty air and
leave no mark on the mind. Dr. Raven's exercised the imagination
which is the kind of extension of experience that the first pioneers of
radio hoped for from this new invention."

But the most substantial contribution to radio which Charles produced was a series published in book form in 1952 under the title
Science and the Christian Man. Here was popularisation in the best sense
of the word, a distillation of the system of thought which he had
recently brought into shape in his Gifford Lectures. It contains nothing
that could be called novel or original but is perhaps noteworthy because
of a passage in which Charles expresses more directly and succinctly
than anywhere else in his writings his personal Christological faith.
Having admitted that "man's religious experience is essentially in-
describable, a moment of ecstasy and abasement for which neither
words or symbols are adequate" he went on to urge that *personal*
categories of interpretation are the highest that we can employ and that
the image of the perfect *person* can best bring God into our comprehension and mode of expression.

"For my own part, I am not prepared to argue that the "image" is
identical with that which it expresses. In confessing that Jesus is God
I mean that He is God for us, God in every sense in which I can conceive
God—a true picture but (perhaps) not the whole picture. For me as man
He satisfies and surpasses all that I can imagine of the divine; He calls out
my adoration; He empties me of my pride; He inspires me as no other
can do. Beyond that I cannot go. If I were an angel or an animal, the
universe and God might look quite different. As a man I cannot know
or conceive God as He is in Himself; but all that I *can* know of Him I
find in the universe and in Jesus, and these two, so far as all my experience goes, belong together. For me "God is in Christ reconciling
the world unto Himself."[3]

In surveying Charles's association with the B.B.C. and the many programmes in which he took part, four very different aspects of this association may be singled out for special comment.

(1)   *The Pacifist Issue.*

The full history of the place of religion in British broadcasting has yet to be written. Much is known of Lord Reith's determination to reserve periods for religious programmes and in Professor Asa Briggs's history of the B.B.C. there is a detailed account of developments during the Second World War. It has never been an easy matter to decide who should be allowed to speak to the huge audience which the mass media command and whether any restriction should be set on what the broadcaster should be allowed to say. The question of the rights of pacifists to be heard during war-time was one of the most delicate and difficult that those in authority have ever been called upon to handle; and Charles was a key-figure in the debates and consultations when decisions had to be made.

It was early in 1940 that the place of pacifism on the air became a live issue. During the first five months of the War broadcast sermons had been given by Charles, George MacLeod and Donald Soper, all well-known pacifists. In their addresses the pacifist position had in no way been renounced but it had not been obtruded. On Sunday, February 11th 1940, however, Leyton Richards, the distinguished minister of Carr's Lane Church in Birmingham, preached a sermon which not only advocated the way of pacifism but did so in a quite explicit and even passionately aggressive manner. This brought a storm of protest, especially from parents whose sons were serving in the Armed Forces, and it became evident that the question of complete freedom of speech in broadcasting must sooner or later arise.

At the time Dr. James Welch was Head of Religious Broadcasting in the B.B.C. He knew Charles reasonably well and later became an intimate friend. He felt that the pacifist position ought to be stated in such a way as to make clear that pacifists and non-pacifists could unite on certain fundamental Christian truths, even in war-time; that in fact the Gospel itself transcended whatever differences there might be about its application to the Christian's participation in War. He therefore

wrote to Charles some days after the Leyton Richards broadcast
inviting him to preach a course of four sermons before the microphone
during the last quarter of 1940. He could select his own dates and the
sermons could be preached in Church or in a studio. The four Sunday
evenings of November were chosen.

Then, however, difficulties began to arise. Welch remembered that
one of the Sundays was Armistice Sunday and it might give offence if
any kind of pacifist utterance went out on that day. Middleton Murry,
by this time a man of note in literary and religious circles but also an
avowed pacifist, had given talks on the radio which led to questions
being raised in Parliament about the degree of licence which could be
given to the B.B.C. to invite to the microphone speakers of this kind.
Then came the dramatic events of May 1940, the declaration of a state
of grave national emergency and the realisation that any open preaching
of pacifism to the nation at large could seem to invite a weakening of
the war-effort in which literally all citizens must now in one way or
another be engaged.

Early in June the Chairman of the B.B.C. Sir Allan Powell handed
Dr. Welch a directive which first made clear what was the position of
the Corporation in regard to Leyton Richards's broadcast and then
proceeded to lay down its policy for the future. It had not in fact been
consulted about the February sermon. The Controller of Programmes
had approved, after the event, Dr. Welch's decision to permit Mr.
Richards to broadcast but the Corporation had obvious doubts about
the wisdom of the action. In any case, for the future,

> "The Governors, considering the war-time situation, are clear that
> there cannot be complete freedom of speech in broadcasting and that
> Christian ministers cannot be given a position of exceptional privilege
> in this regard. They consider that religious broadcasting, and all
> other broadcasting talks which deal with the war, should be in full
> accord with the national effort and with the view that the cause for
> which the nation is fighting is a righteous one, and that in religious
> broadcasting there should be no hesitation in praying regularly for
> victory for our forces.

It would clearly be inconsistent with these aims to invite any known member of an organisation or any individual who does not hold these views, to broadcast."

For the future the duties of Dr. Welch and his colleagues were clearly enough defined. But the question was bound to arise about responsibility for commitments already made. Charles had promised to give the four sermons in November–December; Donald Soper had agreed to do a course in the *Lift up your Hearts* series; George MacLeod was also on the list of future speakers. Were these arrangements to be cancelled? Yes, he was told by the Chairman and Director-General, Raven and MacLeod were well-known and should therefore be excluded. Soper might be allowed to give the *Lift up your Hearts* course but must then be debarred from further broadcasting.

"No one who is shown to belong to an organisation the policy of which is inconsistent with the national effort, or who is shown to have expressed views which are inconsistent with the national effort, may be invited to broadcast in any programme or to contribute material for broadcasting."

These directives raised extremely serious issues for two groups of people within the official structure of broadcasting. First there was the Central Religious Advisory Committee whose Chairman at the time was Dr. Garbett, the Bishop of Winchester. This Committee, representing all the "main-stream" Christian Churches in Britain, has been responsible for relaying the opinions of Christian people as a whole about the manner and content of religious broadcasting to the authorities of the B.B.C. and in particular to the officials of its religious department. At its meeting in September 1940 it considered the directives and minutes reveal that the majority of members were deeply disturbed about their implications. Were they to infer that henceforward no known pacifist could be invited to speak on any subject at all?[4]

To exclude the preaching of direct pacifism was reasonable. But to exclude a Christian minister from preaching the Gospel, only on the grounds that he was a pacifist—this was a far graver matter.

The Chairman of the Governors and the Director-General in long and considered statements justified their policy largely on the grounds that the broadcasts by Richards and Middleton Murry, though including little that was objectionable in the actual scripts, had caused widely-felt offence just because these two men were well known to hold views contrary to the effective execution of the national effort. They believed that ninety-nine per cent of the public supported their decision to exclude such men from broadcasting. On the other hand there was a strong expression of feeling amongst the members of C.R.A.C. that to keep a responsible and devoted Christian off the air just because he held unpopular convictions on a single issue was to create a very dangerous precedent. No resolution was passed at the meeting but the senior officers of the Corporation were made well aware of the deep undercurrent of unease which their directives had created.

For the members of the religious broadcasting department and in particular the two senior officers—Dr. Welch an Anglican and the Rev. Eric Fenn a Persbyterian—the matter became so critical as to cause them to consider resignation. They could not refuse to obey the directives while remaining in their official posts: on the other hand to obey without a protest would be to betray some of their deepest convictions. Neither Welch nor Fenn was a pacifist. They recognised that all the time producers of programmes were involved in keeping some people off the air. And even those who were allowed on had to be willing to submit scripts for what could be regarded as mild censorship. This in effect meant that there need be no direct preaching of pacifism at any time. Yet their directive had insisted that men well-known for their non-co-peration with the national effort must on that account never be allowed to broadcast at all. What would this imply for the future if, say, a left-wing government decided to debar all of its opponents from broadcasting or vice versa? Had not something similar already happened in Germany in connection with the Confessing Church? Hitler had urged all Christians to join in the "national effort" and had assured them that then no disabilities would be placed in their way. But what if they refused to co-operate in what he decided was the detailed nature of the "national effort"? Hitler's answer was clear: exclusion from society, imprisonment! Even if in Britain there was no intention to imprison pacifists, were they not being excluded from society by curtailment of their right to speak over the most public of all media of communication?

Those in authority disclaimed any wish to inaugurate any kind of inquisition into the opinions and convictions of potential broadcasters but took their stand on the concept of "notoriety as pacifists". Of course it was still possible to raise questions about what *degree* of "notoriety" was necessary to merit exclusion or whether the notoriety fairly belonged to the man in question. But in the last resort the Corporation held to its right to decide for or against any particular individual without pronouncing final judgments either on the nature of the Gospel or on the rightness of pacifist doctrine.

When in August 1940 Charles learned of the pressures which were being exercised upon the leaders of the Religious Department in the B.B.C. he wrote to Fenn in the following terms:

"If it were a personal matter or merely a question of saving you (and myself) from embarrassment, I should of course ask leave to withdraw from my undertaking to broadcast in November. But I fear it is impossible for me to take that course: to do so would be to agree that the State has the right to dictate doctrine and use religion as an instrument of propaganda.
So I shall have to proceed to write the sermons; and if I am forbidden to deliver them, shall have to appeal to such Christians as I can reach."

Fenn replied giving a full account of the position as it then stood: the first directive had been received, a memorandum had been submitted to the Director-General pointing out the difficulties that the Religious Department would encounter in trying to implement it, and now there was some hope that the policy enunciated in the directive would be modified.

Charles wrote at once to Fenn, expressing his own concern in even stronger terms:

"If the Minister of Information is not only going to tame the pulpits by his documents to clergy but going to impose tests that the Church does not impose, he is doing exactly what the Minister of Religion did in Germany; and a Confessional Church will be inevitable. I can imagine nothing that will more completely discredit religion in the eyes of the honest layman. So at least you are fighting an issue that is worth an effort.

Of course I realise that the matter is and must remain entirely confidential. But it raises a matter of vital importance for me. If I am forbidden as a pacifist to broadcast and if the authorities of the Church of England and the religious Committee of the B.B.C. acquiesce, I should have to consider resigning my orders or at least raising the whole matter as publicly as possible. For if the Church accepts the right of the M. of I. to dictate its faith, we have dethroned Christ for Caesar. So do please let me know the decision as soon as it can become public."

As already indicated the reply to the memorandum did, in fact, call for the cancellation of Charles's sermons planned for November and for his exclusion from broadcasting for the duration of the War. Welch still hoped that a service might be arranged in which Temple and Charles would each play a part and thereby demonstrate their unity in the Gospel in spite of holding different views on pacifism. But this appears never to have taken place. Moreover Charles did not in fact implement his threat either by resigning his orders or by appealing to the Christian public. Perhaps he realised that in the continuing state of national emergency it would have been impolitic to raise the issue on his own behalf and, so far as the witness of the Church at large was concerned, Archbishop Temple made it clear that a strong body of responsible opinion was in favour of a more liberal attitude being shown to pacifists than seemed to be the policy of the authorities of the B.B.C. He had proposed to move a resolution in the Upper House of the Convocation of York in January 1941, but when it proved impossible for Convocation to meet he wrote to Sir Allan Powell and told him that twelve of the fourteen Bishops would have supported the resolution that:

"Every opportunity should be taken to show unity of faith. In particular those who accept and those who reject the view that Christian discipleship is incompatible with the use of armed force, should respect one another's conscience and maintain their spiritual fellowship in the bond of charity.

That inasmuch as one chief means whereby the Church and the Gospel committed to it are presented to the public is the provision of broadcast services and sermons, no man should be excluded from the privilege of broadcasting the message of the Gospel on the ground that he is known to be a pacifist, provided that he undertakes not to use this occasion to advocate the pacifist position."

But neither continuing representations from within by Dr. Garbett nor resolutions from without by Dr. Temple were sufficient to lift the ban on Raven and Soper in England, MacLeod and Craig in Scotland. The authorities in the B.B.C. were in a strange position for it was accepted that the Ministry of Information had power to forbid any broadcast or the use of any broadcaster in time of War: it had always been admitted that a selective principle governed British broadcasting—no one has the *right* to broadcast whereas the Corporation of the B.B.C. has the right to invite or to cancel an invitation. Further, certain types of propaganda judged inimical to the national effort (e.g. communism and fascism) were excluded from the air. Pacifism might legitimately be regarded as falling under the same ban.

In the last resort the crux seemed to be this. Why should not Charles, who had already established himself as an effective broadcaster, be allowed to preach the Gospel over the radio so long as he did not use the occasion to advocate the pacifist position? The answer in effect was: "Charles is already too well known as a pacifist and as a leading advocate of pacifism for it to be possible for him to come to the microphone in war-time and be regarded other than in this way. If he delivers a course of four sermons on *any* subject, the conclusion can hardly fail to be drawn that the B.B.C. favours the views for which he is famous." Therefore on grounds of expediency the decision was made and for a period of roughly six years Charles's voice on the air was silenced. And he appears finally to have accepted the decision—even in a slightly perverse way to have half welcomed it as an open demonstration that he was being persecuted and made to suffer for his convictions. But beyond anything that happened to Charles the whole question of pacifists broadcasting in war-time raises issues too large to be debated here but of immense importance theologically and sociologically. The Government, the Church, the B.B.C., the People— to frame policies in which all of these shall receive just representation but on which none shall override the others is a task as urgent today as it was in the dark and threatening days of 1940–41.[5]

(2) *Easter 1954*. Charles had agreed to give an Easter broadcast on the Meaning of Eternal Life. When Edwin Robertson, the producer, went to Cambridge to talk to him about the theme and its presentation they went outside and walked together for a while. Suddenly Charles burst out: "Edwin, I'm in love." His face was alight and he told of the plans for his marriage with his long-time friend Ethel Moors, which was to take place in Boston before Easter. He and his bride would come to England after the wedding ceremony and he would be ready for the broadcast at the appointed time.

The engagement had been announced on January 31st, though the proposal of marriage had been accepted in the previous September. Not unnaturally the news was grist to the mill of the popular Press: a widow whose husband had left an estate of more than one million pounds;[6] she a woman eighty years of age while Charles was in his sixty-ninth year; he a Chaplain to the Queen, she a leading figure in Boston society. But in fact there was nothing very surprising about the decision which they had made together. Since 1926 Charles had been an intimate friend of John and Ethel Moors and a frequent visitor to their home. He and Ethel shared an intense concern for every movement directed towards the establishment of peace or the breaking down of barriers of race.[7] She was a devoted member of Trinity Church in which Charles often preached and her father and brother had over a long period supported the Episcopal Theological School in Cambridge where Charles was always a welcome visitor.

He had determined in any case to leave Madingley Hall and now had the prospect of sharing with Ethel in Cambridge a home which could become a centre of hospitality especially for students from other lands. (A house had become available, No. 10 Madingley Road, which seemed admirably suited for their needs and for their work together.)

So Charles went out full of hope and met Ethel on March 22nd. On March 24th, the wedding took place in Trinity Church with Bishop Henry Sherrill, the Presiding Bishop of the Protestant Episcopal Church in the U.S.A. and Ethel's brother, the Rev. George Paine, officiating. As Bishop Sherrill saw Ethel coming into the vestry before the ceremony, she looked so happy and vivacious that he exclaimed: "Who is this young girl coming in to be married to-day?" Her many friends supported her and rejoiced with her and there followed eight days of wonderful happiness for the newly married couple: "The activities of house-arrangements" Charles wrote, "selecting of furniture and books for our home, the parties and visits, the services in Trinity Church, all made an ideal fulfilment of our long friendship and long expectation. It was as she would say an *opus perfectum.*"

They left Boston for New York on March 30th, planning to fly on from there to London, thence to Lyme Regis for a quiet honeymoon, going on from there after Easter to spend the summer in Madingley Hall before setting up home in the newly acquired house in August. But the journey had scarcely begun when Ethel began to show signs of emotional and physical strain. In New York there were symptoms of mental vagueness and of difficult breathing and these were intensified on the plane. From Heathrow they went on by car to Lyme Regis but when they arrived she was quite exhausted and only fit for bed. The next two days saw a slight improvement of her spirits and hopes rose for a complete recovery after an extended rest. On Sunday, April 4th, she seemed better, got up and before lunch dressed and went a short walk to the shore. But as night drew on it was clear that she was desperately ill and by the time the doctor came she had passed into a coma. For a brief moment she rallied and said to Charles "I am quite reconciled—fully reconciled." These were her last words and in the early morning she died.

The funeral took place on the following Friday and Charles once again was left alone. Could he give his broadcast on Easter Day? He had actually written it during the afternoon of the Sunday in Lyme Regis while Ethel was resting and felt that in a very real sense she had shared in it, and that he must bear witness to the Easter Faith, even so soon after his overwhelming loss. On Easter Morning at 4 a.m. he wrote (the broadcast had by this time been recorded.)

> "When one has had a fortnight in heaven one may be sad but one must not and does not grumble when it is over. For (1) it is a possession for ever (2) an experience to be continually remembered and renewed (3) a relationship to be explored and enlarged."

Such a faith and hope he had tried to elaborate more fully in his words on the air. Eternal life, he claimed, is above all a sharing in that life which Jesus possessed and imparted.

> "For this is the Easter message, that men and women who had been with Jesus as He went in and out among them and who had given Him their devotion, their service and their loyalty, knew beyond doubt that His death had not (as they at first and inevitably supposed) destroyed that relationship. Rather, the old links remained and were now unbreakable, the old defects and misunderstandings were removed; life could now be seen as lived as 'all of a piece and all in God'."

It was a memorable broadcast. No reference was made directly to his own bereavement though many who listened knew. Could he still go on after this shattering of so many hopes? Yes, he said, it is the one thing I want to do. The last thing we did together was to discuss the script. (He had read it to her and they had talked together about eternal life.) The tributes to Ethel from those who had known her over many years bore eloquent testimony to her richly cultivated mind, her wide humanitarian concerns, her gaiety and love of beauty, above all her radiant religious faith. For a brief period she and Charles had sealed their long friendship and partnership in common interests.

Now he must reconsider all the plans and arrangements he had made for the coming years and seek again for some integrating centre around which his many activities could revolve. This was to come sooner perhaps than expected through an encounter brought about directly through his broadcasting connections.

(3) *June 17th*, 1956. In 1954 Canon Roy McKay, who was then Chaplain of Canford School in Dorset, entertained in his home a visiting lecturer, a Belgian lady, Mme. Hélène Jeanty, who came to talk to the boys about her war-time experiences. Shortly afterwards he was appointed Head of Religious Broadcasting and moved to London. Mme. Jeanty now often stayed with the McKays while on her lecture tours and on one of these occasions in 1956 he, having frequently discussed religious matters with her said: "You ought to explain your religious views in one of our television programmes". "The only difficulty," he continued, "is to find someone who will pin you down." This is her account of what followed:

> "Suddenly his face brightened. "I've got it," he said. He explained that he had a friend at Cambridge, a certain Canon Raven, who was a specialist in theological debates. If Canon Raven would agree to interview me before the cameras, our show might be an interesting one. He telephoned Dr. Raven. Dr. Raven agreed and a programme was fixed for June 17th, 1956."[8]

Before this date, Mme. Jeanty met Charles twice and almost immediately a warm friendship was established. On the day itself they were called to the studio more than two hours before they were due to go on the air and Charles began to grow increasingly restless. Why so early? Why was the place so hot? As he continued to fume, Hélène, thinking she was unlikely to see him again, said, "Look here. You should not grumble. We shall have nine million viewers. If we can help one bedridden person, don't you think all this will have been worthwhile?". "You are right, my dear" he replied—and relaxed.

Charles's part in the programme was to draw out from Mme. Jeanty some expression of the faith that had sustained her during her extraordinary war-time experiences. These have been described in

M

full in her book *Without Frontiers* which Charles was to help her to write. In brief her story tells (in the words of the book's jacket) how:

"Madame Jeanty Raven was the gay and lovely wife of a Belgian lawyer turned soldier when the war against Nazi oppression broke out. Without hesitation she plunged into what was even then the Resistance, giving cover to those who plotted against the invaders and shelter to a British airman. Before long she was in the hands of the Gestapo and so was her husband. To save him she feigned madness,[9] only so find after years in Nazi prisons and asylums that her husband had been shot in his prison camp.

But instead of bitterness there came a positive turning to the solace of religion, to work for the refugees, to the pursuit of goodwill among all men."

In the programme Charles questioned her about her religious experiences, some of which had been remarkably comparable to his own and at one point exclaimed: "I think for all practical purposes you're a Christian." Madame Jeanty was not prepared, as he put it, to have a label tied round her neck but undoubtedly there had been a meeting of kindred spirits and during the small party arranged by Canon McKay when the programme was over Charles drew her aside and invited her to come and stay "with us" at Cambridge. She imagined that the "us" was Charles and his wife and agreed to go in the following month.

In fact after leaving Madingley Hall Charles had taken up residence with Mary, his daughter, at 10 Madingley Road and she was away when Mme. Jeanty came. In London he had said to Hélène somewhat mysteriously: "I think you have given me the key I'm looking for." Now "he explained that he was seventy-one, that the life he had been living since he was no longer Master of Christ's College, was 'one damn thing after another', that it was time he settled down to a more precise form of activity and that the kind of work I was engaged on appealed to him enormously." (p. 220). He had no altar, no pulpit, no steady mission to perform, no intimate companionship in work. To make 10 Madingley Road the base for the kind of work Hélène was doing, with himself sharing in it, and extending it by his own innumerable contacts—this was the prospect which had suddenly captured his imagination. Within twenty-four hours of their meeting in Cambridge Charles had proposed marriage and although Hélène postponed a formal acceptance, she knew in her heart that she had no wish to say "No". Her son as well as Charles's own children approved and before the end of the year the wedding took place at St. Martin-in-the-Fields with Roy McKay officiating.

This time publicity centred around faith rather than finance, the word having gone round that Madame Jeanty did not call herself a Christian. There was no question, however, about the depth of her mystical experience and of the way in which she had been sustained through her harrowing adventures by her faith in an ultimate Divine providence. She and Charles could now go forward together, she with with a special concern for the arts and religion (she is a keen amateur musician), he with his special concern for science and religion, the two united in their special concern for a deepening of understanding and mutual compassion amongst those of different races, nations and creeds. He introduced her to his friends in Cambridge, she introduced him to her friends in Brussels and Paris. They travelled to America together and organised a series of "colloquies" in their home. In this way new vistas opened out for Charles in the final seven and a half years of his life. His questing, adventurous spirit was searching for new things to observe and wonder at to the very end. Through Hélène's great friend, the Baron Allard, Charles was once introduced to the Queen of the Belgians. She enquired of him how, he judged, life ended. His reply was "Madame, when one has ceased to wonder, one has ceased to live."

(4) *December 2nd, 1959.* Charles's most notable achievement in the realm of broadcasting may well have been his performance in the *Viewpoint* series on the night after the famous *International Science* programme, *What is Life?* appeared. In the latter, brilliant use had been made of camera techniques to illustrate the latest advances of scientific knowledge and to build up a coherent picture of the way in which life could have originated and developed. Charles had seen a preview

of the programme but even so it was a remarkable feat on the part of himself and the producer of *Viewpoint*, Mr. Vernon Sproxton, to construct at such short notice a commentary on it, together with an addendum which did not seem to be sheer anti-claimax. Intense interest was aroused by *What is Life?* Could a sequel entitled *The Within of Things* (a phrase taken from the writings of Teilhard de Chardin) prove to be in any way worthy of comparison with the original?

Charles was at his best when called upon to act quickly in response to a challenge. He rapidly compiled a script which the producer accepted with only a few emendations, and it proved to be of a kind which lent itself readily to visual illustration. In it he began by praising the previous night's programme for its vivid portrayal of the stages in the evolution of plants and animals but, while admitting that it gave a marvellous disclosure of the *outward* characteristics of living things he still found unanswered the question of *the within of things*, the mystery of the nature of the forward drive and of the emergence of consciousness. He then went on to give examples of different types of building: a Meccano-set, a potato virus seen through an electro-microscope, a molecule of D.N.A. All these represent wonderful forms of construction but they are still far removed from the living organism which emerges when a child is born. It is true that a human being is not omnicompetent: bees and birds and animals are capable of sensitivities and resultant actions which are denied to man and which indicate that there are mysteries of life even of a physical kind whose secret is not yet known to us. Even more is it true that life must be evaluated in terms of its ends rather than of its beginnings:

"not at the level of the atom or the virus, or even the vertebrate, but of humanity at its fullest achievement, of the artists, and scientists, the sages and the saints, the Christ. The reality of the Universe will thus be expressed only in terms of the highest and most excellent of the available symbols and instruments; to look to the pit from which we have been digged and not to the peaks to which we may attain is to secure that we shall not make the effort of ascent."

It was only a sketch of his philosophy of life, a philosophy which emphasised potentiality and fulfilment, the embryonic and the integrated whole, all of one substance, all of one piece, with the one Divine Spirit achieving the highest creation of all—a human personality —and still travailing to produce a family sharing the likeness of the highest of all human personalities—the Christ of God. But the response was remarkable. It was not just a spate of congratulatory letters but rather a grateful response by a limited group of thoughtful viewers who had felt vaguely unsatisfied by the first programme, feeling that this was not what life was *all* about and then had found in Charles's presentation the fuller interpretation of the meaning and value of life which the first programme had lacked. It was one of the rare occasions when a "religious" programme succeeded in seizing a theme of major current interest and setting it within the larger context of a "religious" interpretation of life. Perhaps a letter from Enid Blyton, the children's author, expressed most fully the kind of response that the broadcast had evoked.

"I was one of the many thousands who heard you on television last week, the evening after the extraordinary and amazing *Science International* programme. The programme left me in a peculiar state of mind, as it must also have left thousands of others—a state of incredulous wonder at the almost miraculous things man has found out—and awe at his genius in finding them. I was so very glad that I listened to you the following evening. (Who was the genius who thought of such a talk by exactly the right man?) You answered clearly and simply so many of the questions I had asked myself after the programme, and I felt comforted and grateful.

It was not only what you said, of course, or your deliberate and authoritative delivery; it was the fact that your whole personality came across to those who watched and listened. This is not a very common occurrence on television—and it is very good in these days to meet (if only on television) someone of complete integrity and understanding whose natural authority can be used to bring comprehension and comfort to weaker folk. Science is developing too fast for all the implications to be followed by the ordinary mind, it seems sometimes to have left God a long way behind—and we do need someone like yourself to interpret its findings in the kind of language you used—perfectly clear, simple, deliberate, and delivered with authority. (and also "rememberable" as the children say!) I know myself, as a writer for children, how important these clear explanations are when one is trying to interpret difficult concepts for children, and goodness knows we are all children where modern science is concerned. To link God with it so that ordinary people can comprehend and believe is absolutely essential—and you did provide that link—thank you!

Few religious leaders in this century have achieved success on the air. The pulpit, for which they were originally trained is so different a setting from the studio and most have found difficulty in adapting their manner of presentation to the new medium. But Charles was a notable exception. He quickly sensed what was essential if communication was to be effected and he grasped every opportunity which was now offered to him. Possibly no Anglican scholar in the period since the Second World War has attained a higher degree of efficiency in communicating theological insights through the new media in terms and images "understanded of the people."

NOTES TO CHAPTER NINETEEN

1. p. 337: The first recipient was a boy who actually lectured at a meeting of the British Association in 1955 on the head plumage of sparrows. By trapping and ringing more than three hundred, he recorded changes in plumage and weight connected with season and age and discovered a means of sexing and ageing juvenile sparrows, both of which had previously been considered impossible to achieve.

2. p. 341: One of his first broadcasts after the war was on this theme. It was printed in *The Listener* for December 26th. 1946.

3. p. 342: *Science and the Christian Man* p. 21.

4. p. 345:   "Canon F. R. Barry asked whether he understood correctly that Canon Raven could not come to the microphone even to talk about birds? Sir Allan Powell replied that Canon Raven could not use the microphone at all."

5. p. 350:   A lighter side of the pacifist controversy was provided within the musical realm. Hugh Roberton, the celebrated conductor of the Glasgow Orpheus Choir was a pacifist and so was banned from the radio. When this became known Vaughan Williams publicly withdrew the permission he had given to the B.B.C. to perform his most recent symphony. Questions were asked in Parliament and the great war-leader himself declared that he could not see how a man's erroneous views could affect the way he played the fiddle!

6. p. 350:   In view of the fact that there was much speculation at the time about the destiny of this large sum of money it may be well to state here that after his wife's death and the disposal of her estate Charles found himself with an income (including his pension) of roughly £5,000 p.a. The house and furnishings at 10, Madingley Road belonged to him.

7. p. 350:   John Moors used to say: "It's mighty hard to convince Ethel that a white man is equal to a black."

8. p. 353:   Hélène Jeanty Raven. *Without Frontiers* p. 218 f.

9. p. 354:   A lawyer friend managed to inform her that by article 51 of the German criminal code, if one member of a married couple was found by a Court to be not responsible for his or her actions, it was possible that the other member would escape the maximum penalty.

CHAPTER TWENTY

World Traveller

On his sixty-fifth birthday, July 4th, 1950, Charles's reign at Christ's ended. But this did not imply that he would now retreat into a more leisured life. For months he had been looking forward to a round-the-world journey which was to involve him in innumerable speaking engagements in Australia, New Zealand and the United States of America. From mid-July to the end of October he would be absent from England. On his return he would be under pressure to prepare the first series of Gifford Lectures which were due to be delivered in Edinburgh in May 1951.

The visit to Australia and New Zealand had been made possible by a most fortunate set of circumstances. An Inter-Commonwealth Conference of Vice-Chancellors had been arranged to take place in New Zealand in August 1950. Four places were allotted to the committee of Vice-Chancellors and Principals of the Universities of the United Kingdom and although Charles's tenure of office at Cambridge had come to an and in October 1949, he was invited to be one of the four delegates. The opportunity to visit New Zealand in particular brought the fulfilment of a life-long wish and it would be easily possible to fly direct from there to the U.S.A. where he would be delivering the first series of Robert Treat Paine Lectures in October.

Charles was apprehensive about the long air-journey to Australia but with a break at Singapore he suffered no ill-effects. Just under two weeks were spent in the Universities of Melbourne and Sydney and in the National University at Canberra. In Melbourne he preached in the cathedral and lectured on 'Science and Religion' in the University—a lecture afterwards described by the Vice-Chancellor "as one of our rarest treats. I cannot remember when 'Science and Religion' was the subject of a public lecture at our University which in spirit as well as by Act of Parliament is a secular foundation. We are all the better for your having raised the issue." In Canberra the Governor-General was so impressed by newspaper reports of Charles's addresses that he requested through his Secretary that copies might be sent to him for detailed reading. In Sydney, Charles was busy in the University, the Theological Colleges and the Plant Sanctuary and made a personal link with Professor Birch, the Head of the School of Biological Sciences, who was later to draw freely upon his writings in the fine book *Nature and God*.

The programme in New Zealand began with a conference at Wairakei, a beauty spot a few hours' drive from Auckland and concluded with a meeting with the Senate of the University of New Zealand some three weeks later. In between Charles preached in the Cathedrals at Auckland, Christchurch and Wellington and replied in a vigorous speech to the civic welcome in Dunedin. He was happy to recall how his grandfather came to the Dominion in 1853 and he was able to visit the church and homestead which he had established. His childhood, he said, had been so full of legendary stories about New Zealand that when he arrived after taking six days to travel the same distance that took his father six months, (a slight exaggeration!) he almost felt as though he was about to enter a wonderland of swamps, sheep drovers and paradise ducks!

Needless to say Charles grasped every opportunity which time afforded of exploring the "wonderland" and in particular its birds. On one of his detailed programmes of events he pencilled in a note "Albatross" to show how he would spend a brief interval between engagements. And when at one of the many splendid dinners provided during the tour he was replying on behalf of the guests he made special reference to his delight at having seen "the Wairakei geyser valley in the mist of early morning, the dawn painting the snow peaks beyond the lake at Wairakei and the penguins and fur-seals of Sandfly Bay." On another occasion he revealed another aspect of the visit when he declared that though their hosts had not overworked them academically they had been in danger of overplaying them socially: "The strain (if I may speak frankly) has been on our digestions as much as upon our intellects—not least for the Englishmen among us who have been for ten years conditioned to three course dinners (even this a reflection of Cambridge life rather than of the average family) and a mainly vegetarian diet." If the menu of the seven course dinner in the Trans-Tasman Hotel in Auckland at the beginning of their visit is a sample of what was to follow it is a wonder that the delegates' digestions survived the ordeal!

Arriving in the United States at the end of August Charles proceeded by way of Denver, Colorado where he preached in the Cathedral, to an important national conference of the Fellowship of Reconciliation in Evanston, meeting for the first time since the end of the war to consider its policy and programme. From then on he was involved in a typical American lecture-tour: through Delaware, Ohio and Syracuse to Boston and back again via New York, Virginia, South Carolina and Chicago before leaving for home on October 28th. His chief delight was to be a guest once again in the home of John and Ethel Moors in Boston and to meet his many old friends in that area. His most delicate task was that of delivering the lectures on *The Theological Basis of Christian Pacifism* in Union Theological Seminary where neither of the two theological giants, Reinhold Niebuhr and Paul Tillich, shared his views. He was given a courteous hearing—in the opinion of Alexander Miller, who had crossed swords with Charles in *The Presbyter* and now was teaching at Union, a far *too* courteous hearing. In a broadcast issued after the visit he entered "a plea for a godly ferocity". Charles had introduced himself as a liberal and pacifist Daniel in a den of non-liberal and non-pacifist lions. Why then had the lions behaved in such a very un-lion-like fashion? "We owe our guests the freedom of the seminary but that's no reason why we should let them get away with murder. The truth is that Dr. Raven deserved to be theologically scalped and got away unscalped!" Miller went on to defend Barth, who, he felt, had been completely misrepresented and then, more importantly, to indicate why Niebuhr (to whom Charles had been less than fair in a discussion period) deserved to be taken with full seriousness in the pacifist debate.

But with this small exception the tour was in the nature of a triumphal procession. Since his last visit to the United States Charles had gained distinction as Vice-Chancellor of Cambridge University. He was soon to give the Gifford Lectures which the Evanston folder described as the most distinguished theological lectureship in the world. He was honoured as a leading pacifist and recognised as one of the few men capable of speaking on the relations between theology and science with first-hand knowledge of both disciplines. "There are few religious leaders in the world today," a leading Methodist theologian wrote, "who are able to make the challenging contact which you can to the scientific mind." The programme was exhausting but by all outward signs brilliantly successful. It was a very different situation to which he was to return after crossing the Atlantic in the Mauretania.

First he was obviously far from happy about the job which awaited him at Madingley Hall. On the world tour he felt that his preaching and lecturing had won as great appreciation and response as at any time in his life. A permanent position in America had been suggested to him where he could fully serve the Church in a way that seemed impossible in England. Almost bitterly he wrote to a friend, "Madingley is only a makeshift!" And again: "Somehow I hadn't realised till I got back to England how terribly I wanted to have some definitely religious work to do. When the Archbishop[1] told me that there was no work for me to do in the Church, it hurt like hell but I was too busy and too sad at giving up my home and work; so that it was only one more pain. Now to get back here and to find that one had neither an altar nor a pulpit nor any kind of pastoral responsibility and at present no home and no job—I suppose I can carry on; but it isn't going to be easy, partly because I do happen to be immensely fit and to have masses of things that I want to say."

"No home and no job": from letters he had received from Mary he knew that the work of reconstruction at Madingley Hall was going forward much more slowly than had been expected. His appointment dated from October 1950 but it became clear that there would be no proper facilities for residence at the Hall until April 1951. He could be assured of a ready welcome in one of his daughter's homes for a period but Mary had suggested that they should secure a furnished flat in Cambridge for the first three months of 1951 so that he might have quiet and the proximity to libraries for the preparation of his Lectures. At last, however, the Warden's flat was ready and Mary and her father moved in to make the final arrangements for the beginning of the new experiment in Michaelmas Term 1951.

The appointment had been for a term of five years. In the actual operation of the scheme Charles survived for only three. The word survived may be too harsh but it soon became evident that in spite of the many attractions of the house and its environment this was not really his job. The only concrete proposal for work in the Church had come from his old friend the Bishop of Birmingham (Dr. Barnes) who warmly invited him to become Provost of his Cathedral. But for some reason—possibly because of the dominating position of Birmingham's Parish Church—this offer was declined. Consequently the more secular office as Warden of Madingley seemed the best thing immediately available. But his friend the Chancellor (Smuts) had sowed seeds of discontent by urging that surely the Church would have *something* important for him to do. Yet such an offer never came and he prepared himself for his new manner of life, seldom however without the feeling that he was moving into an isolated backwater where his gifts could never be properly used or his energies extended.[2]

At the time many of his friends were delighted that this new prospect was opening out before him. One of his great admirers (a man holding high responsibility himself) wrote of the work and setting of the Hall as the ideal place for Charles to work in.

"If ever there was a square hole for a retiring square peg, this seems to be it. Academically you touch life on more sides than anyone else I know in either University. With the young you have a peerless gift of stimulating confidence and sympathetic understanding. You have more intellectual curosity than most dons under thirty. And you are a born pioneer who will yet give to the new College immense academic distinction. I am immensely encouraged that anything could have gone so immensely right."

And doubtless many others felt the same.

But although Charles exulted in his regular excursions to the country, he was fundamentally, as he often said, a town or city man. Though he could concentrate upon any matter in hand with an almost ferocious intensity, he needed to restore the balance by the stimulus of travelling hither and thither and making contact with a public audience. And although he was quick and efficient in grasping details of business, hitherto, both in College and in the University, there had been a team over which he could preside but which, he knew, would carry out routine matters in their respective spheres without referring everything to him. At Madingley however he would be in almost sole charge and would need to stay closer to the job than ever he had done before.

In a real sense he felt trapped. The Hall was four miles out and public transport was poor. He did not drive himself and so was largely cut off from Cambridge life except when someone came out to see him on a special errand. He could not bring himself to refuse the invitations which still flowed in to lecture, to preach, to attend meetings and conferences. He was chairman of committees which met in London, he was in demand to speak on matters theological and botanical, on field studies and social issues, to university students and to sixth form boys. So the criticism was heard that he was too often away from the Hall. At Christ's he had been free of major responsibilities in the vacations but at Madingley courses were organised for the Colonial Service, for the Extra-mural department of the University and so on and all this was necessary if the Hall was to pay its way and become not only a residence in term-time for graduate students but also a centre for extension courses when space became available. But it was simply not Charles's line to be a resident superintendent, immersing himself in details of on-the-spot organisation and involving himself in the roblems of the general life of the community. The situation, like the parish of Blechingley thirty years previously, was too cramping and confining for one who needed to be free to pursue his own interests and to relate himself to ever new situations.

Not that his time at Madingley was a total failure. Charles widened the scope of what the University had first envisaged for its use and with the help of Mary made it a warm, comfortable and friendly place in which to live and study. In spite of considerable difficulties affecting building and furnishing operations so soon after the War, to say nothing of staffing and catering problems, they launched Madingley on its way and today it is a flourishing institution. But after two years it became clear to Charles that it would be a mistake to continue to the end of his allotted time and as early as February 1953 the Council of the Senate obtained authority to appoint another Warden to take office in the following October in place of Dr. Raven whose resignation had been received. It was of course just at this time that his engagement to Ethel Moors was made public and that the purchase of the house 10 Madingley Road was going forward. So a comparatively brief sojourn in a residence which contained many lovely historical treasures and whose fields and gardens provided much of interest to the natural historian drew to an end and in the summer of 1954 Charles moved back into Cambridge.

Meanwhile, in addition to the Gifford Lectures in Edinburgh in May 1951 and May 1952 which drew some of the largest audiences which this famous series has ever known, Charles gave the Forwood Lectures on the Philosophy of Religion in the University of Liverpool in February 1954 (again largely attended though for some reason not subsequently published.) At the end of May 1952 he flew to Canada to be the first recipient ever of the degree of Doctor of Divinity at McGill University in Montreal. Having thus, as he said in his Convocation address, been given academic citizenship within the Dominion, he went on to Winnipeg and Toronto, delivering in each place the Archbishop Owen Memorial Lecture and receiving at Trinity College in Toronto the Honorary Degree of Doctor of Divinity, being presented there by an old friend Dr. R. S. K. Seeley, the Provost of the College. Seeley had been an undergraduate at Christ's and later Chaplain of St. John's College in Cambridge and spoke of his great debt to Charles who, he said, had influenced him at some of the most crucial periods of his life. Of the many presentations for academic honours to which Charles listened none can have given him greater pleasure than that of Provost Seeley on this occasion. After a brief introduction he went on to say:

"Twenty-five years ago, Charles Raven represented to some of us just entering the University all that was real and vital in the Church. He taught us certain unforgettable lessons both by his words and by his life. He showed us that fear has no place in religion. He emblazoned on our minds that nothing in life can be compared in importance to personal relationships. He taught us above all never to be content with inherited presuppositions. He opened out before us the horizons of the great issues that challenge every sincere Christian. He awakened in us all a divine discontent and led us to a consecration of ourselves, in his own phrase, to strive for the impossible. A few years later, his election to the Regius Professorship of Divinity filled us with delight. We knew that he would be no traditional professor, and he taught us quickly that a theological professor could be also a great evangelist. He taught us that no one has reached the heart of Christianity unless he has both feet on the ground and his heart and mind in the heavenly places. Through him we learned the sacramental nature of the universe, the evidence of the Creator Spirit in every phase of the evolutionary process; but no less we learned to recognise the signs of the glory of God in every human personality. Never was life comfortable for us who followed him. We would achieve some vision of the truth and be ready to rest content with that. But insistent, challenging, and in the prophetic line he would lead us on to something new with which our souls must grapple if we would be real and vital, if indeed we were to justify our living room in the world. It was he who thrust me out from the happiness and comparative security of Cambridge to the unknown challenges of Canada, an act for which at first I thought I should never forgive him but for which I shall always be unboundedly grateful.

I feel tonight like a small and insignificant boy who has impertinently thrust himself into the presence of the great. Never did I dream that there would fall to me the privilege of presenting this giant of the Christian fellowship for an honour such as this. In humble thanksgiving for one who has spent his life teaching the worth of sacrificial and creative living, I present to you, Mr. Pro-Chancellor, to receive the degree of Doctor of Divinity (honoris causa) Charles Earle Raven, scholar, administrator, leader, but above all a passionate disciple of Jesus Christ."

Shortly after his return to England Charles was delivering the four main addresses at the General Conference of the Student Christian Movement at Swanwick. This again was a source of great pleasure to him for the place, though full of memories of conferences in the twenties and thirties, had seemed not to need his particular contribution over the past few years. His old friend Bishop R. O. Hall of Hong Kong was there and the idea may well have germinated while they were together that Charles should come and spend a period in the Far East when free to do so. He had felt unable to accept an earlier suggestion of his friend Max Warren that he should spend a year in China but a limited period in Hong Kong was a different matter—though finally in 1956 the idea had to be abandoned.

Invitations to lecture were in fact coming from all quarters. In England students in Birmingham and London Universities, clergy in conference at Scarborough, the Southgate Council of Christian Churches, the London Society of Jews and Christians, the Fabian Society, the Royal Philosophical Society of Glasgow, the Canterbury Literary Luncheon Club—all were eager to secure Charles as speaker. But in addition a pressing invitation came from the Secretary of the International Missionary Council that he should spend an academic year, either in 1954 or 1955, in Japan and another from his old friend James Welch, formerly Head of Religious Broadcasting and now in Nigeria, to come to Ibadan and give an extra mural vacation course on Religion. Feelers also came from the Gold Coast and British Guiana— there seemed no limit to the contribution to world Christianity which Charles could now make given the necessary time and strength and freedom from other responsibilities.

For varying reasons none of those suggested schemes came to fruition. Only in the winter of 1954–5, after he had left Madingley Hall, and again in the winter of 1955–6, before his marriage to Madame Jeanty, did he go overseas again on any extended missions. These however were of such an unusual kind that some account must be given of them.

One can be briefly described. It was in January 1955 that he flew once again to Montreal to lead a Mission in McGill University. His addresses and final sermon were recorded and published under the title *Christ and the Modern Opportunity*: they provide a notable example of the way in which he appealed both to the intellects and to the wills of his hearers. As R. B. Y. Scott, the distinguished Old Testament scholar wrote subsequently, Charles had established as a fact that the Christian faith can be and has been presented at McGill University on the highest level. At the same time there was the frequent appeal to his own experience—"If I may be personal"—and the invitation to make the venture of faith in face of all that might seem dark and menacing. Less than nine months had passed since his own shattering experience at Lyme Regis and this could not have been far from his mind when he said to the students:

"You will find as you grow into the fullness of maturity that it is precisely those moments in which your world seems to be broken around you, when the sun has been turned into darkness and the moon into blood for you, that it is at these moments that you make sure of the permanence of an eternal relationship."

This kind of Mission was not in any way a new experience for him, though it was the only one that he conducted outside Britain. Another "Mission" in which he had engaged some two months earlier, had, however, brought him a quite unique experience: this was his visit to Russia in November 1954. It came about in a seemingly fortuitous way. He was visiting the University of Hull in June 1953 and happened to meet there a Yorkshire Quaker, Alec Horsley by name, head of a large dairy firm and a pacifist. In March of the previous year Horsley had gone to Russia as one of the members of the English delegation to the Moscow Economic Conference. He had grasped this opportunity partly in order to gain some estimate of the true condition of social life in Russia, partly in the hope of being able to make some contribution to the building of a bridge of peace between Russia and the West. While in Moscow he was introduced to the Metropolitan

Nikolai who expressed some disappointment that the only Christians who had troubled to visit Russia since the War were Quakers.

He reported this conversation to Charles who immediately responded to the effect that he would dearly love to visit Russia but that he could only go as a simple Christian without being entangled with any polit-ical "front". Above all he was anxious not to be identified with the World Peace Council which was playing so large a part in communist propaganda at the time. Having received Charles's assurance of general interest, Horsley went to work immediately to renew contact with the Metropolitan and to sound out the Russian Embassy in London about the possibility of a representative party of Churchmen in Britain being granted permission to visit the Churches of the Soviet Union. Charles was insistent that an invitation must come from official sources in the Russian Church and that no impression should be given that the mission was to be in the nature of a group of curious British invest-igators seeking opportunity to spy out the state of religion in Russia.

There were delays, uncertainties about dates, questions about expense and the size and personnel of the delegation but at length Charles received a letter from Moscow which is historic in character seeing that it was the first invitation of its kind to be issued by any Church leader in Russia to Western Christians after the War and was in a real sense a precursor of closer contacts between East and West which culminated in the admission of the Russian Orthodox Church to membership in the World Council of Churches at New Delhi in 1961. The letter read as follows:

PATRIARCHATE OF MOSCOW—HOLY SYNOD OF THE
RUSSIAN ORTHODOX CHURCH
DEPARTMENT OF FOREIGN ECCLESIASTICAL AFFAIRS.

13 November 1953

Deeply respected Canon,
We have learnt from A. S. Horsley of your desire to visit the Soviet

Union. We are glad to invite you hereby, and also, on your own discretion, up to five ministers of the English Methodist and Congregationalist Churches to come to Moscow at a time convenient both for you and for us.

So far as we are concerned it would suit us very well if you would visit our country in the second half of April 1954 when you will have the opportunity of sharing with us the joy of celebrating our greatest festival, Christ's Easter, and also of observing our people's traditional celebrations of the First of May.

In expectation of your answer I remain with love of the Lord,
> Member of the Holy Synod, Nicholas,
> Metropolitan of Moscow and Kolomna.

Having received the invitation Charles consulted the Archbishop of Canterbury who encouraged him to go forward, it being understood that the party would consist of an informal group of churchmen bearing no official mandate from their own denominations or from such a body as the British Council of Churches. In regard to expense Horsley generously offered to underwrite the cost of air fares to and from Prague; from that point onwards the visitors would be the guests of the Russian Churches or of the Soviet Union.

The only other serious question for Charles was that of how far the delegation would be regarded as a "pacifist" mission to fellow strugglers for world peace in Russia rather than—what he conceived it to be—a visit of goodwill from Christians in Britain to fellow-Christians in the Soviet Union. He wrote to Horsley in January 1954:

Obviously the problem of our attitude to peace wants clearing up. Our whole motive in going is as a ministry of reconciliation—to promote friendship, to speak face to face as Christians, and to be able to bring back a true account of Russian views and intentions. It is for example of vital importance to me to discover the real character of the World Peace Movement. I do not believe that peace can be established by misrepresentation; I do believe that to avoid or counteract this it is important that people who are deeply concerned to get at the truth should have the opportunity to meet, to discuss the situation and to discover what the real position is. So long as English people accept the belief that the World Peace Council is a Communist "wooden horse", and Russians are convinced that Americans are "cannibals" and Britain plotting war against the Soviets, I see something to be done by a visit of Christians, who are passionately desirous of peace but who belive that this must come by reconciliation not by denunciation.

I am fully prepared as I have been for the past twenty years to stand out as a pacifist; I am not prepared to identify pacifism with Communism, or to use the method of propaganda—that is of deliberate misrepresentation.

Horsley found this definition entirely acceptable and the period November 15th to December 3rd was fixed as the most convenient for all concerned. The interval proved none too long for the obtaining of visas etc. and there were hesitations on the Russian side when Charles, who had from the beginning insisted that the party should be allowed to bring their own interpreter, chose a young man Richard Kindersley, at the time a Lecturer in Russian at the Royal Naval College at Dartmouth, to fill this role. However the Embassy finally agreed and showed further goodwill when at the eleventh hour Mary Raven's handbag containing her father's newly visaed passport was stolen and a new visa had to be rushed through. But at the time appointed the six man delegation was ready to leave for Prague and the journey began.

Seeing the original invitation from the Metropolitan had come to Charles he was rather naturally regarded as unofficial leader of the party. The Russians were impressed by his public position—in particular by the fact that he was one of the Queen's Chaplains—and by his firmness in matters that had to be negotiated before and during the mission. But at the airport it was around Donald Soper that the press reporters swarmed. They imagined that it was he who was leading some semi-political mission of enquiry. He, the leading Methodist-Socialist: why was he going to Russia?—a question which he answered with impressive detail in the *News Chronicle* after his return. A third member was a close friend of Charles with whom he had often been associated in joint adventures: Archie Craig, Chaplain of Glasgow University, who was later to become Moderator of the General Assembly of the Church of Scotland. Finally there were three laymen: Horsley the Quaker, Kindersley the interpreter, and a distinguished mathematical physicist from St. John's College, Cambridge, Ebenezer Cunningham who had been elected Chairman of the Congregational Union in 1952 and so shared with Charles the privilege of an official place in the Coronation ceremonies in 1953, and later joined him in this attempt to promote closer relations between the British Churches and Eastern Orthodoxy.

At Prague airport they exchanged greetings with a group of Czech ministers and then flew on via Minsk to Moscow where they were met by representatives of the Church: several bishops, Karpov the head of the Soviet Commission responsible for Church Affairs, and the private secretary of Alexii, the Patriarch of all Russia. Their headquarters was the Hotel National where each was given a suite and where a dining room had been set aside for their exclusive use, members of the Churches, clerical and lay, being brought in to share successive meals with them. The entertainment was lavish and before the end two of the party were feeling the effects of caviare, salmon, vodka and champagne unlimited! But there was no doubt at all of the warmth of the welcome and of the things they had requested of the Patriarch that they might do or see only two were denied them: Dr. Soper wanted to visit a prison and Charles asked if he might meet a professor of Marxist philosophy. Churches, museums, art galleries, universities, theological seminaries, theatres—all were included in the crowded fortnight.

Charles quickly gained the respect of his hosts by the wide range of his knowledge of natural history and of the history of science. His friend Archie Craig recalls the following:

"One small incident gave him unshakable prestige with the group of Russians who accompanied us throughout the visit. One night at dinner we were served for one of the courses with a bird apiece. Raven fiddled about with the creature for a minute or two in an abstracted kind of a way, as though it were distasteful to him. Then he looked up and announced, "There is only one bird in Europe which has a breastbone of this shape. This must be a . . ." Alas, I've forgotten the name he gave it, but I think it was one of the grebes. At any rate, when a dictionary was referred to, it was established that the Russian word for the bird in question was translated by the English name that Raven had given it. After that, he could have said anything he liked about the animal, vegetable or mineral kingdom and been implicitly believed."

When they visited the zoological department of the natural history museum in Leningrad Charles was well able to hold his own with the Director who was happy to find a kindred spirit and presented him with a work he had written on Erasmus Darwin to be deposited in the library at Christ's.

A minor crisis arose early in the visit when the visitors were told that that the Partiarch Alexii, in appreciation of their coming, wished to give each a present of 5,000 roubles (About £100 at the current rate of exchange). They discussed among themselves what action to take and Charles was finally requested to compose a letter asking permission for the money to be devoted to some charitable or educational cause. This he did and handed his letter to the interpreter to be translated into Russian and conveyed to the Patriarch.

19th November.

To His Holiness the Patriarch of Moscow and all the Russias.

Your Holiness,

We your visitors from Britain were overwhelmed at receiving at dinner today your munificent and wholly unexpected gift. We have already been shown by you and indeed by all your fellow-country-men a welcome and hospitality far exceeding our expectation. This further proof of your love leaves us without words to express our feelings.

We have had opportunity of consulting together about this gift to us. We appreciate with profound thankfulness the affection towards us as fellow-Christians and towards our denominations and country which have prompted it. But we cannot accept it for our own personal use or for gifts to our own people. And we must beg you to allow us to employ it for some purpose directly promoting the object which underlies your invitation and our coming.

We should like you to use it as a contribution to a fund which could be dedicated to this end, that is to the promotion of closer and more intimate contacts between your great Church and our own British communions.

We therefore would ask you to give us an opportunity not only to thank you in person for your gift, but to discuss with you the way in which it can best be employed. We have in mind, for example, such possibilities as a fund to enable Christian visitors from Russia to pay visits to us similar to that which we are now paying to you: but other methods may be more appropriate. If we could consider this with you in the near future we should be very happy.

Meanwhile may I once more assure your Holiness of our affection and gratitude.

> And remain,
> Your servant in Christ,

Within ten minutes however the interpreter was back, greatly agitated. He told Charles that there was no precedent for refusing a gift from the Patriarch and then, though himself a communist, added: "Do not forget that for us in Russia the Patriarch is second to God!" There was nothing to do therefore but to spend the money on presents such as rugs and books which could be taken home in addition to the abundant supplies of caviare which were pressed upon them when they left.

Each member of the party was a Christian and therefore deeply concerned to know about Church life in Russia: relations with the State, freedom to worship, freedom to teach. Each member was also a pacifist and therefore concerned about the nature of the peace movement in Russia and how far, for example, the Fellowship of Reconciliation could identify itself with the Partisans of Peace (the official body representing the World Peace Council in Russia). As regards the first concern, though they saw many full churches, they recognised that the congregations were made up chiefly of the elderly and the poor. There had, it was clear, been some betterment of the position of the Churches as the result of Khruschev's recent public letter in which he had given instructions that Christians must not be molested or prevented from carrying on their regular activities of worship while on the other side Soviet citizens were to be free to propagate anti-religious ideas.

When Soper enquired what would happen if he attempted, as on Tower Hill, to preach in Red Square he was told: "It has never happened; there is no precedent." Of the sense of mystery which pervaded the church buildings, of the haunting beauty of the singing, of the manifest fervour of the worshippers the delegates had no doubt. But there seemed in it all little that was related to life in the world outside. And as far as peace was concerned the slogan on display everywhere was "the fight for peace" and it soon became clear to the delegates that this "fight" bore little relationship to their own pacifist position. Charles had regretfully to conclude his report to the International Fellowship of Reconciliation with the words: "Until there is much clearer evidence of a desire for mutual understanding and united penitence, I think our line should be a full measure of friendliness and contact but a plain insistence that Christian pacifism and the fight for peace are fundamentally incompatible."

These were matters which concerned each member of the party. But Charles had a particular concern. It was to know what the prospects were for any kind of rapprochement between "traditional mystical religion and materialist atheist science". He felt that the position in Russia as he saw it was comparable to that which had existed in Britain fifty years previously. Then a great gulf had separated religion from science. But he felt that in his own country great advances had been made towards bridging that gulf. Could there not be a new co-operation between theologians in Britain and in Russia so that a joint challenge could be offerred to atheistic science? Perhaps an account of the changes of outlook on this subject would be acceptable to the Orthodox Church's Journal of Theology. "I could supply this almost at once!"

Charles's enthusiasm, alas, did not immediately evoke an understanding response from Metropolitan Nikolai. He probably failed to understand what Charles was really driving at. He simply replied that in his view science and religion represented two quite separate spheres, the first being concerned with "nature", the second with "man". For Orthodoxy the eternal truth about God and man had been revealed in and through religion. The truth about the world of nature and how man could control it was being revealed in and through science. Few saw any need to attempt to bring the two together.

The visit concluded in an atmosphere of the utmost cordiality with the hope expressed that a delegation from Russia would soon visit Britain and this in fact came to pass in July 1955, when Charles had the pleasure of entertaining them during the day which they spent in Cambridge. His first-hand contact with the life of Soviet Russia brought him a new understanding of its two mystiques: on the one hand the age-long tradition of liturgical and mystical religion in which time seemed to stand still and worshippers were caught up into the heavenlies; on the other hand the Marxist myth of an ultimate salvation through man's harnessing of the powers of nature to his own advantage, a vision of collective well-being sufficient to inspire the individual to present self-sacrifice for the sake of the future. Both of these mystiques made their appeal to Charles, for the first had links with the Platonism of the seventeenth century, the second with the eschatology of St. Paul in the eighth chapter of the Romans. But he could not consent to their being kept separate. The great ambition of his life had been to draw them together and he would willingly have assisted his new-found friends in Russia in the same quest had they been willing. To co-operate, to integrate, to reconcile—these were still his master passions. The sacred and the secular, religion and science, the East and the West, the mystic and the man of action—he wanted to draw all together in mutual understanding and respect. Perhaps he made a modest contribution to this end by his own integrity and enthusiasm. Perhaps he had allowed his own romanticism to make him more optimistic about the future than were other more down-to-earth members of his party. But he had shown himself to be a dignified and resourceful leader to whom the Russians responded with genuine warmth. Cambridge Platonism found itself an acceptable ally of much in the Orthodox theological tradition.

Ever since the time when he was Editor of *The Challenge* Charles had been keenly interested in and an active supporter of the work of Christian Missions. In the thirties he established close friendships with Stephen Neill, a former Fellow of Trinity who had become Bishop of Tinnevelly; with Paul Gibson, the Principal of Ridley Hall who had served in Africa; with Max Warren, Vicar of Holy Trinity Church, who had also served in Africa and was destined to become General Secretary of the Church Missionary Society; and with B. K. Cunningham, the Principal of Westcott House who had for a time served on the staff of St. Stephen's College in Delhi. He often talked with young men who consulted him about their futures and never hesitated to set before them the possibility of spending at least a period in a School or College overseas before settling down in some academic position in Britain. He had a horror of a man being content to spend all his life in some sheltered College situation without experiencing anything of the challenges of a wider world at first hand.

His chief official missionary links in Cambridge were with the Cambridge Mission to Delhi, of which he served for many years as Chairman of its Managing Committee, and with the Asia Colleges Christian Association. His interest in India continued to develop, partly because of the marriage of one of his daughters to a member of the Indian Civil Service, partly because of his friendship with C. F. Andrews, one of the most honoured of all twentieth century missionaries to India, partly because of his encounters with Indian students in his own university. In 1945 a Tagore Institute was founded in Cambridge and this venture owed much to Charles's encouragement. It was designed to promote interest in the literature, art and thought of the sub-continent and to increase the knowledge of Tagore's work and writings. Charles, who had a great admiration for both Tagore and Gandhi, became its first President and acted as intermediary in securing Lord Mountbatten's patronage when he became Viceroy. It was earnestly hoped that this relatively small beginning would lead on to the establishment of a Tagore Professorship of Indian Art and Culture at Cambridge. But in spite of Charles's devoted interest in and work on behalf of the scheme it sadly failed to come to fruition.

As the time for Charles's retirement drew near his friends began to think of possible visits that he might pay to other parts of the world. It was not however until the winter of 1955-6 that a visit to the East became a practical possibility and even then it was not for extended residence in one place. From late November 1955 to late February 1956, Charles was engaged in travelling up and down in India and Ceylon delivering, as he afterwards recorded, one hundred and twelve lectures and addresses in ninety-two days—no mean feat for a man in his seventy-first year who had once suffered a serious heart attack and had never before spent any length of time in the tropics.

The primary reason for this visit was to deliver the first series of Teape lectures at St. Stephen's College, Delhi, in memory of Bishop Westcott, a former Metropolitan of India. The terms of the lectureship involved a consideration of the relationship of Christianity to other faiths and particularly to Hinduism. As the Master of Selwyn, Canon Telfer, who had succeeded Charles as Chairman of the Managing Committee of the Cambridge Mission wrote to him when conveying the invitation:

> "I suppose Teape dreamed of a Catholic Church in which the Upanishads would be read. But how read? As so many Fathers read the *Timaeus* (or commentaries thereon) and were deeply influenced? Can we talk of Plato in the Catholic Church? The popular mind will fix on Upanishads as the key-word. But I should suppose that the opening of the Lectureship was committed to answering the question; "Why could a Western churchman think that the Upanishads could have any relevance to his faith?"

It was a stiff task for Charles.[3] He had never made a specialised study of Hinduism and in India there was a good deal of suspicion of any kind of syncretism. But the subject was one which fascinated him and it was not long before he was finding parallels between the struggle of the Indian Church for an indigenous Christian theology and that of the Church in the first four centuries to find a way between an excessive legalism on the one hand and an excessive idealism on the other.

Charles left no detailed record either of his travel experiences or of the substance of his addresses. But his William Ainslie Memorial Lecture given at St. Martin-in-the-Fields in London in October 1956 and entitled *Hinduism and Christianity: A neglected Crisis* undoubtedly reflected the result of his attempt to relate Christian theology to the particular thought-patterns of the Hindu and Buddhist systems. In the first place this was an appeal to Britain not to loosen cultural and educational ties with India at a time when political and economic relationships had been so radically changed. Secondly, Charles offerred an assessment of the religious situation. He believed that Hinduism was in process of change from its emphasis on other worldly escapism to a recognition "that renunciation must be not for self-fulfilment but for service, that work and worship are one and indivisible, and that in the deliverance of the oppressed, the reshaping of the traditions, the love of the outcast, is the way of salvation." This had been the teaching of Mr. Gandhi who had derived his inspiration very largely from the example of the Christ. Therefore:

> "We have got to help India to realise that in Christ there is the interpretation of religious experience which illuminates the problems of suffering and evil, which discloses the means by which suffering can be made creative and evil be overcome and which not only inspires the believer to give himself to the uttermost in loving service, but also unites him in an organic and integrated community with all those who share the same faith and life. We in the West have had a rigorous training in adjusting traditional beliefs to the changing environments of the modern scientific and technological age. It ought to be our concern to see that others benefit, whether by example or warning from our adventurings, and at least are saved from repeating our blunders or exploring our blind alleys."

"We have got to help"; "see that others benefit, whether by example or warning"—there are still echoes of the old beneficent paternalism. But from that point forward Charles tried to stress the other side: we must recognise the defective way in which we have so far presented the Christ to India, we must learn from the East something of its sensitive awareness of spiritual value and of the sacredness of all life, we must be prepared to work with them towards a deeper understanding of the quality of true mysticism, we must re-discover a theology of fulfilment through sacrifice which the Eastern non-Christian has often exemplified more adequately than have Christians of the West. Charles has little regard for the "legalised, formalised, hierarchical ecclesiasticism of the West." He responds with all his heart to the incarnational, mystical, sacrificial tradition of the East.

During his tour he had long talks with Prime Minister Nehru, with the President of India, with the Vice-Chancellors and staffs of some of the great Universities and with many leaders of the Christian Churches. He lectured on the problems of technological development in relation to social and religious factors in agricultural communities. He was in Delhi, Agra, Calcutta, Serampore, Bangalore and Ceylon and, while everywhere impressed by the place that religion occupied in the life of India, felt that the hold of Christianity on the peoples of the South was far stronger than that existing in the North. He was distressed that the Church of England in its official policies had been so cool to the United Church of the South and so eager to promote a different kind of union in the North.

Finally some reference must be made to Charles's involvement in African affairs though, as it happened, he had to cancel his plans for a visit which at one time seemed full of promise. Friends in West Africa and Uganda would have been delighted to welcome him at any time but the direct responsibilities which he undertook were in connection with central Africa and in particular with St. Faith's Mission Farm in Southern Rhodesia. To this farm a former Head of Oxford House and close friend of Charles, Mr. Guy Clutton-Brock, had gone in 1949 to develop agriculture in a pioneering co-operative way. The work prospered and in March 1952 *The Observer* printed a leading article written by him and entitled *A Practical Hope for Africa*. This aroused considerable interest and encouraging sums of money were sent in to be used for further development. As a result it was decided to establish *The African Development Trust* with Lord Noel-Buxton, Sir Walter Moberly, Charles himself and Michael Scott as Trustees and the formalities were completed by July. Charles thus accepted a definite responsibility in relation to St. Faith's Mission and kept closely in touch with Scott and Clutton-Brock, the key-figures in the A.D.T.

A little earlier in the year a small committee with wider terms of reference had been formed in London to establish a bureau to deal specifically with African affairs. Its chief aims were "to further the best traditions of Britain's policy in relation to Africa, especially with regard to the moral and legal obligation to safeguard the rights of all communities against domination by any minority or majority and to assist peoples in Africa in their struggle against unfair discrimination and inequality of opportunity." Charles was invited to become an Honorary President and to this he readily agreed. By the end of 1952, therefore, he was committed to active interest in African affairs, both through the Bureau and through the Development Trust. And already the issue of Central African Federation and the question of the future of Southern Rhodesia's native policy were becoming critical. In April 1952 the official African delegations from Nyasaland and Northern Rhodesia refused to take part in the conference on Central African Federation and the African Bureau invited them to explain their reasons for abstention at a meeting in May. It was clear that in Southern Rhodesia opposition was also strong though in that area African opinion had no adequate means of expression.

When the Government's intentions with regard to Federation became known, a Memorial was organised and signed by an impressive body of leaders in public affairs in Britain including Charles himself. They pleaded for the implementation of a policy which would give fuller and freer opportunities for educational advance and democratic representation to the African peoples and registered their fear that the new proposals would not in fact make this possible. This led Charles into correspondence with a Land Development Officer in Southern Rhodesia who had been at the King's School, Ely when he was Canon of the Cathedral and at Christ's afterwards and who now wrote at length, comparing the position of natives in Southern Rhodesia with that of the people of the Gold Coast and Nigeria and commending the superior wisdom of the Rhodesian policy. This letter was supported by another from the High Commissioner's Office but Charles was not impressed and renewed his determination to help the Clutton-Brocks in every way possible in their mission of co-operation and friendship.

In 1955 a new issue arose. The Africa Development Trust was anxious to assist in developing adult educational work at St. Faith's and an excellently qualified young man, well-known to Charles, was ready to go out and join the Staff of the Mission for this purpose. The general scheme seemed to have the support of the Colonial Office and of some leading figures in Salisbury, Sir Robert Tredgold the Chief Justice in particular. But there were also certain reservations and dissentient voices in influential quarters, particularly about the young man who was being commended as its leader. Finally in March 1955 an official letter from the Office of the High Commissioner declared that the Federal and Southern Rhodesia Governments having examined the scheme had decided that it would not be possible to fit it into their educational system. Secondary courses in industrial and agricultural subjects they would allow. But any kind of adult education which encouraged natives to think abour politics or social structures could not be encouraged. And no permission to enter the territory for the promotion of such an enterprise would be given.

Charles was now thoroughly aroused. He believed in the Mission's programme, he completely trusted the young man who was being denied entry, he had a high regard for Sir Robert Tredgold and hoped for further support in Salisbury, he had the satisfaction of helping to secure funds from charitable trusts for the adult education scheme. Gradually the conviction grew at St. Faith's and in London that the best thing of all would be for Charles himself to visit the farm and at the same time to have consultations at first hand with Sir Robert and with other responsible persons in the Rhodesian administration. Suitable dates were fixed in Nov–Dec 1956 and all was planned in such a way as to allow a visit to Makerere College and to his friend the Bishop of Uganda in Kampala. In the summer, however, he met Madame Jeanty and a new prospect for the end of the year entered into his calculations. For six weeks in August—September he was in the States combining business and holiday, and on his return found letters which revealed that political developments in Rhodesia were making his visit questionable and that a counter proposal was being made that he should postpone coming until early in 1957.

This left him, as he wrote, "wholly bewildered". He had reserved the autumn for Rhodesia. Now he was being asked at the last minute to let it go to waste and instead to clear the spring. No public protest had yet been made in England about the treatment of the young man who was being denied entry. But those who were holding back their indignation until Charles's visit had clarified the situation were already restless and it was doubtful if they would hold their peace much longer. The exact reason for the postponement had been kept confidential in Salisbury and this made the situation the more bewildering. And finally: "I'm old and tired and much too busy at home to go off for six weeks merely for a pleasure-trip. I have a very heavy list of commitments particularly a big literary job which is being done in partnership"—and so the decision was taken to cancel the whole thing. He wrote to Sir Robert Tredgold on September 22nd, explaining that on the personal side he would have greatly enjoyed a visit. But he had come to the conclusion that in the tense and delicate political situation that existed English visitors might prove an embarrassment to those in official positions like Sir Robert's who were trying to help the Africans towards fuller self-development.

> "To be honest I doubt if a visit from me could do much good and I fear it might easily prove to have been a mistake. It has been a difficult decision: but I am fairly confident that it is a wise one."

To Leslie Brown, the Bishop of Uganda, he could write somewhat more freely. (The Bishop had written in August: "It will be a great strength to me to be able to talk to you whom I have always regarded as my guru!").

> "You will already have heard that after much deliberation and with much regret I have decided that it is wiser to cancel my visit to Southern Rhodesia for the present. You know how suspicious and sensitive opinion has become towards any appearance of interference from England. In the last month it seems that this attitude is being

deliberately intensified, so that anyone like myself associated with Michael Scott and the African Bureau will be received as an enemy and will bring great embarrassment to his friends and their work. In the circumstances my hopes of being able to discuss the present tension, to explain the goodwill that lies behind the work which we have been doing for education and racial co-operation and to warn the Federation that if they persist in a policy of smearing and exclusion they will eventually antagonise British opinion, have disappeared. I feel quite clear that to go would be to do more harm than good. So my plans have been cancelled in the hope that at some future date they may be renewed.

If I could manage it I should dearly like to visit you some day. But this would be for a longer time and with a more considered programme. Perhaps the opportunity may arise before I get too senile. Meanwhile, Russia, Canada, India, Ceylon, U.S.A., is perhaps enough for two years.

What an immensely exciting world it is, with the three major groupings of humanity, race, class and sects, all being radically transformed. There are times when I should like another lifetime to see how you and our children will surmount the difficulties and fulfil the opportunities that await them.

The longer trip to Africa was never made. In fact after his marriage in December 1956 he only travelled outside Europe twice when, accompanied by his wife Ninette,[4] he went to deliver lectures in the United States. Not that he lost interest in world affairs or in his friends who were scattered literally all over the globe. But it was now more a question of the world coming to 10 Madingley Road, especially as Ninette had a wide circle of friends who sought her out in Cambridge, and she, with Charles, began to make their home a centre to which students from many nations in residence at Cambridge were glad to come. Yet the record of travel between July 1950 and September 1956 is a notable one. Few men have used their retirement to better advantage.

N

NOTES TO CHAPTER TWENTY

1. p. 363: He had written to the Archbishop of Canterbury, Dr. Fisher, offering his services after his retirement.

2. p. 364: He wrote to a friend in 1952: "Marooned out here with no clearly defined job in the University and none at all in the Church it is difficult not to feel lonely and useless."

3. p. 379: Though the visit to India led him to reflect on the relation between Hinduism and Christianity, the subject of his Teape Lectures was in fact *Religion, Science and Technology*. The Vice-Chancellor of Delhi University presided at two of the lectures and the attendance was regarded as very satisfactory— possibly the best attended of any that have been given on this foundation. He wrote with much appreciation about the contribution that St. Stephen's College was making to the life of India: he was less certain about some aspects of the discipline of the Brotherhood. The "Lesser Hours" in particular drew his disapproval and a remark over coffee one evening has been long remembered: "How tiresome it must be for anyone to repeat the 119th. Psalm day after day and that too in India!"

4. p. 385: The familiar name by which Hélène Jeanty Raven was known.

CHAPTER TWENTY-ONE

The Last Lap

By the middle of 1956, when Charles was approaching his seventy-first birthday, he began to feel the strain of being constantly on the move. It is true that his friend Professor Macgregor who saw him soon after his return from India declared that he was defying all biological laws—"every year he looks younger than before." But in July, when writing to the Bishop of Portsmouth about an invitation to lecture to his clergy, he included this paragraph:

"Recent events, partly by disclosing that I cannot go on much longer with weeks at a time of conferences and schools and partly by opening a new and more sedentary sphere of work, are compelling me to cut down my future programme very drastically. It looks as if when I get back from Africa I should settle quietly in Cambridge.'

As the visit to Africa failed finally to materialise, the quiet settlement in Cambridge with the more sedentary sphere of work—insofar as Charles ever could be quiet and sedentary—began with his marriage to Ninette in December 1956 and ended with his own death in July 1964.

One kind of occasional ministry which for a while brought him great satisfaction, now virtually ceased. This was at St. Martin-in-the-Fields in London. Some time in 1954 the then Vicar, Mervyn Charles-Edwards, felt the need for some assistance in the heavy work of preaching and lecturing which the organisation of the Church's programme demanded. On a Sunday there would be as many as a thousand present at both morning and evening services; in the week there would often be lectures and discussion groups to medicals, to civil servants, to students from overseas. The happy idea occurred to the Vicar that Charles might be ready to come up from Cambridge fairly regularly and assume

the office of Lecturer in the Church—a post which had for some time
been in abeyance. He was given a room of his own where he could
meet friends or give counsel to those in need. And once again he had a
pulpit which, though not completely his own, was one in which he
could feel at home and could establish a relationship with a regular
congregation.

His preaching was still extraordinarily effective. The combination of
intellectual rigour with sensitivity and passion was rare in London
Churches at that time. He drew constantly upon his knowledge of the
natural world for illustrations and applications; he had a deep concern
for ordinary folk though he never attempted to talk down to them; he
was always willing to expose himself—his struggles for truth, his
visions of the divine splendour, his disappointments and renewals of
hope. Above all he was able to communicate to others his own passionate devotion to the Christ and to see the multitudes as He had done,
often bewildered, looking for the secret of abundant life. He preached
a memorable series of Good Friday addresses and then on the evening of
Easter Day brought home to his listeners with unmistakable power
what the Resurrection had achieved on their behalf.

Charles not only gained stimulus and renewal of spirit by his
association with what in effect was a wide-open public forum at
St. Martin's; he also received consolation and the sympathetic understanding for which he always yearned from the Charles-Edwards
family. At a time of peculiar loneliness, after the plan to leave Madingley Hall and settle with Ethel in Cambridge had been shattered, this
London family accepted him with open-hearted hospitality and Mrs.
Charles-Edwards was ever ready to provide that feminine sympathy
which meant so much to him. He loved to talk with the teenage son of
the family and with medical students who were often being entertained. He made it possible for the family to join him and his daughter
Mary in a superb holiday in the Scilly Isles. The whole association
proved to be a veritable godsend during the bleak period between the
death of Ethel and the first meeting with Ninette.

But in 1956 there were changes on both sides and the regular
ministry at St. Martin's came to an end. Late in 1955 Charles-Edwards

was offered the Bishopric of Worcester. He consulted Charles, hardly
realising at the time how dearly Charles would have loved to be in his
place, and after receiving his encouragement decided to accept. This
meant that he left St. Martin's in the spring of 1956. But it was not long
afterwards that Charles's own plans began to change as a result of his
meeting with Ninette and although he continued to give assistance to
the new Vicar in the autumn and was married in the Church in December a new pattern of life based on 10 Madingley Road began to emerge
in 1957 and this could hardly have included frequent week-end visits
to London.

Charles's writing and botanising, his preaching and lecturing continued though he was much less on the road than formerly. What was
altogether new was his close co-operation with Ninette in the work in
which she had already been engaged and for which she now had a new
base in Cambridge. Her son was in Brussels and she and Charles spent
considerable periods in that city, this enabling him to meet an entirely
new circle of friends and to become aware of a culture very different
from that with which he had been so familiar in Britain and America.
He entered with enthusiasm, however, into this new adventure, often
playing second fiddle in a way he had never done before but always
delighting to listen to Ninette telling her story of her ordeal and to
join with her in her ministry of reconciliation.

This ministry was really four fold. First she continued to give lectures
from time to time in clubs and schools, to religious and medical
organisations, about her wartime experiences and her work with
refugees. Whenever possible Charles sat with the audience, following
her with rapt attention and sometimes joining in the discussion that
followed. Perhaps the most sceptical of these audiences were the occasional groups of professional psychiatrists who were invited to meet her.
They might not have been fooled by her attempt to feign madness but
at least they would have given her the benefit of the doubt. Charles
listened with some amusement, coupled with an unswerving admiration
for what she had achieved. He never tired of hearing her story and
lived through her experiences over and over again.

Secondly there were the Cambridge Colloquies, a new venture in which varied groups of people—varied in age, in background, in nationality, in religious faith—drawn from permanent or temporary residents in Cambridge were invited to 10 Madingley Road to meet and listen to a speaker of distinction. Ninette's circle of friends in London and on the Continent was so wide that there was no difficulty in bringing to the Colloquy a public figure such as Yehudi Menuhin, who would not perhaps normally have been heard in Cambridge, and it was therefore easy to attract an audience, even in the busy weeks of term-time. Charles immensely enjoyed these Colloquies, in no way obtruding himself, but being content to see them as a part of that general movement towards reconciliation which had for so long commanded his devotion and enthusiasm.

Thirdly there was the actual mission of help to refugees. The problem of the refugee has been one of the most acute in world affairs since the end of the Second World War and Ninette with her network of contacts in continental Europe was in a position to play a leading role in tackling it. So in June 1963 we find Charles replying to his friend Sir Richard Acland who had written to tell him of his family home having been taken over by St. Luke's College, Exeter, and of himself having been appointed Warden; and then of his hopes to build up a Library.

My dear Richard,
At the moment I can't sit down and write a cheque. My wife's work with refugees has expanded: we now are responsible through committees in Holland, Brussels and Paris for finding summer hospitality for elderly intellectuals, doctors, diplomats, lawyers, artists who cannot dig, don't want to beg, and in fact are often wholly friendless and desperately poor—the most helpless of all the dispossessed. Lately she has also taken on the refugee students, still very numerous —Rumanians, Hungarians, Poles, etc. Summer vacations and better still summer schools for them mean knowledge of English and the opening of America and the Commonwealth for lives otherwise very restricted. The whole income from Ninette's book and lectures goes in fares and sustenance for such folks and I give all that we can spare.

This year we still have a number of expectant guests for whom funds have still to be found. Our American Tour from which we hoped for gifts has been more expensive than was expected and cost me more than I received. So until the summer is over I can't be sure what I can send. It may have to be spread over a few years: and contrary to press reports I've never had abundance. But you can confidently look for £100, even if it doesn't come at once.

But you speak of books. My house is packed with them from folios of the Christian Fathers to current theology, and from sociology and history to birds and popular science. If (as we expect) we have to move before long into a flat, the books will want a home. Not many are valuable, but I hate throwing them away or sending them to the second-hand market. They may be quite useless to you—they are not a complete library but just the result of sixty years rambling round religious and scientific enquiries and reviewing. Might they be of any interest to you? I don't fancy my family will want them—and apart from a dozen or two they aren't B.M. or even College Library stuff.

Fourthly, there was Ninette's own book published in 1960 under the title *Without Frontiers*. Probably none of Charles's own publications ever gave him greater pleasure than this which was in a very real sense a joint effort. The story was an amazing one. It is told without a trace of self-pity or recrimination and is in fact one of the most notable post-war records of the actual working-out in practice of the spirit of reconciliation. To help Ninette express it in a vivid and readable English style was one of the most agreeable tasks which Charles ever undertook.

But his own writing continued. In addition to the Cincinnati lectures on Medicine and Morals published in 1959 and the Teilhard biography which appeared in 1962 he produced a fresh and vigorous short treatment of New Testament Ethics which he called *St. Paul and the Gospel of Jesus*. This little book is a joy to read if only because of the way in which the language displays the treasures of a richly-stored mind to so great advantage. It could be said that the substance is little different from what Charles would have offered in lectures to undergraduates fifty years previously. He maintains a tenacious hold on the outlines of the historical careers of Jesus and Paul which he had formulated in his own mind all that time ago. Yet it never seems as if he is just traversing well-worn ground. There is still a certain air of enthusiasm, even of excitement, as he tries to draw out from these ancient examples words of wisdom for our contemporary world. As this book so plainly reveals, Charles retained to the end that gift of interpreting the New Testament to layfolk which he had exercised to such marked effect in his Liverpool period during the 1920s.

Soon after he contributed an essay to one of the small volumes which followed the publication of Bishop John Robinson's *Honest to God* in 1963. This he entitled *God through the World of Creation: The New Outlook in Theology*, and attempted to show that what Robinson and others thought was new in 1963 had really been his own concern over the past fifty years. Early in the century he had seen that the task of Christians was threefold: to interpret the historical background of their faith, to interpret the experience there recorded, and to interpret the Christian way of life to a rapidly changing social order. Those were the tasks then: they are still in large measure the tasks now, as the book *Honest to God* reveals. But whether Robinson's trio—Tillich, Bultmann and Bonhoeffer—were the prophets best equipped to guide us in the task of re-interpretation and re-formulation Charles bade leave gravely to doubt.[1] Instead he found the compelling word for our time in the writings of Teilhard de Chardin. He believed that through his painstaking studies of the natural order and his sympathetic understanding of the human lot he had succeeded in declaring the significance of Christ for the future of the world and of mankind in a far more constructive and convincing manner than that of either the existentialists or the "new theologians".

He concluded with a characteristic flourish. "We have some hundred million more years of life on this planet of ours. A long time—but what a thing it is to be alive now! I shan't see, but I should like to be alive to see, how this present younger generation, so easily reviled, and so easily released, and so difficult for the old ones among us to understand, how they will face the next twenty years which will surely decide whether we can enter into an international community or break ourselves by the weight of our possessions."

Charles's final essays and addresses on theology and the modern world were brave re-affirmations of convictions which he had proclaimed over a period of nearly half a century but they somehow failed to come to grips with the most urgent problems of the time. He tried in every way possible to keep in touch with developments in the scientific world but he was really out of sympathy with the new work which was in progress in the worlds of philosophy and theology and found therein little to approve except what was contained in the writings of Teilhard de Chardin. He constantly returned to the theme of the mistakes which theology had made from 1930 onwards—rejecting natural theology, ignoring scientific progress, abandoning the search for firm historical foundations, depreciating the massive achievements of the great pioneers in textual and historical criticism of the Bible, failing to use the new resources available for the construction of a coherent doctrine of the Spirit. When in 1962 a collection of essays by a group of Anglican scholars in Cambridge appeared, Charles reacted to it with less than enthusiasm, even though it was designed to take "Soundings" on the position which Christian theology occupies or could occupy in the world today.

At this time he fastened on two phrases, "The Age of the Bright Idea" and "Emptying out the Baby with the Bath water", and used them freely in commenting on developments in the early sixties. Younger theologians such as John Robinson and Harry Williams (Dean of Trinity College) had in his judgment seized upon some "bright idea" derived from Freudian psychology or communications—theory and jumped to the conclusion that it was sufficient to render obsolete the splendid achievements of liberal scholarship which had preceeded it.

"The arrival of a bright idea often induces competent students to demand for its sake the abandonment of whole realms of previous and arguable conviction. This has been particularly the case among a group of younger theologians for many of whom I have a great respect and affection. The modesty of their title *Soundings*, the courage with which they have faced current problems and the sincerity of their approach to them give the book its relevance and its worth. But it is surely evident in several of the most discussed contributions how exaggerated has been their acceptance and consequently how distorted the picture of the data that appear to them to be discoveries."

The cult of the "Bright Idea", he went on, is no new thing. It has always flourished at a time of economic and political collapse—Augustine after the Fall of Rome, Barth after the First World War and now the existentialists and demythologisers after the Second World War. Caustically and even bitterly he denounced what he called a "root and branch subservience to Lutheran and Reformed extravagances."

"If this were just the glad acknowledgement of the fortitude of those who endured persecution and concentration camps and bore witness unto death, or the triumphant assertion that God has again brought good out of evil and taught us new lessons of his saving power, we could all write to praise Him and His German martyrs. But to behave as if the new religionless Christianity involved the abandonment of every form of creed or code or cultus, would be to denigrate the intellectual, moral and worshipful values which, if religion is the primary obligation and activity of human personality and community, must play their full part in our sanctification."

Whatever may be thought about the views which Charles upheld, it can scarcely be denied that he was still able to express them in the grand style—resonant words and beautifully balanced sentences.

In point of fact, however, it was his apparent unawareness of the problems of language and of other forms of communication which cut him off from the most important developments in the world of theology in the fifties and sixties. In one way this was surprising, for one of his own most faithful friends and ardent admirers was pioneering in this area and grappling seriously with the questions which philosophers were raising about what meaning could be attached to words commonly used in a religious context. Before leaving Christ's to occupy the Chair of the Philosophy of the Christian Religion at Oxford, Ian Ramsey had reviewed one of Charles's books in the College Magazine, favourably but with already a question mark about traditional "religious" words and their capacity to communicate ideas or experiences within modern contexts. In 1957 he published his important book *Religious Language* but Charles has left no record of having read or examined it carefully. He seems to have been so confident of his own ability to communicate meaning through the spoken and written word, so convinced that words or paintings could provide accurate reproductions of phenomena in the world external to the observer, that he never felt the need to examine such themes as the nature of symbolic forms, the structure of language-systems, the psychology of human communication, the critical significance of word-events. In varying ways these themes were attracting the attention of philosophers, anthropologists and dramatists. Theology, if it was to continue to be related to other disciplines must follow suit. But Charles appears never to have realised the importance of the work in progress in this field.

Again there was the more general problem of the relation of religion to culture, a problem constantly in the mind of Paul Tillich and one to which he made outstanding constructive contributions. Charles was unwilling to regard the development of human culture as in any way separate from or even as distinct within the total evolutionary process. This is, of course, an arguable position but it still leaves open the question as to how the great philosophic and artistic and literary creations in human history are to be interpreted. Charles's stereoscopic vision held both together within the unitary movement of the Divine Spirit and saw no need to pay special attention to cultural forms seeing that for him all things in the universe are to be viewed as finding their goal and fulfilment in worship, that worship in which the true life of religion consists. Others however, and notably Tillich, felt bound to make a distinction between the order of nature and the order of culture, the former being by the use of analogy capable of interpretation in terms of freedom or struggle or purpose or progress but only because such terms as these had gained provisional meaning in and through the cultural life of mankind. Moreover man's search for meaning as such could be interpreted, and in Tillich's view should be interpreted, as evidence of his being grasped by the ultimate, the holy, the source of life and meaning, through whose gracious disclosure the final secret of human existence was being revealed.

It is sad in the extreme that Charles never came to terms with Tillich's comprehensive theological system. This could be excused on the grounds that the third volume of the *Systematic Theology* only became available in the year that Charles died. Yet it was partly due to the extraordinary way in which Charles included all German theology within a single packet and determined that he would have none of it. In point of fact Tillich had much in common with Charles—his love of nature, his appreciation of visual imagery, his concern to relate theology to every aspect of human experience, his acceptance of an evolutionary framework and a process vocabulary for interpreting the genesis of species and the development of the universe, his concentration on the significance of particular moments in history when Spiritual Presence becomes supremely manifest. But the major difference between the two men was that whereas Charles never ceased to strive for a more detailed and accurate description of what was in essence a unified and *closed* system, Tillich always insisted that no system could ever be finally closed. His own system was *open* and *transitional* and this was partly the reason that his third volume, which seemed to complete the system, was so long in appearing. In it the key-words are dialectic, paradox, ambiguity—words called forth by aspects of human experience which perforce must be included in any interpretation of life as a whole. The marvellous panorama of universal process could not, for him, be reduced to a single symbolic representation even with the aid of some stereoscopic instrument.

Much could be described in terms of evolution but much could also be described in terms of dialectic. The only final unifying factor for Tillich was to be found in what is most commonly described as *Meaning:* and meaning always involves relationship, interaction, dialectic. Charles's question which he constantly asked for himself and which he believed to be the ultimate question for the world of his time was: How do I find *unity* in a fissiparous and diversified world? Paul Tillich's was: How do I find *meaning* in a bewilderingly ambiguous world? Both are questions of the utmost importance. But whereas the first inevitably seeks an answer which moves towards closure and finality, the second looks ever towards openness and fresh discolosures of meaning. In a paragraph which could be regarded as a summary of his theological convictions Tillich wrote:

"The doctrine of the Trinity is not closed. It can be neither discarded nor accepted in its traditional form. It must be kept open in order to fulfil its original function—to express in embracing symbols the self-manifestation of the Divine Life to man."[2]

Charles on the other hand claimed that:

"the scientific movement and its research into the evolutionary process compel the Christian to discard his conventional and for-mulated systems, to resift the content of his belief and restate its hypotheses."[3]

And as a result he believed it was possible to construct a new and (it seemed) finally satisfying system in which creation, incarnation and sanctification were to be seen as modes and moments in the one univer-sal movement through which the Divine Purpose was being fulfilled. Charles was the apostle of a comprehensive organic unity, Tillich of a dialectical struggle for meaning. The final difference between the two men was that whereas Tillich could include Charles's evolutionary theory within his own system of thought, Charles's own system was bound to exclude the very notion of ongoing dialectical interaction. And this was perhaps the most serious defect within his otherwise remarkably impressive intellectual achievement.

Two noteworthy appreciations of the achievement and of the position which Charles had established for himself in the world of scholarship appeared in the sixties, the first nearly two years before, the second a few months after his death. The first formed part of an extract from a journalist, Paul Ferris's book entitled *The Church of England*. This extract was printed in *The Observer* of October 28th, 1962 and was accompanied by a striking photograph of Charles, the work of Jane Bown. Ferris described Charles as "one of the Cambridge giants", "in the rare category of scientist-theologian, a controversial figure, sometimes battling for pacifism and toleration and half a dozen other causes at once." "Raven is immensely respected, but right outside the orthodox circle of Church authority. He isn't part of the ecclesiastical Them."[4]

In talking to Ferris Charles uttered his customary lament about the eclipse of liberalism in the thirties:

> "The whole liberal Christian movement—whether on the social side or the intellectual side—was swept away by a flood of neo-orthodoxy ... It meant the ice-box for my sort of folk, of whom there are quite a lot in the Church of England. Those of us in academic posts were all right, but it did mean that the sort of thing which the best minds in the previous generation had stood for was abandoned."

He confessed that he was not optimistic about the Church's mood. The unity that he had striven for all his life still seemed far away.

The second more substantial appreciation appeared in the book *Biology and Personality* which, though published in 1965, had its origins in a paper read by Charles to the Annual Conference of the Modern Churchmen's Union in 1961. The original paper was entitled *Christianity and Biology* and in it Charles proposed that the time had come for a group of competent scholars to consider some of the urgent questions arising out of recent progress in the biological sciences in greater detail. As a result a group was organised, papers were written and subsequently edited by Ian Ramsey, and in 1965 the important volume *Biology and Personality* appeared. Such themes as the new perspective of molecular biology, natural selection and human nature, ethics and the theory of evolution, the results of brain surgery, were examined and Charles was accorded the honour of contributing an introductory article to set the book in its appropriate historical perspective. He called it a personal retrospect and went over what had now become, through his writings, familiar ground—the long period of dualism in the history of Christendom, the coming of the new possibility of a

vision of cosmic unity through Bacon's "New Philosophy", the hesitation of the Church, the mechanisation of science—all had been told
before in many different contexts. But Charles always contrived to
maintain his own freshness in the telling and to bring in some vivid
detail from the history of science to illuminate his theme. Writing now
in 1963 he was able to add a new touch by means of a conclusion which
glowed with enthusiasm for the life and work of Teilhard de Chardin.
He still deeply resented the attacks that had been made on him. No one
known to Charles had succeeded as well as he in interpreting the
scientific and the religious data with that stereoscopic perspective
which Lloyd Morgan and his colleagues had so brilliantly exhibited in
England nearly half a century ago.

This vigorous essay was the last of Charles's writings to appear in
book form. Before it was through the press he was dead. His old
friend, Ian Ramsey, the Editor, had written movingly about him in the
Introduction:

"Charles Raven who for long years and through fair weather and
foul has tried to harmonise the two visions of science and religion and
to keep lines of communication open between the two disciplines.
These personal reflections are, as always, inspiringly provocative and
they remind us that in all adventures of the spirit we need to open
wide our ears and eyes in an ever—increasing sensitivity, and to share
our diverse knowledge, common problems and mutual criticisms as
befits those who are explorers together of a common universe."

And he added in a foot-note:

"Dr. Raven died on 8th July 1964, but the breadth and inspiration of
his vision, as it led to this symposium, continues to challenge men of
all disciplines to share in a common adventure of the spirit."

It is fitting that the last book which he promoted and to which he
made so stirring a contribution proved to be one of the really seminal
works of the next ten years. All the contributors shared what might be
termed a general evolutionary outlook but there was by no means
complete agreement concerning the precise nature of the evolutionary

process or of the deductions which were to be drawn from evolutionary theory concerning design in the structure of the universe or purpose in the history of mankind. There were differences of opinion also about the nature of human freedom and of moral responsibility. Nevertheless here was a notable attempt to relate scientific theory and practice to some of the deepest questions of human existence, personal, moral and spiritual. Charles could have wished for no finer company in which to make his final appearance on the stage where the conflict between a purely humanistic and a divinely inspired interpretation of man's earthly existence is being played out.

The last occasion when he gave a major address (afterwards printed in the *Modern Churchman*) was at a Conference in Cambridge in the summer of 1963. The general theme was *Religion in an Age of Science*. Interestingly he turned back in memory to the difficult period at Emmanuel following the publication of the Master's pamphlet entitled *Prove All Things*. Taking the same text Charles proceeded to survey the current scene and to apply his text to the testing of methods currently being employed in the field of theological scholarship. As already indicated the methods used in two recent productions by members of his own University—*Soundings* and *Honest to God*—he viewed with a good deal of dismay. For him the all—important thing was to maintain the vision of wholeness by celebrating the unity, continuity and interrelatedness of the entire cosmic process and by bearing witness to the organic design which conditions every stage of the evolutionary movement. To attempt a theological re-statement without giving proper attention to what can be learned from the study of nature, seemed to him a sheer impossibility. So, defiant to the end, he sounded the alarm and bade his hearers test all things, including the New Theology. If indeed it proved to be indifferent to, or worse still, inimical to natural theology it must be rejected as incompetent to provide that theological reconstruction for which the world was looking and which alone could guide it along the pathway to eternal life.

"A religionless Christianity if it means a Christianity divorced from and inimical to natural theology would be if not meaningless then a contradiction in terms.

May I state this conviction by the record of a personal experience? On the eve of my starting to join the Second Division in France in April 1917 the headmaster of Tonbridge, where I had been teaching for two years, gave me as a parting gift a beautiful copy of *Religio Medici*. He was one of the finest Christians I have ever met; we had worked together and become very closely linked. In the book he, who knew the average death-rate of the front-line soldier, wrote two lines not from the Bible nor from any avowedly Christian source but from a poem by George Meredith

"Into the heart of that which made the rose
Shall I, with shuddering, fall?"[5]

He knew me, as he knew God, very well. If we are to prove all things we must not leave the rose or our appreciation of it out of account."

In the lovely garden at 10 Madingley Road the roses were a constant delight; masses of honeysuckle brought fragrance into the upstairs room where Charles and Ninette shared life together. He did not abandon his former interests completely. Whenever possible he would get to the River, to see the College boat racing, or be on the touch-line when an important College match was being played. He continued his close association with his son John in the pursuit of rare plants and flowers and in the careful recording of every new treasure acquired. More than thirty volumes of Charles's own detailed paintings of flowers are now in his son's possession—possibly a unique collection of its kind. His enthusiasm never waned. His memory was filled with Latin names and exact characteristics of birds, plants, butterflies, moths, any of which he seemed able to recall at a moment's notice.

He occasionally dined at Christ's or as a guest at another College but felt himself to be, as he put it in a letter to a friend, an "exile from the world's theatre". He sometimes assisted at Great St. Mary's, the University Church, rejoicing that Mervyn Stockwood whom he had known since his undergraduate days at Christ's had come to be its

Vicar in 1955. In conversation with Sir Richard Acland, a few months before he died, he revealed an aspect of his own life which those outside might not have suspected. With great earnestness he exclaimed: "I don't think I ever prayed *harder* for anything in my life than for Mervyn Stockwood's success when he came to Great St. Mary's."

So, praying for his friends, preaching and lecturing less perhaps than in the years before 1957 but still always with the arresting voice and the beautifully balanced sentences, writing what were mainly adaptations for particular circumstances of his cherished convictions about science and religion, but in one case—the biography of Teilhard—breaking new ground with astonishing success, revelling in the new experiences which contacts with Ninette's homeland and wide circle of friends brought him, above all finding ever fresh occasions to follow his hero John Ray in observing and wondering at *The Wisdom of God in the Works of Creation*, Charles never ceased to "see life steadily and see it whole" and finally, with but little warning, he "was not found for God had translated him."

NOTES TO CHAPTER TWENTY-ONE

1. p. 392:   Charles once made an interesting reference to Paul Tillich. He said that when the second volume of his *Systematic Theology* appeared, he (Charles) wrote to him saying that the gulf between God and man therein revealed appeared to be so great that it would never be possible for him to formulate a theology of the Holy Spirit in a third volume. Six years had passed and so far, Charles claimed, his prophecy had proved true. However, almost at the very time that he wrote these words, the volume was on its way to the printer for publication in 1964.

2. p. 397:   *Systematic Theology*, Vol. III, p. 314.

3. p. 397:   *Evolution and the Christian Concept of God*, p. 21.

4. p. 398:   After his death a colleague who had worked closely with him in the Peace Movement wrote:

"He loved popularity and languished when it failed him, yet he repeatedly cast it away by his prophetic utterances and his espousal of causes that were distasteful both in Church and State. He coveted preferment and yet jeopardised his career with a cavalier disregard of worldly opinion.

At least he was spared the woe of those of whom all men speak well. If his moral judgements were severe and his animosities sometimes boanergic he had also an endearing courtesy and personal kindness."

5. p. 401: The headmaster of Tonbridge was misquoting from Meredith's *The Spirit of Earth in Autumn*. Or did Charles's memory for once prove inaccurate? The original lines read:

> "Into the breast that gives the rose
> Shall I with shuddering fall?"

CHAPTER TWENTY-TWO

Prospice!

William Temple was more widely known and respected than any other Anglican clergyman of this century. Next to him, at least so far as the Church of England is concerned, the names of George Bell and Charles Raven stand out pre-eminently, the former by reason of his involvement in the arts, in politics, in international relationships, the latter by his involvement in the sciences, in social ethics and in the international fellowship of reconciliation. One of the most distinguished of American preachers declared that a biography of Charles Raven would include "almost everything of any significance that happened in the Church of England in this century": a Yale Professor wrote that "Raven's life and story has always seemed to me to be a transcript of twentieth century English intellectual life": a younger leader in the Church of England expressed the opinion "that most of the main currents of theological controversy focus in the life and work of Charles Raven": a senior theologian from another communion in England described him as "the latest edition of 'renaissance man'— immensely learned in so many fields, now talking theology, now biblical criticism, now science and now art." His interests may have driven him out in too many directions but they made him known far beyond the boundaries of the Church of England or of the discipline of theology. He was not a polymath nor did he gain eminence in the World Council of Churches. But from 1910–1960 he was never far from the place where the most important issues about the relation of Christianity to the twentieth century world were being hammered out. His solutions may often have seemed unsatisfactory but at least he was wrestling with real problems which were of concern to men of liberal outlook and intellectual integrity wherever found.

"Is not one of your most exciting questions: What constitutes greatness?" So a friend wrote when he learned that the task of writing a biography of Charles Raven had been entrusted to me. As I draw towards the end of his life-story I have no doubt that by any reasonable canons of judgment he deserves to be called a "great" man but the question still remains: Wherein precisely did his greatness lie?

What was his own conception of greatness? It was without question *heroic personal leadership*: dramatic, charismatic, yet also balanced and integrated. It was essentially the nineteenth century ideal of the leader, the Bergsonian vision of instinct and intellect working harmoniously together. In it the classical and the romantic were combined. Charles's cultural tastes and ethical standards had been moulded by his classical education: yet his passionate love of nature, almost his worship of nature, belonged to the revolution of feeling which we call Romanticism and which will for ever be specially associated with the nineteenth century. Even Darwin's concept of evolution could be interpreted romantically to become the matrix within which the glory of the classical Christian tradition could be re-expressed in the twentieth century.

So Charles dreamed of a New Reformation, the phrase which recurs again and again in his early writings. It would be a new reformation after the pattern of that which his heroes Paul, Origen, Maurice, had sought to bring about in their own time and that was in fact the pattern supremely delineated in the life-story of Jesus Himself. He did not hesitate to call Jesus Hero, to set Him up as the Hero who was alone worthy to receive man's complete devotion and adoration. Yet any charismatic leader in history who had heard the call of Jesus and had followed Him, regardless of the cost, deserved the title "hero". And from the time of his dramatic encounter with the living Christ in the dingy apartment of an industrial city, Charles's own commitment remained absolute: To be a Knight-errant calling men to Christ's allegiance and to become the Herald of a New Reformation were the dominating constraints of his whole career. He took the nineteenth century ideal of the leader, brought it to a sharply-defined focus in and through the Gospel-portrait of Jesus of Nazareth, and then set to work to dramatise the incarnated ideal in and through his own pattern of activity. And for a time the response to his own leadership was eager and even passionate.

Maurice Druon of the Academie Française has declared that all great statesmen have been writers, all great statesmen have been orators. Demosthenes and Marcus Aurelius in the ancient world, Churchill and De Gaulle in the modern. From the age of seven, Charles was being trained to *write*. Roman history, Roman epics, in the majestic language of Rome, became his daily meat and drink. The discipline which might have been mere drudgery took on elements of romance when the small boy discovered that beloved objects in the natural world could be identified by Latin names. His prodigious memory became a storehouse of Latin words and phrases and his English style became increasingly conformed to the balanced, rhythmical flow of Latin prose. "Style for de Gaulle," Maurice Druon went on to say in his article on De Gaulle, the writer, "was a means of putting on the mantle of the French tradition, and his somewhat unusual classicism reflected his rejection of licence and laxity." The same might have been said of Charles with the substitution of English for French. To the end of his life everything that he wrote was lucid, beautifully phrased, rich in its vocabulary of words of Latin origin, holding the attention of its readers by the very dexterity with which loop after loop of comparisons and contrasts could be brought to a strong and integrating conclusion. When, as mentioned earlier, he was once brought in at short notice to play the part of public orator in a degree-ceremony at Cambridge, his performance was outstanding. He declaimed in Ciceronic fashion and revealed how deeply his English style depended upon its Latin matrix.

Charles loved to quote the maxim: Proportion, gentlemen: proportion! and tried to honour it in his own writing. Perhaps even more he strove to achieve that sense of wholeness which was for him the highest ideal of all. His own mind was not unlike that of the poet as defined by T. S. Eliot: "a receptacle for seizing and storing up numberless feelings, phrasings, images, which remain there until all the particles which can unite to form a new compound are present together."[1] Fusion, synthesis, new wholes—these were the aims of his writing.

To this end the essay and the biography proved peculiarly appropriate forms to use. Some of his essays, inspired by rambles or expeditions, provide brilliant examples of the weaving together of acute observations of the most varied objects into a composite fabric. And when it came to writing about another human being, Charles could quickly select the vivid detail or the noteworthy achievement or the distinctive trait to bring a man to life: he could then summarise in orderly fashion so as to reveal the quality of the whole personality. His writing was rarely analytic or abstract: it was essentially synthetic and personal.

After writing came public *speaking*. Only when his style had been fashioned by constant writing did he launch out into the more exacting discipline in which voice and gesture and timing are of paramount importance. On occasion he wrote a lecture or sermon in full and then committed it to memory like an actor. Far more often he spoke freely with only a few headings to prompt him. Yet he never became verbose or slack; he kept strictly to the time-limit which any particular occasion demanded. To the balance and variety which characterised his essays he added a controlled passion and an empathetic relationship with his audience which made the experience of listening to his voice something very different from that of reading his writings. He was never content simply to read aloud what he had put on paper; when faced by an audience, the whole man became involved. His aim was to fuse his hearers together through the art of oratory into a living body inspired by one dominant interest. On the most notable occasions of all the orator sought to bring his hearers to the place where they could join together freely and naturally in the worship of the One Who, Charles believed, has been revealed as God for us.

In a suggestive essay Donald Davie has contrasted those who tend to be suspicious of language, fearing that it is a trap waiting to ensnare them into saying what they do not mean, and therefore something to be painstakingly analysed and carefully defined, with those who may be called "rhetoricians", who cast themselves "trustingly into the sea of language", confident that its currents will carry them to better purpose than if they insist on swimming against them.[2] There was something of this sense of surrender when Charles arose to speak. Occasionally it might result in a certain flamboyance and almost adolescent defiance of all and sundry. More often it could involve him in repetition—the same tune with slight variations being played again and again. This was in fact the most serious criticism that was levelled against his use of the spoken world. Few denied that at his best he was one of the finest— possibly *the* finest—preacher in the Church of England in this century. But because he tended to repeat the same themes it was sometimes assumed that he had failed to give adequate preparation for a particular occasion or had given insufficient time to reading and thinking. Such criticisms may have been occasionally justified but Charles never treated a public utterance as an event of little consequence and therefore to be treated lightly; and he never ceased to keep his eager mind open to developments in the world of scholarship. The fact was that early in life he constructed a comprehensive trinitarian framework within which his theology and his evangelism were moulded from start to finish. He constantly repeated phrases, quotations, illustrations yet never in a wooden fashion. Each address, rather like a musical composition, had its framework, its controlling theme and its rich development of variations. Variety in unity was the ideal which he pursued in all his public speaking. And in a finally mysterious way he held his hearers captive.

His daughter Betty, aged about seven, was overheard talking one day on a bus between Redhill and Blechingley to a small boy friend:

Betty: Are you going to Church to hear Pa?

Boy: (Doubtfully) A bit long.

Betty: (Firmly) Long and dull!

To a child perhaps. To youth groups and congregations, to university audiences and to mining communities, to soldiers in base-camps and to ordinands in retreat, he was in some strange way compelling, electrify-ing, re-assuring. He disclosed a new vision, he issued a new challenge and few could remain unmoved in the presence of this dynamic and dramatic personality. And as has been well said "whatever the sinking of the spirit, whatever the incentives to inner rebellion, the vision of greatness can operate suddenly as a release, as well as an incentive, to the creative initiation of the spirit."

What then was the actual vision of greatness which he felt constrained to communicate to his fellow-men? As I have already suggested, it was at heart the vision of a heroic figure who had grown up in Nazareth, dedicated himself to God's service, preached the startling message of the Kingdom and restored men to health and fulness of life. But this figure could never be properly viewed or understood in isolation. He must be seen not just as an intruder upon the world's stage, coming from another world to play out a foreordained part and then returning to his former abode. Charles passionately believed that this figure *belonged to the world* and that his actual career in the world was profoundly related to the universal process. From his earliest days he had been fascinated by all living creatures and during his undergraduate career he became equally fascinated by a theory, a story of dramatic movement, which seemed to him to unveil the secret of the whole life of the universe. It was, of course, the story of *evolution* which, half a century after Charles Darwin's pioneering efforts, was gaining increasing attention and acceptance in educated circles. To Charles's mind the theory of evolution seemed to provide a superb means of drawing together his two consuming interests: on the one side Nature, in which the drama of the struggle for survival was being constantly played out, on the other side Jesus the prophet of Galilee, in whose career the same drama reached its climax as in and through Him it became manifest once and for all that the only pathway to fulness of life is that of *sacrifice*.

Might this then be his own destiny—to show his fellow-Christians and the world at large that the concept of evolution which, for the most part, the Church had ignored or rejected, was capable of bringing into a single harmonious system the traditional faith of Christendom and the amazing new understanding of the universe which modern science had discovered? He would try to gain a thorough knowledge of the early development of Christian doctrine, while at the same time he would seize every possible opportunity to acquaint himself with the theory and practice of modern biologists. If he could establish for himself the correspondence of primitive Christian faith with the modern evolutionary interpretation of the universe he would be in a position to lead a crusade whose double aim would be the unification of religion and science and a new interpretation of the Christian verities in evolutionary terms. He already possessed a splendid equipment for this task— a fine literary style, a mastery of the spoken word, a detailed critical knowledge of the New Testament and of the Early Fathers, a record of keen observation and controlled experimentation in the world of nature. Who was better qualified than Charles to take the lead in a New Reformation which could transform the life of Christendom in the twentieth century? It was the grand vision of nineteenth century liberalism, the unification of the world and the perfectibility of man, though in Charles's case his commitment to the Perfect Man meant that in his programme the goal could only be reached if the Christ were accepted as the ideal to be pursued and His Spirit as the inspiration for the process of travail through which alone the dream could be realised.

Then came the War—the critical dividing line between the nineteenth and the twentieth centuries. Its effect upon a man of Charles's sensitivities, physical and emotional, it is impossible for an outsider to conceive. Not only did it produce a traumatic experience in the very depths of his psyche. It also brought a severe challenge both to the liberal view of human nature which he had so ardently espoused and to the evolutionary view of the universe which had seemed so satisfying a framework of interpretation. The intellectual challenges he seems to have met by interpreting the bitter conflict of War as part of the universal struggle for survival. But the deeper horrors which he experienced personally in part sickened him, in part strengthened him as he recalled the intensity of human fellowship in face of danger, in part shamed him for having participated in so evil an enterprise, in part haunted him lest such a thing should ever happen again. He came out of the ordeal a changed man. Henceforward he could speak about enduring values with greater authority for he had himself endured in conditions such as only those who survived had ever been called upon to face. He could go forward with fuller confidence to proclaim the eternal Gospel, for only through the creation of a new spirit and a new brotherhood could there be any hope of lasting peace.

As soon as his work on Christian origins and on nineteenth century Christian socialism were complete, he redoubled his efforts to show that the world, the community and the individual were all governed by the one creative agent operating within them and guiding them forward to their destined fulfilment. The projects of bringing together leading thinkers to consider Christian principles and attitudes in relation to Politics, Economics and Citizenship made an immediate appeal to him. Could this not be a means of discovering the direction in which these important forms of human organisation must develop if God's purpose for humanity at large was to be fulfilled?

That Charles did a marvellous job of preparation for the Copec Conference is clear from the records. Yet this kind of activity did not really satisfy his own innermost passion and concern. His highest ambition was to be the heroic leader rather than the manager, the evangelist rather than the organiser. He wanted to dramatise the present activity of the Christ in persuading and re-directing the individual rather than to work through committees and research projects to re-order the structures of society. Yet, as James Reston so perceptively wrote after the death of de Gaulle, an ideal of personal leadership, however glorious, "does not really work in a world where individualism and nationalism are overwhelmed by the larger needs of common action to deal with common problems in the world. Personal leadership may be exciting and may work for a while but it is not decisive. The modern problems of economics, military arms, imports, exports, unemployment, hunger, balance of payments and all the rest are too complicated to be banished by charisma, by personal magnetism and eloquence."[3] After Copec Charles enjoyed eight years of glorious freedom as evangelist, educator, prophet, charismatic leader. Then world-forces began to close in on his spirit and in what seemed an almost despairing gesture he gathered all his energies to confront the Juggernaut of money, militarism, and racialism with a heroic act of pacifist renunciation: by this means he contrived still to be the dramatic figure on the stage of history. But whereas in the twenties his leadership had assumed the pattern of the first half of the Gospel of Mark, in the thirties it became (at least in its intenser moments) increasingly comparable to the journey up to Jerusalem which the second half of the Gospel records.

Yet the outbreak of the Second World War did not bring the critical dénouement that he might have anticipated. Charles was not imprisoned, he was not persecuted, he was but little restricted in his movements. The only obvious hardship to which he had to submit was the imposition of silence on the air. In the drama of his life the years 1939–45 might have seemed an anti-climax seeing that he now achieved the honourable estate of a College Master. To be sure the years brought depths of private suffering such as he had never known before but his public reputation expanded both by reason of his new role in University life and through his emergence as a historian of science of the first rank. More than twenty years later a leading academic biologist who was familiar with the biography of John Ray but to whom Charles Raven was no more than a name was amazed to learn that the author of this authoritative work on the early history of biology was by trade a professor of divinity. At a time when, both in the ecclesiastical and academic worlds, his fortunes seemed to be fading, Charles made what can only be described as an astonishing comeback by producing within the space of ten years two outstanding books on the history of science and two brilliant series of lectures—the "Open" at Cambridge and the "Giffords" in Edinburgh—on its interpretation. It was not done without toil and even travail. But that it was achieved at all bore witness to the fact that Charles was not only, as sometimes described, the knight-errant, the mountebank, the magnetic orator, the manipulator of audiences, but also the man with an infinite capacity for taking pains, the meticulous investigator of original sources, the master of detail, the pursuer of wholeness both in learning and in life.

If the career of Jesus constituted the primary pattern and inspiration of his life, the writings of St. Paul provided him with a challenge and an example which never grew stale or commonplace. "This one thing I do". What motto could better express Charles's own way of life? Though not exactly a one-dimensional man, he had, since under-graduate days, set his sights on unity and coherence: one evolutionary process, one perfection of personality, one creative giver and sustainer of life. The ideal unity of the family circle, the spiritual unity of a worshipping fellowship, ("We are at one when we are on our knees" was perhaps his most memorable cry at the Copec Conference) the self transcending unity of a company on the battlefield, the almost ecstatic unity of a team struggling to win—these were some of the unities which Charles had experienced and from which he had derived inestimable support. What wonder that he conceived his mission in life to be that of drawing all men into a similar conscious experience of the one creative movement of the Spirit of God? Of course the universe itself revealed unmistakeable marks of travail, of suffering, of the struggle for survival, of progress through sacrifice. But what in the universe was partially veiled, sometimes mysterious, could be seen "in its more condensed and intimate and immediate field" (Charles's own words) in the Passion of Jesus Himself. Charles loved to quote the words of his friend Oliver Quick that there are two unique means of God's revelation, two unique sacraments, the universe itself and the person of Christ. To few men has the study of nature brought a richer sense of being a privileged spectator of a unified system through which the one Divine Purpose is being worked out. Yet it was still in the *personal* career of Jesus that he saw the supreme manifestation of the Divine life in all its self-giving sacrificial power. And it was this that led him to declare, even when War was over, that victory could only be conceived in terms of a broken body, life in terms of the outpouring of blood. "The martyr's way is the way to which Christendom is inescapably committed at all times and in all relationships."

The combination of the concept of emergent evolution with that of "the sublime law of sacrifice", "which Fabre the greatest of field-naturalists declared that he found running through all nature and of which the Cross is the supreme symbol," provided Charles with a satisfying conception of creation, continuity and consummation which governed his field-studies and bird-watching, his painting and photography, his studies of the New Testament and the Early Fathers, his investigations of the Cambridge Platonists and the Christian Socialists, his explorations of the history of the life-sciences. This seemed to him to constitute a systematic theory of the universe, a framework of meaning, a clear direction for the activities both of the community and the individual. He believed that biology, psychology, sociology and theology could alike operate within this unifying framework, using a vocabulary in which such words as synthesis, symbiosis, co-inherence, co-ordination, integration, organism, homology and harmony applied universally whether to the elements in nature or to the individuals in society.

Commenting on what he calls the "rhapsody" of Ephesians 4, Charles expresses his vision of ideal unity in lyrical terms:

"The biological principle of symbiosis, a new principle at the level of the universal human divine community, has found expression. For us it is the co-inherence, the Christification, of mankind in a single organic personality. Like the atoms in a molecule, like the cells in a living creature, like the chromosomes in the zygote, like the analysable elements in the integrated individual, like the several members in the family-life of our dreams, the particular men and women thus combined by the unifying energy of the love of God in Christ emerge as a veritable incarnation of his Spirit in the world. We catch a glimpse of the vast and differing peoples of the world transformed in Christ into the fellowship of a true commonwealth, sharing the same loyalty, serving the same cause, and inspired by the same love. Such a community would live as Jesus lived, in the world but with God; its individuals would find in their membership one of another their own freedom and fulfilment, and its unity would discover for them in the changes and chances of our mortality the permanence of the abiding values and the reality of eternal life."[4]

It is a magnificent ideal magnificently expressed. It is strangely comparable, both in conception and in language, to the vision of Teilhard de Chardin. Each was a man of the nineteenth century, each had been deeply influenced by Bergson, each had a profound sense of the fecundity of "Mother-Earth" and of man's responsibility to honour and co-operate with the processes of Nature, each found it congenial and natural to think in terms of the unity out of which all things emerged and the unity to which in the end all things will converge. Each had a double (though in the last resort single) criterion by which all speculations or theories could be tested: the Book of Nature whose language could be learned and whose messages could be decoded by patient observations and controlled experiments, the Book of the Christ whose language could be learned and whose revelation of true humanity could be apprehended by patient examination of texts and critical comparison of documents. The methods seemed straight-forward; firm and constructive results could be confidently expected.

But neither Charles nor Teilhard was really prepared for the vast changes which have affected man's outlook on the world and on history in this century. Teilhard's specialisation brought him nearer to the problems of the "hard" sciences than did Charles's and this may have made him more ready to wrestle with the question of God's relation to the apparent intractability of matter. Fundamentally, however, each believed that it was possible for man to constuct a single unified symbol –system (and for Charles at least the symbols were to be words in common use) corresponding at all essential points with the universal whole which it was intended to represent. There would of course always be need for adaptation, correction, filling in of detail, change of emphasis in the light of new discoveries and a new understanding of universal processes. But Charles never really swerved from his early conviction that the evolutionary model provided the necessary key to the interpretation of the whole cosmic drama and that within this one all-embracing framework he could include all the essential features of universal life—God, man and the world.

One of the most perceptive comments that I have encountered amongst all the memories of the impressions which Charles made on his contemporaries is the following:

He did not become the leader he might have been because of his utter inability to absorb or relate himself to a contrary idea.[5]

This may seem a severe judgment but there is too much supporting evidence for it to be dismissed as unfair. Again and again, in his writings and speeches, he explodes into a denunciation of dualism in whatever shape or form. If there was one text in the Bible which he hated (perhaps he could register his hate with an easier conscience seeing that he belonged to the tradition which did not include the Apocrypha within Holy Scripture) it was: "The most High has made not one world but two." When Alan Webster, who was at the time Vice-Principal of Westcott House, chose this as the text for a University Sermon,[6] Charles reacted with an almost passionate intensity and seized the opportunity in a public lecture on the following day to demolish this two-headed monster in no uncertain terms. To regard Christ as ladder between an earthly and a heavenly world was, in his view, a perversion of the truth. One world, one universal process, one omnicompetent Divine Spirit—to this conception of unity he was totally committed.

This passionate commitment to the single framework of interpretation made him impatient with questioners who did not appear to share his own basic assumptions. At all times he abhorred any kind of pretentiousness, any dishonesty in refusing to face plain evidence, any sloppiness in argument. As an old friend commented: "Charles did not suffer fools gladly, in fact, it may be said he did not suffer fools." (But added: "He was, however, very gracious to juniors and never displayed the slightest sign of condescension.") But what he found most difficult to tolerate was *the contrary idea*, the suggestion that there could be a quite different approach to reality, the doubt whether his own model was the only conceivable representation of the universal process. Life for him was so completely all of one piece—infinitely rich in variations of form and movement and colour but still *one*—that any suggestion of opposing forces within the human personality or within the world of nature itself was to be resisted to the uttermost.

It was this passion for unity which lay behind his strong, at times almost bitter, aversion to German theology throughout the second half of his life. He had, in his years of study before the First World War, accepted with admiration and gratitude the conclusions of great liberal critical historians such as Harnack and Deissmann while his own celebrated work on Apollinarianism owed an enormous debt to Leitzmann. But it was when the "contrary idea" appeared in German scholarship, represented above all by Barth, that Charles found himself first bewildered, then exasperated. The basic questions at issue were in fact not primarily theological but *historical:* what is history? what is God's relation to history? what language is appropriate for testimony to events in history? is the history of the universe a unity or are there histories which not only are variations on a single theme but which may in fact be seen as existing in dialectical relationship with one another?

For Charles "history" became virtually a synonym for "evolutionary history". History should be regarded as the representation through appropriate language-forms of the long travail of the ages, the struggle of man to survive and to ascend, the emergence of novel but not wholly new forms of life, the temporary wrong-turnings and regressions more than balanced by recoveries and creative advances. He had been disciplined in the study of the history of ancient Rome and had become adept in the use of the ordered flow of the language which described it. The New Testament itself, though not so obviously reducible to a single historical narrative, could by the use of critical skills and careful analysis be organised into a reasonably reliable chronological sequence and its Greek translated into lucid English whose structures and vocabulary owed much to the influence of the Latin "flow".

But now some of the leading voices in Germany were speaking strangely about history, declaring it to be concerned with crisis and dialectic and mighty acts of God and word-events. They were turning their attention to the Old Testament and to the history of Israel and to crises under the Old Covenant—an area which had never seemed to demand Charles's own specialised study or to evoke his particular interest. Moreover they were insisting that the writing of history had all too often been a purely academic exercise with no obvious relation to present concerns. Unless the theologian could bring the past right into the present, they said, unless he could show that the symbolic (in language or otherwise) representation of the past was of critical significance for the life of man today, he might as well leave it in the hands of those who, legitimately enough, were interested in the general

o

recording of human affairs but had no wish to relate the past to the real crisis of their own time.

In the late 1920s echoes of these vigorous questionings about the nature of history began to be heard in England, particularly in the teaching of C. H. Dodd and Sir Edwyn Hoskyns, both of whom had studied in Germany and maintained close touch with German scholarship. But, to put it crudely, Charles found it difficult to understand what all the fuss was about. Had not the essential historical questions about the New Testament literature—documents, dates, authorship, context—been settled once and for all through the magnificent labours of liberal scholars? Of course there could be room for differences of opinion about such matters as the authorship of the fourth Gospel. But the pattern of historical development in the first century of the Christian era was surely hardly now open to question. The authors' messages could be apprehended by patient study and comparison of the texts and transmitted to the world of the twentieth century by the use of clear and accurate language.

Such a view of history depended on the assumption that the symbolic structures of the world of the first century were in all essential points identical with those of the twentieth and that the individual was related to society and nature then much in the same way as he is related to his environment, social and natural, now. But although within the stability of the traditional organic structure of the English environment such a view was tenable, in Germany, where the very foundations of society had been shaken through the War and where there was no longer any stability, political or economic, two questions began to be asked very sharply. Was it any longer possible to assume that the history of the first century in Palestine could be reconstructed in terms of regularities and continuities of symbolic structures such as had been familiar in Western Europe in the early years of the twentieth century? Could it any longer be assumed that first century man, in his recorded words about the world and the reign of God and salvation and the Spirit, was giving answers to the kind of questions that men ask today about the world and human existence and the providence of God?

These were desperately serious questions in the years when liberal institutions were collapsing and totalitarian regimes were assuming control. How could a reading of history as a slowly unfolding pattern mean anything to those involved in daily crisis? How could men resist the tyranny of a dictator by recourse to a world-view framed in organic, evolutionary imagery? They cried out for words crystallised in the furnace of some comparable crisis of history; for an interpretation of their own crisis which would inspire them with courage to stand firm. Might not history itself, or at least all that could be regarded as finally significant in history, be the record of those critical occasions when some man or body of men stood their ground and said: Here I stand: I can no other; so help me God? And such a view of history need not confine itself to *words*. Wherever man has been grasped by a vision of that which transcends the lure or the threat of the immediate, there history is made through the very defiance of that which appears to be natural or progressive or inevitable.

To a degree Charles subscribed to such a view as he showed by his championship of "heretics" such as Origen and Apollinarius and by celebrating the activities of Maurice and his colleagues in the mid-nineteenth century. But he was still inclined to interpret these men as heroic figures within the general evolutionary development of history, men willing to suffer for their convictions but actually aligning themselves with the essential movement of history through their courageous witness. What he seemed unable to accept was the notion that there could be two or more models of world history. His own organic, progressive, "natural selection" view of history was certainly one and this could be exceedingly useful for making sense of a whole host of past events. But the dialectical model, often, it is true, structured by German theologians in such a way as to become a discontinuous and seemingly disconnected series of collisions but in the hands of such men as Tillich and Niebuhr so framed as to suggest a continuous interplay in which each partner in the dialectic can grasp and be grasped by the contrary and thereby move forward to some new creative possibility—this model also is capable of making sense of human history and particularly of its critical turning—points and revolutionary changes.

The evolutionary model alone is inadequate. History, and above all the history of culture, must find place for victory out of the jaws of defeat, for hope out of the depths of despair, for a new *kind* of life[7] out of the apparent finality of death. It is arguable that Barth's early extreme and defiant proclamation of the infinite qualitative difference between heaven and earth may have prevented Charles from ever appreciating the illumination which the dialectical model as structured by such a master of social history as Niebuhr could provide. Be that as it may there can be little doubt that he remained convinced to the end of his life that the seemingly straightforward record of an unfolding purpose and of growth in knowledge through self-surrender even to the point of suffering constituted the true historical reconstruction of the careers both of Jesus Himself and of all those who followed Him in the way of the Cross.

In many contexts and in relation to many parts of the New Testament this reconstruction could be exceedingly moving, especially when expressed through Charles's passionate eloquence. But when made the sole model of interpretation it tended to provoke the reflection contained in a letter from a Yale Professor who had admired Charles and been an eager student of his writings:

> "His picture of the Christian's life seems to me to be a magnification of rather customary ways of living. He has slight room for a more radical and deeper reconstruction of human pathos around the oddities and peculiarities of Jesus and the Biblical story. Instead, his way of construing Christianity seems to me to spread it over the grid of conceptual thought that most of us would construct if we cared to undertake the job from the given flow of daily life as well as the given flow of the natural scene."

This judgment, though penetrating, is not wholly fair. The one radical departure from the given flow was Charles's advocacy of pacifism. Through *passive* resistance he hoped to change the course of history. He was ready to be crushed and broken in the faith that, as in the natural order, new life could spring out of apparent entombment in death. On the other hand he was *not* ready to stretch out and embrace the other side of a radical brokenness which had come about through some commitment to a contrary idea or policy or philosophy of life.

With all his enthusiasm for "modern science" Charles also found it difficult to come to terms with the notions of complementarity and relativity and pluriformity which have played an ever increasing part in twentieth century scientific theory. His dislike of mechanical models was almost as violent as his antipathy to the Barthian view of history. He possessed neither skill nor understanding in the realm of modern technology and never missed the opportunity of pointing out how far superior the life-sciences were to their outwardly more impressive relations—the "hard" sciences of physics and chemistry and engineering. In fact he regarded the most serious perversion of "modern science" to have been its concentration on mechanistic rather than biological models, the celebration of the triumphs of engineering science in spectacular projects rather than the pursuit of the vision of wholeness in which every member plays its part in the life of the total organism.[8]

Yet in many respects mechanical models have proved singularly appropriate for the unravelling of the structure of the universe and pre-eminently useful for the working out of successful policies of action. The search for a single, all-embracing model to represent the operations of the natural order can, it is true, be a waste of time. From one point of view it resembles a clock, from another a living organism, from another a servo-mechanism. Each of these models can provide valuable insights and supply valuable guidance for action. But to attempt to represent through human symbols a single representation of the total process of which man is only a part and of which he is only in part aware, is surely to strive for the impossible.[9]

To a degree Charles accepted this view of man's limitations. When challenged on one occasion about the language problem which arises when any attempt is made to reconcile science and religion, he admitted that language used to describe man's profoundest experiences must always be "pictorial and symbolic and approximate". But at the same time he believed that symbols could become more and more exact in form as a result of developing experience. Even the dialectic between observer and the observed he found it difficult to incorporate into his system. His own powers of observation were so keen, so painstaking and so open to what seemed to be the plain evidence that he found it hard to imagine that a different interpretation of the phenomena in question could possess as strong a claim to truth as his own.

At one point in his fine book *Religion and the Scientific Future*, Langdon Gilkey asks what is the most fundamental basis of scientific enquiry as a human enterprise. It is, he writes:

> "the sense of wonder of which Aristotle spoke, the unremitting eros to know, the unrestricted passion of the rational consciousness to explain, to understand and to judge validly . . . Such passion or eros can take many forms, among them perhaps the following tonalities or commitments: whatever else I might wish, I will assent to nothing that is not established; I am not content to falsify or even to guess; I will accept no surrogate for understanding and verification; and I will continue relentlessly to ask questions, to probe, and to inquire until all the pertinent questions I can raise are answered—even if these questions render my own hypothesis more shaky than if I had desisted."[10]

If this analysis is an any way correct, Charles's ambition to be classified as a scientist can be granted unreservedly. And in those peak experiences when the passion to know was rewarded with a vision of glory and wholeness beyond ordinary human expression he could be forgiven for believing that science and religion had become one: that in the vision of the One all partial knowledge had reached its climax and its crown.

Yet later in his book Gilkey argues that religion if it is to encompass the whole of life must deal with other aspects of man's experience which are not covered by strictly scientific language or even by extensions of that language. There is:

> "the *mystery* of man's freedom in relation to the forces that determine him; the *paradox* of his character and status as a person who thinks and decides as well as an object of theoretical investigation and

technical manipulation; the *tragedy* of his bondage to anxiety and self concern and his strange inability to control himself, and thus the *ambiguity* of his destiny even when he freely seeks to control it—all of these evidences of the mystery of our existence appear." Each of these, he concludes, "points to a dimension of depth in our human being that scientific knowing and common experience cannot explicate."[11]

Charles's speaking and writing had little place for paradox, tragedy, or ambiguity. Yet these words themselves point to man's experience as he stands *over against* the world and his fellow-men. And the peak experiences in this area are those in which man knows himself to be in some sense standing *over against*, even alienated from, the Ultimate, Who is Personal. Charles's system could include suffering and dereliction and a broken spirit; it seemed almost to ignore the existence of contraries and to fail to grapple in depth with tragedy and alienation and broken relationships. In his practice and pastoral care it would be impertinent to suggest that he was unable to speak the Christian word of reconciliation into these kinds of situation. But in the unified system of natural theology to which he clung these elements were little in evidence; indeed they appeared hardly at all. Mutations were admissable; discontinuities were inconceivable.[12]

His intellectual system, his interpretation of the world and of human history, was an imposing structure. It was the creation of a mind (to use words applied by George Steiner to Noam Chomsky) "almost obsessively in pursuit of unification." Charles was always seeking for "the *one* key that will unlock the riddles of human thought and of the dark tangle of history." But as Steiner continues: "Neither language nor the foreign policy of a continent (in Charles's case we might substitute "the mission of the Christian Church") are reducible to a single set of rules and causes. I believe that reality is more ironic, more resistant to human hopes and needs than Noam Chomsky would have it." Singleness of vision concentrates a man's powers wonderfully; it is always dangerous in tempting him to over-simplification and blindness to the "contrary idea".

I have followed Charles through the successive stages of his richly varied life; have tried to give some account of his interests and intellectual achievements as they are revealed in his writings. Now at the end it remains to look back and attempt to summarise the chief impressions left on those who knew him by this remarkable man.

Physically it was his *eyes* that commanded attention. They seemed to miss nothing in the external world. The movement of a bird, the unusual structure of a leaf, the flash of recognition on a human face— he registered them all immediately. And when his eyes were directed penetratingly and expectantly towards an audience, people became aware of an almost hypnotic attraction: this man might be resisted, he could not be ignored. Then there was the *voice*. The tones, the inflexions were not only pleasant to listen to—they somehow demanded a hearing. They were not in the least parsonical or sonorous. The timing and the rhythm seemed exactly right for the listening ear's response and proved to be just as effective in the broadcasting studio as in a cathedral pulpit. And finally the *bodily gestures*. The almost jaunty, half-defiant walking of the gang-plank when lecturing in a room or college chapel; or the pacing to and fro on a platform; the holding of one elbow in the other hand as the whole body twisted around some emphasis he was trying to make—these all became familiar to audiences and somehow helped to make the message more impressive. When talking with a small group in a room he would fold himself into a chair with his legs in a knot and his head in his hand—just like one of Mr. Eliot's Possum Cats the word went round on one occasion to the great delight of his hearers.

Tall and spare, with coal-black hair and prominent eye—brows, he seemed to possess an inexhaustible fount of energy in spite of his lean and hungry look. Once in an after-dinner speech in Trinity Hall he told of a reporter who had described him as looking like St. Sebastian just when he had been struck by the first arrow. And when, soon after he took up residence in Ely, a Verger met the Ravens' cook and she enquired what he thought of the new Canon, he, not knowing of her place in the household replied: "Nice family; but very under nourished!" Yet his capacity for sustained study as well as for endurance in shocking weather conditions when bird-watching was phenomenal.

By temperament, as Charles himself admitted, he was a collector. He was also a classifier. From his earliest days he was attaching names to objects, setting them in order and registering them in his superb memory. He was amazingly quick at mastering detail and equally adept at presenting an ordered account of his discoveries. His was not the deductive mind which begins with propositions or premises and proceeds to weave patterns of logical argument or to build up structures of mathematical proof. He needed to begin with objects or events in the external world and to mirror them in and through patterns of wholeness corresponding to the shapes which he saw with his eyes. He became a characteristic representative of the tradition described in T. R. Glover's *Cambridge Retrospect* as "the predominant feature in Cambridge training and Cambridge thought—that steady interest in the fact, which in its higher flights becomes a burning passion for truth; leading men on to exploration in every field of study and life, and at its worst sinks to a heartless pedantry of accuracy."[13] He examined every aspect of his natural environment with a rapt scrutiny—and then, in the fine phrase of William Carlos Williams, lifted his environment to expression.

He was a collector; he was also in the best sense a "showman". He was criticised for being a "populariser", for seeking the limelight, for constantly acting a part in order to win applause. But having *seen* the wonderful works of God, he believed it to be his task to re-present what he had seen by means of the best devices of the showman's art. This involved discipline of language and movement, the learning of scripts and, when the time came, the projecting of himself into a given situation with immense energy. He repeated himself—but so does every actor. Though he repeated the basic themes of his theological system he never became tiresome in so doing. His rapport with his audience was normally so intimate that he could present his dramatic monologue as if for the first time. He was "the last of true orators," writes one; "the best preacher I have ever heard," writes another. Great preaching has always had a near kinship with great acting. Charles mastered the art of solo performance in a way that was not uncommon in the nineteenth century but of which he was almost the last representative in the twentieth.[14]

Two words may serve to draw together the outstanding impressions which Charles made upon those who came to know him in any way that was more than casual or fleeting: they are *Personality* and *Passion*. In his own philosophy personality was the term which represented the highest level within the grand hierarchy of Life itself. Not the life-force, not life-structures, not even life-values, but the living personality. And some men and women seemed to stand head and shoulders above their fellows in displaying gifts of personality which were higher than physical prowess or intellectual cleverness or even artistic genius— *whole* persons in the sense that all their faculties combined in harmonious fashion in the service of God and their fellow-men, "every activity of body, mind and spirit", as he once said, fulfilling a common and compelling purpose.

It was, he felt, the men and women in history who had in some measure attained this ideal that qualified as *saints*. He admired men of great learning as well as those who displayed great powers of physical endurance. But his highest regard was for those of either sex who approached nearest to the perfect personality whose life-story is recorded in the Gospels and whose character constitutes the crown of the whole cosmic process. "In our Blessed Lord," Charles wrote in one of the Copec Reports," we see a personality perfectly co-ordinated; He responded with every atom of His being to the accomplishment of the divine will; He showed us perfect manhood because in Him each instinct and emotion, thought and action, was related to, united with and sublimated by the presence of God." This was Charles's vision of the true goal of life. In his vocabulary, co-operation and co-ordination were key words, constantly in use. Personality at its highest level displayed unity, harmony, co-ordination: this he had seen in full splendour in Jesus the Christ: this was to be the goal of his own striving from the day when first the vision gripped him in the dreary lodgings at Stoke-on-Trent.

How far his own "personality" depended upon and reflected the "personality" of the One to Whom he had given his allegiance is not for any human observer to judge. That he possessed what would normally be termed a strong, a vivid, a commanding personality is hardly open to question. A senior Cambridge figure, who knew Charles over a very long period, declared that his "personality" was so powerful that he could bring off the espousal of unpopular causes without ceasing to be accepted by the establishment or respected by his colleagues.

The second word that almost inevitably comes to mind as one reflects on his total career is the word *Passion*. Not that it was in the least an uncontrolled or irrational passion. In a review Mrs. A. S. Byatt once described Thomas Mann's *Magic Mountain* as having been presented "with icy clarity and a feverish passion". Perhaps "icy" and "feverish" suggest too strong a contrast to be wholly appropriate in Charles's case. Yet he combined in an extraordinary way a capacity for cool, patient, judicious clarification of scientific observations or historical data with an inner passion which could lift him to some height of ecstatic vision or send him forward in utter dedication to some compelling cause. And he himself had no doubt about the source from which his passion came: he had seen the vision of Jesus going up to Jerusalem, had tried to keep company with him in the Garden of Gethsemane, had been prepared to follow Him even to the Cross.[15]

In the 1920s he returned again and again to the strangely haunting words of Mark 10. 32: "And they were in the way going up to Jerusalem; and Jesus went before them; and they were amazed; and as they followed, they were afraid." Later in life he returned more often to the Johannine passage which, having pictured a corn of wheat falling into the ground and "dying", goes on to apply the parable to the life of man: "He that loveth his life shall lose it; and he that hateth his life in this world shall keep it unto life eternal." These were the more directly personal constraints which seemed to come from the lips of the Christ Who had lived and died in Galilee. But in constant interplay with the particular, incarnated expression of the law of sacrifice supremely revealed in Jesus there was, in Charles's total philosophy of life, the general, all-embracing expression of this law in the universe itself. From the time when he first studied the Epistle to the Romans in depth at the conclusion of his undergraduate days in Cambridge, to the time when near the end of his life he took up his pen again to write about *St. Paul and the Gospel of Jesus*, the passage Romans 8. 18–28 never ceased to awaken in him renewals of wonder, inspiration and hope. The world which he so deeply loved was not, as some would have it, just running down into darkness and death. Rather, he believed, it was to be viewed in terms of travail and pregnancy and the hope of new life—the bringing to birth of the total family of the children of God. And amidst all the suffering which the universe undoubtedly contains:

"We are not alone. God is not a distant spectator watching the conflict and praising or condemning its participants. He is himself involved. His Spirit is engaged alongside and within the effort, sharing in its agony and inspiring its direction. With us and in us is the divine, manifested in Christ and dwelling in his people."[16]

And nothing can finally separate us from the love of God.

This was the faith which fed and constantly renewed the passion which drove him forward through fair weather and through foul, through success and disappointment, through pleasure and through pain. He failed—sometimes grievously—to live up to or to commend the ideal to which he was so passionately committed. But no one could ever say that he willingly turned aside from following the Christ or ceased to believe that the Way of the Cross was the only road to blessedness and fullness of life.

Only rarely did he quote poetry. When he did, the poet was almost certain to be Robert Browning. And when back in the dark days of the First World War he was teaching Latin at Tonbridge and, apparently for his own satisfaction, translating passages of English into Latin verse, he chose for one of his exercises Browning's *Prospice*. Perhaps the prospect of death had already become real to him as the names of friends from Cambridge days were appearing on the casualty lists and as his own call to chaplaincy service remained an open possibility. In Flanders he came very near to death but he escaped and for almost half a century he, who hated war but was "ever a fighter",[17] never spared himself in the struggle for truth and justice and peace. *Prospice* can stand as the epitaph of an enthusiastic natural historian, a brave crusader for what were often unpopular causes and above all an unwearying exponent of and advocate for the Christian faith.

Prospice

Fear death?—to feel the fog in my throat,
    The mist in my face,
When the snows begin, and the blasts denote
    I am nearing the place,
The power of the night, the press of the storm,
    The post of the foe;
Where he stands, the Arch Fear in a visible form,
    Yet the strong man must go:
For the journey is done and the summit attained,
    And the barriers fall,
Though a battle's to fight ere the guerdon be gained,
    The reward of it all.
I was ever a fighter, so—one fight more,
    The best and the last!
I would hate that death bandaged my eyes, and forbore,
    And bade me creep past.
No! let me taste the whole of it, fare like my peers
    The heroes of old,
Bear the brunt, in a minute pay glad life's arrears
    Of pain, darkness and cold.
For sudden the worst turns the best to the brave,
    The black minute's at end,
And the elements' rage, the fiend-voices that rave,
    Shall dwindle, shall blend,
Shall change, shall become first a peace out of pain,
    Then a light, then thy breast,
O thou soul of my soul! I shall clasp thee again,
    And with God be the rest!
                        Robert Browning.

Eurydice Orpheus.

Mors venit haud fugienda viris: in faucibus haeret
　　Spiritus et crepitat vox; timeamne rogas.
Ecce seni cano leti penetrabile frigus
　　Nuntiat inferni regna propinqua dei:
Nox oculos velat, resonant clangoribus aures,
　　Assurgit Ditis mox ineunda domus,
Cernitur ad portas Acherontis terribilis rex,
　　Nec forti potis est usque referre pedem:
Nam finitur iter, nam vitae terminus adstat,
　　Nulla brevis restant impedimenta viae;
Res tamen una manet; prius est certamen habendum,
　　Quam tandem victor praemia iusta capit.
Pugnax semper eram, nee iam pugnare timebo;
　　Optima pugna manet pugna suprema mihi.
Mors mihi nec saevos miserescens leniat ictus,
　　Me nec in insolita pace latere sinat.
Tale nego: liceat fati mihi pocla bibisse
　　Heroumque pari par petiisse decus;
Temporis et puncto mea debita cuncta resolvam,
　　Si laetus carui nocte dolore fame.
Pessima nam passo succedunt optima forti,
　　Fugit momentum perniciesque simul;
Omnia mutantur; stridor strepitusque silescunt
　　Et rauca in dulces desinit ira modos;
Angorem sequitur requies; lux discutit umbras;
　　Notum pectus adest Eurydiceque mea
Amplectar te, cara, iterum; nihil amplius opto;
　　Sint curae faustis cetera cuncta deis.

13. II. 1915.

NOTES TO CHAPTER TWENTY-TWO

1. p. 406: J. Hillis Miller. *Poets of Reality*, p. 148.

2. p. 407: *Eliot in Perspective*, ed. Graham Martin p. 72.

3. p. 411: *The Times*, November 13th, 1970.

4. p. 414: *St. Paul and the Gospel of Jesus*, p. 122 ff.

5. p. 415: Another who knew him expressed the same kind of judgment in a slightly different way: "He was a man of almost all the talents and interests in an age of specialists. But he was so sure of the rightness of his position that he could not be self-critical of it."

6. p. 416: On January 22nd, 1950. *The Otherworldly Character of the Christian Religion.*

7. p. 420: Charles could not accept the possibility of a change in *kind* as distinct from a change in *degree*— which may be true enough in the world of nature.

8. p. 421: The honorary degree which Charles valued most of all was the Doctorate of Science conferred upon him by the University of Manchester. But he failed to achieve the still higher distinction, a Fellowship of the Royal Society. The only cleric of this century awarded this honour was his friend, Bishop Barnes. Charles might have read with a certain wry feeling of consolation a passage from an article in *Encounter*, April 1974, written by Professor John Passmore.
"There is a pecking-order in science;" he comments: "almost everybody pecks the 'natural historian'. The field naturalist is unlikely to find himself awarded a Nobel Prize or even a Fellowship of the Royal Society. But there are already signs that such a revolution is under way, if still very tentatively."

9. p. 421: Charles rarely used the term symbol and I know no instance of his using the concept of the *model* which played so large a part in the philosophical theology of his friend and former student, Ian Ramsey. Ramsey expresses his own position succinctly and admirably at an early stage of his book *Models and Mystery*. "The whole of my argument presupposes a new era in science, a new way of theorising in terms of models; and I shall argue that the result is to make science not a picture language about the universe, but a collection of distinctive, reliable and easily specifiable techniques for talking about a universe which is ultimately mysterious; and further, that the revolution in science is not without its lessons for theology." p. 4. Charles remained impervious to this notion of a "new era" and never relinquished his supreme confidence in the capacities of "picture language."

10. p. 422:   *Religion, and the Scientific Future*, by Langdon Gilkey, p. 48 ff.

11. p. 422:   Ibid. p. 124 ff.

12. p. 423:   In Paul Tillich's *Travel Diary* there is an interesting reference to these contrasting outlooks. He meets his old friend Karolus Mennicke. "In the evening Karolus and I discuss our respective positions. Result: his is progressive—optimistic, while mine is tragic—dialectic; his Erasmic—mine Lutheran. He rejects the idea of the daemonic and of catastrophe, which explains his completely negative stand on Communism. I am glad that the perpetual, palpable tension between us has at last been given clear conceptual expression."

                          My Travel Diary. 1936, p. 82.

13. p. 425:   *Cambridge Retrospect*, p. 17. Glover makes a charming remark later: "Oxford's most characteristic contribution to the nineteenth century was Newman; Cambridge gave Darwin and said less about it." Charles had a profound admiration for Darwin but showed no interest in Newman. What a happy thing it would have been, however, if the Church of England had been so organised that it could in the end have given Charles a Cardinal's hat even though he had been denied the episcopal office. Perhaps the red cassock of a Royal Chaplain was the nearest equivalent.

14. p. 426:   Dr. Kenneth Slack, Minister of the City Temple, recalls a broadcast sermon on the last Sunday of 1935 of which the opening sentence ran: "This year which began with the martyrdom of Abyssinia has ended with the suicide of Spain." "When I was at Westminster College, Cambridge," he writes, "I used to take every opportunity that afforded of hearing him as a preacher, for I would put him as one of the most naturally gifted preachers I ever heard. I mean by that—not just his superb content but the combination of the magisterial and the spontaneous in the actual manner in which the sermon was formulated and delivered."

15. p. 427:   It is doubtful whether Charles ever attained a more eloquent and passionate expression of his devotion to the crucified Christ than in the Three Hours Good Friday Services which he conducted from time to time in Great Britain and America. For those present these were unforgettable occasions.

16. p. 428:   *St. Paul and the Gospel of Jesus*, p. 93.

17. p. 428:   "I remember," a correspondent writes, "on almost the last occasion when he spoke at Swanwick it was almost a case of 'Charles contra mundum'. He could not away with Barth and his disciples!"

APPENDIX ONE

Charles never abandoned the quest for scientific *truth*. Many of his observations and discoveries were gladly accepted by expert scientists of his time as valuable data for inclusion in their collections of attested evidence. Where he often failed to win their assent, however, was when he attempted to show that certain detailed sequences or concurrent events could not just have happened by chance, or by some impersonal process called "natural selection". This can be illustrated by his disagreement with a fellow-ornithologist whom he regarded with respect and friendship. David Lack[1] in his book *Evolutionary Theory and Christian Belief* has a chapter entitled *Creative Evolution*. In this he considers objections to the doctrine that the whole development of life in the universe may be described in terms of natural selection and refers in particular to the postulate that "a force outside the animal provides the driving impulse and purposive direction of evolution—a Universal Mind, a Life Force, Creative Evolution, Emergent Evolution, Holistic Urge—various terms have been used." He names as authors of such views Samuel Butler, J. C. Smuts, Canon Smethurst and in particular Canon Raven, quoting both from the Cambridge Open Lectures and from the Giffords. In assessing their arguments he does not deny that there *could* be such a Force. What he cannot allow is that its existence could be regarded as established by any strictly *scientific* evidence.

Charles had a great interest in the cuckoo and often referred to the phenomenon of the cuckoo's egg. He argued that "a sequence of at least five distinct events, outside the run of normal behaviour and structure" must take place before the cuckoo could safely leave its egg in the nest to be reared by another bird. Yet each of these alone would

433

have been useless. The combination of the five seemed to Charles so impossible to conceive in terms of random coincidence that he felt obliged to view this phenomenon as the result of purposive force of some kind. But Lack replied that the European cuckoo is a very specialised species. Other cuckoos succeed though they possess only one or two of the features named by Charles.

> "Thus various species do not have abnormally small eggs but lay in the nests of birds of their own size, in many species the young cuckoo does not eject the young of its host but is raised with them, and in some forms the egg bears little or no resemblance in colour to the eggs of the host. Hence there is little difficulty in seeing how the parasitism of the European cuckoo could have been evolved in a series of gradual and functional stages."[2]

Charles's second oft-repeated appeal was to the case of a fossil bird-reptile, the Archaeopteryx. Its progression from reptile to bird seemed to Charles to illustrate an intricate synchronisation of adaptations rather than a series of steps. But Lack produced evidence which had not been available when Charles gave his Gifford Lectures to show that the synchronisation argument could no longer be regarded as conclusive. He and Charles had shared a deep interest in birds and bird-behaviour but with all his admiration for Charles's field-work Lack could not follow him in some of the chief deductions he tried to draw from phenomena in the bird-world to demonstrate the existence of a teleological Life-Force to be spoken of in terms of purpose or creativity or originality. It was Charles's conviction that whereas "natural selection" was a fit title to describe a process of sifting and fixing and developing, it was quite inadequate to represent the evidence in nature of what he called inauguration and creation. Lack was ready to allow that certain qualities in man might be regarded as owing their origin to a supernatural source rather than to natural selection alone. Charles on the other hand clung to the view that the universe is *one* and that God is working at all times in and through the natural in order to achieve the fulfilment of His one purpose which is Christ in man and man in Christ.[3]

NOTES TO APPENDIX ONE

1: Director of the Edward Grey Institute of Field Ornithology, Oxford 1945–73. A noted authority on the robin and the swift.

2: *Evolutionary Theory and Christian Belief,* D. Lack, p. 58.

3: In a manuscript prepared in 1959 Charles attempted to answer Lack's criticism in an appendix entitled *Occam's Razor and Nelson's Telescope.* He claimed that Lack had turned a blind eye to the instances which Charles himself had tabulated of "simultaneous change in an interdependent series of events."

APPENDIX TWO

A remarkable summary of and commentary on the Raven–Hildbrandt debate appeared in *The Record* of January 19, 1945. It was written by Max Warren who was intimately associated with both men in the early years of the War and who held both in high esteem and affection. He pointed out how different had been the two situations within which each had been living and working in the thirties. Charles had been trying to speak to man bemused by science, fascinated by its achievements and possibilities yet unable to apply them to the urgent moral questions of the day. He had attempted to get alongside them and to learn their language and to set before them a worthy goal for their striving. Hildebrandt, on the other hand, had been trying to bear witness to Christian faith in a situation where there seemed no longer to be any common ground to which appeal could be made, where language had been perverted and false gods enthroned. Max Warren points out how untypical Cambridge was in the total world-situation: "one of the islands of liberal culture in a naughty world of grotesque intolerances."

How hard it was for a long-time resident *within* the island to imagine the lengths to which intolerance would go outside! How hard it was for one *from outside*, who had seen with his own eyes what intolerance meant and bore its marks in his own status as exile and alien, to adjust to the tolerant liberalism which must at times have seemed nearer to isolationism and indifferentism! Charles was concerned to bring together fragmented and broken parts into an integrated whole; Hildebrandt was concerned to resist the demonic forces which were breaking men in pieces and at the same time to proclaim the message of salvation to the bruised and broken-hearted.

Charles deeply appreciated his friend Max's article and wrote him the following letter:

26th January 1945.

My dear Max,

Your article in *The Record* has only just reached me: my faith isn't strong enough to survive the regular reading of Church papers and my press agent is woefully dilatory. But now it has come and I am most deeply grateful for it. It seems to me a real piece of reconciling and interpretation—too kind, I fear, to me but at least saying for me what I should like to have been able to say for myself. I am particularly grateful that you have answered those who attack Franz for impropriety or ingratitude: he is, as I told him from the first, wholly within his rights in view both of the importance of the issue and of our joint responsibility: one or two small points I wish that he had altered or omitted—curiously enough the use of my Christian name on the dust-cover is the one that I dislike most and that my friends are apt to resent: but these are only matters of trivial failure to appreciate the nuances of English manners. He has cut out nearly all the points of this sort that hurt me in his first draft.

You fasten upon the heart of the matter when you say that it is in my doctrine of the Spirit that my answer to his charges lies. It is indeed something of an irony that having spent many years and several books in trying to re-affirm the doctrine of the Holy Spirit so as to give meaning to words like "every virtue we possess and every victory won are His alone" I should be singled out as a Pelagian, a Secularist and a "Mystik". I think he ought to have known me well enough to realise that however one-sided certain of my phrases may be when detached, the solid structure of my position is not only Christo-centric but non-Pelagian.

But of course the particular book with which he deals was sent to the Press unrevised and at a time when I expected not to live to revise it. Bee and I got it done—I dictating to her as best I could: and then I just murmured a sort of Nunc Dimittis as we sent it off to

H and S. Months later it was returned to me in page-proof: and it seemed hopeless—and undesirable—to attempt a rewriting. Under such circumstances I have no right nor desire to escape criticism.

Your main point—that in fact he does not really meet my arguments— was to my great surprise made by Pastor Schweitzer at the C.I.S. meeting last night. After praising Franz's book and saying that he regarded it as a fine statement of faith as against heresy, he added "Then I read our Chairman's book and found that it was not at all what I had expected: the two do not meet: they are parallel." To what extent this is true I am not the person to judge. My book was not a criticism of Franz but an exposition and a warning. But the differences between him and me are, as I have always known, pretty radical: and his book accentuates them . . .

I am most grateful for the brilliant and lovely way in which you have fulfilled your task.

Ever affectionately,
Charles.

BIBLIOGRAPHY OF CHARLES RAVEN

Theological

What Think Ye Of Christ? London 1916
Christian Socialism: 1848–1854 London 1920
Apollinarianism Cambridge 1923
Our Salvation London 1925
The Eternal Spirit Liverpool 1926
The Creator Spirit London 1927
The Quest of Religion London 1928
Women and Holy Orders London 1928
Christ and Modern Education London 1928
Jesus and the Gospel of Love London 1931
Is War Obsolete? London 1935
Evolution and the Christian Concept of God Oxford 1936
War and the Christian London 1938
The Gospel and the Church London 1939
The Cross and the Crisis London 1940
Lessons of the Prince of Peace London 1942
Science, Religion and the Future Cambridge 1943
Good News of God London 1943
Science and the Christian Man London 1952
The Theological Basis of Pacifism London 1952
Natural Religion and Christian Theology Gifford Lectures Series 1 and 2,
    Cambridge 1953
Christ and the Modern Opportunity London 1956
Science, Medicine and Morals London 1959
St. Paul and the Gospel of Jesus London 1961
Teilhard de Chardin: Scientist and Seer London 1962

Natural History

In Praise of Birds London 1925. New Edition 1950
Ramblings of a Bird Lover London 1927
Bird Haunts and Bird Behaviour London 1929
Musings and Memories London 1931

History of Science

John Ray: Naturalist Cambridge 1942. Second Edition 1950
English Naturalists from Neckam to Ray Cambridge 1947

Autobiographical

A Wanderer's Way London 1928

Index